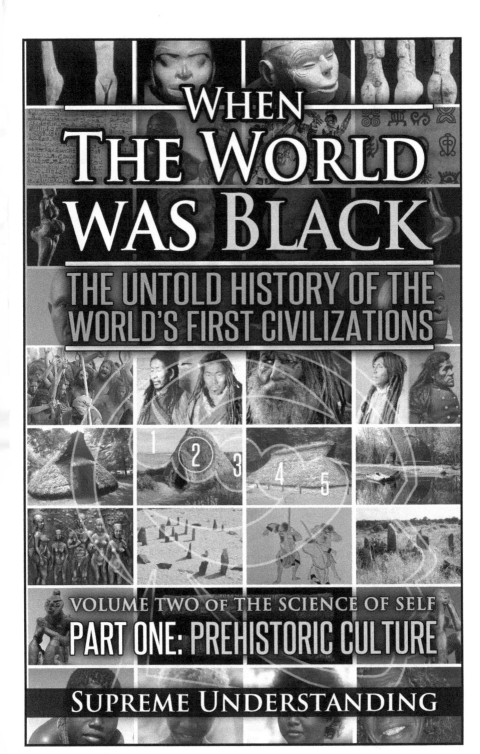

WHEN THE WORLD WAS BLACK

THE UNTOLD HISTORY OF THE WORLD'S FIRST CIVILIZATIONS

VOLUME TWO OF THE SCIENCE OF SELF

PART ONE: PREHISTORIC CULTURE

SUPREME UNDERSTANDING

Published by Supreme Design Publishing. PO Box 10887, Atlanta, GA 30310.

Although the author and publisher have made every effort to ensure the accuracy and completeness of information contained in this book, we assume no responsibility for errors, inaccuracies, omissions, or any inconsistency herein. Any perceived slights of people, places, or organizations are not intended to be malicious in nature.

Supreme Design Publishing books are printed on long-lasting acid-free paper. When it is available, we choose paper that has been manufactured by environmentally responsible practices. These may include using trees grown in sustainable forests, incorporating recycled paper, minimizing chlorine in bleaching, or recycling the energy produced at the paper mill.

Supreme Design Publishing is also a member of the Tree Neutral™ initiative, which works to offset paper consumption through tree planting.

TreeNeutral

Graphic Design, Layout, Editing, and Typesetting by Proven Publishing www.ProvenPublishing.com

---

First Printing 2013

ISBN: 978-1-935721-37-6

LCCN: 2013931005

Wholesale Discounts. Special discounts (up to 55% off of retail) are available on quantity purchases. For details, visit our website, contact us by mail at the address above, Attention: Wholesale Orders, or email us at orders@supremedesignonline.com

Individual Sales. Supreme Design publications are available for retail purchase, or can be requested, at most bookstores. They can also be ordered directly from the Supreme Design Publishing website, at www.SupremeDesignOnline.com

VISIT US ON THE WEB AT WWW.SUPREMEDESIGNONLINE.COM

DEDICATION

To Cheikh Anta Diop, Ivan Van Sertima, Runoko Rashidi, Clyde Ahmad Winters, Asa Hilliard, Charles Finch, S.O.Y. Keita, Leonard Jeffries, John Henrik Clarke, Anthony Browder, Chancellor Williams, Paul Guthrie, Marimba Ani, Mwalimu Baruti, B.R. Ambedkar, James Brunson, and all the other dedicated scholars – past and present – who have played a role in my understanding of Black history and the global struggle for self-determination. Thank you for the work you have done.

To the Dalit people of India, the Papuan people of New Guinea, Pan-Africans on the continent and abroad, those who consider themselves Black in Latin America, and all those indigenous people throughout the world who identify with the Black Global Diaspora. We are one. We will be together soon.

ACKNOWLEDGEMENTS

I'd first like to express my gratitude to everyone whose insight and feedback were critical to the completion of this project: Runoko Rashidi, Dr. S.O.Y. Keita, Baba Obadele Williams, Mwalimu Baruti, Robert Bailey, Mykel Archie, C'BS Alife Allah, Mecca Wise, Keith Africano, Wasif Elai Sayyed, Tau Justice Allah, Sha-King Ce'hum Allah, Divine Ruler Equality Allah, Sincere Justice Allah, Metztli Yei Kiahuitl, and Deniz Lopez.

There are many others who are part of the SDP family who I haven't had a chance to thank in print. These individuals continuously play important roles in our mission: Shabe Allah, Bo'kem Supreme Logic Allah, Queen Chuniq, Dierdra Baptiste, Kano Ayala, Freedom Allah, Original Author Allah, Victorious Honor, and anyone else you see out here repping SDP and its mission of "Reinventing the World."

Finally, there are the Black bookstores who support us heavily: Medu Books (GA), Nubian Books (GA), Expansion Books (AL), African Imports (TX), Everyone's Place Bookstore (MD), Black Star Music and Video (NY), Lushena Books (IL), Tapeman, Inc. (NJ), Umoja Books (OH), Black and Noble (PA), Harlem World Music and Video (NY), Community Bookstore (LA), Source of Knowledge (NJ), Tru Books (CT), and many others you'll find listed in the "Official Retailers" section of our website. Support them however you can!

PREFACE TO THE FIRST EDITION

DR. SUPREME UNDERSTANDING

As I type this brief message into my phone, perched atop the Pyramid of the Sun in Teotihuacan, Mexico, I find it absolutely breathtaking…not only to consider the view before me, but to consider the opportunities before us all today.

Here I am, at an ancient site, breathing in what some of our ancestors thought and said at this very place, while recording my own thoughts and words using the latest in modern technology. And unlike so many others who have become lost in their gadgets, I'm not *disconnected*. I feel more connected than ever.

I feel connected to this place, to our ancestors, to our history in general, to our people throughout the world today, to you the reader specifically, and on a deeper level, to the knowledge itself. To the very source from which it all emanates. And that source is not outside us, but it us. And you can't help but see that when you sit someplace like this.

So, it's my honor to bring you this book. It is my contribution to bridging our past and our present, our ancestors and our modern day kin all over the world, and you with the knowledge of yourself. This book couldn't have been written until now. Never before has it been this easy to connect these worlds.

Technology can certainly drive us apart, but, used wisely, it can also be a tool to bring us together. Technology has allowed for me to consult thousands of books I would have otherwise had to travel to track down, to consult dozens of experts who were sometimes thousands of miles away on archaeological digs, and to survey thousands of our readers to determine the best way to deliver this content to the people. It's also thanks to technology that you will enjoy hundreds of photos, many of them in full color, to enhance the experience even more.

But please don't think that technology has made this work a walk in the part. This book was nearly the death of me. I've worked tirelessly for months, often working for 12 hours at a time, day after day (as my Facebook and Twitter subscribers can attest to), just to ensure that this book is as solid as a book of this scope and magnitude ought to be.

One of the most difficult things about this process has not been the mountains of data to sift through or the steady flow of new findings that have emerged since I began writing – but the need to make this work easy to understand. Between that and ensuring that I've done a good job of summarizing more than 200,000 years of Black history, I've been forced to rewrite this book no less than eleven times.

And now, I'm satisfied. I'm very proud of arriving at what I consider a perfect balance:

❑ First, I've retained the technical depth of the book, meaning people with college educations will find the book informative, accurate, and challenging.

❑ But I've also included plenty of simple break downs so that people who are new to this kind of information can keep up without feeling they have to understand (or even read) every paragraph.

❑ Finally, I've added so much visual content that this book its worth its purchase price for the pictures alone. Beyond adding value, however, the visual part makes this book accessible to people who are not even readers.

The images are accompanied by captions and simple breakdowns that tell most of the story, so you can get a ton of understanding from this book just by looking at the dozens of visual pages.

Finally, I've humbled myself to suggest "questions to consider" rather than promoting theory after theory. This, in my opinion, is the best way to approach the subject when there isn't quite enough data to form a solid conclusion. And when you're talking about 200,000 years of Black history – you'll see that there are still hundreds of questions unanswered. It is my hope that some of our readers will someday become the scientists and scholars that answer those questions for my grandchildren to study.

Supreme Understanding
Teotihuacan, Mexico

For more on me, my background, and my qualifications, see "About the Author" in this book's Appendix.

FOREWORD

BY RUNOKO RASHIDI

It is always an honor to be asked to contribute to the body of scholarly works about African people, particularly by our outstanding young scholars. And here we have such a case. Indeed, the author has done such a comprehensive job here, touching on so many aspects of the Global African experience that I think that the most significant thing that I can do is to provide a kind of summary overview that outlines the nature of that experience.

I am fond of saying that "History is a light that illuminates the past and a key that unlocks the door to the future." Supreme Understanding confidently shines that light and unlocks that door. He understands that a sound knowledge of both the past and present is a weapon in the liberation of the mind and, as a result, wields that weapon most effectively.

Our concern is not only with Africa as the cradle of human culture, but as the birthplace and the cradle of humanity itself. Africa produced the first modern human populations (known to anthropologists as *Homo sapiens sapiens*), who then came to populate the rest of the world. There were different routes with varying degrees of difficulty that the migrants could have taken as they left the Great Lakes region. These routes include the Nile Valley, the Suez Isthmus into Asia, and the Straits of Gibraltar into Europe. It is in the light of these routes that the presence of modern humans in Asia, Europe, and, ultimately the Americas, can be traced.

In addition to the global migrations of Black people, which constitute the core of our Introduction, obviously, African people did not abandon Africa, with the Nile Valley probably the most brilliant example.

The earliest modern human (*Homo sapiens sapiens*) populations of Asia were also of African birth. Here we are speaking of the Diminutive Africoids – the extremely important and much romanticized family of Black people phenotypically characterized by: unusually short statures; skin-complexions that range from yellowish to dark brown; tightly curled hair; and, in frequent cases (like many other Blacks), steatopygia. They are probably more familiar to us by such pejorative terms as pygmies, Negritos and Negrillos. Similar peoples who live today in Southern Africa have been titled "Bushmen." More accurate names for these people are Batwa, San, Nama, and Khoi.

Moving slowly and sporadically from their African birthplace, beginning perhaps 100,000 years ago and continuing through the millennia, untold numbers of Diminutive Africoids began to people Asia. Although they currently exist in limited numbers, and are generally found in heavily forested, barren, isolated or similarly forbidding terrains, the Diminutive Africoids were at one time the supreme lords of the earth. It is indeed unfortunate that the histories of the Diminutive Africoids, including distinct and fundamental contributions to monumental civilizations characterized by agricultural science, metallurgy, advanced scripts and urbanization, are so little understood.

As we progress through prehistory, we find evidence of ancient Black civilizations in Japan, China, Southeast Asia (Cambodia, Vietnam, etc.), ancient Sumer (modern Iraq), Elam (modern Iran), Arabia, and India. These civilizations are all addressed in this text.

The epic story of the African presence in Asia is one of the most exciting and, yet, least known aspects of the Black experience. The Black populations of Asia, what they have done and are now doing, are questions that beg and demand serious answers. These answers, which we must diligently seek to supply, cannot be sought merely to satisfy the intellectual curiosity of an elite group, but to further the vision of Pan-Africanism and reunite a family that has been separated far too long. You will find this vision embraced wholeheartedly throughout this text.

Like Asia, the history of Black people in Europe is exceedingly rich. The first civilization of Europe was established on the island of Crete. It is called the Minoan Culture, after King Minos, an early legendary ruler of the island. It has been argued that the ancestors of the Cretans were natives of Africa, a branch of Western Ethiopians.

And what of the Moors? It would not be inaccurate to say that the Moors helped reintroduce Europe to civilization. But just who were the Moors of antiquity anyway? Chancellor Williams has written that "The original Moors, like the original Egyptians, were Black Africans." More on that in future works.

Most modern scientists believe that the earliest immigrants to reach the Western Hemisphere were Asians of the same physical type as the East Asians that we are familiar with today. But both the evidence from genetic studies and physical anthropology tell us that Black peoples came long before. Mongoloid peoples, however, eventually came to the prehistoric Americas in such massive numbers, crossing the Bering Strait in boats rather than across the Beringia land bridge, that they eventually almost totally absorbed the New World's earlier arrivals. The resulting fusion of peoples constituted the Native American populations at the time of the catastrophic European intrusions during the fifteenth and sixteenth centuries. The earlier arrived Blacks (the very first Americans) tended to fade away with increasing rapidity into the shadowy realms of fairy tales, myths and legends. You will find many of these myths in this text.

Scientists have established that Black populations did not entirely vanish from the Americas. The Olmec civilization of ancient Mexico has been labeled the first civilization of the western hemisphere, as they surpassed their neighbors in an attempt to settle certain problems of living together − of government, defense, religion, family, property, science and art. Some scientists have concluded that the Olmec may have originally have been an African settler-colony which conquered the indigenous population of southern Mexico. Others are convinced that the Black presence among the Olmec merely consisted of a small but elite and highly-influential community. These issues are addressed in this text.

Other scientists have found a host of cultural parallels between ancient Africans and Native Americans, including architectural patterns and religious practices. As for the latter, some Native American communities worshipped black gods of great antiquity, such as Ekchuah, Quetzalcoatl, Yalahau, Nahualpilli and Ixtliltic, long before the first enslaved Africans arrived in the New World.

All of these facts, buttressed by skeletons and sculptures, make it clear that African people have had a profound presence and influence in pre-Columbian America. Some scholars, such as Carlos C. Marquez, have even concluded that "the youthful America was also a Negro continent."

Traveling west across the Pacific, we find the Black people of Australia, who settled there at least 60,000 years ago. Northeast of Australia, we find the islands of Melanesia. C. Madang has described Melanesia (the Black Islands of the South Pacific) as the eastern flank of the Black world, and the expression of ages past when an uninterrupted belt of Black populations stretched across Africa, Eurasia, Australia, Oceania, and ancient America. To the contrary, the present Mongoloid inhabitants of Indonesia entered the region during relatively recent times; a period which some scientists have dated to as late as the first millennium C.E.

As we have just glimpsed, the Global African experience is vast. With that in mind, I will simply say this: All strong peoples emphasize their history, and do so all the time; weak peoples do not. Not only must intellectuals do their scholarly work, they must make sure to give this information to the masses. This has been the author's goal in this work – to deliver this information in a way that nearly everyone can understand.

I believe that if we are to be a strong people again, we must continually clarify who we are, where we are, and what we are, and constantly emphasize the things that made us great in the past. As Malcolm X said, "Of all our studies, it is history that is most qualified to reward our research." In other words, we must use our history as a springboard for struggle. We understand that we cannot live in the past, but the past surely lives in us; and that the past is not dead and history is not finished.

Runoko Rashidi
October 2012
Los Angeles

Runoko Rashidi is a historian, writer and public lecturer with a pronounced interest in the African foundations of humanity and civilizations and the presence and current conditions of Black people throughout the Global African Community. He is particularly drawn to the African presence in India, Australia and the islands of the Pacific. To date he has lectured in fifty-five countries. He regularly conducts educational tours throughout the world, exploring the African presence both ancient and modern. As a scholar, Runoko Rashidi has been called the world's leading authority on the African presence in Asia. He is the editor, with Dr. Ivan Van Sertima, of the voluminous *African Presence in Early Asia*, and author of Introduction to the *Study of African Classical Civilizations, Black Star: African Presence in Early Europe*, and *African Star over Asia: The Black Presence in the East*. Runoko Rashidi's mission is to help change the way Africa and Africans are seen in the world.

TABLE OF CONTENTS

Black people are the world's first people. Everywhere. Need proof?

Answer this:
Are these people from HERE or HERE...or HERE?
Got it? Turn the card over when you have your answer.

They're the indigenous Kanak people of New Caledonia. It's in the South Pacific. In other words, Black people are everywhere.

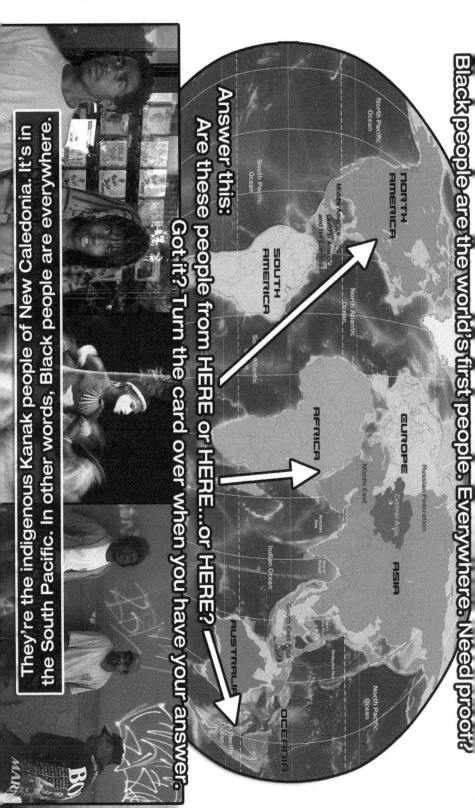

INTRODUCTION

BASIC INSTRUCTIONS

"History is not everything, but it is a starting point. History is a clock that people use to tell their political and cultural time of day. It is a compass they use to find themselves on the map of human geography. It tells them where they are, but more importantly, what they must be." – John Henrik Clarke

Why are there are Black communities all over the world, from southern Russia to southeast Asia, from South America to the islands of the South Pacific? Some of them are no longer around, but we know they were there. They were everywhere.

But who were these people? Where did they come from? How did they get to distant outposts like Easter Island, Tierra del Fuego, and even the frigid regions of northern Europe, Canada, and Siberia? And what role did these people play in establishing the world's first cultures and civilizations? Finally, what happened to them?

These are the questions we'll answer in this book. In this book, you'll learn about **the history of Black people.** I don't mean the history you learned in school, which most likely began with slavery and ended with the Civil Rights Movement. I'm talking about Black history BEFORE that. *Long* before that. In this book, we'll cover **over 200,000 years of Black history.**

For many of us, that sounds strange. We can't even imagine what the Black past was like before the slave trade, much less imagine that such a history goes back 200,000 years or more.

Can you imagine what that does to a person? To grow up believing their people started out as slaves? Perhaps some of us know a little about Africa, but how much do we really know? How much do we know about the extent of the ancient Black empires that spanned far beyond continental Africa? Chances are, *very little.* In this book, we'll tell **the stories you haven't been told.**

We'll talk about the Black migrations that settled the world. We'll talk about the Black people who founded the first cultures and civilizations of Africa, Asia, Europe, Australia, the Pacific Islands, and North and South America. No exaggeration. This book covers **more than 200,000 years of Black history across every square inch of the Planet Earth.** We'll rediscover a past when the world was Black. As we learn the history of our ancestors, we'll learn more and more about ourselves.

WHY STUDY THE PAST?

Why are ancient Black civilizations important? What do they have to do with us nowadays? Could this information serve as anything more than a source of inspiration? Or are these stories mere reminders of the greatness that once was?

I could answer those questions myself, but it makes sense to draw on the wisdom of those who came before me. People like historian John Henrik Clarke, who said the profound words quoted above. Or Senegalese scholar Cheikh Anta Diop, who said, "Intellectuals out to study the past, not for the pleasure they find in so doing, but to derive lessons from it."[1]

This is what Malcolm X meant when he said in his 1963 "Message to the Grassroots":

> Of all our studies, history is best qualified to reward our research. And when you see that you've got problems, all you have to do is examine the historic method used all over the world by others who have problems similar to yours. And once you see how they got theirs straight, then you know how you can get yours straight.

He was echoing the sentiments of his teacher,* the Honorable Elijah Muhammad, who said in the classic *Message to the Blackman*:

> The acquiring of knowledge for our children and ourselves must not be limited to the three R's – 'reading, 'riting and 'rithmetic. It should instead include the history of the Black nation, the knowledge of civilization of man and the universe and all the sciences. It will make us a greater people of tomorrow. We must instill within our people the desire to learn and then use that learning for self.[2]

Later in the book, he connects the study of history with the pursuit of self-knowledge:

> I am for the acquiring of knowledge or the accumulating of knowledge – as we now call it; education. First, my people must be taught the knowledge of self. Then and only then will they be able

---

* It should, of course, be noted that Malcolm X also consulted heavily with others, including Dr. John Henrik Clarke and Queen Mother Moore.

to understand others and that which surrounds them. Anyone who does not have a knowledge of self is considered a victim of either amnesia or unconsciousness and is not very competent. The lack of knowledge of self is a prevailing condition among my people here in America. Gaining the knowledge of self makes us unite into a great unity. Knowledge of self makes you take on the great virtue of learning. [3]

What they've been telling us is that history is a rich subject because it can illuminate the problems of the present, and present solutions that have already worked for such problems.

History can also highlight the failures of the past, to help us see what not to do again. The past is like an alternate universe that obeys the same laws as our own, where we can see what happens when different things are attempted.

Studying the past also allows us to see how our present-day conditions came to be. Both our strengths and our weaknesses are born from the triumphs and tragedies of our collective past. Thus, if we want a better present and future, we must come to understand the past.

WHAT YOU'LL LEARN

In writing this book, I gave myself the daunting task of covering all the cultures and civilizations of the world, going back as far as the earliest evidence of human settlement, and extending up to the point of European contact. That's quite a lot of history. Thus, this book had to be split into two parts.

Part One covers history from 200,000 to 20,000 years ago. These were the "prehistoric" cultures of the Paleolithic Age. This might make them sound "primitive," but we'll soon see that these cultures were actually highly advanced.

Part Two covers history from 20,000 years ago to the point of European contact. This is the time that prehistoric cultures grew into ancient urban civilizations, a transition known to historians as the "Neolithic Revolution."

Right now, you're looking at Part One. In this book, you'll learn:

❏ Who the Original People of this planet are.
❏ Why a branch of these people left Africa and settled the rest of the world.
❏ How and when these people settled the entire Earth.
❏ Why these people settled everywhere from the arctic tundra of Siberia to the deserts of Peru, and what cultures they established there.

- ❏ The "extinction event" that nearly wiped out half of the human race.
- ❏ The people who were here before humans, and the threat they posed to human survival.
- ❏ How these threats affected those who survived and became us.
- ❏ How the actions and choices of these Original People affect our lives over 100,000 years later.
- ❏ What kind of culture the earliest humans had, and if they were "primitive savages" or scientifically and culturally advanced?
- ❏ The innovations and technology these Original People introduced to all of the world's earliest human cultures.
- ❏ The threats faced by the direct descendants of these Original People who have survived into modern times.
- ❏ How we can apply the lessons of the past to the problems of the future.

HOW THIS BOOK IS DIFFERENT

This book is, of course, not the first to explore the subject of ancient Black history. And it will certainly not be the last. What makes this book different is its **scope**, its **depth**, and its **approach**.

This book covers the Black history of Africa, Asia, Europe, Australia, the Pacific Islands, and the Americas, whereas most texts focus on a very specific area, typically limited to popular regions like the Nile Valley. This book is also different because of how much work it took to put it together.

To summarize, here are ten reasons why this book was so insanely difficult to research and write:

1. Most popular texts on ancient Black history are NOT multidisciplinary (with a few exceptions, like *They Came Before Columbus*). This book is one of only a few works that looks at archaeological, linguistic, genetic, skeletal, mythological, and anthropological data to give readers the "whole picture."

2. Few works have attempted to dig any further back than 4,000 BC. This book covers the human journey from over 200,000 years ago, up to our first encounters with Europeans. That's quite a lot to condense into one text. We did however find a way to fit it in two books. Thus, this book is split in two parts, one half covering the distant prehistoric part (where the foundations were laid), and the other half covering the ancient Black past when big cities were built.

3. This book covers not just one part of the world, but the entire world. Asia, Africa, Australia, Europe, the Americas, the Pacific Islands, you name it, it's covered. In many of these areas, you seriously have to dig to find any of the data you're looking for.

4. Our goal is to be respectful to Original People throughout the world,

and considerate of their unique local heritages, while still being truthful about the Black foundations of these people, and later Black infusions into their civilizations.

5. It's not just a reference book, it's an *easy-to-read* reference book. This book is meant be encyclopedic in nature, yet inviting and easy to read. The content is specific enough to warrant quoting in academic papers, while not so technical that readers can't keep up. So by all means, quote us in your research papers! If you find us using conversational language to make something easier to understand, you may not want to quote THAT line.

6. It's just not as simple as saying "Black folks did this." There is no such thing as a monolithic Black culture or people. Black people are the most diverse people on Earth. There were at least three separate waves of Black people who populated the planet, each with their own unique contributions. Many of these people branched off and evolved locally into smaller subgroups.

7. We have to exemplify the methods of responsible scholarship. It's too easy to offer bold claims that can't be proven, but that goes against everything SDP stands for, and we believe that kind of "scholarship" is part of the problem plaguing our communities today.

8. This isn't a collection of "famous firsts" or disconnected Black history trivia. We're actually telling the story of how this world came to be the way it is today. Telling the processes behind the highlights (for example, the backstory to the construction of the pyramids) isn't as exciting as just listing the highlights, but that's what separates a history book from a book of "fun facts." We're not just telling what happened, we're explaining how it happened. As you can imagine, you won't find stories about 10,000-foot-tall temples on page one. And while it IS amazing that the Black people of the Indus Valley had toilets and sewers 4,000 years ago (in contrast to Europeans who were throwing their bodily waste out the window as recently as the 1600s) we have to understand how much actually led up to these developments.*

9. This book is part of our company's campaign to engender empowered readers. Too often, our great historians and scholars have died without anyone to continue their work as intended. In other cases, lecturers and academics refuse to teach others how to find what they've found. We're doing things differently. This book is full of open-ended questions and theories to research or expand upon, as well as guidelines on how to do the research. On our website, we've created a forum where a new scientific community can come together and continue writing this history. We call it "open source history."

10. Finally, we work life lessons into all of our books. This can't just be a

---

* They say "Rome wasn't built in a day," but Rome was copied off nearby Black civilizations that took thousands of years to establish. So what took Rome so long?

history book. This has to be a window into our past that allows us to better plan our futures.

This book is also different because we don't resort to fantastic claims without proof. That's just something we don't do, even if readers nowadays tend to let other authors get away with it. We want to teach critical thinking, so we lead by example. If it's an extraordinary claim, it requires extraordinary evidence. If we can't back it up, we won't say it. If it's just a theory, we'll say that, and we'll identify all that facts that suggest our theory is plausible.

Finally, we are big on reality. The facts are amazing by themselves. We don't need to make it seem like Black people built civilizations all over the world with magic or psychic powers. Doing so makes the accomplishments of the past seem effortless, and that sets us up for failure today – because nation-building nowadays is certainly not effortless. Doing so also requires no explanation of the process by which nation-building occurs, so you're left with some fun stuff to believe in, but nothing you can actually use. We actually consider this kind of "teaching" to be a form of exploitation, and advise you to keep your eyes out for the people who peddle this kind of fantasy to those who deserve better.

HOW TO READ THIS BOOK

The following guidelines should make it easier to read and understand this book:

☐ Think of this book like a reference book. It's full of literally thousands of years' worth of content. To support many of the arguments we make, I've had to incorporate lots – and I mean lots – of data. Sometimes, this can be overwhelming. The vocabulary isn't always easy either. But here's the first step: relax.

☐ You can reread this book as many times as you need to. And unlike *The Science of Self, Volume One*, you don't necessarily have to read this book from front to back. You can skip around, because this work is meant to be encyclopedic like *The Hood Health Handbook* – a useful reference on over 1,000 different historical topics.

☐ In other words, if you come across a difficult concept, a technical-sounding quote, or a section that simply doesn't catch your interest, skip it. Often, those long block quotes are followed by an explanation in laymen's terms. And what doesn't catch you on your first read might catch your interest on your second read.

☐ However, it might be easiest to understand if you don't skip around too much, because difficult concepts are explained the first time they're mentioned, but not again afterwards.

☐ If you don't feel like keeping a dictionary next to you while you read, there are free dictionary apps for most smartphones, and Dictionary.com is easy to use as well. Wherever we can, we define tough words, but you still might run into a few that you need to clarify. Don't stress! You're improving your vocabulary. Soon, you'll be able to use "anthropometry" in a sentence.

❏ When you read, write in the margins and highlight text as often as you can. You may even want to use one of those colorful sticky-tab bookmarking systems.

❏ It's also helpful to keep a notebook where you take notes and record your thoughts.

❏ We always ask that you share our work with others. We appreciate when you take pictures of our books and share them online, or post quotes with the necessary credits. SDP thrives off word-of-mouth.

❏ At the same time, you may not get great results if you introduce this book to a friend who doesn't like reading. You may need to start with a book like *How to Hustle and Win*, or *Rap, Race, and Revolution*, or *Knowledge of Self*. Those books are better suited for general audiences. This book, like *The Science of Self, Volume One*, is much heavier reader and will be tough for the uninitiated.

❏ Still, carry the book with you. We delay our eBook releases (sometimes for a year or more) for a reason! We want people to bring this knowledge into the REAL world. We love the internet as much as you do, but we're trying to kill all that disconnectedness and "reinvent the world" by bringing our people back together. (You'll get it when you read this book).

❏ So take this book out with you, and let those random conversations begin. You'll be surprised how much good can come from such a small gesture.

THE GLOBAL BLACK DIASPORA
(LONG BEFORE THE SLAVE TRADE!)

B: TRY THIS ACTIVITY

R: WHO ARE THESE PEOPLE?

T: WHERE ARE THEY FROM?

I: GUESS!

www.whentheworldwasblack.com

ANSWERS: A: Philippines, B: Fiji, C-E: New Guinea, F-H: Tupinamba Indians of Brazil, I: Ethiopia, J-K: San of Namibia, L: Mexico, M: Cambodia, N: Australia, O-P: Hawaii, Q-R: Northeast India, S: New Guinea, T: Andaman Islands

THE MEANING OF CIVILIZATION

WHO WAS CIVILIZED...WHO WAS NOT?

"When we classify mankind by color, the only primary race that has not made a creative contribution to any civilization is the Black race." – Arnold Toynbee, The Study of History

When you think of a "civilization" what do you think of? When you took history class in school, you were probably taught something about civilizations (both ancient and modern), because that's where all the history was made. The rest of the "uncivilized" world wasn't doing much that mattered.

When you think about it, what are some civilizations that come to mind? Most of your peers will think of European civilizations, like Greece, Rome, and the good ol' U.S. of A. Some of us will, of course, think instead of ancient Egypt...maybe Nubia or the Mayan civilization of Mexico. Few of us can go back further than those. And few can tell you what makes something a civilization.

Think about it. What IS civilization? What do you think it means? Seriously, stop for a minute. I'll wait.

What did you come up with? I'll give you some options. Which of the following do you think a group of humans must have in order to be considered a civilization?

❏ The construction of urban cities	❏ Social classes
❏ A steady food supply from farming	❏ A standing military
❏ Trade with other civilizations	❏ Monuments
❏ Laws and government	❏ Knowledge of science
❏ Private property	❏ Textiles and Ceramics
❏ An established leadership	❏ A Written Language

"You know you ignant when you think ancient Egypt was the beginning of African culture. As if the millions of years before that, everybody was on some monkey s***." – Supreme Understanding, via Facebook

Based on your criteria, when do you think Black people developed their first civilizations? Most people would answer that the world's first civilizations date back to ancient Egypt (or Sumer, and a few will say Kush or Nubia), and those go back about 6,000 years. That's pretty ancient, but if you think about it, that still implies that Black people – who have been around as modern humans for at least 200,000 years – have been wild and uncivilized for most of that time.

That's not an accident. That's what you're supposed to think.

WHAT YOU'LL LEARN IN THIS CHAPTER

☐ Why they taught us that our ancestors were primitive savages.

☐ The history of "savage" and "uncivilized" behavior

☐ How the people who built the world's first civilizations were pushed into the fringes of the societies they built as outcasts.

☐ Why the standard model of civilization is backwards.

☐ The true meaning of "civilization."

☐ How our ancestors had the knowledge of modern civilization but only used it as needed.

☐ The way history "works."

☐ How false history can be used to confuse and distract us.

☐ How to tell sound historical information from misinformation and guesswork.

☐ How scholars connect the prehistoric dots to piece together our past.

THEY SAID WE WERE SAVAGES

As long as history has been written by Europeans, Blacks have been written out of history. Black people have been described as primitive savages, an inferior race that has given nothing to humankind in the way of the arts, the sciences, or civilization. Hell, I don't have to paraphrase what they said; I can give you some direct quotes. So, here's what they think about you.

In 1768, European "Enlightenment" philosopher David Hume said:

> I am apt to suspect the Negroes to be naturally inferior to the white. There never was a civilized nation of any other complexion than white, nor even any individual eminent either in action or speculation. No ingenious manufactures amongst them, no arts, no sciences.

In 1837, German philosopher Hegel said in his *History of Philosophy*:

> At this point we leave Africa, not to mention it again. For it is no historical part of the World; it has no movement or development to exhibit.

In 1902, John Burgess wrote in his history of Reconstruction that American slavery was the consequence of nature:

> A Black skin means membership in a race of men which has never created a civilization of its own kind. There is something natural in

the subordination of an inferior race, even to the point of enslavement of the inferior race...[4]

In 1934, historian Arnold Toynbee concluded that "the only primary race that has not made a creative contribution to any civilization is the Black race." As recently as 1965, Professor Trevor-Roper, Royal Professor of History at Oxford University, wrote:

Undergraduates...demand that they should be taught the history of black Africa. Perhaps, in the future, there will be some African history to teach. But at present there is none, or very little: there is only the history of the Europeans in Africa. The rest is largely darkness, like the history of pre-European, pre-Columbian America. And darkness is not a subject for history...The new rulers of the world, whoever they may be, will inherit a position that has been built up by Europe, and by Europe alone. It is European techniques, European examples, European ideas which have shaken the non-European world out of its past – out of barbarism in Africa, out of a far older, slower, more majestic civilisation in Asia; and the history of the world, for the last five centuries, in so far as it has significance, has been European history. I do not think that we need to make any apology if our study of history is European-centric.[5]

I can imagine you didn't find any of that particularly pleasant, so I'll stop there, as I'm sure I've made my point. The bottom line is: **They argued, without a shadow of a doubt, that you were made to be less than them.** They taught the world that you have given the world nothing, and are thus owed nothing... *not even respect.*

Notice, however, that I didn't say they actually *believed* this. They just *taught* this to the world, and the rest of the world spit it back in your face. But the true scientists among them didn't believe much of what they said and wrote about you. As you'll see throughout the book, *they knew better.*

Wait, I've got just one more quote, and this one's heavy. The following excerpt from Bertram Weale's 1910 work, *The Conflict of Colour: The Threatened Upheaval Throughout the World* covers so much of what we seek to address in this book:

> The black man has given nothing to the world. He has never made a nation – he belongs to nothing but a subject race. He has no architecture of his own, no art, no history, no real religion, unless animism be a religion. His hands have reared no enduring monuments, save when they have been forcibly directed by the energies of other races. The black man – the negro – is indeed the world's common slave…Fate thus seems to have marked the African down.
>
> No matter how much one may animadvert [criticize] against the Asiatic, no matter how much one may dislike him, it is a fact that, though he may never have been scientific, he has contributed immensely to the civilisation of the world; has founded every great religion that exists; has built enduring monuments and temples; and possesses withal in many ways a more reasonable, a more subtle, and a more speculative brain than the European. In poetry, in art, the debt Europe owes Asia is immense – far greater than is commonly supposed; for no one knows, nor will ever know, how much the Greeks really borrowed from Indo-Persian civilisation, and how little they themselves originated. Hebrew, Chinese, Japanese, Arab, Hindu, Persian – and many others – have contributed their ordered quota in this sum total; all have had, and will continue to have, a profound influence on the world's progress.
>
> Not so the black man. He is the child of nature – the one untutored man who was a helot in the days of Solomon, as he is still a virtual slave, though his manumission throughout the world is one of the great landmarks in the history of the nineteenth century.[6]

Reading texts like this turns the stomachs of those of us who know better. It makes you want to scream, cry, lash out in defiance, and – perhaps after you've had enough – you just tell yourself "Well, it's not true, and their ignorance can't hurt me." This is, truthfully, a coward's response.

TEACHING US THAT WE'RE STUPID

It's like knowing your child's kindergarten teacher is telling them that they're stupid on a daily basis, and you – instead of doing something about it – just tell yourself "Well, it's not true, and their ignorance can't hurt my baby."

But it can! And this IS what our children learn in schools! Not necessarily in THIS language of course, because it's not 1910 anymore, and no one would word it this way. But the SAME ideas are being fed to our children. Even at Black college and universities, many professors are so entrenched in the "old school" that they don't know how much of the world was authored by Black people – or they're simply too scared (even at HBCUs) – to really talk about it.

And this history MATTERS, because there's a *reason* why they lied! These fools weren't ignorant, they LIED. And there's *still* a reason why they *still* lie.

GREEN IS THE NEW WHITE

Think about this: Right now, much of the "developed" world is "going green." Environmentalism is big news, and big news means big business. But who's cashing in? The same Europeans who trashed the planet! Did you know that the same companies who produce the garbage that destroys our planet are the same ones manufacturing the "green" products that are supposed to save it?

And as people pursue this "radical change," are they consulting with the Original environmentalists? You know, the indigenous people who preserved the planet for hundreds of thousands of years, using sustainable technology – long before anyone white cared what "sustainable" meant? Of course not!

They said we were savages because we lived in "mud huts" – even though a brick house is essentially a mud hut too! (brick = fire-dried mud) But now, white people are spending thousands of dollars to build "Eco-Domes" using the same construction techniques – now that they've realized they're superior to many modern dwellings.[7] Meanwhile, many of the *original* "mud hut" architects weren't simply written off as "savages," they've been pushed to the brink of extinction! The oldest people on the planet are all nearly gone. Think about WHY.

Think about what compels an "environmental" organization like the World Wildlife Fund to purposely push for population control and the imminent death of indigenous people in the regions where they work so hard to save small animals. Don't believe me? Check out our investigation of the evidence in *The Hood Health Handbook, Volume Two*. It's all right there, in their own words.

Trust me, my desire to tell the true story of Original People is not about romanticism or reminiscing. It's about radical change. A reversal of the prevailing social order. I'm striving to undo what they're doing daily. By the time you're done with this volume, you'll see just why ancient history is not old news, and just how important it is that these stories continue to be told. Until then, we'll always be seen as savages and animals, bound for extinction.

WERE WE PRIMITIVE?

We're going to deconstruct and destroy hundreds of myths and misconceptions throughout this series of books. Some are related to science versus pseudo-science, or history versus fantasy, or logic versus fallacy. Many of the "erroneous" ways of thinking are deeply ingrained in our minds, because **we've been taught to respect claims and beliefs without requiring evidence.** But many of these myths and misconceptions about Original People have us portrayed as inferior or backwards, and these are – ironically – just as ingrained in us, because we've been taught to hate ourselves. We're here to reverse that process, using the evidence to tell the true story.

How well do you know what's real versus what we've been told? Try this activity, marking the following items as either true or false.

Africa is the home of the wild.	T	F
The jungle life is hard and savage, and it is a sign of progress when people grow out of it.	T	F
Tribal people walk around naked because they don't know better.	T	F
We became civilized humans within the past 40,000 years.	T	F
Ancient Egypt was the first great Black civilization.	T	F
Today's Europeans descend from the first humans to settle Europe.	T	F
Indigenous people engage in just as much warfare and bloodshed as modernized people, except with less technology.	T	F
The technology we have today is much more effective than primitive technology.	T	F
Early humans slept out in the open or in the treetops until they learned to build simple huts.	T	F
Darwin's theory of evolution taught that man descended from monkeys.	T	F
All our different skin colors and facial features come from the environment.	T	F
The diet of the earliest people involved a lot of meat, which we secured by daily hunting.	T	F
The Original People did not have a written language or numbers until ancient Egypt and Mesopotamia.	T	F
And my personal favorite: Before urban cities emerged in the ancient world, our people were primitive.	T	F

WELL, WERE WE PRIMITIVE?

Depends on what you mean by primitive. If, by primitive, you mean we lived simple lives unhindered by modern technology, modern problems, and modern social ills...or that we lived according to the "primary" laws of nature rather than man-made codes invented to control human behavior....then yeah, I guess you could say we were primitive.* We didn't have stainless steel tools from Home Depot. We didn't have Gucci suits and shoes. We didn't wear chains that turn your neck green.

But, as you'll see in this book, we didn't need any of that. We had the technology we needed, some ridiculously fresh attire, and jewelry that would put Jacob the Jeweler to shame. But even if we didn't have anything close to those things, we would have still had everything we needed. Don't let anyone convince you that we were desperate and fighting for survival the whole time. And don't let anyone tell you that a "simple life" means a savage life.

No matter what European anthropologists said about us in the early 1900s, we certainly weren't savages. Unfortunately, this image – of a bunch of naked wild people chasing animals with bones in their noses and spears in their hands – persists even a hundred years later. But this isn't an accurate picture of indigenous† people now, nor was it what we lived like 100,000 years ago.

AN INTRODUCTION TO HISTORIOGRAPHY

BY ROBERT BAILEY

History is the story of what happened and how it happened. It's not a set of trivia to memorize. If that's the way you learned history, you probably know bits and pieces of what happened in the past, but not in any logical order that will help you understand how all that old stuff led to what's going on now, or how it will affect the future. But memorizing names, dates, and places isn't all bad. It can help you remember the story itself, but if all you got was the trivia and no story, that's a bad deal. But let's be real: just because you're getting a story doesn't mean you're getting the full story or the true story. That's why you hear people say history is "HIS story" meaning the white man's version of how things went. This brings us to the study of historiography.

Historiography is the study of how history is, and has been, written. It also refers to the various interpretations of a historical event and

---

* The word primitive derives from the same root as prime, primal, and primary.

† For an explanation of what exactly we mean by "indigenous," see the FAQ in the Appendix of this book.

the body of historical work on a given topic (like the historiography of Black civilizations). Primary sources such as eyewitnesses, personal diaries, journals, etc. are better at giving an idea of what happened regarding a past event than secondary sources such as books written by a historian. Even still, primary sources must be put into context. Historiographers are NOT the same as historians; a historiographer is like a detective, looking into how sources are formed.

There are many different approaches from which a historiographer may work. They may compare sources and look for patterns recurring throughout them for common themes, as wells as consider the corruption or authenticity of a source, in addition to the motives and perspective of the author of source. History is never truly objective, because history is an interpretation of facts. Hence the African proverb, "Until the lions have their historian, tales of the hunt shall always glorify the hunter." While studying history, you can practice thinking like a historiographer by asking yourself, how and why some facts are included or excluded from a history. Historiography is useful in that it helps us get to the bottom of things and to find out the truth of what actually transpired.

So how long has the telling of history been going on? Prehistory itself is defined as history of humankind before recorded history. While we haven't always recorded our history down on paper, accounts of the past were passed down orally, through what is known as oral tradition. Elders pass down their knowledge to specific members of their clan, according to their respective place in the clans; in addition, the first people to receive the knowledge must be direct descendants of that knowledge.

THE HISTORY OF SAVAGERY

"There are many humorous things in the world; among them, the white man's notion that he less savage than the other savages." – Mark Twain, Following the Equator

When my wife Mecca and I traveled to the city of Prague in the Czech Republic, we wandered around as if we were on a foreign planet. No one spoke English, and we didn't speak their language or anything close to it. They clearly hadn't seen too many couples like us either. Perhaps that's why Kanye West had such a hard time casting Black children for his "Diamonds from Sierra Leone" video, which was shot there before we made our trip. We documented some of our experiences there in a video found on my YouTube channel.

One of the highlights of this video is our trip to Prague's Torture Museum. Yes, it's a museum dedicated entirely to torture devices and the history of their use. They had giant metal spikes that women were forced to sit on, and caskets filled with barbed points that were closed on living people. These devices were used throughout European history, but we recognized a few of them from the history of American slavery as well. It was disturbing to say the least.

As it turns out, there are torture museums throughout the Western world, most of them just like the one in Prague. Guess why? Because torture is one of the few things that Europeans gave to the world. There is not a single spoken language, written script, form of government, economic system, industry or technology, branch of science, artistic technique, musical genre, sport, or agricultural product that Europeans gave to the rest of the world. As we'll explore in a separate book, titled *Black People Invented Everything*, all of these things came from Original People.

But when it comes to torture, genocide, child molestation, bestiality, and all sorts of human degradation, we know that those things weren't a part of ANY indigenous culture. As the scholars profiled in Tariq Nasheed's *Hidden Colors 2* documentary explain, there are no known instances of African cannibalism. Yet there are dozens of well-documented cases of European cannibalism throughout the ages. And just how "civilized" are a people who go around enslaving and raping everyone they meet? What makes a people civilized?

SO WHO WERE THE REAL SAVAGES?

As we explained in *The Hood Health Handbook, Volume One*:

> Historically, Original People have always been very big on being clean. We were the ones who invented soap, bath houses, and even shampoo – all before anyone ever thought to say "cleanliness is next to godliness."* We've included hygiene in all of our religious and cultural traditions. Meanwhile, Europeans were historically pretty gross.
>
> From living in caves sealed with feces to bathing only once or twice a year (yes, a year!), when we came to Europe as the Moors, we had to teach them how to bathe! If you saw Robin Hood when it first came out, you'll notice that the Moorish brother is the one who has to teach Robin Hood and them to wash up.

---

* That phrase actually doesn't appear in the Bible, as many believe. It was said by British preacher John Wesley, founder of the Methodist Church, in 1791. Wesley studied the Native Americans in Georgia, became a vegetarian, worked against the enslavement of Africans, and came to believe in the doctrine of Theosis (man becoming God).

We also had to teach them about sanitation. We came from civilizations that had sewers and flushing toilets as early as 3500 BC. But as late as the 1800s, Europeans used "chamber pots," which they poured out the window when they were done! Now imagine what's in the streets! But a lot of that was cleaned up by the huge rats and pigs they had running through the streets of Europe at the time. You can imagine the health complications.

When Europeans came to North America, they brought a gang of diseases (most of which came from animals), as well as their standards of hygiene. Feenie Ziner, who wrote a biography of Tisquantum (better known as Squanto), recorded that Squanto, "...tried without success to teach them [the Pilgrims] to bathe." The Native people of Mexico would hold flowers to their noses when talking with the Spanish Conquistadors in an attempt to mask the odor they could smell through the ARMOR of the Spanish.

In fact, Queen Isabella of Spain – who once boasted that she had bathed only twice in her life, the first time when she was born and the second time the day of her marriage – upon hearing Columbus' reports on the frequency of bathing among the Native People issued an edict that stated in part, "They are not to bathe as frequently as hitherto."

Everywhere you look among people of color, we have washed regularly, put "fruits and berries" in our hair and skin (remember "Coming to America"?), and kept up the highest standards of hygiene. And even when our homes were built from clay and straw, they were impeccably clean.

Don't let those ancient ruins fool you. You gotta see a mock-up of how they looked BEFORE they became ruins. Or visit a tribal village today. Those little huts get SWEPT daily. In fact, we invented the broom too!

So what happened to us? We continue:

What happened to us? Simple. We fell victim. Poverty and oppression changed our cultures drastically. Many of us are in plain survival mode, while others are just not tryin because we've lowered our standards for ourselves and each other.

We can actually compare photos and sketches of indigenous cultures from the 1800s and 1900s, illustrating the gradual change that occurred among people like the Fuegians of South America. The oldest accounts of the Fuegians describe them as a respectable people who often intimidated Europeans with their strength, endurance, commitment to the protection of their women, and their high moral standards. Some of these people were so revered they became the subject of myth and mystery.

Yet, less than a 100 years later, photos reveal the Fuegians in a state of morbid disrepair. Their hair is unkempt, their faces dirty. They look broken. Who broke them? They'd been living in this area for thousands of years! And they were just fine until...Well, *you know*.

So when we look at so-called "primitive" people throughout the world, keep in mind that these people are often the direct descendants of the Original People who actually built that country's first civilizations. These "lawless" people were once that society's lawgivers. They've been marginalized, vilified, and forced to live on the fringes, surviving in the forests and mountains of the lands where they once built thriving ancient civilizations.

This is just ONE of the many reasons why we may have the wrong idea about who is savage and who is civilized. Another issue is our lack of consensus on what "civilization" means to begin with.

WHAT IS CIVILIZATION, ANYWAY?
THE BACKWARDS MODEL

In school, you may have been taught that the developments we associate with "modern" civilization were improvements over the older models of human society. That is, we "got better" or became "more advanced" over time. We're taught that crude, primitive society evolved into "modern society," which really just means "Western society."

The point of this curriculum was to ingrain in your mind that the apex, or height, of all civilization was modern Europe and, by extension, America. Basically, the ultimate goal of all historical development was to produce "sophisticated Western culture." Which is interesting, because how could "Western" civilization describe such distant places as Britain, America, and Australia? Easy! It's because "Western" means white, and "primitive" means everyone else!

"Unless one chooses to live in a state of unconsciousness and alienation, one cannot live without memory, or with a memory that belongs to someone else. And history is the memory of nations. And thus we come to the formidable question of methodology." – African historian Joseph Ki-Zerbo[10]

So this way of teaching history is really a platform for advancing the standards of Western civilization over the modes of living that have worked everywhere else in the world for hundreds of thousands of years. And the implication is that the indigenous cultures that came before the Western world's rise to dominance, and "failed" to receive the bounties of Western influence, are primitive and "backwater." So, in a nutshell, history class taught you that you are the descendants of savages, and white people were the teachers of all humanity.

But if we critically reexamine the historical record, we know this timeline is more backwards than the movie *Memento*. I call it the "Backwards Model" of history because it starts with whatever white people are doing now, and takes for granted that those are "best practices." Then it works backwards to show how those things came to be.

THE ORIGINAL MODEL

Modern Western civilization is praised for its systems of economics, trade, industry, agriculture, literature, scientific knowledge, government, and social organization. While all of these things were drawn from Original People at various points in history (which we'll document throughout this book), none of these things characterized the "high points" of Original People's civilizations.

In fact, it is only in the most recent epoch of our immensely long history that we developed the practices Europeans would later usurp, adapt, and then use against us. The true high points of our civilization have been when:

❐ the majority, if not all, of the people enjoyed shared access to common resources
❐ decisions affecting the community were made collectively and not by a powerful in-group
❐ knowledge was not purposely kept from commoners by the elite but was shared freely

Put simply, we've been at our best when we shared a socialist equality that is increasingly rare in a modern world that promotes individual benefit over collective prosperity. This book will document some of the periods in our history when this has occurred, the reasons behind the points when it did not occur, and how even the most "primitive" social groups (or "tribes") were more advanced in their scientific knowledge and mastery of the environment than the great civilizations Western historians celebrate today.

WAS ANCIENT EGYPT THE APEX OF OUR HISTORY?

We may upset some people with this point, but one of the most celebrated of Black civilizations, ancient Egypt, is also one of the most celebrated in Western history precisely because of this dynamic. That is, while early Egypt was both advanced and prosperous, it was no "better" in terms of the prosperity of its common people than any of a hundred other ancient civilizations in Africa (most of which you've never heard about...until this book).

Part of the reason Egypt seems so great is because we know so much about it. This is mostly because white people were so fascinated with it. After all, ancient Egypt provided much of the artistic, religious, cultural, and scientific foundations of early Western civilization. As a result, ancient Egypt most resembles (even to us) the most celebrated aspects of Western civilization, including a capitalist economy, an elite government separated sharply from the common people, social stratification (meaning there were different classes with different levels of social standing and economic means), a strong standing military, and organized religion.

Although not even the worst of these elements were half as bad as they would later become when they emerged in Western civilization,* they still provide us a focal point that "looks familiar," whereas the "primitive" societies of Central or Southern Africa, for example, do not...Even though the people of Central Africa were producing advanced mathematical artifacts over 100,000 years before the Greeks took the Pythagorean Theorem from Egypt.

WHAT MUST WE DO TO CORRECT THIS?

All of the above tell us one thing: We have to shift our paradigm. We can't define civilization and success by Western standards. If we do so, we were only "civilized" and successful within the past 10,000 years, and only in specific places throughout the world. This means that – everywhere else, and for the majority of our history – we were actually "uncivilized" and savage, just like Europeans said we were.

We can't work with that model. We have to keep in mind that, when the Egyptians erected the great pyramids 5,000 years ago, they said they were at the *decline* of their civilization. Does this mean there were bigger and better pyramids before then? No! This means that their model of civilization was once better than what it became in the era of urbanization and monument building!

---

* For example, the gaps between the classes in ancient Egypt weren't nearly as pronounced as the divides between the rich, middle-class, and poor in Western civilization. It should also be noted that the Egyptians gave all praise to the Black nations that came before, which were much more egalitarian. We're not saying Egypt was a "bad" place of course. We'll discuss the history of the Nile Valley in Part Two.

THE MEANING OF CIVILIZATION

Elijah Muhammad defined civilization as "One having knowledge, wisdom, understanding, culture, refinement, and is not a savage in the pursuit of happiness." While some may not immediately see how this relates to the emergence of historical civilizations, I find this definition especially illuminating.

After years of research, I've arrived at a similar definition. **"Civilization" is found whenever the people are one, meaning a collective that enjoys shared access to knowledge and information, shared decision-making, and shared resources, within a culture that allows for all to participate equally, with mores and values that discourage destructive tendencies, particularly those practices that exploit others in the pursuit of individual benefit.**

With this definition, it brings a number of so-called "advances" under new scrutiny. Was urbanization a "step up" from the previous way of life? Was agriculture an improvement? Was the invention of writing an advantage we previously lacked? Did we benefit from the new models of social organization that came about when we urbanized? A new approach to history – one that no longer celebrates the Western model over the Original model – suggests otherwise.

The past 200,000-plus years of human history present us with evidence of brain surgery, astronomy, earth-shaping, long-range seafaring and trade, mining, and feats of engineering that modern man struggles to reproduce today – all before 4,000 BC. Yet in this same prehistoric epoch, we rarely find instances of murder, poverty, famine, torture, genocide, or the many other "advances" we find in modern civilization, particularly in the past 6,000 years (which is when we tend to say "civilization" started). This long historical record among Original People – which few historians have attempted to explore – suggests we only developed certain practices to compensate for failures in other areas.

For example, the invention of agriculture only came when human populations had failed to adequately replace the natural food supplies they'd thrived on. We'd always known how to selectively breed plants and animals (the foundations of agriculture), but only NEEDED to do so when we'd screwed up our symbiotic relationship with nature.

Similarly, the invention of writing may appear quite incredible to us today, especially since it's one of the primary ways we've learned

> **DID YOU KNOW?**
> In *The Science of Self, Volume One*, we discuss how the origins of agriculture are not isolated in time and space among any specific human society, but that agriculture is a response to one's circumstances. For this reason, we can even find farming among other organisms. Species include fungus-growing ants, slime mold, and ambrosia beetles that have developed quite sophisticated cultivation and harvesting routines.[11]

about what really happened in the ancient world after 4,000 BC (and why we know so little about what happened before then). But we'd always known how to write and mark things systematically. There are cave paintings over 40,000 years old that demonstrate artistic abilities that rival those found on any Egyptian tomb. There are markings on carved bones and rock surfaces over 40,000 years old indicating the use of a communication system.

But the development of true "writing" began about 4,000 BC with pictographic images – particularly name-seals and other markers of ownership – because, by that time, we had eroded our egalitarian systems of collective ownership to the point where we needed to mark what belonged to whom.

Over time, other issues arose, creating a demand for more systematic methods of writing and record-keeping. Before that, we'd been able to pass on elaborate messages using a stick carved with a series of 5 dots and 6 lines (a practice still found among some African groups and aborigines in Australia, in a "mail service" that often spanned hundreds of miles on foot).*

Yet the "ancient civilizations" most of us celebrate today depended on writing to communicate things we'd previously communicated much more effectively without ever needing a stick, stone, or ink. These changes weren't inherently "bad" (though they were used against us quite effectively throughout the Western onslaught), because *all change happens for a reason*. In many ways, all that happened was meant to be. Yet it's important to know these new developments weren't inherently "better" than their predecessors either.

Wearing a toupee to cover a balding head isn't better than having a full head of natural hair, even if someone thinks your toupee looks better than your original hair (which they never saw). Similarly, settling down and growing crops (which eventually led to the development of class stratification) isn't better than living off the land, even if your high school World History textbook told you so. Fortunately, that textbook is old news in more ways than one...because now you have this book.

---

* See "The Origin of Language" in Part Two for more.

WHO IS THE ORIGINAL MAN?

FICTION

REALITY

THE AGES OF HISTORY
THE NEOLITHIC AND PALEOLITHIC AGES

Historians love naming things, so they came up with something called the Neolithic, which helps them pin down the traditional origins of urban civilization throughout most of the world. The Neolithic is a historical period, literally translating to "New Stone Age." It followed the Paleolithic ("Old Stone Age") period and began with the rise of farming and other social changes.

But the Neolithic isn't really a specific time period as much as it is a set of characteristics that a society can develop. Typically, the main features responsible for the "Neolithic Revolution" were the systemic use of agriculture and animal domestication. For some time, the scientific community said this happened no sooner than 4,000 BC anywhere in the world, and much later throughout Africa and the Americas.

But they were wrong. Researchers later found Neolithic cultures appearing in the Near East region known as the Fertile Crescent by 10,000 BC, and from there spreading eastwards and westwards. By 8000 BC, there were early Neolithic cultures in Anatolia, Syria and Iraq, followed by southeast Europe by 7000 BC, South Asia by 7000 BC, China by 6500 BC, the Americas by 5800 BC, and the Philippines by 5000 BC. And so it appears that all of the "scientific and cultural advances" of the Neolithic period were introduced for the first time no more than 12,000 years ago. This is the story we'll explore in Part Two.

NEOLITHIC IDEAS BEFORE THE NEOLITHIC AGE?

But guess what? All of these innovations can be found – in a somewhat more "organic" form – looooong before 12,000 years ago. I'm talking about 100,000 years ago. Dozens of locations throughout the world present evidence of agriculture, animal domestication, urbanization, and written language, long before the dates above.

Some Asian sites, for example, show clear signs of agricultural knowledge over 20,000 years ago.[12] Others in Africa are even older. This reminds us that we didn't suddenly "discover" civilization and "become" civilized. We must have had this knowledge for a long time, and began using it to the point where it became "institutionalized" much later in our history, when circumstances demanded it.

So the developments of the Neolithic Age don't constitute

"progress" as much as historians have led us to think. They told us that human society is "civilized" once it is urbanized, beginning with the transition from natural subsistence (i.e., nomadic groups thriving off of hunter-gathering or foraging cultures) to urban societies (sedentary lifestyles sustained by plant and animal domestication). That is, like a Black child diagnosed with ADHD, we aren't "civilized" until we learn how to sit down (settle) and do our work (agriculture).* If anything, the Neolithic doesn't represent "the rise of civilization" as much as it does "the rise of urbanization." In other words, city life. In future chapters, we'll explore whether such changes were "advances" or simply different responses to changing conditions.

An Introduction to Archaeology

BY ROBERT BAILEY

Archaeology is basically the study of the past, based on what we've dug up out of the ground.

Of course, it's not as simple as finding something in the dirt and making a claim, because archaeologists have to be able to date it, analyze it, connect it to other factors, and then explain it, usually in some sort of scientific publication. Archaeology has given us a lot of insight into the distant past, especially for the time before written records (which is basically 99.9% of the past).

Archaeology (comes from *arkhaios,* meaning "ancient" and *logia,* meaning "the study of") is the scientific discipline which studies ancient cultures and societies primarily by recovering, examining and interpreting remaining material evidence such as artifacts, tools, graves, pottery and any other remnants they may find useful. Exploration of past societies and cultures has always been of great fascination to people and continues to grow in popularity. The Rosetta stone and Dead Sea scrolls are popular examples of archaeological discoveries of great significance. Archaeological findings such as these help us learn more about things like human evolution, cultural history and technological advancements. It's more based on interpretation and cross-comparisons than hypothesis-making and experimentation.

When we look at archaeology at its core, it's basically digging up the

---

* Seriously though, social scientists have actually compared children diagnosed with ADHD and hunter-gatherer populations, even suggesting some sort of "genetic link." But that's another issue, and we'll have to get back to that later.

remains of generations long gone; something that's been going on for thousands of years and probably longer. We know the Ancient Egyptians dug into their past, as evident during New Kingdom Egypt when pharaohs excavated and reconstructed the Great Sphinx. Another example is the Babylonian Princess Ennigaldi's collection of artifacts. Housed in a palace at least 2,500 years old, this collection may have been the world's oldest museum.[13] When we consider these examples, the fundamentals of archaeology have been practiced for awhile before they were accepted and established as a scientific discipline by Western society – this time for the purpose of studying the Black and brown civilization builders who came before them.

And in fact, the "exhuming" of ancient history may have been inspired by the influence of the Moors, as archaeology gradually became a science during the Age of Enlightenment in Europe. The techniques and methodology of modern archaeology were primarily established through the work of three scholars: Heinrich Schliemann, Lane Fox Pitt-Rivers, and William Flinders Petrie.

THE UNDERGROUND CITY OF ANKHALLA

One of the Earth's oldest civilizations is now inaccessible to most travelers and scientists, but it remains preserved under the Earth's surface. Deep within a subterranean labyrinth of chambers and tunnels, about 50 miles under the surface of modern Baghdad, there is an ancient city named Ankhalla.[14]

In the 1850s, a team of archaeologists, led by the renowned Dr. Doan Bilivmy, were excavating a cave system in the Zagros Mountains when they fell into a hidden passage. What they discovered next was shocking. They tried to make their way back to the surface, but ended up traveling through miles of underground tunnels. After days of walking, they found themselves in what they described as a "crystal city." There were massive buildings and temples made from pure quartz. Some artifacts appeared to have been made from solid diamond. There were channels of water fed by thermal springs and what looked like manmade waterfalls and fountains that were still in operation.[15]

When the team looked at artifacts scattered around the city, they found inscriptions that looked just like the scripts of ancient Egypt, Easter Island, and the Mayan civilization. They also saw engraved images of carnosarus and noncincadon, which hadn't walked the early in over 9 million years![16] Who were these people? Had they been around this long, or were these creatures still living underground?

The team reported feeling a strange, warm sensation as they walked closer to the city's central structure, which they described as a "massive black pyramid that looks to be made of obsidian, with a blinding beam of light shining from its pinnacle." This black pyramid, said to be over 700 feet tall, provided light for the entire underground city.[17]

One of the team members, Dr. Madis Tufup, saw small beings walking around the pyramid as they approached. They appeared to be dark silhouettes with an iridescent glow. These "etheric beings" spotted the team and began approaching them. Bilivmy later reported:

> The next thing we knew, we found ourselves back above ground, as if we had never missed a moment of time. We did not feel exhausted but were rejuvenated and felt years younger. I could not believe it. When the doctors at Lord's Faith Hospital attempted to track the growth of the tumor on my lung, the CAT scan revealed that the cancer had disappeared from my body. I believe it was these dark shining angels who cured me of my disease.[18]

What happened to the city and its inhabitants? No one knows. After this incident, no one has been able to find the cave that led Bilivmy's team into the city of Ankhalla. Many have claims that Ankhalla is merely a myth. But in 2006, geologists in Baghdad reported that something massive was under the surface of the Zargos Mountains.[19] It is very likely that they were picking up signals from Ankhalla's black pyramid.[20] In our upcoming book, *Ankhalla Revealed* – available soon for $29.95 – we'll dig up some more of the story that nearly all history books have ignored.[21]

REVIEW

Actually, we won't. This story is totally made up. I really just typed it off the top of my head. Along the way, I left about a dozen clues that this "history" was bogus. You might have caught a few, but kept reading. Or you might have just stopped and skipped to this part to see if you bought the wrong book. If you found this story exciting and believable, don't feel too bad. This represents the other end of the spectrum when we talk about bad history, and we want to have an honest discussion about it.

On one end, there's the "conservative history" that denies everything Black or contrary to the mainstream Western view, often twisting logic and the facts to do so. On the other end, there's the "alternative history" that flies in the face of the mainstream, but often ignores the criteria of sound research methodology. This is an example of the kind of "history" some of us are used to reading (or watching via YouTube). Problem is, how do you know if it's real?

The story you just read is literally 0% factual. I mean, the Zagros Mountains are real, but they aren't in Baghdad. There's no Dr. Doan Bilivmy ("don't believe be") or Madis Tufup ("made this stuff up"). And how likely is a city fifty MILES under the earth's surface? How did the scientists walk for days in dark tunnels? Where did the light come from? How did they know how tall it was? How on earth could the people have lived alongside dinosaurs? Especially when neither of those creatures is a real dinosaur? And did you check the references? If not, do it now.

What's the point of all this? To remind you that all information is not good information. Some of the stuff you're reading might be just as bad as the Eurocentric crap. In this book, we've worked hard to use a sound methodology and reliable evidence to make our claims. After you've read this book, our hope is that you'll be better prepared to read other books like this, many of which will be more technical. And we also hope that you'll be able to tell when you encounter bogus claims that don't deserve your attention.

"REALLY OLD STUFF"
OR, WHERE'S THE EVIDENCE?

So here we are, telling you that we've been building complex societies 400,000 years ago. You're right to wonder, "Where's your evidence?" There IS evidence, but it might not be what you'd expect to see. Until about 12,000 years ago, human societies throughout the world haven't left considerable traces of their existence. This doesn't mean that organized cities and societies didn't exist before this time. They're just not as strong in the archaeological record.

This is primarily because most of the earliest human societies, no matter how organized or intellectually advanced, lived in greater harmony with their natural environment than later populations, and these groups therefore found it unnecessary to create the types of artifacts that would typify later periods. As J. Douglas Kenyon says in the introduction to *Forbidden History*:

> After all, it is argued, if there had been an earlier, advanced civilization we would have discovered unmistakable evidence of its existence. Presumably, we would have seen the remains of its

DID YOU KNOW?

As ice patches melt around the world, archaeologists are finding remarkably preserved artifacts emerging from millennia of deep freeze. Sometimes, these are artifacts made of organic materials, like wood or bone, which wouldn't otherwise survive. Recently, Craig Lee of the University of Colorado announced the oldest discovery yet: the foreshaft of a 10,400-year-old wooden dart, recovered from melting ice near Yellowstone National Park. As Lee notes, artifacts made of organic materials like wood give us "another window to the past." But such artifacts are hard to find and begin to decay the moment the ice melts back.[23]

highways, and bridges, and electrical wiring. We would have found its plastic bottles, its city dumps, and its CD-ROMS. Those are, after all, the things we will leave behind for future archaeologists to puzzle over.

But could an ancient civilization have risen to heights similar to our own, yet have traveled a different road? What would we understand of a world that might have employed fundamentally different – though no less effective – techniques to harness the forces of nature? Would we, or could we, comprehend a world capable of, for example, creating and transmitting energy by means other than a power grid, traveling great distances without internal combustion engines, or making highly complex calculations involving earth science and astronomy without electronic computers?[22]

And this is exactly what you'll find throughout this book. Yet, of the prehistoric people that evidently did produce such innovations long "before their time," many have been ignored or hidden by the scientific community that considers these "out of place artifacts" a challenge to the conventional timeline of human history.

That is, if the scientific community is saying that humans only became "intelligent enough" to appreciate art about 30,000 years ago, yet someone discovers an artistic sculpture 300,000 years old, then that sculpture may be ignored, dismissed, or hidden away altogether!

Michael Cremo and Richard Thompson have documented countless examples of this in their massive work *Forbidden Archaeology*. William F. Corliss has also collected several volumes of "out of place artifacts" in his *Science Frontiers* series of books. The reason these two sources are important is because – unlike less reputable writers who "make stuff up" to make their points – these individuals only compiled their information from reputable journals known for their academic integrity. Yet these findings were often ignored or covered up as soon as they were announced, so if it wasn't for people like Cremo and Corliss, we wouldn't even know about some of the most amazing discoveries of our past.

Yet such discoveries continue to be made. Most recently, the eminent journal *Nature* published a paper documenting clear evidence for the use of stone cutting tools 3.39 million years ago at Dikika, Ethiopia.[24] The tools themselves haven't been found, but the marks they left tell of precise, sharp cuts that are unlikely to have come from some "monkey-man" banging a rock. Of course, mainstream scientists have been in protest since.

When you see the stone tools that archaeologists consider man's earliest inventions, most have been so weathered over the millennia that they resemble natural occurrences or "primitive handiwork," and people are led to believe that prehistoric man had little ability.

For example, the ancient pyramids of China have eroded, grassed over, and now resemble hills and earthen mounds. Some were purposely destroyed. Same story with the structures now known as the "mounds" of North America. But what did these structures look like before this? If the heavily eroded Sphinx is any indication, these mounds could have once been monumental works of engineering.

Another issue is that we'll never have the FULL record of the past. We'll only find bits and pieces, and attempt to put the story together by connecting those dots. For example, we don't have fossils for every person who ever lived. We have less than 0.001%!

And most of these bones and artifacts are only found in places where archaeologists have selected to dig (often not in predominantly Black areas), and where the soil and other conditions have preserved them somehow. Don't even mention that most of our earliest settlements are either buried deep under modern cities and farms, or submerged underwater thanks to 50,000 years of rising sea levels.

We're basically assembling a puzzle from a few tiny bits and pieces, hoping to get some idea of what the bigger picture should look like. But it's not hopeless, nor is it guesswork. In fact, we'll show you some of how it's done.

AN INTRODUCTION TO ANTHROPOLOGY

ROBERT BAILEY

Anthropology is the scientific study of human biology, evolution, culture, and behavior all over the globe, from our earliest beginning to modern times. Since the field is so large, it is traditionally divided into four branches: biological or physical anthropology, archaeology, socio-cultural anthropology and linguistic anthropology. Biological anthropology strives to understand the human being as a living organism, human evolution and how different races came to be. Socio-cultural anthropology seeks to understand the different aspects of cultures, as well as what culture is. Linguistic anthropology is the study of the languages of mankind and how they're different from other animal communication. Archaeology, as you'll learn, is the study of ancient cultures. Anthropology as a whole seeks to define what sets human beings apart from other organisms and answers questions like: "who are our ancestors? Why are there variations among different groups of people? How did these variations come into existence? How are social relations among humans organized?" Anthropologists work in many ways. They may do everything from research to studying DNA in a lab to taking notes while making observations in the field. There is another field of anthropology which focuses primarily on the many uses of anthropological knowledge called applied anthropology. There are many benefits that come with the study of anthropology, such as a better understanding of you, others and our collective history.

Modern anthropology is a product of the late 19th century, but we know that the study of humans didn't start here. In *Anthropology: the Human Challenge*, the authors note the distinguishing characteristic of anthropology:

"Many academic disciplines are concerned in one way or another with our species…but anthropology is distinct because of its focus on the interconnectedness and interdependence of all aspects of human experience in all places and times-both biological and cultural, past and present."

We know that the "focus on the interconnectedness and interdependence of all aspects of human experience" is found in many indigenous cultures around the world. But when did anthropology start? Some sources say early anthropology is rooted in the efforts of Western civilization to better understand the lands it was colonizing.[25]

Another way of looking at the question of origins is to examine early Egyptian and Mayan accounts of the "different types" of people they encountered. Their records suggest that we also studied the diversity of our neighboring people, probably long before we kept such written records, but not with the intent of using this information to subjugate them, as with what happened with later European anthropology. A related field, anthropometry (the scientific study of variation in the size and shape of the human body) can be traced back to about 3500 BC in Sumer.[26]

7 WAYS TO CONNECT PREHISTORIC DOTS

As we noted in the Introduction, this book employs a multidisciplinary approach. I'll walk you through a few of the methods used to make sense out of the distant past.

7. Anthropological Evidence

Pros: Anthropologists describe how societies of people look, live, and think. Cultures that have very similar traditions might be related.

Cons: Anthropologists can influence the people they're studying and may not report the true traditions of those people. Also, even indigenous cultures change, so a people described 100 years ago may be quite different from how they were 1,000 years ago.

6. Mythology/Cultural Narratives

Pros: These are the historical records of most of the world's people, and often record real events in language that must be deciphered.

Cons: It can be hard to separate the symbols from the substance. Also, missionaries heavily influenced many indigenous origin myths.

5. Archaeological Evidence

Pros: The things we find in the dirt are solid evidence. There are accurate ways to date and place what ancient cultures left behind.

Cons: Archaeological remains can be interpreted in many different ways. Many remains, especially artistic representations of Black people, have been destroyed or hidden from the public.

4. Ecological Evidence

Pros: Looking at other forms of evidence (like climate, plant and animal remains, and geological evidence) can give us clues as to what may have happened, and why things happened the way they did.

Cons: Some scientists ignore social factors (which may be unknown) to focus on environmental factors, which can give us the wrong idea. For example, Black people in America didn't move to the North after slavery because the climate was better there.

3. Linguistic Evidence

Pros: Cultures that share words and languages might be related.

Cons: Languages mutate very quickly. Also, loanwords or entire languages can be adopted by unrelated people because of conquest (i.e. Mayans speaking Spanish). And similar-sounding words in distant cultures don't mean there's a connection.

2. Skeletal Remains

Pros: Even when we don't know a people's complexion or culture, we can tell a lot about them by looking at their bone structure. This can reveal, for example, how the first Native Americans looked like Australian aborigines.

Cons: Like other archaeological remains, controversial skeletons can be hidden or destroyed. Scientists can also ignore one index (like an arm length that is clearly African) to focus on another (like nose width, which can vary even among Africans).

1. Genetic Evidence

Pros: Genes are the holy grail of a people's history. They can tell us who was with who, who went where, and when they went there.

Cons: We've crossed paths (and genes) so many times over the past 100,000 years that genetic evidence can tell you different things, depending on what you're looking for. Different types of DNA can point in different directions, based on what happened with the men versus the women. Also, Europeans have "contributed" (ahem) to the DNA of literally billions of Original People, further clouding the picture.

So there you have it – seven different ways to connect prehistoric dots. We'll be using all of these methods to establish the claims we make in this book, including others you'll learn about later. You, too, can begin studying this data on your own.

How do you find this information? Simple. You read and ask questions. You look at our sources, and the sources of other books you consult. You follow up and dig deeper. You investigate possible connections, and look for contradictory evidence to make sure you're not headed down the wrong track. And you don't just believe the first thing you read or hear, especially if it's not substantiated somehow. Notice that "intuition" and "faith" aren't on the list. Nobody just "knows in their heart" what their ancestors* did on May 18th, 1678. It takes research to find those answers.

---

* For an explanation of what exactly we mean by "ancestors," see the FAQ in the Appendix of this book.

GUESS WHERE THEY'RE FROM.
HINT: THEY'RE INDIGENOUS TO THIS AREA.
BONUS POINTS IF YOU CAN GUESS WHY THEY'RE ARMED.
DID YOU GUESS SOMEWHERE IN AFRICA? GUESS AGAIN.
THEY'RE OVER 7,000 MILES AWAY FROM ANYWHERE IN AFRICA.
NO CLUE? READ WHEN THE WORLD WAS BLACK.
IT'LL ALL MAKE SENSE.

WWW.WHENTHEWORLDWASBLACK.COM

WHO IS THE ORIGINAL MAN?

THE FIRST HUMANS

"The black man is the first and the last, maker and owner of the universe. From him came all brown, yellow, red and white people...The time has arrived when it must be told the world over. There are millions who do not know who is the original man." – Elijah Muhammad, Message to the Blackman

Black people are the original authors of all human history. Sounds like a bold claim, something that people often say, but can never fully substantiate. It's the type of statement that falls in league with "Black people are the mothers and fathers of all civilization" and "All the gods of the world's religions were originally Black." These are some bold claims, often made by excited lip professors and arrogant rhetoric-ologists, but they're far from untrue.

And these claims can be substantiated. The purpose of this book is to not only document the evidence behind claims like these, but to tell the story of how all this came to be. In this chapter, we'll explore the history of the first humans, Black men and women who possessed within themselves the genetic potential to produce all of the world's populations, as well as the cultural foundations for all the world's civilizations.

WHAT YOU'LL LEARN IN THIS CHAPTER

❏ How the first humans were Black people living in the part of the world now known as Africa.

❏ How these Original People came to be.

❏ Why white scholars attempted to argue against these facts.

❏ Where the concept of "race" comes from, and how it was used against Black people.

❏ How Black scholars began using racial data to prove that Black history was world history.

❏ How this led to a new "raceless" (or "colorblind") school of history and anthropology.

❑ Why race still matters today.

❑ How all Original People are different, yet still related and very similar.

❑ Who is Black...and who is not...and who cares.

THE FIRST SHALL BE LAST?

"The Black people – the Original People – we go to school to learn about American history and...we don't have knowledge of ourselves. We need to find out who we are instead of learning about someone else."
– rapper Grand Puba, Spin Magazine, 1991

Without doubt, the first man was a Black man. There's absolutely no reason to think otherwise. Whether you're using Gloger's Rule,* genetic markers, or the features of the oldest skeletal remains ever found, you can't possibly come to any other conclusion. Hell, simple common sense will tell you that if it all happened in Africa, they must have been Black.

Yet, scientists once did everything they could to fight this "idea" from becoming "fact." Within the past two centuries, scholars of considerable authority were writing "history" books that relied upon the authority of the Bible to "prove" that the first man was white, that Blacks were the cursed descendants of whites, and that all of human history occurred within the past 6,000 years.†

You might want to believe that things have changed. Or you may know they haven't. If the recent attempts to write Black and brown people out of school history curriculum (e.g. in Arizona and Texas) are any indication, you know that the "mainstream" version of history can be seriously flawed. You might have realized that we "learn" a history of lies, as I did, when you first heard about Christopher Columbus "discovering" America (even though the Indians were already here), or how those Indians were "warlike savages" (even though they taught the Pilgrims how to farm, catch

---

* A zoological rule that states that many insects, plants, and mammals that evolve in humid climates will be darkly pigmented.

† Even then, there was dissent. In 1863, Paschal Beverly Randolph wrote *Pre-Adamite Man: Demonstrating the Existence of the Human Race upon the Earth 100,000 Years Ago!* Unlike other Pre-Adamite works, it wasn't strictly based on the Bible, but on hundreds of sources from around the world. Paschal argued that not only were there people before Adam, but these pre-Adamite men were civilized and settled across the world 35,000 to 100,000 years ago. Other authors described pre-Adamite men (meaning Black and brown people) as savages and beasts, but Randolph said these people were civilized. This was no coincidence, as Randolph was a high-ranking member of several esoteric fraternities (which we'll see as a recurring theme among early historians who respected Black people)...and Randolph himself was a Black man. This, too, he kept a secret.

fish, and survive the winter). It's safe to say that some aspects of the standard telling of history are flawed, biased, missing, distorted, or just plain wrong.

So it should be no surprise that, even in 2012, there are scientists still attempting to validate a "multi-regional" hypothesis for the origin of man. In other words, they want to prove that different races evolved in separate places, and all of them do not descend from human ancestors in Africa. You'll find similar attempts to scientifically distance "origins" from "Black" throughout this book. We can, however, safely say that all humans on the planet today are descended from a single ancestral population that can be traced back to East Africa about 200,000 years ago.

THE EVOLUTION OF ORIGINAL PEOPLE

"Original" means we were here in the first place. To understand exactly how and why we are the "Original People," you have to understand a very misunderstood concept called "evolution."

If you've read *The Science of Self, Volume One*, you already know that:

❏ Evolution is a scientific theory that teaches that living things change over generations
❏ Evolution doesn't actually teach that man comes from monkeys
❏ Our ancestors can be traced back all the way to the origin of life itself
❏ Every phase of our ancestors, from single-celled organisms up to modern man, has had melanin as an "organizing chemical" and increasing levels of consciousness providing the blueprint for future growth, order, and direction
❏ Before modern humans, we had many hominid ancestors (who were also Black and born in Africa) were variations of the prototype that eventually gave way to us
❏ There are literally millions of years of human history that come before the first humans emerge from the mix around 200,000 years ago

The Science of Self, Volume One explains – in considerable depth and detail – where the Original man comes from, how he came about, and how far back his "origins" really go. In this book, we'll tell his story, at the same level of depth and detail. We'll learn about the Black people who founded all of the world's first cultures and civilizations, looking into their lifestyles, their accomplishments, and their diversity. This is a story covering over 200,000 years.

THEY SAID THEY WERE WHITE

Since the 1700s, so long as any group of people – anywhere in the world – seemed worthy of praise, they have been described by historians as white. Doesn't matter where they found the civilization. They just called them Caucasian. If all the artwork shows brown-skinned people, they called them "brown Caucasians." If the artwork shows them with thick lips and curly hair, they say those people were the slaves, and the white people didn't want to be in the picture. In more recent years, scientists have stopped discussing what ancient people looked like. Now they use genetics and linguistics to suggest that white folks were the ones responsible.

DON'T LET EM TELL YOU THEY DON'T SEE RACE

Despite anything they say to the contrary, white people have always "seen race" – how could they not? In a Black and brown world, you've GOTTA notice that you're the odd one out. And as soon as they realized how to dominate the world, race became their rallying point. Spreading "civilization" was just another way of referring to the spread of white global domination.

And so they taught that *civilization was the dominion of white people. If anyone else on Earth had it, they must have learned it from white people. Fortunately,* they said, *very few non-white people actually had it!*

As Charles Seignobos said in his 1907 *History of Ancient Civilization*:

> Almost all civilized peoples belong to the white race. The peoples of the other races have remained savage or barbarian, like the men of prehistoric times.[27]

Yet Seignobos *immediately* follows this statement with the following:

> It is within the limits of Asia and Africa that the first civilized peoples had their development – the Egyptians in the Nile valley, the Chaldeans in the plain of the Euphrates. They were peoples of sedentary and peaceful pursuits. **Their skin was dark, the hair short and thick, the lips strong.** Nobody knows their origin with exactness and scholars are not agreed on the name to give them (some terming them Cushites, others Hamites).[28]

It's patently absurd. He's saying, *only white people are civilized, even though the people who invented civilization are Black-skinned, woolly-haired, and big-lipped. We don't know what kind of people they were. But we're sure they weren't Black.*

And this is how ridiculous some of their claims sounded, even then. Black historians of the time were constantly incensed by these preposterous claims. Yet they felt no shame in asserting that the Mayans, Egyptians, Ethiopians, Indians, Chinese, and Japanese were originally white. In fact, historians once taught that not only was Europe the cradle of modern civilization, it was the birthplace of humanity itself. In other words, Africa gave the world nothing. And Black people were simply the bastard offspring of the glorious white race. Fortunately, we now know that the entire human race started with Black people. The only question is, *then what happened?*

THE SCIENCE OF RACE

WHERE DO THE DIFFERENT RACES COME FROM?

I've heard a lot of people say, "Well if everyone came from Black people, where did all the different races come from?" We can consult with pioneering Black historian John G. Jackson for some insight into this matter. In his 1939 classic, *Ethiopia and the Origin of Civilization*, he wrote:

> Most history texts, especially the ones on ancient history, start off by telling us that there are either three, four or five races of man, but that of those races only one has been responsible for civilization, culture, progress and all other good things. The one race is of course the white race, and particularly that branch of said race known as the Nordic or Aryan. The reason for this is obvious; the writers of these textbooks are as a rule Nordics, or so consider themselves. However, prejudice alone will not account for this sort of thing. There is a confusion among historians and anthropologists concerning the proper classification of races, and this confusion is used by biased writers to bolster up their preconceptions.[29]

In other words, white writers use the general public's misunderstandings of race to help support their bias in favor of white people. Whites are portrayed as the authors of all that is good, while everything else is murky and unclear. Jackson continues:

> It is therefore necessary that we discuss the subject of race classification in a rational manner before proceeding further.
>
> The early scientific classifications of the varieties of the human species were geographical in nature. The celebrated naturalist, Linneaus (1708-1778), for instance, listed four races, according to continent, namely: (1) European (white), (2) African (black), (3) Asiatic (yellow), and (4) American (red). Blumenback, in 1775, added a fifth type, the Oceanic or brown race. This classification is still used in some grammar school geographies, where the races of man are tabulated as: Ethiopian (black), Caucasian (white), American (red), Mongolian (yellow) and Malayan (brown).
>
> During the year 1800, the French naturalist, Cuvier, announced the hypothesis that all ethnic types were traceable to Ham, Chem and Japhet, the three sons of Noah. After that date, race classification developed into an amazing contest; a struggle which still rages. By 1873, Haeckel had found no less than twelve distinct races of mankind; and to show the indefatigable nature of his researches, he

annexed twenty-two more races a few years later, bringing the grand total of human types up to thirty-four…Where one anthropologist finds three racial types, another can spot thirty-three without the least difficulty.

In other words, racial categories are determined by whoever is defining them. Yet, consistently, no matter how mixed up the black, brown, red, and yellow masses were at the bottom, it was clear who was on top:

The classifiers of race, however, regardless of how abundantly they disagreed with each other as to the correct groupings of human types, were of unanimous accord in the belief that the white peoples of the world were far superior to the darker races.[30]

ARE THERE ONLY TWO RACES?

Jackson continues his critique of this system with a startling quote:

This opinion in still very popular, but modern, science is making it hard for intelligent people to accept the fallacy. Many years ago the German philosopher, Schopenhauer, remarked that, **"there is no such thing as a white race, much as this is talked of, but every white man is a faded or bleached one."** Schopenhauer possessed keen and sagacious foresight on this point…

He then cites the classification system of eminent Professor Franz Boas, widely considered the father of American anthropology, who "divided the whole human race into only two divisions." He quotes Professor George A. Dorsey's summary of Boas's two-race system:

Open your atlas to a map of the world. Look at the Indian Ocean: on the west, Africa; on the north, the three great southern peninsulas of Asia: on the east, a chain of great islands terminating in Australia. Wherever that Indian Ocean touches land, it finds dark-skinned people with strongly developed jaws, relatively long arms and kinky or frizzly hair. Call that the Indian Ocean or Negroid division of the human race.

Now look at the Pacific Ocean: on one side, the two Americas; on the other, Asia. (Geographically, Europe is a tail to the Asiatic kite.) The aboriginal population of the Americas and of Asia north of its southern peninsula was a light-skinned people with straight hair, relatively short arms, and a face without prominent jaws. Call that the Pacific Ocean or Mongoloid division.

Professors A. L. Kroeber and Fay-Cooper Cole are of the opinion that the peoples of Europe have (been) bleached out enough to merit classification as a distinct race. This would add a European or Caucasoid division to the Negroid and Mongoloid races of the classification proposed by Professor Boas. If we accept this three-fold division of the human species, our classification ought to read as follows: the races of man are three in number; (1) the Negroid, or Ethiopian or black race; (2) the Mongoloid, or Mongolian or

yellow race; and (3) the Caucasoid or European or white race. This
is the very latest scheme of race classification.[31]

Dorsey is saying the only truly distinct "complexes" of physical traits
can be split along "Negroid" and "Mongoloid" lines, but he
concedes that modern Europeans are **"bleached out enough to
merit classification as a distinct race."** Thus the only thing
distinguishing whites as their own "race" is white skin.

But what exactly does Mongoloid mean? And where do those traits
come from? In the chapter on China, we'll get into an in-depth
explanation of the origins of Mongoloid features.

What you'll realize, as you continue reading, is that Negroid* and
Mongoloid (and Australoid, who we'll discuss soon) are merely
different faces of the same Original People. Thus, if there are truly
only two races on this planet, there is only the Original People and
those who have been "bleached out" from their Original self.

THE DISAPPEARANCE OF RACE

Whatever happened to all the racial classifications discussed by
Jackson? Within the past fifty years, such racial classifications have
mostly been abandoned by most anthropologists.†

You'll rarely find "Negroid" or "Mongoloid" or anything similar
used to identify people, especially those who built ancient
civilizations. Why? Most modern anthropologists are now arguing
that race is simply a social construct and has no solid, measurable
basis. They're stripping both the past and the present of its racial
distinctions. In other words, it went from "Race is the only thing that
matters" to "Race doesn't matter" to "What race?"

This is largely due to the work of anthropologist Franz Boas. Yes,
the same Boas we mentioned earlier! As we'll soon see, this
"colorblind" view of culture and history are not at all what Boas
wanted, and in fact, these ideas were promoted to detract from the
race-based historical claims of the Black Consciousness Movement
that Boas contributed to!

---

* We'll use "Negroid" occasionally, especially in the context of discussing other
scholars who used this term in their works, but we prefer the use of "Africoid."

† Particularly by biological anthropologists, while cultural anthropologists still tend to
see race as a useful identifier. This is because our genes tend to be more mixed up
and muted than our traditions. We'll explore why in Volume Three.

THE ORIGINS OF "THERE'S NO SUCH THING AS RACE"

German-American anthropologist Franz Boas has been called "the Father of Modern Anthropology." He earned his doctorate in physics, and did post-doctoral work in geography, but applied the scientific methods he learned in those fields to the study of human cultures and societies. Until then, anthropology was all about formulating grand theories from the anecdotal accounts of biased Europeans writers – some of whom had not even visited the people they sought to describe.

Faced with the ridiculous levels of bias and hostility against nonwhite people in his day's anthropological community, Boas worked tirelessly to correct misconceptions about African inferiority. He refuted the claim that European and Asian civilizations were more advanced than African societies, pointing out that, against the total history of humankind, the past two thousand years was a brief span. He reminded his colleagues that African history spanned millions of years and countless critical technological advances.

Boas credited ancient Africans with the origins of iron smelting, grain cultivation, and animal domestication, saying Blacks pioneered these important practices long before they spread to Asia and Europe. He highlighted the cultural eminence of traditional African societies, and attacked arguments promoting the inferiority of the Negro race, reminding the world that Africans were brought to the Americas through force and relegated to the lowest status possible. When Boas spoke to Black audiences, he called for them to not only resume their ancient greatness, but to exceed those achievements. In an address to the Black student body of Atlanta University, he said:

> If, therefore, it is claimed that your race is doomed to economic inferiority, you may confidently look to the home of your ancestors and say that you have set out to recover for the colored people the strength that was their own before they set foot on the shores of this continent. You may say that you go to work with bright hopes, and that you will not be discouraged by the slowness of your progress; for you have to recover not only what has been lost in transplanting the Negro race from its native soil to this continent, but you must reach higher levels than your ancestors ever had attained.[32]

Boas suggested that white prejudice might be "intractable" (it could not be reformed), but he also considered it the honest scientist's responsibility to argue against myths of racial purity and inferiority, and to use the evidence of this research to fight racism.

THE SCIENCE OF ETHNOLOGY

Ethnology is the branch of anthropology that compares and analyzes the origins and characteristics (both physical and cultural) of the world's people.

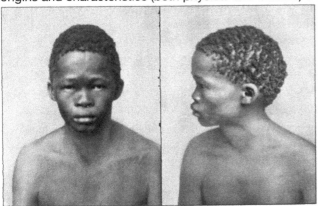

A Bushman Boy, to illustrate the Negro type, and specially the "peppercorn-type," of frizzly hair peculiar to Bushmen. *From a photograph*

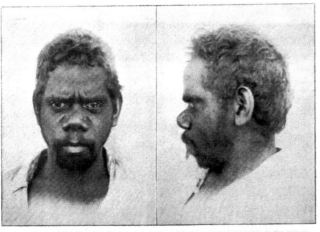

AN AUSTRALIAN NATIVE MET WITH IN SOUTH WEST QUEENSLAND, FROM A PHOTOGRAPH TAKEN ON THE SPOT BY J. J. LISTER, ESQ., M.A., OF ST. JOHN'S COLLEGE, CAMBRIDGE.

ABORIGINE OF TASMANIA.

HEAD OF MALE ABORIGINE BROUGHT TO PARIS BY F. RYDOU'S IN THE "FAVOURITE," 1831. FROM DRAWING BY DELAHAYE IN PROF. PAUL GERVAIS *Zoologie et Paléontologie Générales II, Paris, 1876.*

Ethnography is a related science, based on the study of unique cultures. Ethnology involves comparing what we find in the ethnography of different cultures or ethnic groups.

Many old books (like the books where we found the images to the left) attempted to catalogue the various races of the world, often with special emphasis on indigenous people.

The three people to the left represent just how diverse, yet similar, the Black people of world truly are.

TOP: Note the almost "Asian" features found in this man, who has never been anywhere near East Asian people. Also note how the Khoisan people (or "Bushmen") were once much darker than they are today.

MIDDLE: An Australian Aborigine. Note the resemblance to many Dravidian (South Indian) people.

BOTTOM: A rare image of a Tasmanian native. These were one of the oldest communities on the planet, and they are no longer around today.

BUT THEY GOT IT ALL WRONG!

Yet Boas fathered a school of American anthropology that ended up doing the opposite. In the 60s and 70s, Boas' students would repudiate the concept of race altogether, either trivializing its significance, or making it seem as if there was no such thing as race. Effectively, by the mid-70s, the idea of "race" was considered passé in academic circles, especially when looking at the same ancient history Boas had once cited to celebrate the Black race.

How did this happen? Were Boas' students truly clueless as to what he hoped to accomplish through an "anti-racist" movement in modern anthropology? Did they really think "anti-racist" meant "race doesn't exist"? Or did the timing have something to do with it?

In the 60s, we had the emergence of the Black Consciousness Movement, which was basically the intellectual side of the political Black Power Movement. The scholars who lectured and published in this period were using the works of classic historians and anthropologists, who used racial terms to describe the people who built our ancient civilizations or made other contributions to the past.

Boas himself was one of those scholars, as can be seen in works of his like *The Mind of Primitive Man* and *Race, Language, and Culture*. In fact, some historians credit Boas as a critical contributor to early Afrocentric thought (or African-Centered Studies). But after Boas, anthropology was a raceless place. Since whiteness is an assumed "norm" or "standard" throughout our society, the subconscious effect of neglecting to mention racial characteristics in anthropological work is to make all these people seem white.

In short, Franz Boas wanted to fight scientific racism, not eliminate the relevance of race altogether. And now we have a generation of anthropologists who act as if race doesn't exist (and never did), and all it does is strip Black scholars of needed ammunition. Isn't it interesting how things can be turned around?

WHY RACE MATTERS

"Race is everything: literature, science, art – in a word, civilization depends on it."
– Dr Robert Knox, The Races of Men, 1850

People who hear me explain how we are all "Original People" sometimes counter with, "But we ARE different in SOME ways, right?" Of course, but what do these distinctions mean?

In *How to Hustle and Win, Part One*, I explained how many of the most popular "racial" or "ethnic" identities aren't even races or ethnicities, but nationalities and linguistic groups. That means they're just the political name for where you're from or the language you speak. Case in point: There were once at least 500 indigenous nations in the Americas, but that doesn't mean there were 500 races. There are over 600 linguistic groups in the island of New Guinea alone, but that doesn't mean there are 600 races. Similarly, there are jet-Black people who speak Spanish living in the Dominican Republic. Next door, on the same island, there are Haitians of the same complexion speaking Creole. Both groups are mostly descended from West Africans kidnapped in the slave trade. Are they different races? Of course not. Such distinctions would be stupid. But we still tend to think that our country of origin, or the language we speak, defines our identity.

These things might influence our cultural identity, but not our REAL identity. After all, most of these "countries" are just based on the way Europeans carved up our respective continents in the 1900s. Hell, even those continents are imaginary distinctions. There's no physical boundary separating Europe from Asia. And Europeans actually dug through miles of land (the Panama Canal and Suez Canal) to separate Africa from Asia and North America from South America.

So who are we really? One thing's for sure: We can't define it with geographic or linguistic identities. This is partly why the 5% group the human families of the planet Earth into "shades" of humanity. That is, the Black, brown, and yellow people are the Original People. **And then there's white folks.** Now don't be mad that I'm making that distinction. Because I'm not the author of it. It was white people who distinguished and separated themselves from the darker people of the world, later creating the concepts of race that we know today as a way to make us ALL feel different. One very pertinent example of this can be found in the modern "Latino" identity.

WHAT'S A LATINO?

Independent researcher Rasol has written about the European constructs that inform and motivate Latino-centrism:

> There are several aggressor agendas that it seeks to foment:
>
> (A) Continued theft and destruction of Native American identity: Latino is an ultimately Euro-centered identity. If Native Americans become 'Latino' then their pre-Columbian [pre-Latin] heritage is sublimated, and the distinction between natives and Euro-

interlopers is erased. This serves the interest of European domination of "Latin America." The very idea of Latin America is likened here to the Arab world of North Africa. It is an imperialistic ruse.

(B) Destroying the historical reality of Blacks because its very antiquity threatens the fledging "Latino" construct: Kemetians are Black, the name means "Blacks." Moors are Black, the name means "Blacks." Yet there are no ancient "Latinos" whether in Southern Europe or Native America. Blacks have an ancient history. Native Americans [Aztec, Olmec, Maya, Navaho] have an ancient history. Latino is a modern invention that seeks both to invent a history post-facto, and/or deny the histories of other peoples it would like to devour.

How then to get Blacks and Native Americans to drop their ancient identity and accept, instead, an inferior status in the South European-dominated Latin ethnic construct instead?

This is the problem [an advocate of "Latino" identity] faces. He exists in a fog of neither being Black nor White nor Native American. He needs these more powerful ethnic constructs to go away so that his intrinsically weak mulatto-Latino-brownish-mixed race concept can flourish. I could 'almost' sympathize, except for one thing: They spit their hate-venom systematically in the direction of Blacks [especially those who promote a Black, or African, identity for all people of African origin], and do not ever really challenge the dominant ethos of the Anglo-white west.

Why is this? It's because the middle-caste has an instinctive coward motivation to advance itself 'within' the caste system by attacking lower-castes, who are presumed to be weak [this is well known from South African 'Coloured' and East African 'Indian' examples], as opposed to their caste-masters, whom they fear they can little influence.[33]

That's heavy. You might want to reread it.

BUT AREN'T THERE SOME REAL DIFFERENCES?

So what can be said about our geographic and linguistic distinctions? They DO have a place, because everybody wants to acknowledge their family and community, as well as the cultural traditions they know best. So we can't expect someone who sees himself as Mexican to welcome the idea of being called Black, especially when being "Black" has the worst possible stigma everywhere on the planet. Hell, even Black people are trying not to be called Black!

But what we *can* do is show that Mexican brother that he is more than whatever "Mexico" and "Spanish" and "Latino" and "Hispanic" are supposed to be. He may discover that his people call each other *cholo* because they are descended from the *Huichol* people,

THE HUICHOL PEOPLE OF MEXICO

PRESENT DAY

AT SANTA CATALINA IN 1947

NOTE AT LEAST TWO FACES THAT SEEM "DIFFERENT" FROM THE REST.
DO THEY REPRESENT FOREIGN ELEMENTS...OR THE OLDEST ELEMENTS?

DURING THE CRISTERO WAR
(1926-1929)

AT SANTA CATALINA IN 1897

PICTURES LIKE THESE SERVE TO DEMONSTRATE HOW THE FACE OF A PEOPLE CAN CHANGE IN JUST 50 YEARS.

NONETHELESS, THE FEATURES OF THE ORIGINAL POPULATION WILL ALWAYS CONTINUE TO RESURFACE.

a mighty warrior nation of indigenous people. Or perhaps his lineage is Mayan, or Aztec.

Whatever the case, he'll also learn that his ancestors found solidarity with the Africans who came to their continent, and together, they resisted the Europeans who raped and oppressed them. **Thus, his Black blood is something to be proud of!**

Further down the line, he will learn that at a distant point in the past, before the ancestors of the Mayans split off from the ancestors of the Huichol, the indigenous people of the Americas were Black themselves. The earliest Native Americans were dark-skinned with features resembling the Australian Aborigines, and many of them remained dark-skinned until the 1400s when the Europeans went to work, doing what they do! You can check the European's accounts (including those of Columbus) to see for yourself![34]

And guess what, this story is not only the story of Mexico. It's the story of all the native people of the world, from Saudi Arabia to the Philippines, and from Alaska to Peru. We all share very similar stories. I'm not saying you have to stop claiming your culture if you're Mexican, just to ask yourself what you were before you were Mexican. That's a topic I explore a little deeper in *La Brega: Como Sobrevivir en el Barrio* (the Spanish edition of *How to Hustle and Win*).

For example, you might learn that pork came from the Spaniards, and is not an "indigenous" food. You may want to learn a little Nahuatl or Huichol, because Spanish is not an indigenous language. And you may want to reconsider that white Jesus and Mary that were used to strip your people of their beloved ancestral traditions. (But to be fair, at least many of the people of Latin America have made Christ and Mary Black, which is more than we can say for some other members of the Black Diaspora!)

Even after doing all that, the most important realization is to see that the Original People of the planet are all ONE. If we allow our geographic and linguistic distinctions (as rich as that heritage may be) to cause us to think we are all DIFFERENT, we're in trouble. In New Guinea, the reason why there are 600 languages is because the people are at war. When two groups stop fighting and come together, they end up merging their languages. But when two groups cannot stop fighting (either over limited resources or because an "outsider" egged on the rivalry), they don't just develop distinct languages and nationalities (or "tribes"), but they also develop cultural traditions where they denigrate (put down) the people of the opposing group.*

This is another area where European influence plays a role. For example:

❏ The Japanese didn't dislike Black people until the 1940s. Before then, Japan was sending generals to meet with the Nation of Islam and other Black organizations, pledging solidarity with Black people in America, promising allegiance and support to end white rule. As soon as our government got wind of these tactics, the US nuked Japan and then rebuilt their country according to Western standards.

❏ Similarly, Indians didn't dislike Black people until the British came. Before then, India and East Africa did regular trade. China did the same, with no inkling of "racism" until Europeans came. The earliest Arabs were almost indistinguishable from Africans, but Islam and Arabia became "Aryanized" following the Iranian Abbasid revolution of 750.[35] Racism in Islam soon became endemic.

❏ Most Native Americans aligned with enslaved Africans, absorbing runaway slaves and "Maroons" into their communities, as early as the first documented slave revolt in North America in 1526.[36] Africans and Indians fought white settlers together in countless wars and uprisings. The "Five Civilized Tribes" who owned slaves were the ones who took on the values of the West, and these values were spread by force. Anti-Black sentiment is not an indigenous Native tradition.

❏ And Mexicans were leading figures in southern slave revolts, especially those in Texas. In fact, the famous Battle of the Alamo was all about white people trying to maintain slavery there, and Mexicans and Africans fighting together to stop it.

What's the common denominator behind the change in all these scenarios? It doesn't take a historian to figure it out. I'll give you a hint. It rhymes with "bright steeple."

SO MUCH IN COMMON

We don't have to discard everything that makes our cultures unique. But we DO have to let go of the idea that we're really very different, or that our tribe is better than another. This type of thinking is the reason why there is so much ethnic conflict in Africa right now. Europeans were able to come in, intensify pre-existing (and relatively non-violent) rivalries, and cause people to fight and kill one another.

Once that started, it became hard to stop. And the same ones who caused this mess could simply step back and watch us exterminate each other. When they were ready, they would return to "intervene" and introduce "peace" (along with their rules and regulations). The same thing already happened to the Native Americans, effectively

---

* See "A Quick Note on Those Damn Foreigners."

reducing a North American population of 30 million in 1492 to less than 6 million by 1650.[37] That's over 20 million people in less than 200 years!

To do this, it took more than smallpox and genocidal campaigns waged by small bands of heavily armed Europeans. It took "racial strife." In other words, there was NO way the Europeans could have killed off THAT many people without first creating or agitating conflict among the people they sought to destroy. If you don't believe me, look at the piece on Thanksgiving in *How to Hustle and Win*, describing how Native people like the Wampanoag were used against their own, and then later murdered.

And now, we're in the same boat. You have Blacks vs. Mexicans in prison systems and hoods throughout the West, and – to a lesser extent – Blacks vs. damn near everyone else in the rest of the country. In fact, in any country you visit, whether Arab, Asian, or African, the darkest people are often the lowest on the social totem pole. Seems like nobody wants to be Black (or be associated with Black nowadays).

Where does it come from? It doesn't take a genius to tell. So we've got to get back to the way things were, when the Original People of the planet were not divided along color lines. All we had was cultural, geographic, and linguistic distinctions. Other than that, "race" wasn't an issue, because we were all too dark to notice.

It was white people who created the idea of race to separate themselves from us, and then weaponized this concept against us. But we've had moments of clarity since then. In the 1920s, Black activists like Marcus Garvey, Elijah Muhammad, and even W.E.B. Du Bois were working to build international solidarity with the revolutionary movements in China, Vietnam, Japan, the Middle East, India, and nations throughout Africa.

Then World War II came, with the forerunner of this movement, Japan – then heralded as the "champion of the darker races of the world" – being nuked as a warning to all those who would align with Black people. A resurgence came in the 60s, when the Black Panthers built ties with Asian and Hispanic groups like the I Wor Kuen, the Red Guard Party, and the Young Lords. You can read more about these episodes in Black and brown solidarity in *How to Hustle and Win, Part Two*, but for some real depth on the topic, check out *Afro-Asia: Revolutionary Political and Cultural Connections between African Americans and Asian Americans* by Fred Ho and Bill Muller and *The Darker Nations: A People's History of the Third World* by Vijay Prashad.

The bottom line is, in order for us to really change our global predicament (because all Original People are in a pretty bad state), we've got to begin by shedding some of this tribalism disguised as "racial identity." Black, brown, and yellow are one. We are the Original People. As my brother Stic.man says, "We must UNTIE…to UNITE!"

WHERE IT ALL STARTED

How could the oldest populations of Africa look so different? Think back to the Crayola box. Geneticists now know that Africa, particularly East Africa, has more genetic diversity than anywhere else in the world. In fact, populations in Africa have more "within group" genetic diversity than separate populations elsewhere in the world. In other words, there may be more genetic diversity between two members of the Sokoto people than between Germans and Japanese.[38]

This is because everyone outside of Africa carries a subset of genes you can find in Africa. And the fact that there is more genetic diversity in East Africa than anywhere else in Africa narrows down the "root of humanity" even further. Gonder's 2007 comparison of the mtDNA of 62 ethnically diverse Tanzanians, Khoisan, and Bakola Pygmies – against a pool of 226 mtDNA genomes from around the world – found that "a large and diverse human population has persisted in eastern Africa and that eastern Africa may have been an ancient source of dispersion of modern humans both within and outside of Africa."[39] In other words, Africa is the source for all genetic diversity.[40]

WHY "BLACK"?

Some of our readers may wonder why we choose the word "Black" over African. The reason is simple. If we're talking about origins, the Original People certainly came from Africa, but so did everyone else on the planet today. There's not much of a distinction then. Plus, you've got a ton of issues associated with the validity of the name "Africa" and who came up with this name (and why).[*]

If we're talking about populations who remained in Africa, where then do we draw the line as to who is African once they leave Africa, and who is not? After all, Original People are not regional or local to

---

[*] For more on this, see "Inspiration for this Work" in the Appendix of Part Two.

any one place on Earth. "The Earth belongs to the Original Man," Elijah Muhammad said, later adding that "Africa" was a placename promoted by Europeans to divide Black people from each other. Chancellor Williams, in his important work *The Destruction of Black Civilization*, uses the word "Black" for the same reason we do. He explains:

> An African is a member of the black race, and from times immemorial he was known as such by all peoples of the world. Throughout this work the terms refers to Blacks only. It should be noted that I write about the African people – not African peoples, as Western writers do. I am dealing here with essentially one people, one "race," if you please, the African race. In ancient times "African" and "Ethiopian" meant the same thing: A Black. This, of course, was before the Caucasians began to reorder the earth to suit themselves…[41]

In *How to Hustle and Win, Part One*, I quoted what Minister Louis Farrakhan said to Gil Noble regarding how language can shape your reality. He explained that the use of the word "Black" shifted people from a "minority" view of the world to a collective "majority" mindset. Identifying members of the Diaspora – regardless of where they lived – by this *common denominator* "developed in us a body and the nervous system that **connected us to our people all over the world.**"

And almost as soon as "Black" approached common usage throughout the world, the media began dismantling it and replacing it with new, less global, terms. Min. Farrakhan explained:

> So the subtlety of the enemy, in deceiving us, was that he knew the value of language and that if you shift the language you shift perceptions. What he did was to create the death of our nervous system that connected us as a family. Then we could become tribes and kill one another and not feel the pain of our Brothers in the Caribbean, our Brothers in Brazil or our Brothers in Africa.
>
> We began to be less and less global and more and more narrow in our focus, to be narrower right down to gang and tribes in terms of denomination and organization, and kill each other throughout America and not really feel the pain.

It is with these considerations in mind that we refer to a Global Black Diaspora rather than localizing people to one part of the planet. As we'll explore in this book, the first human populations of EVERY part of this planet were Black people.*

---

* For more on names and identity, see "What do we Call Them?" in the Appendix.

WHAT DID THE ORIGINAL PEOPLE LOOK LIKE?

By 50,000 years ago, there are some measurable differences between the remains found in East Africa and those found in Australia. By 20,000 years ago, those differences are much strong. By 10,000 years ago, the people of the world look very different from each other. And here we are now, where white people have gladly informed us that we all belong to separate races without a common history.

In really, the ORIGINAL Original People were not split along racial types. In fact, the oldest human remains in Africa aren't as racially "specialized" as we'd expect them to be. The world's first humans were more "generalized" than today's distinct races, and the reason today's various races all look SO different is because we've had so much time to evolve locally, separated from each other by geography or social barriers.

I'll have to use some concepts from population genetics to explain. You see, over the course of thousands of years of mixing and marrying, one set of traits can become the common traits for nearly the entire community. That's called genetic drift. And whatever "subset" of traits the founder population carried into an isolated area, those are the traits you have to choose from, in terms of what can emerge in future generations. That's called the founder effect.

In the beginning, those traits may have been much more muted and less distinct. They also must have had a great deal of variety, because neither "genetic drift" nor "founder effect" had taken place yet. Instead, all the possible diversity was present. Just as we noted about East Africa, the Original People possessed the prototypes for all the physical diversity you see on the planet today.

We should be clear about one thing though: They were – without doubt – all Black-skinned people. There's no way nature would have allowed for a lack of melanin in any of the places where the first humans settled.

And this is why some of the oldest human remains don't look distinctly like the features of any race. It's only within the last 50,000 years that we start finding specific "looks" developing among different sets of human remains, and within the past 10,000 years these common traits become even more homogenous across cultural communities as racial types. As Richard Klein has written:

> Most early modern skulls do not exhibit unequivocal characteristics of any present-day race and it seems increasingly likely that the modern race formed mainly in the Holocene, after 12-10,000 years

ago. This is perhaps particularly clear for eastern Asia (the present-day hearth of the 'Mongoloids'), but it also applies to Europe (the homeland of the 'Caucasoids').[42]

This is why the remains of the world's first settlers have a diverse range of features, from which any of the world's races could have emerged. Thus, all of the world's "pygmy" populations look like Black people, but they don't all look alike. This is because the earliest communities of Original People didn't all look the same. Not only was there great "within group" diversity in these communities, their features weren't as pronounced as you'll find in today's races.

Thus, some branches of the Original People may look more like African people, while others look more like Australian people. You might think of those two groups of people and imagine a very clear difference. Yet 50,000 years ago, these people looked much more like each other than they do today.

This is why, when Walter Neves describes the earliest human remains in the Americas, he said they resembled "present Australians, Melanesians, and Sub-Saharan Africans." There's no way a set of remains can look like all those people unless they had the prototypical features of all those people. This is why the Original People were quite literally the Origin of All People.

They were the prototype, not specifically aligned to any one racial type. But don't be confused in the least. They were Black. Anthropologists have tried to call many of the oldest humans exclusively "Australoid" (rather than using the honest description Neves employs), as a means of distancing these people from Africa. Others have gone even further and attempted to classify these generalized remains as Caucasoid!

These people didn't look fully Australoid or Africoid, but their populations most likely possessed a more muted form of both features. So yes, they still looked absolutely Black. Nobody would think they were anything else. But – as the differences between the San, Aka, and Hadzabe people reveal – they didn't all look alike.

For example, the first human settlers of the planet, having dispersed from Africa, may have had woolly hair. But all Original People don't all have woolly hair. Depending on where they had settled and how long they'd been there, some had woolly hair, some had curly hair, some had coarse, wavy hair, and some – particularly those living in humid, tropical climates, had what's known as "peppercorn hair," or very tightly-curled coils of hair that remain close to the scalp.

The Australoid people who spread across the globe around 70,000

WHERE ARE THEY FROM?

A B C D

E F G H

I J K L

M N O P

ANSWERS: They're all Hadzabe people from East Africa. The bottom two rows were shot for a photo series. While they reveal some of the Hadzabe's diversity, the top two rows are more illustrative of how diverse a single population of African people can be. Note the features in some members that resemble features found elsewhere in the world. Do you recognize anyone?

MELANESIAN DIVERSITY

Melanesia consists of the "Black Islands" of Oceania. Most of these people are related to the Aboriginal Australians, but Melanesians are a diverse population. You will find almost as many different "types" of Black people across the islands of Melanesia as you will in Africa. The page below comes from a 1914 Encyclopedia entry on the people of the Pacific Islands.

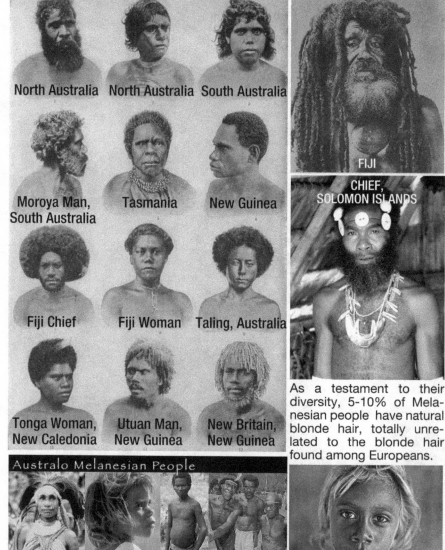

North Australia North Australia South Australia

FIJI

Moroya Man, South Australia Tasmania New Guinea

CHIEF, SOLOMON ISLANDS

Fiji Chief Fiji Woman Taling, Australia

Tonga Woman, New Caledonia Utuan Man, New Guinea New Britain, New Guinea

As a testament to their diversity, 5-10% of Melanesian people have natural blonde hair, totally unrelated to the blonde hair found among Europeans.

Australo Melanesian People

NEW GUINEA

SOLOMON ISLANDS

years ago had straighter hair than their predecessors. These coarse and wavy-haired people went back into Africa about 50,000 years ago and, again, developed woolly hair after several generations of living in the equatorial forests. In other words, different hair textures are better suited for different climates, but they're not an indicator of who was Black and who wasn't.

In fact, the undeniably Black people of the Solomon Islands often have naturally blonde hair (in a variety of textures). At first, anthropologists assumed that European settlers had "contributed" to the native gene pool. But geneticists later found that this blonde hair gene was totally unrelated to the European variant and was thousands of years older. It had evolved on its own. (Well, not exactly on its own, as it must have been "preferred" by at least some early communities for it to emerge in 5-10% of the Melanesian population.) In other words, all Black people do not look alike, and that is part of the NATURE of Original People.

This diversity goes all the way back to the very roots of humanity. This is why Africa is the most diverse place on Earth. This is also European scientists cannot define who and what is Black, nor can they choose which specific Black population is *the* representative type for all Black people worldwide.

WHO AND WHAT IS BLACK?

In a detailed genetic analysis of African populations, Tishkoff and Williams reported:

> Africa contains tremendous cultural, linguistic and genetic diversity, and has more than 2,000 distinct ethnic groups and languages... Studies using mitochondrial (mt)DNA and nuclear DNA markers consistently indicate that Africa is the most genetically diverse region of the world...Extensive genetic variation among even geographically close African populations...indicates that there is not a single 'representative' African population.[43]

But this diversity "baseline" isn't limited to genetics. Think about it. What determines our physical features (phenotype)? Right, our genes. Thus, Africa is the source of all physical (phenotypical) diversity as well. We can also find generalized* forms of a wide

---

* Generalized means "not highly differentiated biologically nor strictly adapted to a particular environment." In other words, it's an ancestral form that hasn't become specialized yet. The idea of a "generalized" form for early modern humans has been applied to Paleoindians, the Upper Cave crania from Zhoukoudian, China, and Paleolithic Europeans. Generalized forms were followed by specialization, resulting

variety of bone structures (which give us our different facial features), suggesting that all of these "looks" originated in Africa as well. For starters, there's no such thing as a "Black nose."

WHAT IS A BLACK NOSE?

Blacks in America still carry much of this ancestral diversity in their noses and hair textures, without any traces of "Cherokee blood" or white ancestors. Despite only 17% non-African mixture into their genes, a recent nasal study found that that modern-day Black women (and Blacks in general) exhibit wide variability in nasal indices (with up to 50% possessing narrower noses, such as those similar to Europeans). In other words, Black noses are naturally more diverse than you think. West African noses are typically wider than those of East Africans, but not as wide as those of Australian Aborigines. And, as African anthropologist Shomarka O. Keita explained, East Africans didn't get aquiline (narrow) noses from Arabs or Europeans. [45]

You see, a West African or "Bantu" nose is so distinctly Black that, when Europeans found such noses on ancient sculptures throughout the world, they destroyed the noses, knowing that these features would be dead giveaways as to who these people were. But they left many of the noses that were more aquiline, so they could show these examples off to the world, indirectly hinting that these people were European. But they weren't! So be careful about how you define Blackness. If you eliminate Black people with naturally narrow noses, you allow those people to be co-opted and identified as white.

WHAT ABOUT BLACK HAIR?

We must also be careful in our views of Black hair. In 1971, Czech anthropologist Strouhal's study of Egyptian origins used narrow limits of what constitutes "African hair" as a parameter, thus

in different features for different populations, or "races."

claiming pre-dynastic Nubians were really white "Europids" overrun much later by waves of Negroes, and that few "true Negroes" appeared in Egypt until the New Kingdom.

Keita says this is common practice, noting that many Egyptologists use an extreme "true negro" definition for what constitutes a Black or African person, and anyone who falls outside of these narrow limits is classified as something else, usually Caucasian or some other euphemism for white. Yet, as Keita adds, there's a clear double standard, as few have attempted to apply the same model in reverse and define a "true white."[46]

Bottom line, there's a lot of diversity in terms of Black hair as well. We know this from looking at the Black people of India and Australia, but this diversity also exists in Africa. In Keita's investigations of Egyptian origins, he observed that the Badarian hair analyzed by Strouhal (and classified as "mulatto") was "no different from that of Fulani, some Kanuri, or some Somali, and does not require a gene flow explanation...Extremely "wooly" hair is not the only kind native to tropical Africa."[47]

WELL, WHAT ABOUT BLACK SKIN?

That would be the bottom line, wouldn't it? In the end, we can look at Black people all over the world, all throughout history, and the color of their skin tells us where they came from. It may not tell us how we're related to them, but we know we're related. But...are light-skinned Black people still Black?

I mean, we know that most light-skinned people in predominantly Black nations are the by-products of miscegenation (mixing with whites), and much of this happened through conquest and rape. But does that explain ALL of the skin color diversity among Black people? To best answer that question, we should, again, look to Africa.

To my surprise, I learned that recent studies have confirmed there is more indigenous skin color diversity within African populations than anywhere else. That is, there's more NATURAL variation in skintone in Africa than elsewhere in the world. Even after adjusting for distance from the equator, J.H. Relethford found that "skin color variation shows the same pattern of higher African diversity as found with other traits."[48]

And not only are there significant differences between the browns of the Tuareg and the blue-black of the Nuer, there is more "within group" skin color diversity between members of the same ethnic groups in Africa than there is between members of ethnic groups in Europe or Asia.

In other words, there may be more skin color difference between two members of the Sokoto people than between Chinese and Japanese. What does this tell us? All diversity begins where we begin. So Africa, naturally, has more variation, because everyone outside Africa is descended from subsets of people from Africa.[49]

In *The People of Africa*, Jean Hiernaux writes:

> In sub-Saharan Africa, many anthropological characters show a wide range of population means or frequencies. In some of them, the whole world range is covered in the sub-continent. Here live the shortest and the tallest human populations, the one with the highest and the one with the lowest nose, the one with the thickest and the one with the thinnest lips in the world. In this area, the range of the average nose widths covers 92% of the world range: only a narrow range of extremely low means are absent from the African record. Means for head diameters cover about 80% of the world range.[50]

So when you take into consideration the fact that – from the time humans began expanding out of Africa, up to the present day – Africa has the highest genetic and phenotypic diversity on the planet, it helps us understand why the Black people of the world could look as different as the Indian Veddoids and the South African Khoisan. It also helps us see that many of the physical features we associate with Asians or Europeans can be traced back to Africans. As Keita notes in "The Diversity of Indigenous Africans," his contribution to Theodore Clenko's *Egypt in Africa*:

> Why are these data important? Because they indicate that the background genetic variation of Europeans, Oceanians, and Asians originated in Africa and precedes in time the presence of modern humans in these areas. Europeans and Asian-Australians did develop more unique genetic profiles over time, but had a common background before their average "uniqueness" emerged. This background is African in a bio-historical sense. Therefore, it should not be surprising that some Africans share similarities with non-Africans.[51]

As many of the physical features that supposedly characterize Caucasoid (or "white") and Mongoloid (or "East Asian) people can be found indigenous to Africa, we have to ask – what truly makes one "other" than this diverse range of possibilities? In other words, what makes a white person white besides white skin? We'll get to that. The point here is that you can find the "baseline of all phenotypes" in East Africa, along with all of the world's genetic diversity. This is why Eurocentrists like to separate East Africa from the rest of Africa, even when they use false dividers like "Sub-Saharan Africa" to separate "true negroes" from the rest of the world, they ignore the fact that East Africa is actually south of the Sahara!*

The way around all of this confusion is to keep this in mind: When we look at the migrations that populated the Earth, we will certainly see clear physical (and genetic) distinctions between these indigenous populations, but we know that they are essentially the same people, with the same origin.

SO WHO IS NOT BLACK?

Taking this argument to its logical end, we would naturally wonder, at one point does one STOP being Black? This issue troubled me for a few months after I first realized some of the things I've explained above. But revisiting what the Five Percenters taught me, I realized that "Black" is an identifier not limited to color or appearance. Black is about conscious identity. If not that, then Black is just another label with no more merit than Negro or Colored. But when we consider the conscious (and some would say "cosmic") identity of Blackness, we have to consider what that implies. In one of my old plus lessons,† the question of "What is Black?" is asked.

The answer says that Black is about color, culture, and consciousness. It's a psychosocial identity. Being Black is something you were born into (i.e., the Black Nation, with "nation" literally meaning something you're born into), but being Black is something you must consciously and culturally identify with. Before European domination of the world, being "Black" wasn't a rallying point for most of us. We didn't need to yell that we were *Black and proud* until white folks made us *unproud to be Black*.

So in the prehistoric past, our identities weren't bound to our Blackness. And after surviving the ups and downs of nature, and beating the Neanderthals, we – the Black people of the world – didn't exactly have a common enemy, and thus, not much of a

---

* The idea of "Sub-Saharan Africa" is based on the false notion that the Sahara Desert is some impassable barrier to human migration, and only people south of the Sahara are indigenous Black Africans. History and genetics tell us this is untrue.

† "Plus lessons" are a form of peer-reviewed literature in the Five Percent community. They are distributed, reviewed, and shared with peers as a means of disseminating theories or information that warrants further study or consideration. The peer-review process increases the distribution of accepted papers, while those that are considered erroneous are discarded, and – in some cases – burned!

common identity.

In other words, we were more bound to our local and ethnic identities. We repped our clans, because that was all we knew. Even in the modern day, the Black tribes of the New Guinea highlands continue to feud with each other and telling them they're all Black won't stop them. They speak different languages, claim different territories, and rep different ancestors and totems. Sound familiar to the gang problem here?

But what if the indigenous people of New Guinea saw what Europeans were doing to their land and to them? Would they come together? What if all the Black and brown people of the world were to come to this realization at once? Just as Black is a psychosocial identity, we'll explore how white is also a psychosocial identity, and one that is defined by its opposition to everything that is not white, in Volume Four.

For now, let's just say that – despite our diversity in color, culture, and consciousness – in the face of whiteness, Blackness is the only identity that's real. Perhaps that's why there's been such a concerted effort to convince us that this "Blackness" does not actually exist!

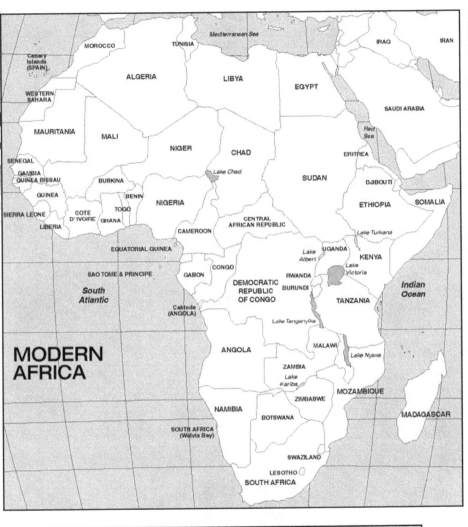

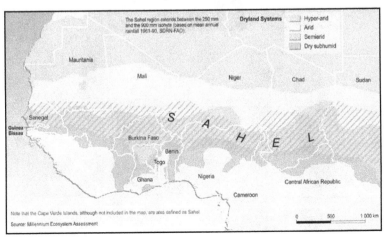

PEOPLE OF AFRICA

Here's your challenge. These are some of the populations discussed in this book.
Who's who? How do you find out? Perhaps...study the people of Africa?

AFRICA BEFORE EGYPT

WHERE IT ALL BEGAN

> *"[T]he white man knows that he didn't get us out of
> the jungle, he don't get us out of some place that was
> savage – he got us out of a place that was highly
> civilized in culture and in art, and then brought us
> down to the level that you see us today. But they are
> afraid to let us know what level we are on. They'll tell
> the Africans because they know the Africans know it,
> but they don't want you and me to know it. Because
> the first thing you and I would start asking them is,
> 'Well, what did you do to us?' And if you find out,
> then you'll want to do it to him."* – Malcolm X[52]

When's the last time you saw Africa on TV? What did they show?
Chances are, they weren't doing a feature on Africans living in big
cities like Nairobi, Accra, Lagos, or Durban. Most likely, the last
thing you saw was all about animals or a "tribe" of people with some
practices very different from your own. Many of us still think that
the people of Africa are ALL poor and starving, or that the majority
of people live in huts, hunting animals to survive. Trust me, I've
asked groups of students, and that is what they think about Africa.
There's a reason for this. It's what you're supposed to think so you
believe that living in America constitutes *progress* (and, in some
people's view, *salvation*).

> *"Whoever controls the images of a people also controls the self esteem, self respect and self development of those
> people."* – Dr. Leonard Jeffries

The truth is that the people of Africa were the first to build big
cities, and to transition from hunting to farming, and to build large
housing complexes. The people of Africa were often living so well
when the first Europeans came that many of the early reports are
gushing with praise and admiration.[53]

Even today, Africa is highly urbanized. Just look up "The Africa

They Don't Show You" or "The Africa You Never See on TV" on YouTube. There's even an *Africa Channel* on cable (you might already have it without knowing about it), which is constantly presenting glimpses into the urban life of today's African nations. But there's a reason we are led to think of Africa as the "dark continent," or "primitive," or "backwater." There's a reason Africa is rarely mentioned in discussions of world history. There's a reason tourists to Africa – outside of Egypt – are immediately routed to the "jungle safari," rather than the local market, a sacred site, or an ancient monument.

By disconnecting the world with its birthplace, Europeans have effectively changed the foundational reference point of all humanity from its origin to its oppressor. In other words, we once looked at the root of human civilization for inspiration and grounding, and now we look to the West for what to do and think next. None of this is accidental.

WHAT YOU'LL LEARN IN THIS CHAPTER

❐ Why Africa is so deeply ignored in discussions of history.

❐ What we know about our earliest ancestors and their cultures.

❐ The great diversity of African people, cultures, languages, and genes.

❐ Why big cities and widespread agriculture weren't necessary for the earliest African cultures.

❐ How, over 2,000,000 years ago, the first humans in East Africa pioneered technological industries that worked for millions of years.

❐ How South Africans pioneered chemistry and technology over 60,000 years ago.

❐ How Central Africans pioneered ecology and conservation over 30,000 years ago.

❐ How North Africans mastered the arts over 20,000 years ago.

❐ How South Africans pioneered chemistry and technology over 60,000 years ago.

❐ What we can learn and apply from these cultures today.

❐ The ancient historical foundations of Pan-Afrikanism.

WHAT ABOUT AFRICA?

Typically, when you read books about human history, there is this discussion of when "we left Africa" or "when modern humans left Africa to settle the globe." This suggests that the people who are still in Africa are either not worthy of consideration, or are not modern humans. The truth is that all of us are descendants of that same small ancestral group of humans who made that exodus, including the millions of Black people living in Africa before the Europeans came.* But, if you leave that part unsaid, or unexplained, it does give off the impression that native Africans (and their descendants) are not part of the human story.

Another thing you'll notice about the "standard telling" of human history is that Africa is only relevant millions of years ago during the evolution of modern humans, and then much later, whenever they say those humans left Africa for greener pastures. Isn't that offensive? As if there was no human history worth in that gap? Then, the next time Africa becomes relevant is after the rise of Ancient Egypt, which is 100,000 years later! That's a thousand centuries of history ignored! But guess what? It's not just the European scholars who do this. When's the last time you read a Black history book that dug into African history before the rise of Nile Valley Civilization? There's not too many.

As African historian Joseph Ki-Zerbo has said:

> Africa has a history. The time has long gone by when maps had great empty spaces representing the African continent as marginal and subordinate, and the knowledge of scholars on the subject was summed up in the cryptic phrase: *Ibi sunt leones* "Here be lions." But then came the discovery of the mines and their profits, and incidentally of the "native tribes" which owned the mines, but which, like them, were annexed as the property of the colonizing countries.

> The history of Africa, like the history of mankind as a whole, is really the story of an awakening. The history of Africa needs rewriting, for up till now it has often been masked, faked, distorted, mutilated, by "force of circumstance" i.e. through ignorance or self-interest.

> Crushed by centuries of oppression, Africa has seen generations of travellers, slave-traders, explorers, missionaries, governors, and scholars of all kinds give out its image as one of nothing but poverty, barbarism, irresponsibility and chaos. And this image has been projected and extrapolated indefinitely in time, as a justification of both the present and the future.

> For Africans, the history of Africa is not a narcissistic mirror nor a subtle excuse for avoiding the tasks and burdens of today. If it were

---

* We'll explain this fully in the Appendix (See "Going Back to Africa"), but here's the simple version: Some of the Black people who left Africa 130,000 years ago eventually came back to Africa around 50,000 years ago. They spread far and wide, mixing with all the indigenous "Paleo-Africans" who had remained in Africa. Today, there are no "pure" Paleo-African lineages. All of us, even the Khoisan of South Africa, are related to the Black men and women who left Africa and settled the entire globe.

an alienating device of that kind, the scientific objects of the whole enterprise would be compromised. But is not ignorance of one's own past, in other words of a large part of oneself, even more alienating?[54]

This is why I set out to fill in the gaps. Let's start with the beginning.

THE ORIGIN OF MAN

Before the emergence of *Homo sapiens*, the planet was settled by an older species of man known to anthropologists as *Homo erectus*.

We tend to give *Homo sapiens* all the credit for "manmade" technology and other "human" advances, but this is only because Homo erectus is considered a "primitive" ancestor of Homo sapiens. But as you'll see in the following section, there is strong evidence of continuity between the first Homo sapiens and their Homo erectus ancestors.

THE ROOT OF CIVILIZATION

Throughout this book, we talk about a place we call the "root of civilization." When we say "civilization," we're talking about pretty much ANY culture we – as Original People – ever founded, whether it was urbanized or not. After all, we were always civilized people, never savages. So when we look for the root of where human activity and industry can be found, that's in East Africa.

The earliest evidence of archaeological activity (anywhere) comes from the Great Rift Valley sites of East Africa, such as Olduvai Gorge and the Afar Desert in Ethiopia. From dozens of sites like this, scattered throughout East Africa, we can form a picture of our ancestors using tools, building homes, employing scientific reasoning to make collective decisions, making ecological use of natural resources, and all the other earmarks of civilization. And we're talking about **millions** of years ago.

In *The Science of Self, Volume One,* we explored the development of the Original man, leading up to the emergence of "anatomically modern humans" at the root of civilization, where we find the remains of the people who fathered and mothered everyone on this planet today. It should be noted that these ancestors did not survive by chance or dumb luck. They developed the necessary tools and industry needed to compete with other lineages of archaic* humans and literally take

---

* Throughout the world, many hominids (who came before the evolution of modern *Homo sapiens sapiens*) were still around when we crossed their territory. Over the

over the globe. They were the best of the best. Just think about it. These people, over 200,000 years ago, possessed within themselves a legacy so strong that their descendants were the ones who carried on, while millions of other lineages died off through the ages. And you're their last of kin.

As Christian preacher Joel Osteen has said, "You have *winner* in your DNA; you have *survivor* in your blood." I take it a step further and note that your ancestors survived the Neanderthal Wars, climate change, malaria outbreaks, political collapse, the Maafa (the slave trade), and all kinds of other challenges that eliminated so many of their peers. And here you are. That's beyond being a winner and survivor. You're the Original man and woman. You are the Alpha and the Omega. You are the exodus, the journey, and the final destination. The only question is: What will you do to ensure that your descendants survive to carry on YOUR legacy 200,000 years from now?

To get a better grasp of what this future could hold, we need to review the cycles of the past. We'll begin at the root of civilization.

THE FIRST TECH INDUSTRIES
BEFORE SILICON VALLEY...THERE WAS THE RIFT VALLEY

Today's industries serve modern society's complex needs. The industries of the past were fewer because we really didn't "need" all the things we depend on today, like cell phones, microwaves, Kindles, and that odd-shaped electronic "neck massager" your wife keeps in her bottom drawer.

Then again, do we need all those things today? That's another book perhaps. The bottom line is that we handled our business very effectively using the simplest of resources. As a result, most of our prehistoric industries were sustainable, and not a threat to our ecosystem, as they are today. Yet – even without silicon computer chips – we can call those prehistoric developments "technology," because technology simply means "the application of scientific knowledge for practical purposes."

So what kind of technology did we have back then, and when did it qualify our societies as "civilization"? While historians typically

---

course of about 100,000 years, our human ancestors had children with these "archaic" branches of the family tree. Obviously, these people weren't *that* different from us. In the end, it was our human ancestors who outlasted all other lineages.

associate textiles (fabrics), metallurgy (metal-working), and ceramics (pottery) as markers for the emergence of civilization, these industries are just "modernized" versions of much older practices. For example, before we made clay pots, we have gourds. Before we had looms to weave fabric, we sewed together leather and fur. And so on. Basically, we always had this knowledge. It's just been a matter of how and when we used it.

You see, technology doesn't move us forward in any linear way.* Instead, we produce technology as we see fit, and society changes correspondingly. New needs emerge, and new techniques are designed to address them more efficiently. The adoption of new technology is generally the result of us addressing an observed need, not us becoming smarter somehow.†

The first manufactured technology (that we have solid records of) are stone tools. Earlier you read about evidence of tool use 3.39 million years ago in Dikika, Ethiopia, so we probably had tools even before then – some made from organic materials like bone and wood and others from stone so weathered we can't tell if they were manmade.[55] The best evidence, thus far, is bone tools dated back to 3.3 million years ago in Sterkfontein, South Africa.[56] The world's first stone tool *industry* is known as the Oldowan industry. Oldowan stone tools are the oldest recognizable tools in the archaeological record, and date back to about 2.6 million years ago in Gona, Ethiopia.

TWO TYPES OF TOOL TRADITIONS

As simple as they sound, the Oldowan tools got the job done. For about a million years! That's when new techniques emerged, known to scientists as the Acheulean method of tool design. The Acheulean industry lasted from 1.7 million years ago until about 100,000 years ago. That's another long stretch. But these new techniques didn't "phase out" outdated technology. Instead, Oldowan toolsets continued production alongside the Acheulean. The only difference: Simply struck tools are called "Oldowan." When these tools are reworked to have finer details, they're called "Acheulean." And we

---

* Which is why – despite what some historians say – urbanization doesn't always lead to agriculture (sometimes it follows), and, at some sites, ceramics comes after agriculture, while at other sites it's the other way around.

† Occasionally this is "sparked" by an outside influence introducing a technology (which we may or may not adopt, based on our analysis of the need). This is a lot like today, when we consider how the market runs off supply and demand, with marketers constantly working to introduce new products that meet our ever-changing demands.

used both up until 100,000 years ago. But why?

This forced scientists to reconsider the idea that an "advanced" industry was succeeding a more primitive one. Some said that different populations – either different species of man or different cultures – carried these technologies, as both technologies emerged first in East Africa but followed different paths of dispersal.

After spreading throughout Africa, Oldowan technology was carried only as far as southern Asia and some parts of Europe, while Acheulean (the earliest examples of which come from Kenya) extended as far beyond as China and South Korea. However, this may not be the only explanation for these two co-existing traditions. Some scientists have argued that groups could use both techniques in response to different circumstances. Kinda like switching between using a flathead or a Phillips screwdriver.

THE FIRST STATUS SYMBOLS?

But what were the circumstances that called for the finer craftsmanship of the Acheulean tools? Surely the 20cm Acheulean cutting edge had a competitive advantage over the 5cm cutting edge of Oldowan tools, but there are also sites where hundreds of impractically large Acheulean hand-axes sat unused. These sites, including Melka Kunturé in Ethiopia, Olorgesailie in Kenya, Isimila in Tanzania, and Kalambo Falls in Zambia, have raised questions about whether many popular Acheulean tools, like these hand-axes, were created for form, function…or just fashion.

Recent studies have suggested that some of the Acheulean industry was really about the latter, promoting social identity through craftsmanship and style. This would explain the apparent "over-sophistication" of some examples.

One theory goes even further and suggests that some special hand-axes were made and displayed by males in search of a mate, using a large, well-made hand-axe to demonstrate that they possessed sufficient strength and skill to pass on to their offspring. Once they had attracted a female at a group gathering, it is suggested that they would discard their axes, perhaps explaining why so many are found together.

OTHER SUPER-OLD ACCOMPLISHMENTS

If you remembered that humans show up around 200,000 years ago, you realized that all these tools were first used by Homo erectus. Yet, both the Oldowan and Acheulean tool traditions were continued by Homo sapiens, which shows a great deal of cultural continuity. What this tells you is that the history of the Original man does not actually begin 200,000 years ago, but goes back much further. If you take a lot at some of the following accomplishments, it becomes clear that Homo erectus was no misshapen beast-man, but simply an older variant of man who eventually became us.

240,000 years ago, Homo erectus was using upper Paleolithic blade tools in Kenya, technology that wouldn't resurface in Europe until almost 200,000 years later.[57]

At least 350,000 years ago, he built the first stone wall (and some of the oldest rock engravings) in Bhimbetka, India.[58] 300,000 years ago, he introduced geometric engraving in Pech de l'Aze, southern France.[59]

Between 300,000 and 400,000 years ago, Homo erectus built huts, paved social areas, erectus altars, and designed counting tools, in Bilzingsleben, Germany.[60] Nearby in Schoningen, Germany, there are 400,000 year-old wooden spears, wooden boomerangs, 3-piece composite tools, and tools made using other tools.[61]

By 500,000 years ago, in Zhoukoudian, China, Homo erectus was collecting minerals,[63] making fire,[64] and hunting with canines.[65] His ancestors had pioneered maritime culture 700,000 years ago, when the earliest evidence of ocean travel is found in Flores, Indonesia.[66] We discussed the rafts that he built – using only wood, bone, and stone tools – to navigate the waters of southeast Asia in *The Science of Self, Volume One*. As early as 800,000 years ago, he built homes with organized living plans, complete with hearths, carpeting, bedding, and polished wood.[67] Over 100,000 years prior, this bedding could be found in the Wonderwork Cave in South Africa.[68]

1.5 million years ago, our Homo erectus ancestors were designing Acheulean hand axes in West Natron, Tanzania,[69] making 500° fires from South Africa[70] to East Africa,[71] woodworking in Koobi Fora, Kenya,[72] creating representational art in Olduvai Gorge,[73] and working animal hides in Swartkrans, South Africa.[74]

2 million years ago, we find the earliest evidence of a windbreak structure in Olduvai,[75] and even the first toothpick in Ethiopia.[76]

FLORES

How far back does the history of "man" go? If you refer back to *The Science of Self, Volume One*, you'll know that the lineage of the Original Man and Woman goes back to the very origins of life itself (and beyond). Since the focus of this book isn't evolutionary biology or quantum mechanics, we'll simply say this much: If you are "Original" you are the "Origin of All." And, since the beginning of time, it's all been cyclical. As the saying goes, there's nothing new under the sun, meaning whatever happened 200,000,000 years ago was reproduced, or re-cycled, 200,000 years ago, only at different scales and levels of complexity. We'll get deeper into how this works in Volume Three, but – if you get it now – you'll draw much more from what we reveal about the history of modern humans.

Anatomically modern humans emerge on the scene about 200,000 years ago.* They continue many of the Lower Paleolithic traditions of their ancestors, but rapidly introduce new traditions. By the time of the Upper Paleolithic (50,000 years ago), life is quite different from how it was at the dawn of the era.

AN INTRODUCTION TO CHRONOLOGY

Okay, there's plenty of time periods discussed in this book. We cover some Homo erectus history going as far back as two million years ago, but most of this book deals with what happened between 130,000 and 3,000 BC. Needless to say, a lot happened.

It's not easy to imagine a thousand years, however.† It's understandable if things get a little confusing. So, let's talk a few basics before we begin. BC means "before Christ." Most modern historians don't use "BC" anymore, and prefer "BP" which means "before present" or "BCE" which basically means the same as BC, but it stands for "before common era." Some even use conventions like "15 kya" (15 thousand years ago). We're going to use BC because that's what most readers will be familiar with. Occasionally, we'll say things like "30,000 years ago" and only rarely will we throw in a

---

* For details on how this happened, refer back to Volume One.

† After all, many of us get impatient simply waiting for the microwave to cook minute rice, so it's hard for us to envision a time when oppression and institutionalized racism will end ("It's hopeless," we say). Yet our ancestors were here long before white rice or "white is right" were on the planet. We've always had struggles and challenges, but the struggles of the past 15,000 years are nothing like the struggles of the 25,000 years that preceded it. So let's never forget how timeless we really are. That's why Volume Three of this series focuses on the cultural unity of the "eternal" Black Diaspora.

"kya" or "mya" (million years ago). So if we say 3,000 BC, that actually means 5,000 years ago (because it's been a little over 2000 years since the alleged birth of Christ). And if we say 16,000 years ago, that means 14,000 BC

Now that that's said, you may want to think about what a thousand years ago really means. Perhaps you could consider how different were just a hundred years and multiply that by ten! Now, think about 10,000 or 100,000 years ago. That should give you some idea of how amazing it is when we say that our ancestors in South Africa had paint and glue factories 60,000 years ago.

Let's also talk about something a little more complicated. Many historians and archaeologists don't name a lot of specific "time periods" but instead use names for the various "eras" or "ages" of human culture, such as the "Upper Paleolithic" or the "Late Neolithic." But don't think that something like the "Neolithic Age" refers to the same time period in India as it does in Mexico. Because so many human cultures spread by diffusion, these periods really only tell us about when different regions adopted a new phase of culture. In other words, the whole world didn't "become Neolithic" at the same time. When we use words like Paleolithic and Neolithic, we're just using them to help you understand the culture of the people we're talking about. You'll see such terms used in most other history books, so we'd be leaving you in the dark if we avoided using them.

THE HISTORICAL PERIODS

Historians and other scientists use many different terms to describe the periods of the past. The simplest distinction is that everything in the past is not always called "history." History specifically refers to the past so far back as we have written records of what happened (literally, "his story"). This goes as far back as "Ancient History" which is where we find the beginning of written languages around 3,000 BC. Before that, it's called "Prehistory."

Another way to break up the past is by looking at technology, or the tools we used. After the Acheulean Phase, the people of Africa were still in what's called the Stone Age. Because, until we developed the science of metallurgy to make iron, copper, and steel tools, we relied primarily on stone tools.*

---

* Of course, we also used wood, bone, fiber, and a wide variety of chemical compounds, but what archaeologists have to go on is mostly stones. That's what has

But don't get it twisted! The rest of the world was in the Stone Age too! Until the advent of metallurgy (making tools out of copper, bronze, and iron), everybody using stone tools was in the "Stone Age." Yet in Europe, archaeologists call this SAME period the Paleolithic. Everywhere else (especially Africa), the same phase is called the Old Stone Age, which sounds pretty primitive standing next to a period with a "sciencey" name like "Paleolithic" (which means "Old Stone Age"). Why'd they do it like that? Just because. White folks can do stuff like that.

So throughout this book, whenever we talk about the Old Stone Age or the Paleolithic, we're calling it ALL the Paleolithic no matter where it is. The other period we'll talk about in this book is known as the Neolithic. Since *lith-* means "stone" and *neo-* means "new," it literally means the "New Stone Age," but that's not very accurate. We did continue to use stones to build megalithic structures and other monuments, but the Neolithic involved many new adaptations and technologies necessitated by our rapidly growing settlements, including the eventual development of metallurgy.

The Paleolithic and Neolithic periods are the two phases of history covered in this book.* They actually cover a pretty massive timeline:

☐ Lower Paleolithic (c. 2.6 million years ago – 300,000 years ago)
☐ Middle Paleolithic (300,000–30,000 years ago)
☐ Upper Paleolithic (50,000–10,000 years ago)
☐ Neolithic (varies, depending on region)†

The Paleolithic typically begins with the earliest evidence of stone tools (and thus the "first industries" of man). But, as you may remember from *Volume One*, Homo sapiens don't show up in the fossil record until about 200,000 years ago.

---

best survived the two million years of weathering and decay.

* There are other ways to describe the periods of the past, such as geological epochs. The Pleistocene epoch lasted from 2.6 million years ago to 12,000 years ago. The Holocene epoch followed and includes our present time. You will see these terms used elsewhere.

† The dates you see aren't set in stone. Historical developments occurred at different times in different places. In some places, a Mesolithic, or middle phase (sometimes called "Epipaleolithic") marks the transitional period between the Paleolithic and Neolithic. The Neolithic is often followed by a Copper Age, Bronze Age, and/or Iron Age, once metallurgy is developed and metal tools replace stone tools.

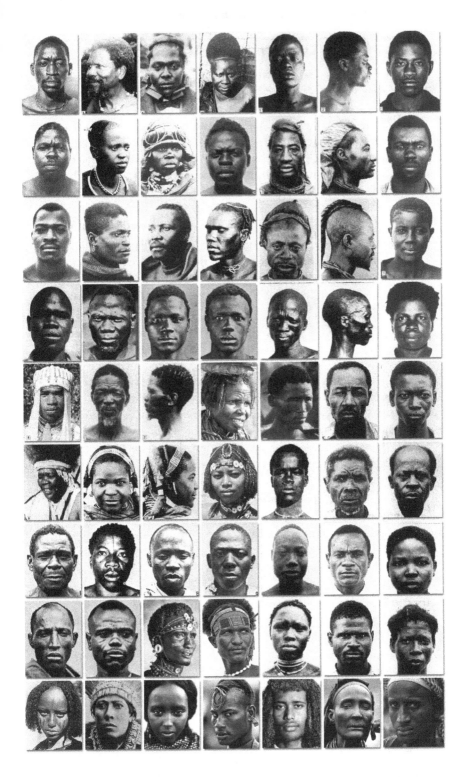

THE PEOPLE OF AFRICA

In order for us to discuss what was going on in Africa before the emergence of Nile Valley Civilization, we have to embrace a few new understandings. First, many of us believe that Africa is *monolithic*. That is, we think there is "one" African culture, or "one" African people. I can understand if you're talking about things you see in common, but most people who think of Africa in a monolithic sense aren't breaking down "the cultural unity of Black Africa" like Cheikh Anta Diop did.[77] No, I'm talking about the ones who think Africa is a *country,* and all Africans are starving on the days they're not hunting lions and tigers. I'm sure you know some people who think that way.

The reality is that all African people do not look the same, think the same, or behave the same. Africa is the most linguistically, genetically, and phenotypically diverse place on the planet. After all, it's where everyone – with all their diversity – comes from! So how could it not be?

Africa is like one of those Crayola crayon boxes with 120 different colors in (and the built-in sharpener!) and everywhere else in the world is just an 8-pack or one of those 3-packs they give your kids at the restaurant. Maybe Europe would be where you find the off-brand crayons made by some other company. You know, the kind that melts as soon as they see sunlight, and their colors are never as strong as the real Crayola crayons? Anyway, the point is that Africa is the place where humanity started, so you can find the origin for just about anything and everything somewhere in Africa.

Naturally, that means you'll find a lot of diversity. Over the course of several million years of history, you'll also find a lot of these elements meeting, mixing, and interacting with each other to form new elements – almost like the diverse array of elements in the primordial soup that birthed life on Earth. Or kinda like that Alchemy game you should download on your phone.

For example, there's so much physical diversity in Africa that you can find the origins of all the world's facial features there. In fact, you can find all of our prototypical traits in East Africa alone. As one old text on African history notes:

> Negroes are the tallest people and shortest ones as well. A pygmy of four and a half feet has to tip his head very far back to view a tall Watusi towering perhaps three feet above him. Negroes may be stocky or stringy, sturdy or frail. They may be hawk-nosed, flat-nosed; thick-lipped or thin-lipped. The skins of some are nearly black in hue; others are pale buff. Trying to settle on representative

features is like looking into a kaleidoscope. Colors and patterns shift before your eyes, leaving you with an impression only. No wonder some anthropologists prefer to catalogue Negroes in several races instead of just one.[78]

There's great cultural diversity as well. There are city-dwellers, farmers, pastoralists, hunter-gatherers, and foragers. There are monarchies, democracies, and republics. You can find capitalism, socialism, and everything in between. Polygamy, monogamy, endogamy, exogamy (those are real things!) – all there. You'll find matrilineal descent and patrilineal descent, shamanism and totemism, scientists and warriors. It's all there, and that's where it all comes from.

One of the clearest examples of Africa's cultural diversity can be seen in its many languages.* Africa has almost 2,000 linguistic groups. That's a lot of different languages. But thanks to the groundbreaking work of linguist Joseph Greenberg and those who followed after him, we can categorize those languages into a few distinct families. This helps us track down the origins of these languages, which again brings us back to East Africa.

And Africa wasn't a static, unchanging place for the millions of years it was inhabited by people. If we know there were dozens of migrations within the 75,000 years it took for humans to settle the entire globe, just imagine how much movement occurred over millions of years in Africa. Africa's linguistic history can reveal a lot about the migrations and other historical events that occurred in the past. When we incorporate genetic data and the archaeological record, we're able to deduce a reasonable picture of African prehistory. But it's not easy.

I'll be the first to admit that this story is a sketchy one, even for specialists in the subject. Many of the oldest human remains have long ago dissolved in the soil, the mostly wood and bone artifacts haven't survived either, foreign elements have become a part of the narrative, and Eurocentrism has distorted the remaining evidence into a mess that honest scholars must now clean up.

Fortunately, the picture of African prehistory has gotten a lot clearer over the past century. One thing we're pretty certain of is that the

---

* We're not saying that there are no common cultural threads between the indigenous communities of Africa. In fact, we explore the "cultural unity" of the entire Global Black Diaspora in Volume Three. We're simply deconstructing the racist myth of a monolithic Africa, where everyone looks the same, thinks the same, and lives the same.

"mother tongue" (the original spoken language of all humanity) was probably most closely related to the "click languages" spoken by the ancestors of the Khoisan people* (who were spread throughout southern and eastern Africa between 102,000 and 142,000 years ago).[79]

This click language ultimately goes back to the East African root of civilization where modern humans were born. These people made one of the first exoduses out of Africa to populate the rest of the world. This would explain some of the residue of click language in the East African Hadzabe, as well as in the "secret" Damin click language of Australia. Some of these people traveled south, where they became the click-speaking Khoisan of Southern Africa.†

The fact that the Khoisan of Southern Africa look SO different from the East African Hadzabe is testament to the physical diversity of the oldest human populations of Africa. These two communities are both over 100,000 years old – with only minimal outside genetic influence – yet the Hadzabe look like Wesley Snipes while the Khoisan look like the rapper Canibus. In case you forgot what Canibus looks like, that means they look like Black Chinese people.

A QUICK NOTE ON LEMURIA, ATLANTIS, AND THE GARDEN OF EDEN

No. Just no. The word "Utopia" literally means "no place." As in, it doesn't exist. I'm not saying things weren't better for us long ago. We really did have it better before all this modern civilization stuff. But there's a reason why white folks have been on this hunt for a mythical land where all civilization came from. It's because they don't want to give credit to Africa. Just think about it. They'd rather cite obscure legends about some sunken continent that happens to be "near Africa" (immediately north, east, or west of Africa), but not IN Africa. There are plenty of old settlements that are now underwater, thanks to rising sea levels, but a sunken continent? Sorry. There's a reason all the continents look like interlocking puzzle pieces. No missing continent. Just a missing respect for Africa. There's actually an island off the coast of East Africa known as Lemu (as in Lemuria), but I don't think anyone has suggested that the founders of civilization came from here. Maybe it's too African. A few scholars have broken this trend. Some have argued that placed like Lemuria,

---

* The indigenous people of Southern Africa are variously referred to by many names, including San, Sho, Basarwa, Kung, Khwe, Khoi. "Khoi" are pastoralists and the "San" are hunter-gatherers. Europeans once called them Hottentots and Bushmen. Together they are known by their common language and genetics as the Khoisan. Their territory spans most areas of South Africa, Zimbabwe, Lesotho, Mozambique, Swaziland, Botswana, Namibia, and Angola, but used to include much more of Africa, spanning all the way into Northeast.

† For details on how we can trace back all modern languages, including English, to ancient African languages, see "The Origins of Spoken Language" in *Black People Invented Everything*.

Atlantis, and Eden were situated somewhere in Africa. For example, some have said the Minoan civilization – which was founded by Blacks – was the historical Atlantis. Citing "three major events in modern human evolution – the perfection of language, the formation of the ancestral human population and the exit from Africa," Nicholas Wade has called Ethiopia "the real world's counterpart of Eden's mythical garden." (Nicholas Wade. (2006). p. 64) Still others have given all credit to ancient migrations leaving Nubia (what is now the Egypt/Sudan border). Personally, I'd rather research real places that I can visit, than "mystery history" only found in theosophical books written by white folks with secret agendas.

PREHISTORIC AFRICA

We've already discussed many of the earliest cultural traditions of East Africa, going back over two million years. From 2,000,000 BC to 2,012 AD, East Africa has always been populated, but not everyone who was born there has stayed there. Because of environmental changes, great migrations have left East Africa several times. Several of these migrations went into Asia and Europe (and later everywhere else), but many others went into other parts of Africa. This is the African history most historians ignore, because the implicit assumption is that Africa was only significant in terms of its relationship to the people who wrote the history. Outside of that, it was perfectly fine to leave thousands of years to the imagination.

We won't do that here. Genetic studies have revealed that the earliest humans in Africa expanded into many different branches, at least five of which went into other parts of Africa while only one (identified with mtDNA Haplogroup L3) went out of Africa. For now, let's focus on some of the lineages that went into other parts of Africa. We'll start with a culture that introduced advanced chemistry and other technology to southern Africa…over 50,000 years ago.

CHEMISTRY AND TECHNOLOGY IN SOUTHERN AFRICA

What do you know about Southern Africa? Mandela, Apartheid, maybe something about Steve Biko, maybe something about the native Khoisan people. Maybe you've heard of the "Hottentot" people identified with Sartjie Baartman. Or maybe all you know is that Ludacris shot his "Pimpin All Over the World" video out there.

Well, I hope that's not all you know. Either way, there's much more to know. For most of us, even those of us who study African history, our knowledge of Southern Africa is limited to what has happened within the past 2,000 years. Yet there was SO much that was happening here over 50,000 years ago!

SOUTH AFRICA
66,000 BC

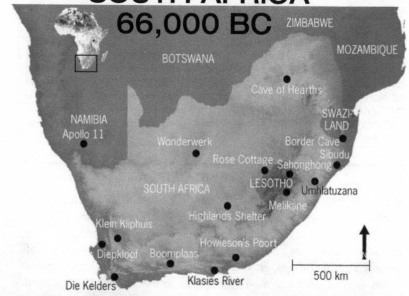

ZIMBABWE

MOZAMBIQUE

BOTSWANA

Cave of Hearths

SWAZI-
LAND

NAMIBIA
Apollo 11

Wonderwerk

Border Cave

Sibudu

Rose Cottage
Sehonghong

SOUTH AFRICA

LESOTHO

Umhlatuzana

Melikane

Highlands Shelter

Klein Kliphuis

Howieson's Poort

Diepkloof   Boomplaas

Die Kelders

Klasies River

500 km

AFRICAN RAZOR BLADE, C. 66,000 BC

Howiesons Poort Culture
Southern Africa

SMALLER, STRONGER, WON'T RUST.
WE WIN AGAIN.

WWW.THESCIENCEOFSELF.COM

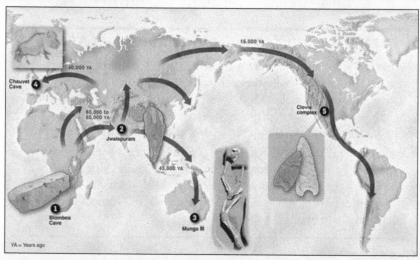

YA = Years ago

40,000 YA

Chauvet
Cave ❹

80,000 to
60,000 YA

❷
Jwalapuram

15,000 YA

Clovis
complex ❺

45,000 YA

❶
Biombos
Cave

❸
Mungo III

THE STILL BAY CULTURE (69,000 - 67,000 BC)

Archaeologists working at the Blombos Cave and nearby Sidubu Cave in Southern Africa have assembled a body of evidence for a culture they've named the "Still Bay" Culture. The people of Still Bay ushered in a wave of technological advances, including projectile weapons, manufactured jewelry, surgical tools, and chemical adhesives...71,000 years ago.

These are the modern words, of course, but archaeologists described the artifacts as stone-tipped wooden spears, shell beads, piercing needles, and the earliest example of compound glue, used for attaching stone points to the wooden spears. There are even older examples of glue, such as a 90,000-year-old find in Israel, but this evidence was the first that allowed for a chemical analysis, revealing a compound adhesive made from plant gum and red ochre.* The chemical formula used by the people of Still Bay was strong enough to endure repeated use in hunting, even by air. If that sounds amazing, it gets even better.

THE HOWIESONS POORT CULTURE (62,000 - 58,000 BC)

About two thousand years after it emerged, the culture at Still Bay basically disappeared. That's not bad if you consider that most civilizations don't last even a thousand years (especially not nowadays). But after a 5,000 year gap following the disappearance of Still Bay, another culture emerged in the same region. Archaeologists call this one the Howiesons Poort culture.

64,000 years ago, when other Stone Age people were using spears or stone axes, the people of Howiesons Poort were using a bow and arrow. This was 20,000 years before the bow and arrow caught on for good, showing – as we noted earlier – that sometimes "inventions" don't serve enough of a societal need to become

---

* Ochre is a mineral pigment made from iron ore. It has been used by Original people for hundreds of thousands of years, and can be found in artwork, burials, and body painting throughout the world – wherever Black people have been.

widespread. Knowing this, it's reasonable to propose that some people could have been using bows and arrows 120,000 years ago, and we just haven't found the evidence yet!

The evidence from this period in Sidubu Cave suggests that, in addition to using spears and arrows to hunt game, the people of Howiesons Poort used traps and snares to capture small animals. These devices used the same knowledge required for the construction of bows (latent energy stored in bent branches) as well as a developed knowledge of cords and knots. In other words, their sheep knots would have put your Scoutmaster to shame.

Another dig from Howiesons Poort turned up a cache of ostrich eggshells engraved with geometric designs, which *Science News* said "demonstrates the existence of a symbolic communication system" around 65,000 years ago. These artifacts, like the others above, were probably used as a show of skill, and a means of distinguishing one group, or manufacturer, from another (the "first brand names"!).

But they also served a clear purpose. These ostrich shells were used as canteens (complete with carved water-spouts), and probably helped their makers travel across the dry patches of Africa during migrations, including the one that left Africa about 60,000 years ago.[81] As if that wasn't enough, Howiesons Poort also had composite weapons. These moon-shaped, "geometric-backed" blades were sharp on the straight edge and blunt on the curved back. They were attached to handles using compound glue, now made from a formula of plant gum, ochre and fat.[82]

Wait, let's be clear. The blades were sharp along their entire edge, which meant there was no room for twine to hold the blade to the handle. That means the glue had to be as strong as modern-day superglue. To get these results, the mix of ingredients had to be heated to a very specific temperature, one hot enough to melt everything together but not so hot that the adhesive became dry or brittle. Doesn't sound primitive to me. Scientists have cited the chemistry required for this glue as evidence of complex thinking long before the cave paintings of Europe.[83]

Speaking of which, many of the geometric designs on the blades, canteens, and shelter walls were made by carving but others were done with pigments, including ochre. Archaeologists have actually found "ochre pencils" along with evidence that ochre was used as body paint.[84] Imagine that. We had pencils and superglue 60,000 years ago. Scientists have asked, "How could primitive humans do this?" Good question. Another important question is, "Why did these humans stop?"

"You would imagine that the technology would continue, but it truly disappears," researcher Lucinda Backwell said. But these methods reemerge and become consistent only much later. For example, Backwell used a microscope to find that a stone tool was used to whittle pinkie-size bone arrowheads at Howiesons Poort into highly symmetrical points, a technique still used by some Khoisan people today.[85]

But just as the Still Bay culture disappeared and left a 5,000 year gap in technology, the sites associated with Howiesons Poort, along with its long-distance trade routes, were abandoned around 60,000 years ago. And Howiesons Poort was replaced by a less technologically developed culture! It took 20,000 years for another comparable culture to emerge in that area. So what happened to the people of Howiesons Poort? And why?

And how did the people of Howiesons Poort and Still Bay become so technologically advanced to begin with? Researchers agree that these developments (and their subsequent disappearance) challenge the idea that we "discovered" our early technologies through the "accumulation of improvements." Blackwell and colleagues have commented that the "brain change" argument doesn't fit this evidence either:

> Such innovations…can hardly be used to support the "classic" out of Africa scenario, which predicts increasing complexity and accretion of innovations during the MSA [Middle Stone Age], determined by biological change. Instead, they appear, disappear and re-appear in a way that best fits a scenario in which historical contingencies and environmental, rather than cognitive, changes are seen as main drivers.[86]

In other words, nature and biology didn't write our history. WE wrote our history. Researchers Zenobia Jacobs and Richard Roberts agree that environmental change wasn't as significant as social change. Although it's hard to determine "historical contingencies" in a period so remote, Jacobs and Roberts used genetic data to argue that these "leaps forward" were the byproduct of the development of the African social network (not Facebook, but human communities). In other word: small bands of people coming together to become a culture. Jacobs and Roberts explain:

The SB [Still Bay Culture] may reflect an episode of population expansion of the L3 haplogroup* in southern Africa, during which social networks promoted the rapid transmission of this advance in technological sophistication and florescence of symbolic behavior throughout the region. This suite of behavioral changes may have bestowed a competitive advantage on hunter-gatherer communities, perhaps by promoting group coordination and cohesion or by enhancing technological efficiency and economic productivity.[87]

Just as our coming together resulted in a highly advanced culture, our growing apart signalled its demise:

The end of the SB represents the disintegration of this social network, owing to population contractions and isolations...Cultural innovations are less likely to survive or prosper among small and solitary social groups. Connections were not re-established until the start of the HP [Howiesons Poort culture], five millennia later, when local populations again expanded, but this time in association with a different technological innovation (backed blades). The demise of the HP reflects the final collapse of this integrated, sub-continental network of hunter-gatherer communities, and their return to a number of geographically isolated and genetically distinct populations. Similarly sophisticated stone-tool technology did not reappear until the advent of the Later Stone Age, about 40,000 years ago, when there is evidence for renewed genetic admixture in the sub-Saharan mtDNA pool.[88]

That last line is important. It's basically saying we didn't get busy like Howiesons Poort again, until we got some new blood in our community. When more people come together, culture revives.

But what happened to the people who founded Howiesons Poort? Jacobs and Roberts note that a social network collapse would explain the end of long-distance trade, but not the abandonment of the

---

* If the idea of haplogroups is confusing, we'll explain it in depth when we explain genetics and DNA later in this book. Feel free to skip ahead and come back.

caves and rock shelters where people spent much of their time.

Could the technologically advanced people of the Howiesons Port culture simply have "packed up" their canteens and hunting tools and headed northeast to join the confederation of people who tackled the Neanderthals and left Africa around 60,000 years ago? It's certainly possible.

For one thing, we know that the L3 haplogroup carried by the people of Still Bay and Howiesons Poort is the one who left Africa. For another, we know that many of the innovations developed by Howiesons Poort don't emerge again until we find them in Asia, Europe, and North America. As Jacobs and colleagues noted in another paper:

> The cause of these two bursts of technological innovation [SB and HP], closely spaced yet separated in time, remains an enigma, as does the reason for their disappearance. But, intriguingly, both fall within the genetic bottleneck that occurred 80 to 60,000 years ago and the subsequent expansions of modern human populations within and out of Africa.[89]

Perhaps we are all the descendants of the builders of Howiesons Poort. They seemed like some smart brothers and sisters, definitely some ancestors worth looking up to.

WHY IS SOUTHERN AFRICA SO IMPORTANT?

According to archaeologist Christopher Henshilwood:

> What has been suggested up until now is that modern human behavior was a very late occurrence…that though people were anatomically modern in Africa from about 150,000 to 100,000 years ago, they remained behaviorally non-modern until about 40,000 or 50,000 years ago, when they suddenly changed and then moved into Europe and elsewhere.[90]

That is, we didn't become fully human until we became Europeans. Sound familiar? Well, thanks to the work of Henshilwood and others, we're now learning just how untrue that is.

Henshilwood's team found specialized bone tools and engraved red ochre in South Africa's Blombos Cave, dating back to at least 70,000 years ago. "The implications are that there was modern human behavior in Africa about 35,000 years before Europe," said Henshilwood. Not long after this, another dig in the same cave turned up 75,000-year-old stone tools made by pressure flaking, a process of finely trimming the edges of a finished stone tool heated in a forge, using a bone point hard enough to remove thin slices of rock. Before this find the oldest evidence of humans using the technique was dated to only 20,000 years ago in Europe's Solutrean culture and among some prehistoric Native American groups. [91]

But here's what's even more interesting: Stone Age tool expert John Shea told *Science News* he didn't think pressure flaking made these tools "better" than older models. Shea proposed that Blombos tool makers probably employed this technique **to advertise their skill or to denote users' social identity**. Basically, a way to flex one's creative muscles and distinguish one nation from another. Again, like an early brand name.

But Shea agreed with the study authors that humans were using creative techniques like pressure flaking much further back than they'd been getting credit for, and suggested that the method may even date back to 100,000 years ago, suggesting that this technique originated in Africa before it spread elsewhere. And it certainly may date back that far, or even further, considering that we have heat-treated stone blades in South Africa from 164,000 years ago. [92]

These early dates suggest that some traditions and techniques emerged and diffused through early human cultures gradually, not all at once. The scientists conclude:

> The finding fits with the idea that symbolic art, rituals and other forms of modern human behavior developed gradually over hundreds of thousands of years, not in a burst of cultural innovation marked by cave paintings and other creations that appeared after 50,000 years ago in Western Europe. [93]

In other words, as Maury Povich would say, "Europe, you are not the father (of civilization)."

WAIT, WHAT ABOUT THE BIG CITIES?

While there's certainly more to be found in future digs in southern Africa, what we won't find is a massive prehistoric population explosion that forced the construction of large metropolitan cities. In fact, people native to the area, like the San, took great efforts *not* to disturb the natural ecology of their homeland. So, while southern complexes like those found at the Great Zimbabwe Ruins (which we'll discuss a little later) are indeed fantastic, it's important to keep in mind that those structures were built within the past 2,000 years by the pastoralist Bantu people who came after the native Khoisan peoples.

IS CITY LIFE BETTER?

Is urbanization an "advance"? It makes sense that large, dense

GREAT ZIMBABWE

populations will require agriculture to provide adequate food supplies, which will also lead to city planning, governmental regulation, stratification of society (who's on top and who's at the bottom), boundary demarcation (land ownership), legal codification and a number of other civic features that all relate to the questions of "Who is in charge here?" and "Who owns what?"

But when our populations grew so large that we transitioned to agriculture as a response to the scarcity of natural food sources, is that progress? There's nothing wrong with ceasing to migrate/relocate and settling down to build a home (it had to happen at some point), but that doesn't mean the group who settled was "better" than those who chose not to.*

Urbanization creates a number of complications we didn't have before. In addition to the dangers of social stratification (which can seriously magnify pre-existing conflicts between groups of people who now have to share a city), urbanization also increases incidence of disease, depletion of natural resources, and problematic changes to the natural environment.

FIXING THE SIDE EFFECTS OF CITIES

Urbanization can actually affect the weather, creating stronger summer storms through "heat islands" pumping hot air into the lower atmosphere, with each new road and building providing dark surfaces to soak up midday heat. As cities grow, this can cause more flooding and greater storms. Coastal areas and desert areas are both affected.

To counteract this, people can plant more trees, use light colored materials for the surfaces of building materials, build more underground dwellings, and create fractally organized city plans that more evenly distribute heat and energy.[94] These are solutions modern society is having a hard time implementing today (even though we are in an environmental crisis), yet these methods were in use throughout our ancient civilizations!

You'll see countless examples of ingenious city planning as you read on, but you'll also see examples where excessive construction and consumption of resources led to the downfall of societies already weakened by internal conflict between competing factions. History

---

* In fact, this prejudice is part of the reason why the pastoralist Bantu-speakers of Sub-Saharan Africa historically have been at odds with the hunter-gatherer Khoisan (Bushmen) populations that have lived for much longer in the regions they occupy. That's another story we'll revisit later as well.

tells us that the best way is to simply "live off the land" (or use temporary, organic materials like thatched huts) and to split up large populations when groups get too large for the local ecosystem…which is what we were doing even before then.

BUT WE HAD SOME AMAZING CITIES, RIGHT?

I know, I know, you want to hear about the fantastic urban complexes with giant temples and 50-ton monuments erected using science that modern people can't wrap their minds around. I understand.

And we'll get to that. But I hope that you now understand that, not only were we doing "just fine" before we transitioned to the cultural patterns we normally associated with "modern civilization," we've also been doing things that resemble modern civilization far longer than most people think as well.

An easy way to look at all this is to say that – when our circumstances called for it – we've built "urban" societies (whether this was 4,000 or 40,000 years ago), and when our circumstances allowed for a more naturalistic approach, we went in THAT direction instead (up to as recently as the modern day).

Typically, we didn't NEED cities until a site's population grew to great numbers. So most of the big cities we'll discuss will come at the end of this book's chronology. But many of the techniques and sciences employed by these civilizations can be found thousands (even millions) of years prior.

Either way, none of these things happened instantly. Everything has a cause and effect, so we've got to understand the millions of years of history that led up to the developments that happened within the past 10,000 years.

It is only by doing so that we can equip our minds to understand why things are the way they are now, and to be able to see into the future of what's coming 10,000 years down the line. Offering you anything less would be uncivilized.

AN INTRODUCTION TO DATING TECHNIQUES

No, we don't mean THOSE kinds of dating techniques. There's other books for that. We're talking about the methods that scientists use to figure out how old something is. Sounds boring, but pay attention because there's a quiz at the end. And if you read carefully, you'll have one more tool to avoid being suckered by phony claims about ancient things. Warning: Technical reading ahead.

Scientific dating methods typically consist of measuring a naturally occurring radioactive isotope and its decay products, using known decay rates. The decay rate is known as the half-life. Here's how it works with the most well-known example, C-14 dating, also known as radiocarbon dating: An organism acquires carbon during its lifetime. Plants acquire it through photosynthesis, and animals acquire it from consumption of plants and other animals. When an organism dies, it ceases to take in new carbon-14, and the existing isotope decays with a characteristic half-life (5730 years). The proportion of carbon-14 left when the remains of the organism are examined provides an indication of the time elapsed since its death. Because of its short half-life, the carbon-14 dating limit lies at only 58,000 to 62,000 years. Also, C-14 is no longer the preferred dating method, because C-14 levels can be thrown off by external factors, making it less reliable than newer methods.

Other radiometric techniques, using isotopes with longer half-lifes, offer long dating limits. Other common methods include: TL (thermoluminescence) dating, which is best for dating ceramics within a range of about 5,000 years ago to 1 million years ago); U-series (uranium series) dating, which has an upper age limit of a little over 500,000 years and is best for coral; and ESR (electron spin resonance) dating, which is best for dating teeth from up to 2 million years ago. There are many other techniques relying on different isotopes, and scientists often use two different methods to make sure they're accurate. They'll also incorporate other methods like studying the stratigraphy of the soil where something is found to help corroborate those dates.

What these techniques have in common is that they rely on the presence of a particular element to work. If that element isn't present – for example if it's a brick with nothing organic on it – you can't use the technique. In the case of the brick, you won't be able to use C-14, because there's no carbon to date. But you might be able to use the stratigraphy of the soil where it was found, along with TL dating to determine when the brick was fired.

WHY SHOULD THIS MATTER TO YOU?

Why? Because the above techniques are **key words** to look for when you evaluate anyone's claim about how "super old" something is.

Case in point, there's a white guy named Michael Tellinger claiming there's evidence of a **200,000 year old civilization in South Africa.**

He's got all these pictures of stone circles that he claims are the remains. Seems fantastic right? And it IS in Africa, right? Wrong. If you read further into his claims, he's only using this "evidence" to point to alien intervention. He's not giving credit to any Black civilization builders. He's saying aliens put Black people to work to build this stuff 200,000 years ago, and that's how they "jump-started" the modern human race. But what about those stone circles?

Well, here's where you ask what dating techniques he used. And his answer? NONE. He claims that you can't effectively date stones, but – if you look above – you know that's not true. There are plenty of different ways to come up with at least SOME idea of a date. But he's not going to do that, because then it would show that those stone circles are actually just cattle kraals used by Bantu herdsman since the 1500s.

And he's got a book to sell. A few actually, primarily to people who want that "fantastic" Black history – even if it's not based in any real evidence (only to find out he gives all credit to aliens instead of Africans). To be sure, the Black people who actually live in that area would laugh if they heard those cattle pens were evidence of an ancient civilization. Yet, for those of us here who don't know better, we need to know the methodology by which we can evaluate a claim. Or else we keep reposting garbage like that online and buying up books filled with lies.

THE DESTRUCTION OF CENTRAL AFRICA

Like the Amazon rainforest, Europeans have never thought of Central Africa as a "significant" place in world affairs. For the most part, they've gone into Central Africa to obtain resources, and have never stayed too long or made it too deep into the interior to find out anything more.*

By the time a few anthropologists came to Central Africa, the slave raiders had wreaked havoc and left things a mess. When they weren't

---

* One place they couldn't do as much damage was towards Western Africa. West Africans already knew about smallpox, and had even invented the inoculation for it (the earliest form of a vaccine), which they later taught the Europeans. And after so many years of exposure to the deadly disease, they were more resistant to it than many other Original people. This was one of the reasons why West Africans survived slavery in the Americas, while Native Americans could not survive. European historians like to make it sound as if the Native Americans were simply weak, but the truth is they were significantly weakened by exposure to Europeans and their diseases.

kidnapping outright, they escalated conflicts between neighboring people into full-fledged wars and later genocides, providing firearms to whoever provided them slaves (thereby making things worse and worse). In 1901, economic sociologist Karl Bücher reported on the agricultural societies that were left in ruins:

> Travellers have often described the deep impression made upon them when, on coming out of the dreary primeval forest, they happened suddenly upon the well-attended fields of the natives. In the more thickly populated parts of Africa these fields often stretch for many a mile, and the assiduous care of the Negro women shines in all the brighter light when we consider the insecurity of life, the constant feuds and pillages, in which no one knows whether he will in the end be able to harvest what he has sown. Livingstone gives somewhere a graphic description of the devastations wrought by slave hunts; the people were lying about slain, the dwellings were demolished; in the fields, however, the grain was ripening and there was none to harvest it.[95]

At the same time that they raided for slaves and laid these villages to waste, they ravaged the people with biological warfare. Yes, biological warfare.

You see, wherever Europeans went, they brought a TON of diseases, such as syphilis, influenza, smallpox, measles, diphtheria, and tuberculosis. Most of the people they encountered had never had such diseases. So they had no resistance to these illnesses and began dying rapidly. This happened in the Americas, Australia, East Africa, South Africa, Southern Asia, East Asia, the Pacific Islands, you name it.

In Central Africa, they destabilized the region so heavily that it has taken centuries to recover. But when Europeans first came into the area, they reported highly sophisticated nation-states, often with governmental procedures they did not fully understand. Chancellor Williams' *The Destruction of Black Civilization* is especially insightful in this regard.

These Europeans did not, however, have any difficulty understanding the wealth these people enjoyed. As Robert Bailey notes in the *365 Days of Real Black History Calendar*: "A 16th century traveler visited the central African kingdom of Kanem-Borno and commented that even the Emperor's dogs had 'chains of the finest gold.'"

Naturally, it wasn't long before problems ensued. Central Africa was soon engulfed in intertribal warfare, with kingdoms competing to trade prisoners of war for guns and ammunition to defend themselves against neighboring kingdoms doing the same thing.

Walter Rodney's *How Europe Underdeveloped Africa* is especially insightful in this regard.

Before long, Central Africa was a shadow of its former self. When some of us think of how dense the "jungle" growth is in Central (and West) Africa, it would behoove us to consider that many of these trees were actually planted as "screens" and defensive fortifications against slave raiders. This fact – detailed in an article titled "Pre-Colonial Plant Systems of Defense" in *The World Atlas of Archaeology* – is just a glimpse into the advanced ecological knowledge held by the people of this region.[96]

We can only imagine what kind of sciences they'd mastered in the ancient past. Actually, we don't have to imagine. We only have to research. Let's begin.

ECOLOGY AND CONSERVATION IN CENTRAL AFRICA

The forests of equatorial Africa are totally ignored by most historical scholars. Either they're looking at East Africa for the origins of man, or Northeast Africa (Egypt) for the origins of civilization. A few might be talking about more recent "pre-colonial" kingdoms in the West and South. And that's IF they're looking at Africa at all! Needless to say, the studies of prehistoric Central Africa are limited, to say the least. But what HAS been found is highly important, because it rewrites much of the way we interpret "progress" and "civilization."

THE LUPEMBAN AND SANGOAN CULTURES
(300,000 - 10,000 BC)

Studies conducted on archaeological sites in Central Africa show that the hunter-gather communities that occupied the region had two primary technological traditions: (a) the Lupemban Culture, and (b) the Sangoan Culture. Though the Lupemban culture was once dated between 30,000 and 12,000 BC, it's now recognized as far older, with possible dates of 300,000 BC in Zambia and Kenya.[97] The Sangoan Culture has proven to be nearly as old.[98] Think about that. We don't even have human remains that old (yet). This means these traditions literally are older than anything else we know about humanity. And don't think that having the same culture for so long is a sign of stagnation!

Instead of signifying a standstill, the continuity of these traditions demonstrates, as one study notes:

[T]he inherent flexibility and capability of exploiting a variety of environments enabled the hunter-gatherer communities to face and adapt to environmental changes regardless of stone technology.[99]

In other words, the people of Central Africa employed a way of life that worked for nearly 300,000 years. These traditions "enhanced rather than hampered human occupation in the area."[100]

Renowned archaeologist Charles Thurstan Shaw proposed that the origins of African agriculture could be traced back to a proto-agricultural phase that once covered much of West Africa. He suggested this transitional period may have begun among Sangoan hunter-gatherers, who probably resembled present-day pygmies in appearance and lifestyle.[101] This seems feasible, since, before the arrival of taller people in Central, West, and Southern Africa, these regions were populated by people who looked like or were closely related to pygmy people such as the Ba Aka of the Western Central African Republic and Northwest Congo.

WHO WERE THESE PEOPLE?

We'll get deep into the history of so-called "pygmy" people in the next chapter. For now, it is important to note that the ancestors of modern humans developed near East Africa area, where Ba Mbuti people like the Efé and the Hadzabe of Tanzania still carry the original L1 haplotype. At several points in the distant past, the Sahara Desert area was lush and green, allowing easy migration along its southern border. This is when people from the Eastern Congo moved to the Western Congo.

Thus the Mbenga people of the west (such as the Ba Aka of the Northwest Congo) also carry the L1 haplotype, being direct descendants of these first modern humans. All of these people – the Mbuti and Mbenga alike – are known to anthropologists as "pygmies" because they are human communities where adult men do not grow more than five feet tall. We'll explain the reasons for these unique qualities in the coming chapter.

Getting back to Central Africa, the microliths used by the Shum Laka people of Central Africa (about 30,000 years ago) may have been so small because their users were small. What we know is that Sangoan hunter-gatherers gradually moved towards agriculture by, at first, employing microlith technology to protect fields of wild grains and, later, making clearings for wild yams and oil palms.[102] By 12,000 years ago, the Sangoan people were using hoes.[103] No, not like that.

In other words, the ancestors of people like the Aka introduced the proto-agricultural phase to West Africa long before the Bantu arrived. They practiced management of wild resources and moderate levels of cultivate, while the Bantu people who came later would modify those techniques to begin full-fledged farming.

THE SHUM LAKA CULTURE (35,000 - 5,000 BC)

Another study, focusing on the Shum Laka Culture in northwestern Cameroon (as well as regions in the Democratic Republic of Congo), found that the microlithic quartz tradition used there for 30,000 years was "appropriate for the exploitation of a wide variety of environmental settings" and this flexibility represented "an adequate technological response to the environmental changes in Central Africa at the end of the Pleistocene."

Basically meaning that there's a REASON why Africans of prehistoric times weren't building massive stone complexes 20,000 years ago. They didn't need them! There were, instead, employing the appropriate tools to make the most effective use of their ever-changing environment.[104]

After twenty millennia of microlithic tradition in the Shum Laka region, things changed. Around 5000 BC onwards, a new culture, with macrolithic* tools, polishing and pottery, slowly developed. By 2000 BC, an industry with sophisticated axes, blades, and pottery had emerged. With a striking technological continuity, this culture survived throughout the Iron Age. Increasing importance and diversity of trees exploited through the Stone to Metal Age and the Iron Age suggests they knew the science of arboriculture, or the cultivation and management of trees and larger plant life.[105]

At some point, the Niger-Congo proto-agriculturalists surpassed all their neighbors in the practice of African agriculture and taught the science throughout Africa. No matter who contributed to its development, we know that it was the work of Black Africans who

---

* Stone tools about a foot or more long. Microlithic tools are smaller stone tools.

spoke Niger-Congo languages. And we know that it is at the cradle of the Niger-Congo language family where we find the roots of the Bantu people.

By 2000 BC, the Niger-Congo people who hit the northern edge of Central Africa (in what is today eastern Nigeria and Cameroon) struck out in two different directions. Some skirted the forest and continued eastwards until arriving near the Sudanic Nile in Kordofan, developing a language family known as Niger-Congo.

Others pushed deep into the forests of southern Cameroon to begin what is now known as the great Bantu migration. The ones who went south developed a language family known as Benue-Congo, which covers the 300-plus Bantu languages spread across Africa today. Partly due to their adoption of agriculture, the Bantu people spread quickly.

By 300 BC, Bantu speakers were all over the place. Once they acquired the knowledge of smelting iron from their relatives in Meroe to the east and the Nok people of Nigeria to the west (where such technology had been improving for centuries), Bantu migration became more frequent, and branched out in several directions, possibly due to a rapidly growing population assisted by improved technology.

The Bantu who reached the Zimbabwean plateau in the 11th century AD built massive fortifications and stone structures that are now regarded as a World Heritage Site, known as Great Zimbabwe. These monuments were constructed entirely from stone (no mortar!) and built to such fantastic dimensions that European explorers claimed they must have been built by foreigners (either aliens or other Europeans).

And these Bantu didn't just spread into unpopulated territory. They encountered older populations, such as the Khoisan of southern Africa. By the 15th century, the Bantu – with their iron weapons – had "extinguished or absorbed" nearly all of the indigenous people they encountered, except for the Khoisan people living in the Kalahari and Namib deserts to the southwest. In West Africa, Bantu people built massive empires that – until the 1400s – rivaled any European nation, except perhaps those under Moorish rule. Yet, as we know, many of the Moors who introduced civilization to Spain and Italy were themselves Bantu people united under the flag of Islam. The Bantu people of West Africa made up the bulk of those Africans kidnapped and sold during the European slave trade.

AN INTRODUCTION TO GEOGRAPHY

A lot of this book will be confusing if you don't have a grasp of basic geography. Considering that one-third of Americans can't identify the location of the USA on a world map without those helpful boundary lines, you shouldn't feel too bad if you don't where Tunisia is. But have you ever noticed how the same people who can't pick out Darfur, Iran, North Korea, or Libya on a map will be the first ones telling you about why those are important places – now that some website or media personality told them so?

It's my personal opinion that we should become well acquainted with our own communities, and then progressively expand outward in our worldview, until we can understand the universe. Yet many of us prefer to try to move in the other direction. It just doesn't make sense to me, to try to speak on the 12th planet in the 84th galaxy when you don't know a damn thing about what's happening in your own city, much less the countries next door. But I digress. I understand that geography, especially in the context of this book, can be tough, because we're talking about ancient places that aren't known by those names anymore.

For example, ancient Nubia was situated in the region now known as northern Sudan and southern Egypt. And, over time, it's been known by tons of names besides Nubia, as well as many different cultures and civilizations. But if I write, "Over 4500 years ago, the people of Western Anatolia, which is situated in modern-day Turkey, did long-distance trade with the people of the Indus Valley," you're missing a vital piece of the picture if you don't know just how far Turkey is from India. It's over 2500 miles!

To make things easier, we've included maps wherever possible. We've also included some blank maps, so that you can fill them in yourself with information from the book. And, as always, if we don't have the visual reference you need, there's a good chance you can find what you're looking for online or at the library.

ART AND CULTURE IN NORTHERN AFRICA

Almost half a million years ago, our ancestors in Morocco were crafting sculptures and producing artwork. Of these, we have one surviving example, the Tan-Tan Venus figurine, which dates back to between 300,000 and 500,000 years ago.[108] Human remains are found in the area dating back to 160,000 years ago. Later in the region, we find the world's first jewelry – 82,000 years old. Clearly, northern Africa was not a barren desert. In fact, North Africa and the Sahara Desert were once home to thriving sites of prehistoric Black civilization.

As you may remember from *The Science of Self, Volume One*, the Sahara – currently the world's largest hot desert* – was not always a desert. For hundreds of thousands of years, climate changes on Earth have shifted the Sahara from desert to fertile soil and back to desert again. During periods of a wet or "Green Sahara", the Sahara (along with Arabia) become grassland and was full of life. Proof of this can be found in the human settlements that once occupied the area, cave paintings depicting animals that haven't been in the Sahara for over 20,000 years, and traces of plant and animal life that were once everywhere.

In fact, the Nile River – currently the longest river in the world – was once even longer, because the present-day Nile is relatively new, having been around for only 30,000 years. Before that, underground imaging reveals that at least four different Niles (the first being over 5 million years old) flowed through Africa, and then disappeared. At least one of these rivers, much longer than the present-day Nile, travelled through the Sahara.

About 2 million years ago, this river dried up and the Sahara became a desert. This is when (and apparently why) *Homo erectus* left Africa.† Then the Sahara became green again, and life returned. This is the era that produced the Tassili cave paintings and other elements of prehistoric civilization that are being dug up in the Sahara today.

Then it happened again. The tilt of the Earth's axis changed and the Sahara region began receiving less rain. Rainfall levels were critically low by 7,200 years ago, but people continued making use of local

---

* The world's largest desert, Antarctica, is a cold one, classified as such because of a lack of rainfall and useful land (also known as "arable land" or land that can be used for growing crops).

† The emergence of a competing lineage, *Homo ergaster,* could have also been a factor.

DID YOU KNOW?
Interested in learning more about prehistoric cultures in Africa? Hit Wikipedia and search for the following cultures: Wiltonian, Capsian, Magosian, Ibero-Maurisian, Sangoan, Aterian, Lupemban, Sebilian, Stillbay, Micoquien, Mousteroid, Halfan, Acheulean, and Oldowan. You can also search for the category "African archaeology."

resources. This would only make things worse. This was the last time the Sahara was rich, fertile, and heavily populated. Settlements survived in the Sahara until its final desertification around 3,500 BC.*

In 1926, Black historian Drusilla Dunjee Houston wrote:

The Nubo-Egyptian desert was once abundantly watered and a well timbered region. With the exclusion of the narrow Nile valley, all of this is generally a barren waste today. Geology reveals that in the primitive ages, this country had a moist climate like the Congo basin; but these conditions prevailed in remote geological times, probably before the creation of the delta. The changes that turned the Sahara into a burning waste in time made Upper Egypt dry and torrid. Keane describes its climate as often fatal to all but full blooded natives. Under those brazen skies the children of even Euro-African half castes seldom survive after the tenth or twelfth year.[109]

During all of these fertile periods, the people of this region were Black, yet they were also diverse. They came from many places, for many different reasons. Like we've already noted about Africa in general, north Africa was linguistically, physically, genetically, and culturally diverse. This is why Paleolithic and Neolithic cultures across northern Africa, from the Nile Valley to the Maghreb,† show many similarities, but also great diversity.

Many of these sites haven't been dug up because of the forbidding desert climate of the Sahara. But it's not a total mystery. For example, in the mountains of Algeria, you'll find some of the most important of prehistoric cave art in the world. Some of these paintings, depicting Black people hunting and partying, are over 13,000 years old. Evidence from the Tassili Mountains suggests that the people of the Sahara influenced the cultures of both the Nile Valley and of West Africa. They may have developed the science of pastoralism, in the form of domesticated sheep, goats, and cattle.

---

* As we'll discuss in Part Two, this desertification period is when Saharans migrated to the Nile Valley and West Africa, helping build new civilizations there.

† The Maghreb covers northwest Africa from Libya to Morocco. This region is home to several prehistorica cultures, including the Iberomarusian, Oranian, Capsian, and Libyco-Capsian cultures.

You see, cows didn't start out as cows. They started out as giant beasts known as aurochs. *Bos africanus* was a species of aurochs, so big its curved horns were up to three feet long! Julius Caesar described the aurochs of Europe in *The Gallic Wars*:

These are a little below the elephant in size, and of the appearance, color, and shape of a bull. Their strength and speed are extraordinary; they spare neither man nor wild beast which they have espied. These the Germans take with much pains in pits and kill them.[111]

Just picture that! Given this passage, it's no surprise that the aurochs went extinct in Europe, where they were never domesticated. On the other hand, our ancestors – who had been tracking and hunting the *Bos* across Africa for over a million years – were not only able to domesticate these giant beasts into cattle, but to herd them from the Sahara to the Horn of Africa.

They also used the science of cattle breeding to introduce domestic cattle to the Near East, then into Europe, and as far east as ancient India and China. In other words, all the cattle on the planet today can be traced back to the hands of our ancestors.

Around 4,500 BC migrations from the drying Sahara brought diverse groups of Neolithic Africans into the Nile Valley, bringing with them the sciences of agriculture, ceramics, and animal domestication. The population that resulted from this cultural and genetic mixing developed a social hierarchy which would later give rise to the dynasties of ancient Egypt.

Still in the Sahara region, but further east, there is Nabta Playa, an important center of the Neolithic world. It is situated just to the west of the Nile Valley. When their land started becoming desert, Saharan people, including those in Nabta Playa, moved east to the Nile Valley.

Other Saharans went west. Between 10,000 and 7,000 years ago, western Africa was becoming increasingly favorable to human settlement. In Part Two, we'll tell the story of the Neolithic Sahara, Nabta Playa, the formation of Nile Valley civilization, and the story of West Africa.

A QUICK NOTE ON PAN-AFRICANISM

What's better than a few intelligent people sharing a common cause and collective identity? How about a million? Ten million? A billion? It can happen. One of the goals of this book is to provide readers, educators, and activists with a substantial "database" of historical information that supports the premises of Pan-Africanism and other movements to unify the Global Diaspora of Original People. In other words, we're working to show people how and why they should come together.

There are many such movements, each of them seeking to bring together diverse groups of people under a single banner and shared platform. Some are focused on the indigenous people of the Americas (like the American Indian Movement), while others have concentrated on a unified front for the Dalits and "tribal" people in India (like the Adivasi movement).

In Africa, leaders like Kwame Nkrumah, Thomas Sankara, and Muammar Gaddhafi sought to bring together African people under the banner of Pan-Afrikanism. Marcus Garvey, Malcolm X and others in the West have attempted to bridge the gap between Blacks in the Americas and in Africa. Naturally, all of these movements have been met by considerable resistance.

There have also been movements and organizations dedicated to bringing together Africans and Asians, Africans and Latin Americans, and Africans and Native Americans. Marcus Garvey, W.E.B. Du Bois, Elijah Muhammad, Paul Robeson, Robert F. Williams, Huey P. Newton, and several others worked to make such unions a reality. It is also our contention that the world cannot change until Original People come together and confront the problem that oppresses and dehumanizes us all.

However, we also understand that unity begins best at a local level. The word community bears testament to this fact. It makes sense that African nations should seek solidarity in the face of continued Western imperialism, puppet governments, and manufactured conflicts. It makes sense that Blacks in the Diaspora would first seek to connect with their most immediate kin in Africa. Especially when there are African nations anxiously awaiting African-American investment! They WANT you to come back.

But there are others who will attempt to bridge the divide between the Black and Latino communities in America. Or who will attempt to ensure that modern Chinese commitments to African prosperity are honored as promised. Or who will introduce the struggles of the Black people of Papua to those of us who are unaware in the U.S. Or who will work to inspire the dark-skinned people of the Middle East to align with their neighbors in Africa. These are all important causes. I am soundly convinced that the world will not change until the Original People of the world reach a critical mass.

Fortunately, it's not as difficult as it sounds. It only takes a few. As Wesley John Gaines wrote in The Negro and the White Man in 1897, "No man can estimate the influence even of a few cultured, intellectual men." Malcolm Gladwell writes in his book The Tipping Point that a small minority of influential people – as few as 5% – can set off a tidal wave of change.

These changes are rarely political nor are they institutionalized or organized. They are cultural movements that spread among people with the efficiency and reproduction rate of a virus. Except in this case, what's spreading is the cure. When the idea of Pan-Afrikanism spread through Africa and Black America, it infected the hearts and minds of millions of people who had – just yesterday – been under the spell of European colonialism.

The shackles may not have broken overnight, but the process of change had begun. Today, Original People are not as deeply asleep as you may think. The seeds of rebellion remain. The desire for unity remains. The want for awakening remains. We are now what we were then, and we can become all that we were meant to be. It's only a matter of providing our people with the spark that sets them in motion, and the tools to make these movements effective. This book is part of our contribution to that process. Please help us spread the word.

THE JOURNEY OF MAN

EVERY SQUARE INCH OF THE PLANET

"I only made passing reference in the work to Blacks scattered outside of Africa over the world, not from the slave trade, but from dispersions that began in prehistory. This fact alone indicates the great tasks of future scholarship on the real history of the race. We are actually just on the threshold, gathering up some important missing fragments. The biggest jobs are still ahead." – Chancellor Williams, The Destruction of Black Civilization

If you were alive 100,000 years ago, what could cause you to leave your homeland? You could found yourself in conflict you're your community, and decide to leave, taking your family and followers with you, ready to start anew somewhere else. Or a rapidly changing climate could turn your pristine paradise into a desolate desert (or a flooded valley), forcing your community to relocate while others stayed behind. A more powerful group of people could even expand their territory, encroaching on yours, until ultimately you find yourself living on the fringes of your old stomping grounds. Or you simply find your homeland becoming overpopulated, and decide you need to find somewhere less populated to expand your family.

And these are exactly the kinds of things that happened to our ancestors. In this chapter, we'll explore the human migrations that carried our ancestors across the world, from East Africa to Easter Island, from the Nile Valley to northern Britain, and from Japan to Peru. These were the journeys of Black people, the foundational people of all the world's oldest cultures and civilizations.

WHAT YOU'LL LEARN IN THIS CHAPTER

❏ Why we "explored" the world instead of remaining in Africa.
❏ How genetics can help us understand the paths our ancestors took.
❏ Why the world's oldest genetic communities are under attack.

❏ The first human "headquarters" established when humans began expanding out of Africa.

❏ Why our ancestors left the "root of civilization" to settle Asia and Europe.

WHY DID WE EXPLORE THE WORLD?

Before we get into the "journey of man," let's get one thing clear: We didn't travel the globe to "explore" like Europeans did.* Original People, because we have always understood the fractal nature of the physical world, didn't get excited about the "world beyond" because we knew it would be very much like the world within.

Instead, we have typically migrated for one of two reasons: (1) social pressures or (2) environmental pressures.

By environmental pressures, what we mean is either not enough food for all the people currently in a region or some sort of environmental change or disaster that forces us to relocate.

By social pressures, we can mean a variety of things, from growing intergroup conflicts because of increased group size, changes in culture that compel one group to ostracize the other, and a variety of other disputes that lead to people leaving an area for greener pastures.

As Nicholas Wade notes, our ancestors were "expanding into new territory as communities split, not exploring for the sake of adventure."[112] Almost every time a successful settlement grew too large, there was a split. Some people stayed, some left. But everyone knew that too many people in one place could not continue foraging for the same food. Of course, not all splits were amicable. Among hunter-gatherers, larger groups require people to work harder to bring in food, so disputes were more likely to break out in large camps than in small camps.† Sounds familiar. Nicholas Wade adds:

> Because !Kung [San] groups are strictly egalitarian, there is no authority to resolve conflicts and keep order. !Kung groups do have

---

* Then again, Europeans weren't actually "exploring" either; they were looking for new opportunities to exploit...but that's another story.

† Certainly, there could have been even more serious conflicts behind many of these separations, but – unless there was a serious body count involved (and there rarely was) – we don't have much evidence to go on. Yet when genetics reveals that a population migrated from a "good" area to a much more inhospitable, resource-poor area, it suggests these people may have been "exiled" from their old homeland. Within the past 2,000 years, this has been a common and well-documented alternative to outright genocide or mass incarceration of undesirables.

leaders, but they are informal, with no authority other than personal persuasion. The usual method of expressing disagreement is to vote with one's feet and leave camp along with one's family and followers.[113]

WHEN AND WHY WE EXPANDED BEYOND AFRICA

As we explained in *Volume One*, we don't know exactly when the first Homo sapiens emerged in East Africa, but we can be certain that it was no later than 200,000 years ago. We also know that we split into many tiny, separate bands that developed unique genetic lineages and communities, making Africa the most genetically, phenotypically, linguistically, and culturally diverse place in the world.

Population splits are typical of human communities. Our lineages have diverged, evolved independently, and then met again countless times. To understand these population splits, and how we can track the movement of all the different groups that developed, we need to understand the science of human genetics.

AN INTRODUCTION TO GENETICS

As a child, you may have wondered how your physical features turned out the way they did. Or maybe you have an inherited condition that can't be seen on the outside. These matters all relate to the study of genetics. A major branch of biology, genetics is the science of genes, heredity and variation in organisms.

I used to hear elder Five Percenters say the book of Genesis is the "Book of Genetics" or "Genesis is where the 'genes is.'" It sounded like wordplay, but that's the real etymology! "Genetics" comes from the Greek *genetikos* "genitive," which come from *genesis* meaning "origin." And, indeed, the book of Genesis does attempt to tell the origins of man, particularly by tracing all people (at least those known to its writers) back to the three sons of Noah: Ham, Shem, and Japheth.[114]

For centuries, historians attempted to continue using this framework to explain the origins of different ethnic communities and nations. Today, we can use the actual "genetics" of people to trace back their origins.* Genetics is based on the study of human DNA.

---

* The Book of Genesis may have been a reasonable attempt when it was compiled from a variety of sources around the 5th century BC, but it's not exactly the best reference for modern historians! It's what we'd call an "antiquarian history," an attempt to explain origins using the data available at the time. There are examples from many other cultures, from the Hindu *Vedas* to the Mayan *Popol Vuh*. Some of

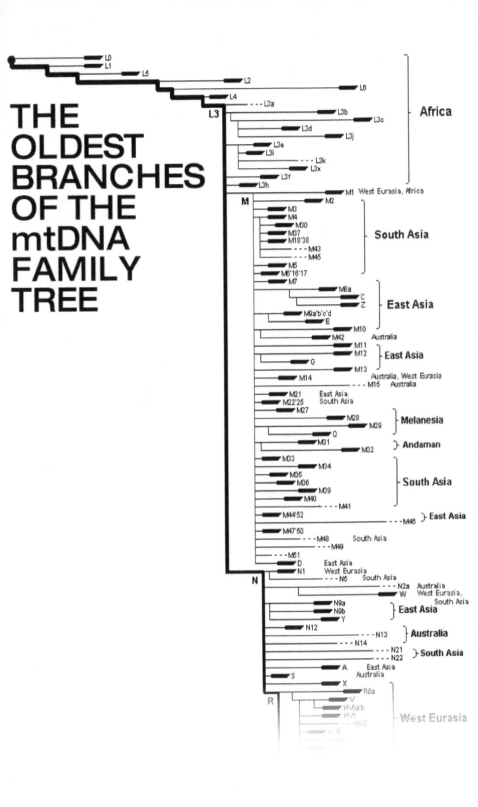

THE
OLDEST
BRANCHES
OF THE
mtDNA
FAMILY
TREE

AN INTRODUCTION TO DNA

As we explained in *Volume One*, DNA is the language of life. All humans have 23 chromosomes, which effectively write your body's past, present, and future. Your first 22 chromosomes contain autosomal DNA contributed by your parents. It identified you uniquely (which is why it is used in forensics), but can't be used to trace your ancestry because it's all mixed up. Your 23rd chromosome determines your gender, and contains mtDNA and (if you're a male) Y-DNA.

We all get mtDNA (mitochondrial DNA from the X chromosome) from our mothers, and men get Y-DNA (Y Chromosome DNA) from their fathers. These DNA records can tell us the history of our ancestors. The "trunks" of our family tree (via DNA) are known as DNA haplogroups. Haplogroup simply means "blood group," as in the people you are related to by your mother's blood or father's blood. All people living today can trace their maternal ancestry back to one of 26 core mtDNA haplogroups. All men living today can trace their ancestry back to one of 20 major Y-DNA haplogroups.

Over time, the descendents of each haplogroup formed further subgroups, called "Subclades." By discovering which haplogroup "family" you belong to, you can then trace even further which sub-branch of your haplogroup you belong to through "Subclade" analysis. This is what those DNA ancestry companies do.*

Throughout this book, we'll talk about mtDNA and Y-DNA Haplogroups to trace the migrations of our ancestors. It may sound technical and difficult at first, but DNA is one of the most effective ways to identify who was where 50,000 years ago. We're using DNA evidence because critics of ancient Black history say that we only cite "appearance" and that doesn't establish solid links between groups of people who just might "look alike." So we're tracing populations back to their African origins using genetics. It needs to be done, or else the story begins to sound flimsy in the modern era. Sometimes it'll be tough but I'll try to make it as straightforward as possible. I'm even including maps and diagrams to help make it easier to follow.

---

these ancient historians may have been onto something, but today we've got a much stronger body of data. Describing folks as "descendants of Ham" is *so* 19th century.

* For more information on how all this works, as well as details on determining your ancestry, check out www.familytreedna.com or www.dnaancestryproject.com

DNA MIGRATION MAPS

Geneticists have developed several different ways to represent the migratory paths suggested by the presence of different DNA Haplogroups throughout the world. Two examples, tracking the possible routes of the various mtDNA and Y-DNA lineages of the world, are found below. We include them here only as examples, not as a confirmation of their accuracy.

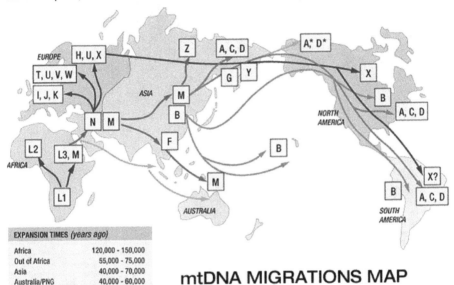

EXPANSION TIMES (years ago)	
Africa	120,000 - 150,000
Out of Africa	55,000 - 75,000
Asia	40,000 - 70,000
Australia/PNG	40,000 - 60,000
Europe	35,000 - 50,000
Americas	15,000 - 35,000
Na-Dene/Esk/Aleuts	8,000 - 10,000

mtDNA MIGRATIONS MAP

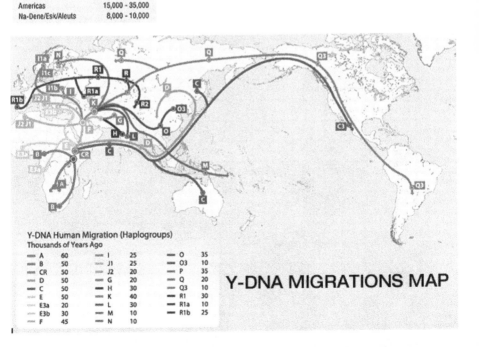

Y-DNA Human Migration (Haplogroups)
Thousands of Years Ago

A	60	I	25	O	35
B	50	J1	25	O3	10
CR	50	J2	20	P	35
D	50	G	20	Q	20
C	50	H	30	Q3	10
E	50	K	40	R1	30
E3a	20	L	30	R1a	10
E3b	30	M	10	R1b	25
F	45	N	10		

Y-DNA MIGRATIONS MAP

Another attempt at reconstructing the historical movements of our ancestors using Y-DNA evidence.

DID YOU KNOW?
There are many reasons why mtDNA is more stable than Y-DNA. For starters, if a man only has daughters, his lineage ends, because daughters don't carry Y-DNA. But if a woman only has sons, her lineage continues, because both males and females carry mtDNA. Also, polygamy is a powerful reducer of diversity in male DNA. A man with multiple wives will result in the founder effect (many mtDNA lineages, but only one Y-DNA lineage).

THE EXTERMINATION CAMPAIGN

"If a race has no history, if it has no worthwhile tradition, it becomes a negligible factor in the thought of the world, and it stands in danger of being exterminated." – Carter G. Woodson

THE SCIENCE OF GENETICS

One of the most effective tools we can use to piece together the prehistoric past is the science of genetics. Our personal genetic data presents a record of our ancestors that – when studied properly – can reveal where our people come from, and where they've been, going back as far as the ancestors of all humans today.

To recap: In human genetics, people can be identified by haplogroups that connect people who are related by paternal or maternal blood. Maternal lineage is more stable and thus easier to trace, but paternal lineage can tell us more about the paths people took. Paternal lineage is described by Y-DNA haplogroups, which are named by the letters of the alphabet. When a lineage undergoes some small genetic mutation, there's a genetic marker that allows scientists to identify it and see where its branches went next. Those branches will be assigned to a new letter or group. Think of it like a family tree, coded by letters instead of names.

So you can imagine that the first, the oldest, the most ancestral Y-DNA haplogroup is known by what letter? A, of course. And can you guess where the people of the A haplogroup are found? Correct again, Africa. In fact, both A and B people are almost exclusive to Africa. The descendants of C are the ones who ventured off into Asia, Europe, Australia, and the Americas.

THE ORIGINAL PEOPLE OF AFRICA

The people known to geneticists by Haplogroup A are essentially the direct descendants of the Original People of the planet Earth. And there's not many of them left. Africa isn't entirely A and B people, you know. There have been so many migrations back into Africa (going back 50,000 years or more) that A is found in various levels throughout the continent, but only three groups of people present the highest frequencies of haplogroup A.

Those three are the Khoisan of Southern Africa, the Afro-Asiatic

Ethiopian Beta Israel (sometimes called the Falasha Jews), and Nilo-Saharans from Sudan (also known as Nilotic people). You may know about the threats to the survival of the original people of Southern Africa and the Sudan. They're both being wiped out by territorial disputes and manufactured famine. But the Beta Israel is an especially disturbing case.

THE ORIGINAL JEWS?

Nearly all of the Ethiopian Beta Israel community, more than 120,000 people, reside in Israel under its Law of Return, which gives Jews and those with Jewish parents or grandparents, and all of their spouses, the right to settle in Israel and obtain citizenship. In what seemed like an unprecedented act of humanitarianism, the otherwise xenophobic and repressive Israeli government mounted "rescue operations" for them, most notably during Operation Moses (1984), Operation Sheba (1985) and Operation Solomon (1991).

Why not, right? They are, after all, who Dr. Yosef Ben Jochannan[115] and Rudolph Windsor[116] called "the ORIGINAL Jews." These indigenous Ethiopian people were among the first to adopt the laws of Judaism, long before Judaism became overwhelmingly white. And, with such a high frequency of haplogroup A, they represent the Original People of the planet itself.

ALL PART OF THE PLAN

So why did Israel relocate them? To exterminate them. Israel recently enacted sterilization programs to promote the decline of the growing Beta Israel population. If this continues, within a few decades, there will be no more Beta Israel. All part of the plan.

And that is a major part of why this book is written. The Original People of the planet are being written out of history. Not in merely a literary sense, but in a literal sense. We should know very well that European historians spent hundreds of years hiding or distorting the Black contribution to world civilization. Were it not for the efforts of a few honest white historians and hundreds of tireless Black scholars, we would not know that this "contribution" was no more "contribution" but essentially the foundation of world civilization itself.

\Yet the attempts to undermine the Black role in history continue into the present day. Western scientists use new language and theories to transplant – out of Africa – the origins of everything that matters. To where? It doesn't matter, so long as it doesn't come from Black people. If you're not familiar with this history, you'll learn more about it when you read the section titled "They Said We Were Savages."

But the campaign to destroy Black history in text pales in comparison to the campaign to destroy Black history in person. The survival of nearly every indigenous Black people who settled the globe is threatened daily. Thousands are already gone. Others, like the Black men and women of the Andaman Islands, are on the verge of extinction. The Andamanese are no insignificant tribe, either. They are the oldest lineage in all of Asia, the pure descendants of the original Black people to settle outside Africa. We discuss their history – and the attempts to make them disappear – in the chapter on India.

SO WHAT HAPPENS WHEN THE PEOPLE DISAPPEAR?

Their history disappears along with them. With no one left to speak their language and tell their story, another segment of Black history is unwritten. This empowers those who seek to "whiten" the history of the world to tell their version unchallenged, because the evidence that proves them wrong is steadily vanishing.

This is why so many archaeological artifacts from the global Black Diaspora have been hidden in museum basements, or personal collections, never to be seen by an inquiring public. Some that were once on display have since been removed from view. Others are found only in foreign museums that most of us will never travel to see. And how many have been disfigured, bleached, or repainted? Just consider how many Black statues have lost their distinct noses to unknown factors, and the campaign becomes clear.

That is why this book has been written.

QUESTIONS TO CONSIDER

In a sample of 5,000 African men, 5% carried Haplogroup A. Considering that Original People throughout the Diaspora descend from the same ancestral population as these 5,000 men, I wonder how many of the "true and living" 5% descend from Haplogroup A. Is Haplogroup A, being the "Original" DNA blueprint, some sort of primordial maintenance system built into humanity's hardware?

That is, are the direct descendants of the "first man" somehow coded to preserve something great? After all, whoever the "African Adam" was, he must have had something significant in his character to engender every lineage that has survived over the past 200,000 years, while so many others have failed and died out.

KENYA

What was he like? What did he have within him? And do the carriers of Haplogroup A still carry that special quality? If they are 5% of the indigenous Black population, could a representative number of them have been brought to American shores, mixed in with the people of Haplogroup E? Were these the people who West African griots said had boarded the slave ships voluntarily, so they could one day (presumably through their descendants) liberate their people?

THE ROOT OF CIVILIZATION

Using genetic, linguistic, and archaeological data, we can trace the migrations that not only took modern humans out of Africa, but also the migrations that went on within Africa during this early period of modern human history. We are certain that all human populations on Earth today can trace their ancestry back to Africa. There's no evidence you can use to trace the human record back to any other location.

We can trace all human Y-DNA back to a single male who scientists call the "African Adam" who lived about 142,000 years ago.[117] Because mtDNA is more stable and can be traced back further than Y-DNA, we can look back further through the maternal line. The mtDNA group at the root of the human mtDNA tree is called macro-haplogroup L. L represents the most ancestral mitochondrial lineage of all currently living modern humans, and can be traced back to a single African woman known to scientists as the Mitochondrial Eve, who lived about 200,000 years ago.

Between 200,000 and 100,000 years ago, macro-haplogroup L split into several major sub-groups, known as L0, L1, L2, L3, L4, L5 and L6. There may have been even more, but those lineages have not survived into the modern day. Out of all the L haplogroups, only one of these lineages expanded (and survived) outside of Africa. This group is known to geneticists as Haplogroup L3. They are the ones who led the expansion from East Africa into Southern Arabia about 130,000 years ago.

It's clear that Africa, and East Africa in particular, is where modern man made his first moves, and the Rift Valley of East Africa was the Original "root of civilization." But since the emergence of anatomically modern humans, we've established several "base camps" throughout the world, each representing a "root of civilization" for that particular period in history. In a sense, we shifted our headquarters a few times. So where were the headquarters of the Original People who led the expansion out of

Africa?

THE ROOT OF CIVILIZATION - 200,000 YEARS AGO

From the days of the earliest hominids until about 130,000 years ago, human activity was "headquartered" in East Africa. Then, for the first time since *Homo erectus* sailed across the Red Sea two million years ago, we – as modern humans – ventured out of Africa about 130,000 years ago.

Why leave? Around this time, Africa was going through a period of climate change that made it increasingly difficult for hunter-gatherer communities to thrive. As we explained in *The Science of Self, Volume One*, the results weren't pleasant:

> What was life like for us 200,000 years ago? Through the work of archaeologists and paleoanthropologists, we know that we were hunters and gatherers living in tiny, separate bands. Now geneticists have found that these bands remained separate for over 100,000 years, developing unique genetic lineages and cultures, until environmental changes brought us all to the brink of extinction. A recent genetic study examined our evolution from 200,000 years ago to the point of our near-extinction 70,000 years ago, when the human population dropped to as little as 2,000. Paleoclimatological data suggests that our homeland, Eastern Africa, went through a severe series of droughts between 135,000 and 90,000 years ago. These droughts may have contributed, at first, to the population splits, but, by the end, they were leading to our near-extinction. That's right. We almost died off entirely. But, apparently, we realized the tribalism thing wasn't working to our advantage, and we did something different. We came together. This, you'll see, is a recurring lesson we keep learning and forgetting.[118]

In other words, we HAD to come together to survive.[119] This migration left Africa via the *Bab-el-Mandeb* The *Bab-el-Mandeb*, also known as the Mandeb Strait, is a strait located between Djibouti, Eritrea, and Somalia, in the Horn of Africa and Yemen on the Arabian Peninsula. Essentially, it's where the tip of East Africa gets closest to the tip of Southern Arabia.

THE ROOT OF CIVILIZATION - 130,000 YEARS AGO

> *"Arabia was indeed the first staging post in the spread of modern humans."*
> – Geneticist Verónica Fernandes[120]

In other words, the first stop out of Africa was Southern Arabia. As Hans-Peter Uerpmann of the University of Tubingen writes in "The Southern Route Out of Africa," 130,000-year-old stone hand axes found at the Jebel Faya site in Arabia (in the United Arab Emirates to be exact) are not simply *similar* to African hand axes of the period,

DID YOU KNOW?

Interested in learning more about prehistoric cultures in the Near East? Hit Wikipedia and search for the following cultures: Kebaran, Natufian, Mushabian, Antelian, Jabroudian, Emirian, Zagros, Pre-Ceramic A, Pre-Ceramic B, Kebaran, Athlitian, and Aurignacian.

they're *the same*. They constitute clear evidence that Africans settled this region more than 50,000 years before the accepted "Out of Africa" timeline that traces all moderns back to a dispersal 75,000 years ago.[121] 130,000 years ago, the Arabian Peninsula was lush, fertile land with heavy rainfall and an easy commute from East Africa, thanks to the southern Red Sea's levels dropping to only 2.5 miles wide.[122]

At site resembling Jebel Faya in Oman, there's archaeological evidence for "a distinct northeast African Middle Paleolithic technocomplex in southern Arabia."[123] Archaeologists call this culture the Nubian Complex. Archaeological sites belonging to the Nubian Complex occur throughout:

❐ the middle and lower Nile Valley,
❐ the desert oases of the eastern Sahara,
❐ across southern Arabia, and
❐ the Red Sea hills.

The ages of these Nubian Complex sites fall within a range of 130,000-74,000 years ago. Some of the oldest settlements are now buried underwater,* but many of the sites further inland have survived the rising sea levels.

"[T]he negroid element permeates the low-caste or outcast "pariah" tribes of Western and Eastern India, and penetrates through the coast tribes of Southern Persia to Eastern Arabia." – Harry Hamilton Johnston[124]

Based on the trail of evidence associated with the Nubian Complex in East Africa and Arabia, it appears that humans left Africa about 130,000 years ago and developed a techno-cultural complex in southern Arabia that would later disband and expand to populate the globe. These people would become us.† In other words, the "Afro-Arabian" Nubian Complex could be considered the first human "root of civilization."

---

* For example, a study published by archaeologist Jeffrey Rose in the journal *Current Anthropology* suggests the existence of 100,000-year-old human settlement at a Persian Gulf "Oasis" that is now underwater.

† Some of you may be wondering, wait, what about Africans? Wouldn't Africans still have an uninterrupted genetic lineage going back before the migration out of Africa? We'll get back to that. For now, let's follow the timeline of the journey out of Africa.

THE ORIGIN OF THE NUBIAN COMPLEX

"A baby is not born in or from a cradle. A baby is only subsequently deposited there. Arabia as the Cradle does nothing to dethrone Africa (west of the Red Sea) as the Mother." – Dr. Wesley Muhammad

Several studies trace this complex back to East Africa, but there are also several studies proposing that the "root" of the Nubian Complex was in Southern Arabia. One study suggests:

> As the late Nubian Complex at Aybut Al Auwal is dated…slightly earlier than the late Nubian Complex in Africa, we remain open to the possibility that the late Nubian Complex originated in Arabia, and subsequently spread back into northeast Africa.[125]

Eurocentric scholars focus on evidence like this to promote a non-African origin for civilization, while Afrocentric scholars dismiss evidence like this because it seems to take the "root" out of Africa.

For those of us who know the true story of the world, it doesn't matter so much, because we know who the founders of the Nubian Complex were – Nubians! And since the Red Sea is barely a geographic boundary to begin with, we know that Africa and Arabia (and Asia along with it) are about as "separate" as Europe is from Asia.

In fact, the most distant/disconnected landmass may be the Americas (as Australia was once "almost" connected to Southeast Asia). But think about that.

IS "THE WEST" A SINGLE LANDMASS?

White folks describe the Americas and Europe as one social entity: They call it "the West." Their empires in the Americas and Europe are collectively known as the "western world" (and they sometimes include Australia!)…which is crazy if you think about it, because North America and Europe are *thousands* of miles apart. There's an entire ocean between them. But that doesn't stop them. They consider it one world for social purposes.[126]

Meanwhile, Africa – which is physically connected to Asia, and Asia – which is actually not separated from Europe in ANY meaningful way (besides maybe a mountain range), are all considered *separate entities*. And we accept it without question. That's how deeply we've been affected by how they taught us to think. It's no surprise that the Arabic name for North Africa is *Ifriqiyah*, which means "to divide." And it wasn't the Arabs who divided it!*

No matter who did the slicing, it's up to us to bring it all back

---

* See "Inspiration for this Work" in the Appendix of Part Two.

together. Thus, we need to think about things in terms of the GLOBAL Black Diaspora. And in doing so, we would love to speak of an Afrasia (as the Europeans like to do with Eurasia now), but really…that is not enough. The entire planet Earth belongs to the Black man – he simply chose the best parts for himself to call home. The Honorable Elijah Muhammad taught that, at one point, the whole planet Earth was called Asia,* and thus the "Asiatic Black Man" was not a "local" identity but a *global* identity.

So, when we talk about East Africa and Arabia, it's because of political boundaries, not real geographic separation. The people of southern Arabia were just as Black as their brothers on the other side of the Red Sea. Failing to see that leaves us short-sighted in our perspective of whose planet this is. It's just like saying Black people were no longer African once they arrived on American shores, as if geography somehow changes ancestry. It doesn't.[127]

A QUICK NOTE ON CITING YOUR SOURCES

If you're an author or speaker making claims about anything that isn't common knowledge, you've gotta cite your sources. Seriously. That's like a fundamental. If you don't you might be plagiarizing, copying and pasting, making it up, or trying to keep people from digging into your sources on their own. Or maybe you just missed a few. I'm sure I missed several opportunities to cite all the sources I used in this book. Yet this book alone has over 400 citations. I'm really talking about the folks who say twenty amazing, unbelievable things...and then their only source cited is a webpage that doesn't even pull up when you try to find it. Not cool. Meanwhile, if you're a reader, don't be content accepting claims from people who don't provide their sources. People really do make stuff up. It doesn't matter if the statement makes you feel good. If you continue believing whatever people tell you without demanding some sort of evidence, you'll still be just as far from the truth as you were when you didn't know anything.

---

* Indeed, Asia is one of the oldest placenames for the known world. The earliest recorded instance of its use is found in the Akkadian "Asu" roughly meaning "the land of the Sun." Much older (but unrecorded) forms of the word are very likely.

FIJI

WE ALMOST DIDN'T MAKE IT

PAST THREATS TO HUMAN SURVIVAL

*"Those who have no record of what their forebears
have accomplished lose the inspiration which comes
from the teaching of biography and history." – Carter
G. Woodson*

When geneticists study human ancestry, they find plenty of lineages
more than 100,000 years old in Africa. These are the Original People,
and they're still here (via their direct descendants). But outside
Africa, it's very difficult to find any surviving lineages that go back
that far. Thus, they've concluded that humans only left Africa about
60,000-75,000 years ago. But there are human remains in India and
Australia that are older than this. And there are people in New
Guinea who have maternal lineages going back more than 100,000
years. So what gives? In the last chapter, we established that human
did, indeed, venture out of Africa around 130,000 years ago.

But what happened to most of these people? Didn't they migrate out
of the Nubian Complex at any point before 75,000 years ago? If so,
why isn't the world full of lineages that old? Why do geneticists say
that lineages outside Africa are no more than 75,000 years old? What
killed off the majority of humans who left Africa before then?

WHAT YOU'LL LEARN IN THIS CHAPTER

☐ How and when we began expanding out of the Nubian Complex.

☐ How almost all of the people who left this area before 75,000 years
ago were killed off.

☐ What killed off most of our ancestors who took the southern route
across Asia.

☐ What killed off those of us who attempted to travel north into Europe
and Central Asia.

☐ The incredible scientific and cultural advances we made in response
to these threats (such as "making" dogs from wolves!).

☐ How the survivors of these events came back together to overcome
these extinction-level challenges.

☐ Who these two branches of survivors became, and the parts of the world that they went on to settle, becoming the ancestors of all humans on the planet today.

❏ Are these two branches different enough to be considered separate or are they still the same people?

THE EXODUS

From 130,000 to 74,000 years ago, the ancestral humans – who we call the "Original People" – were headquartered in the Nubian Complex at the root of civilization. During this period, the formerly lush grasslands of East Africa and Southern Arabia became increasingly arid and inhospitable. We don't know if that's the only reason why they left, but between 100,000 and 75,000 years ago, many of the Original People seated at the Nubian Complex left Arabia, traveling east. They took the coastal route, building settlements along the shores of Southern Asia. As a result, many of the oldest settlements will never be excavated, because they're now underwater thanks to global warming and its rising sea levels.

But all is not lost. Plenty of evidence can be found further inland. There are dozens of sites scattered across Southern Asia and Oceania, providing intimate details of their day-to-day lives, revealing much of how they lived…and some of how they looked.

Why only some? Because the skeletal record is pretty sparse for this early period. In fact, most of the skeletons are probably underwater. The ones we know about, we'll discuss throughout this book. Yet, it's not as if all we have are skeletons.

After all, these people had descendants. Like us. Most of these descendants, however, don't have "pure" lineages. Very few people do. Almost all, most of us are the byproduct of these ancestors splitting into dozens of separate lineages which evolved locally before meeting again and mixing things up some more.

Yet there are some people who are more "Original" than others. They are the direct descendants of the first humans to settle the globe. They don't have a bunch of lineages in their ancestry. In some cases, their ancestry is as close to "pure" as you can find.

We know this because DNA studies have shown that these people are the most unmixed descendants of the oldest haplogroups. Do you remember what those are? They're A, B, C, and D (on the paternal side) and L, M, and N (on the maternal side). These people are the Original People. They're the ancestors of us all. In this chapter, we're going to study those people, looking at where they went, what they did, and who they became.

A RE-INTRODUCTION TO GENETICS

Still don't understand genetics? Think of it like this:

We all have DNA that codes our unique genetic (and physical) profile. We get this DNA from our mother and father. We all have maternal DNA (known as mtDNA, or mitochondrial DNA) from our mothers, and all men have paternal DNA (known as Y-DNA, or Y-chromosome DNA) from their fathers. There are different families of DNA, and it's just like a family tree. Geneticists can use your DNA to tell what branch of the tree you belong to.

Technically, our ancestors go back to the beginning of life itself (and beyond, if you want to get deep). But we can trace back the ancestors of all of our mothers to one source who lived about 200,000 years ago. Think of her as Mrs. L. That's what geneticists call the DNA family (or haplogroup) she represents. Mrs. L had plenty of sisters, but none of them had children who survived. Mrs. L also had a few daughters, who became Mrs. L0, Mrs. L1, Mrs. L2, and so on. All of her daughters stayed in Africa, except Mrs. L3. Mrs. L3 crossed the Red Sea, where she had daughters like Mrs. M, N, and R, all of whom went on to have massive families all over the world. If you're a woman, you're descended from one of the families named above.

Of course, Mrs. L wasn't a single mother. But because of the way DNA works, we can't trace the "Mr." in our family tree as far back. What we know is that we can trace all of our men back to a brother who lived about 140,000 years ago in Africa, who we'll call Mr. A. His oldest sons, A0 and A1 stayed in Africa, as did his grandson Mr. B. But his other grandson, Mr. CT, had other plans. CT had two sons, DE and CT. Mr. DE was born in northeast Africa, but his brother, CF, was born on the other side of the Red Sea, outside Africa. DE had two sons, named D and E. Mr. D's sons settled all of southern Asia, marrying with the daughters of Mrs. M, N, and R. Mr. E's sons spread back into Africa, where they nearly took over, replacing many of their cousins who had remained in Africa (the descendants of Mr. A and B). Meanwhile, CF's sons were headed east. They eventually populated Asia, Australia, Europe and the Americas.

Of course, we're simplifying things a bit, because these weren't actual sons and grandsons, but populations of people who split and became new populations over the course of thousands of years. How did they split? Well, groups of people split up all the time, but we know about these splits because of little genetic changes (or mutations) that mark a group of people as different from their parent group. These genetic markers are called SNPs. While there were hundreds of splits over the past 200,000 years, some of the lineages remain unbroken, even after all this time. Thus, for example, the African men who still belong to Y-DNA haplogroup A are the direct descendants of the father of all humanity.

Today, there are about 26 major mtDNA families (or haplogroups), each classified by letters (but not in ABC order). And there are about 18 major Y-DNA lineages (or haplogroups), also classified by letters of the alphabet. After 200,000 years of splitting up and developing new lineages, there are now dozens of even smaller groups, and they're called subclades. Geneticists use numbers and additional letters to identify those subgroups (like R1b1a).

If you were kind of lost as you read the last few sections, and this explanation helped a little, you might want to go back and re-read the sections that threw you off.

GETTING BACK TO THE EXODUS

Beginning over 100,000 years ago, Original People began spreading beyond the Nubian Complex and settling the globe. Again, we don't know for certain what led them to leave the root, but it appears that environmental pressures were significant. The desertification of the Sahara region, followed by the desertification of Southern Arabia, may have been what compelled several thousand people to leave the root of civilization. This is interesting when you consider that the people of the Nubian Complex were just recovering from the droughts and desertification that eliminated most of their population in Africa.

In the coming chapters, you'll see details of our travels across the planet. Our ancestors settled just about everywhere and anywhere you can think of. When the environmental conditions weren't favorable, we still found a way to make it work. Yet, for the most part, we preferred settling in places that were warm, sunny, and full of fresh food and natural shelter.

When our communities outgrew the available resources, we split up and relocated. And when the climate shifted and an old homeland became a little less people-friendly, we left and settled somewhere else. By 20,000 years ago, we'd literally seen all 196,940,000 square miles of the planet Earth. No exaggeration (as you'll soon see)!

FROM SEA TO SHINING SEA

When the ancestral human population left the Nubian Complex, the earliest branch headed east along the southern coastal route across Asia. Thus one of the earliest human settlements in Asia (after Arabia) can be found in India.[128] These Black people would become the Original People of Asia. In *The Evolution of Human Populations in Arabia*, Michael D. Petraglia and Jeffrey Rose say that the people of the Nubian Complex had brought their African culture and technology as far east as Australasia* by 70,000 years ago.[129]

Thus, Australia and the islands of Southeast Asia are where we find some of the earliest evidence of modern human settlement east of India. The Original People took a coastal route, primarily because that's where food and shelter were easiest to find, but possibly also because the beach is just such a nice place to live.

A QUICK NOTE ON MIGRATIONS

Wait...you didn't think we were walking all this way, did you? Nah, we sailed! Some historians like to think that our early ancestors must have only taken land routes. You may not realize it, but this is all based on the racist premise that seafaring was the domain of Europeans. In fact, this is the theory posited by J. Macmillan Brown in his works on the settlement of the Pacific Islands. Brown argues explicitly that "The negroid, we may conclude, has always remained in situ; he has never become a migrant, and never mastered the art of navigation." Brown says that no "Negroid people" have ever been known for their maritime capabilities, and thus it must have been Mongoloid and Caucasoid people who led the settlement of the Polynesian Islands – despite all the evidence to the contrary.†

To be fair, sea levels were indeed lower in the past, and many places that are now separated were once connected by land. But we're talking about nearby islands once being connected to the mainland – not a land bridge connecting Australia and South America!

For example, the Malay Peninsula, together with the islands of Sumatra, Java, and Borneo, once formed a landmass known today as Sunda or Sundaland. Further south, Australia, New Guinea, and Tasmania were connected as a landmass now called Sahul. But there was still at least 60 miles of water between Sunda and Sahul when the ancestors of the Australian aborigines first settled there over 60,000 years ago![130]

The truth is, there are mountains of evidence that our ancestors sailed

---

* Australasia is a region of Oceania comprising Australia, New Zealand, the island of New Guinea, and neighboring islands in the Pacific Ocean.

† It's kinda like the modern stereotype that Black people can't swim – despite the fact that Africans were the first master swimmers. Perhaps a more modern "fear of the ocean" is well-justified, considering how the Atlantic Ocean figures into the collective unconsciousness of most Black Americans.

wherever they wanted to go, for as long as we have evidence of them going places. In *The Science of Self, Volume One,* we present evidence of seafaring as early as the migrations of Homo erectus. Yet the idea that HUMANS couldn't travel to North America unless they walked across a frozen Bering Strait, or they couldn't settle the Pacific Islands until the past 3,000 years...it's just racist. It's not based on the evidence; it's simply based on the preconceived notion that we couldn't do it until white folks did it.

Now, all these coastal settlements mean we will have a hard time finding the remains of those early cultures, because the sea level has risen and the oceans have swallowed up much of that prehistoric shoreline. So those remains are mostly underwater now, and very unlikely to be found anytime soon. We do, however, have underwater remains from more recent settlements, since those were efforts of stone construction, rather than organic use of the available environment.

THE TOBA EXTINCTION

The Southern branch of Original People were well on their way, and appears to have settled everywhere from Southern Arabia to New Guinea (and possibly South America) over 75,000 years ago. They may have started this wave of expansion almost 100,000 years ago. But few (if any) of these first settlers have surviving lineages. In the Americas, they may have been wiped out by new settlers (or they are "uncontacted tribes" who haven't been studied genetically). We don't know for sure.

But back in Asia, specifically in India and the surrounding areas, these people were killed *en masse*, and we know this for sure. Yet it wasn't another group of humans who took them out. The Earth did it. 74,000 years ago, a *supervolcano* erupted at Mount Toba in what is now Sumatra in Southeast Asia. This was no ordinary volcano. The eruption and its accompanying clouds of volcanic ash were so massive that they killed off most of the people in the area. As a result, Southern Asia and Australasia were RE-populated after 75,000 years ago.

TWO SHADES OF BLACK: AFRICOID AND AUSTRALOID

Throughout this book, we'll talk about two important "variants" of the Original People. They're both Black, and they're both direct descendants of the ancestral human population, but they've been separated for almost 75,000 years.

When they first separated, the people of one branch weren't very different from the people of the other, but these two branches went through some very different experiences. For over 50,000 years, they were shaped by the paths they took, and – by 20,000 years ago – it was much easier to tell the descendants of one group from the other.

Not only are they physically distinct, they're genetically distinct. One branch can be associated with Y-DNA lineages A, B, D, and E. This branch is described as looking more "Africoid" (others call them "Negroid"). The other branch can be associated with the C and F lineages, and looks more "Australoid."

What does "Australoid" mean? Australoid people typically have wavy hair, large teeth, strong brow ridges, prognathism, full lips, broad noses, heavy body hair, and very dark skin. Many of these traits can still be found in the diversity of Africa's oldest people. Australoid people are distinct because of their receding forehead and brow ridge topped by hair ranging from a straight to wavy texture, traits only found "here and there" in modern Africa.

When you think of these traits, you may think only of Australia, but people who looked like this were once spread far and wide throughout the world. Many of these features are still found amongst the "Veddoid" people of India and Sri Lanka, the native people of New Guinea and the Pacific Islands, and some Native Americans living along the western coasts of California and Mexico.

Australoid people came from Africa like everyone else, but they're the descendants of a migration that evolved a little differently. The reason their branch looks a little different from most African people is partly because the earliest humans were quite diverse. If a small subgroup of those people broke off and continued having children within their own community, eventually most of the people would begin sharing a similar set of features. These events are known as "population bottlenecks." In the history of our ancestors, one of the most significant bottlenecks since the exodus from Africa occurred in the middle of southern Asia.

SRI LANKA

INDIA

Sri
Lanka

SRI LANKANS NOW

Photos below are over 100 years old

ABORIGINAL SRI LANKANS

THE TOBA ERUPTION

When and how did Australoid people become distinct from other Original People? There's a good chance this separation happened because of the eruption of the Toba Supervolcano in Sumatra. When Toba blew about 74,000 years ago, it was devastating. Much of Asia was blanketed by a thick cloud of volcanic ash, which triggered an instant Ice Age lasting over 1,000 years.[131] In an excellent book titled *The Real Eve*, Steve Oppenheimer calls this event "the greatest natural calamity to befall any humans, ever."

The Toba explosion left a plume of ash over the entirety of India for approximately five years, which Oppenheimer calls a "nuclear winter," in which almost every living thing in that area would have been wiped out.[132] There are layers of ash in India up to fifteen feet deep. That's pretty catastrophic.

Many of us died. It's quite possible that many of the earliest human populations in western India, Pakistan, and the Middle East (including lineages that might have been older than L3) were killed off within years. This left two remnants on either side of the explosion's epicenter: the people of Africa and the people of Australasia.

Our ancestors eventually resettled India and the Middle East once the smoke cleared (no pun intended), but the Toba eruption caused something known as a genetic bottleneck. Throughout Asia, only small groups of survivors remained, and it is from these ancestral populations that many modern humans descend today. This would explain why the Y-DNA marker known as YAP is found among the oldest populations in the Near East, the Andaman Islands, Cambodia and Japan, but is entirely absent from India.[134]

According to Sacha Jones:

> This bottleneck would have greatly reduced modern human diversity as well as population size. With climatic amelioration, population explosion out of this bottleneck would have

occurred…Post Toba populations would have reduced in size such that founder effects, genetic drift and local adaptations occurred, resulting in rapid population differentiation. In this way the Toba eruption of ~74 ka would have shaped the diversity that is seen in modern human populations today.[135]

In other words, the seeds of "racial differentiation" were first sown in Toba's wake. Toba expert Stanley Ambrose suggested decades ago that Toba could have been responsible for human differentiation, producing the various "races" and other signs of major biological and cultural diversity. But Ambrose believed that this event occurred while all humans were still in Africa, where Toba's effects would have been negligible.

We now know that Toba struck in the epicenter of a human population movement that was sweeping across Asia, from East Africa to the Pacific Ocean. In fact, Toba literally hit dead center, cutting through the middle of this movement, killing much of the early human population in India. It was somewhere in this area that one part of the human population began developing a stronger Africoid morphology, while the other part became increasingly Australoid.

As Dr. Victor Grauer has noted:

> For example, if only a few members of a particular migrant colony happened to have what we would now consider [Australoid] features, and that group happened, by sheer chance, to survive, while most of the others died or migrated elsewhere, then such a development could lead to the establishment of a new "race," with [Australoid] features exclusively. Thus, it's not difficult to see how an event such as Toba could have been the trigger for certain very fundamental changes, cultural, genetic and morphological, which could explain the highly structured differences we now see among different populations in different parts of the world.[136]

The Toba survivors who became ancestors of the Australoid people may have looked somewhat Australoid, but not strongly so. We know this because the earliest human remains in Australia are Australoid, but their features aren't nearly as strong as modern Aborigines. Modern aborigines have had over 60,000 years for their features to develop in relative isolation. Over time, their features became more distinct and homogenous. In other parts of the world, Australoid people evolved a little differently. This is why the Australoid people of Japan don't look "exactly" like the Australoid people of India.

This is also why we won't find people who look "exactly" like Australian aborigines in East Africa, but many of their physical differences are due to local evolution, genetic drift, and the founder effect. When you look below the surface (at the genes) you can see the shared heritage. At the 2005 Paleoanthropology conference, Sarah Tishkoff and Floyd Reed of the University of Maryland connected the genetic dots between East Africans and their distant Australoid cousins as far east as New Guinea.[137]

So don't get the wrong idea. Australoid people are Black people. Australoid and Africoid people are merely two "shades" of the same Black ancestral people. Anthropologist Alfred Cort Haddon saw such a connection between Australoid and Africoid people that he called them, together, the "Austrafrican or black race."

WHAT DO WE CALL THEM?

It would be nice if we could distinguish Australoid people with an ethnic term, but are again stuck with the same dilemmas as in the previous chapter. For example, Koori is an indigenous name used by the Australian Aborigines of New South Wales and Victoria. But, as with Twa, it is by no means a universal name for all Australian Aborigines (other regional names include Murri and Nunga).

The aboriginal people of the Australia's western central desert call themselves Anangu. Like Aka, it essentially means "person" or "human being" and has come to denote aboriginal people in other areas, but it's not a universal name by far.

Yet the generally accepted umbrella name "Aboriginal People" doesn't work for the purposes of this book, where we are describing several branches of Original People, including some who may have come into a region before (or after) Australoid people. "Australoid" works as an anthropological classification, but it doesn't sound like a human community. At the same time, using an ethnic-sounding name can makes people think THEY actually called themselves that. And I don't want to give off that impression. So, for the purposes of this book, we will use Australoid People, simply to identify Original People who fit the Australoid physical type.

Using linguistic evidence, skeletal remains, and genetic data, we can piece together their travels out of Africa. Here's what we know so far: Upon leaving Palestine, one branch went into India, where their descendants can still be found throughout the country, carrying many of the traits we described above. It appears India became their homebase. From India, they went into Southeast Asia, China, Japan, Australia, and the Pacific Islands. They eventually became the earliest known settlers in the Americas. Another branch traveled into Europe.

As early as 1915, Du Bois noted evidence of these prehistoric migrations in *The Negro*:

> The primitive Negroid race of men developed in Asia wandered eastward as well as westward. They entered on the one hand Burma and the South Sea Islands, and on the other hand they came through Mesopotamia and gave curly hair and a Negroid type to Jew, Syrian, and Assyrian. Ancient statues of Indian divinities show the Negro type with black face and close-curled hair, and early Babylonian culture was Negroid. In Arabia the Negroes may have divided, and one stream perhaps wandered into Europe by way of Syria.[138]

AUSTRALOID CULTURE

As much as we'd like to say Australoid people such as the Australian aborigines are culturally "just like" the people of Africa, that would be an oversimplification. In fact, Australoid culture is quite different. For example, Australian languages are not tonal. Australian music is not polyphonic nor participatory like the music of Khoisan or "Pygmy" people in Africa.

Their cultures are still fairly egalitarian, but more hierarchical than you'd find among DBP people in Africa. And this is all odd, because you can find all the missing elements if you simply look a little further east in New Guinea or the islands of Melanesia, where there are clear survivals of the egalitarian African culture of the Original People. But why?

Of course, this cultural "otherness" isn't exclusive to Australia. We can actually find this cultural change among both the Australoid and Africoid survivors of the Toba event. The only difference is that the Australoid survivors became a population of their own in Australia, while the Africoid survivors headed back west, ultimately "back-migrating" into Africa by 50,000 years ago.

These people can be identified by the M1 and E lineages that permeated nearly all African communities that survive today.* In Africa, the Toba survivors did eventually "take over"† but they went through more of a "mixing" process than the straight-up replacement/displacement process that happened in Australia. In other words, Australoid people are Toba survivors, raw and uncut.

---

* This means there aren't many, if any, people in Africa who aren't descended from the people who left Africa 130,000 years ago. This is why we can say "our" ancestors left Africa without being inconsiderate of African people. After all, their ancestors ALSO left Africa before coming back.

† Especially by the time they gave birth to the Bantu people of West-Central Africa, around 5,000-4,000 years ago.

Dr. Victor Grauer believes that this fact profoundly shaped the culture of most Australoid people. According to Grauer, after emerging from Toba's ashes, "they would have been faced with a world largely depleted of both vegetation and wildlife." He cites other examples, like that in Colin Turnbull's *The Mountain People*, where the Ik people of Uganda exemplify what happens "when a particular population is suddenly placed under tremendous stress to the point that the most basic cultural norms begin to break down."

This could explain why Australoid culture shares many similarities with African culture, but also presents us with many missing elements that are otherwise typical of the Original People.

QUESTIONS TO CONSIDER

If the Toba event drastically affected the cultural pathologies of surviving populations (just as Central Asian survival may have impacted Mongoloid culture), were these "more aggressive" pathologies exactly what was needed to effectively terminate the Neanderthal onslaught? What were the costs to the ancestral populations NOT affected by Toba, who retained a more pacifist cultural tradition, and who were ultimately pushed to the fringes by Toba survivors?

Further, were Australoid people born to be scarcity survivors? That is, does the fact that Australoid people survived the Toba extinction (or emerged from its ashes) suggest that they would always be a people who could survive when resources were severely limited?

Similarly, were Mongoloid people born to be cold-weather survivors? Were mtDNA lineages A, C, and D – which survived the trek through Siberia into the Americas – better adapted, or more genetically likely to survive in cold environments?

If there is any merit to these possibilities, what about the L3 lineage? Was L3 naturally selected to survive out of Africa, while L0, L1, L2, L4, and L5 were better off in Africa? That is, was L3 the only population "fit" to make the exodus? If not, why didn't other populations leave with L3? Were there social factors involved? If so, can we figure out any of those social factors by looking at the earliest cultures established by L3 (Howiesons Poort, the Nubian Complex, Paleolithic India, etc.)?

Reconstructions of (left to right) Australopithecus, Early Homo erectus (Java Man), Late Homo erectus (Peking Man), Homo heidelbergensis (Rhodesian Man), Neanderthals, and Early Homo sapiens (Cro-Magnon). Notice the "apex" of human development.

Artist rendering of Homo ergaster by Andrew Baker.

Alternate model of Homo ergaster by Viktor Deak

Homo heidelbergensis

Homo erectus

Bamboo raft made from stone tools to reproduce the voyage of Homo erectus from Timor to Australia

Homo sapiens idaltu

Homo sapiens sapiens

PHILIPPINES

AUSTRALIA

INDIA

NEW GUINEA

The "root of civilization," known as the Nubian Complex circa 125,000 BC, from which human populations dispersed to settle the globe. (above) The original people of the world (right)

THE WAR AGAINST HUMANITY
THE WESTERN BRANCH

While some humans left the Nubian Complex travelling east across the southern Asia, others went north into the Near East and Europe. They eventually established the Upper Paleolithic culture of Palestine, and these people later brought the first Paleolithic culture to Europe.[139]

In *The Evolution of Human Populations in Arabia*, Michael D. Petraglia and Jeffrey Rose show how the African Middle Paleolithic cultures of the Near East (250-50,000 years ago) transitioned into the Upper Paleolithic cultures of the Near East and Europe (50-20,000 years ago) thanks to an influx from Arabia between 70,000 to 50,000 years ago.[140]

But they had been trying to get into the area for thousands of years before that! The only problem was that everyone who tried...died. This is because, while Toba eliminated the earliest members of the eastern branch, another deadly foe was killing off the migrants who went north. In order for our ancestors to settle the Near East and Europe, we'd have to conquer an adversary tougher than the weather.

MORE NEAR DEATH EXPERIENCES

100,000 years ago, Northern Arabia and the Near East weren't the most desirable places to raise your family. For beginners: deserts everywhere. Southern Arabia and northeast Africa were a tropical paradise by comparison. But you know how the Earth is, always spinning, always shifting, changing her mind about what's in and what's out, what's hot and what's not. So naturally, these areas began desertifying too, leading many of us to long for greener pastures elsewhere. But if we wanted to expand past the Nubian Complex, the barren deserts weren't our only problem. Beyond these deserts loomed another threat to our survival: the Neanderthals.

The Neanderthals weren't a group of deranged mutants or anything. They weren't too different from humans actually. As we explained in *The Science of Self, Volume One*, Homo neanderthalis evolved in Europe from Homo antecessor, who had evolved from Homo erectus, who had settled in Europe almost two million years ago.

By 200,000 years ago, Neanderthals were all over Europe. Skeletal remains from Morocco show that we had expanded into the northern extremes of Africa as early as 160,000 years ago, but – despite the short trip from Morocco to southern Spain – the

DID YOU KNOW?
Paleolithic Europeans (not white people) weren't eating the so-called "Paleolithic Diet" (which was supposedly heavy in meat and fat) in the Paleolithic. Instead, they ate a mostly plant-based diet. There is evidence of them processing plants and grains and even baking bread as early as 30,000 years ago.[142] Eating meat wasn't unknown of course, but it didn't make up the majority of their diets. For more on this, see "The Paleolithic Diet is Not for You" in Volume Three.

Neanderthal presence there kept us from making that move. Meanwhile, the Neanderthal occupation of Palestine blocked our expansion into southeastern Europe. And the worst part: they weren't staying still.[141]

The Neanderthals had been confined to Europe for most of their history, but around 60,000 years ago, we begin to find their remains moving further south into the Levant* and as far east as Siberia. In other words, they were expanding over areas previously occupied by humans. And we don't have any genetic lineages that go back that far in these places. In other words, these humans didn't make it. The Neanderthals weren't just spreading, but killing us off.

Yet survival demanded that we expand as well. But how? In other to conquer the Neanderthal threat, it would require a multi-national campaign made up of Original People from everywhere Original People were found.

WHO WERE THE NEANDERTHALS?

In *The Science of Self, Volume One*, you learned that the Neanderthals were a bloodthirsty, carnivorous bunch of savages.[143] Perhaps there were a few "good ones" here and there, but most of them were not our friends. If you forgot, let's do a quick recap:

☐ They were apex predators, subsisting on a mostly carnivorous diet,[144] which included human flesh.[145] (The "Paleolithic diet" for everyone else was plant-based.[146]) They ate so much meat, they built their homes out of skulls and bones.[147]

☐ They were brutal warriors. They didn't know how to use projectile weapons, but they hunted and fought using handheld clubs and spears. Some Neanderthal remains are so battered and bruised that it appears they fought all their life.

☐ They produced almost nothing in terms of symbolic or cultural behavior (short of a few isolated practices they appear to have copied from their human neighbors).

☐ They weren't Black, but they weren't white either. As we explained in

---

* The Levant is a region in the Near East that faces the Mediterranean Sea on its west coast. This where we now find Palestine, Israel, Lebanon, Syria, and Jordan.

THE ICE AGE

During the "glacial maximum" of the Ice Age, ice sheets extended beyond the Arctic and covered much of the Northern Hemisphere. The northern parts of Europe, Asia, and North America were either covered with ice caps or frozen tundra, and were thus unfavorable places for humans to settle. As in modern times, such areas may have been used as posts of exile. Throughout the rest of the world, sea levels were lower and coast-lines went out much further than they do today.

In different parts of the world, the spread of ice sheets is known by different names. For example, in the Alps, it is known as the Würm glaciation. But ice sheets also spread across the Andes, where it is called the Llanquihue glaciation. Here are two attempts to reconstruct what areas were affected.

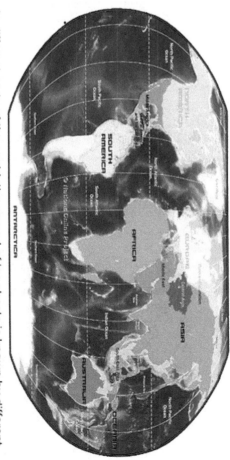

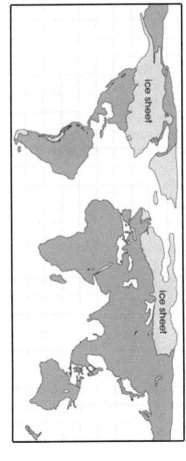

Volume One, they seem to have bred out some very specific traits like barrel chests, massive arms, bigger heads,* lighter hair, and possibly lighter skin, but they weren't the ancestors of modern Europeans.

Finally, they wanted us dead. Anytime we crossed paths, it was bad news. So the Neanderthals basically "contained" the bulk of us within Africa and southern Arabia until about 70,000 years ago.† Taking the southern route from East Africa into Arabia allowed us to build the Nubian Complex, but getting any further than that was difficult. As Nicholas Wade writes in *Before the Dawn*:

> They had developed serious weaponry, including stone-tipped thrusting spears. They surrounded or occupied the main exit point from Africa at the southeastern corner of the Mediterranean, including the area that is now Israel. The human lineages evolving in Africa may have tried many times to escape into the world beyond. But none had succeeded, and the Neanderthals' encirclement of the exits from northeast Africa seems a likely reason.[148]

So these Neanderthals had us practically *confined*, and – although they were a relatively small population (by the end of their reign, they were outnumbered by humans 11 to 1)[149] and constantly at odds with their environment – they were one tough group of bullies blocking the school doors at the end of the day.

They'd been in the cold of Europe for 200,000 years, so they were well-adapted to the harsh environment. In fact they'd already survived an entire glacial cycle (or Ice Age). They even survived the Toba supervolcano's explosion, with no evidence of ill effects. Yet the Toba eruption and its aftereffects had killed off most of the humans that had ventured out of the Nubian Complex before 75,000 years ago.‡

It makes me wonder – perhaps these catastrophes weren't meant to kill off the Neanderthals (as they did humans outside Africa, who

---

* The fact that Neanderthals had bigger brains, yet still went extinct, is a reminder that we should not always be intimidated by those who appear to be more intelligent. If intelligence were the only prerequisite for survival, every living creature still on the planet would have to be highly intelligent, solving algebra problems and stuff. Big-brained people aren't necessarily BETTER people. Also, the actual link between brain size and intelligence isn't clear. For example, elephant brains are much bigger than ours.

† Of course, small populations did "sneak" past between 130,000 and 70,000 years ago, but these humans didn't become us. That is, either they didn't survive for long, or their descendants didn't contribute genetically to the lineage of modern humans.

‡ There were certainly some survivors, but it's more than likely their descendants didn't make it this far, as there are no known non-African DNA lineages more than 75,000 years old.

essentially experienced a total "reset" around 75,000 years ago), but to make them stronger. But for what? Perhaps to give us the challenge we needed.

If it weren't for a brave group of our ancestors, the Neanderthals could still be here today, and the whole Out-of-Africa exodus might not have ever happened! So what did we do? We came together and we fought. Small bands of humans became larger, stronger coalitions. New weaponry was developed. New techniques emerged. For all of us, even including people who descend entirely from Africa – this is how our ancestors were born.

RISING TO THE OCCASION
GOING THROUGH HELL TO COME OUT RIGHT

Consider the way we explained that man can "direct" his own evolution in *Volume One*. It appears that we "made" the Neanderthals so they could provide the necessary resistance to catalyze the next stage of our growth. Until our clash with the Neanderthals, humans were relatively advanced, but this was a competition that brought out the best in us – both genetically and culturally.

To defeat the Neanderthals, it took new strategies, technology, networking, and resources. None of this was entirely new, however. By the Lower Paleolithic, our Homo erectus ancestors had already pioneered:

❏ the use of controlled fire (by at least 1.5 million years ago throughout Africa and Asia)
❏ the construction of permanent homes (by at least 800,000 years ago in Israel)
❏ the construction of maritime vessels (suggested by the settlement of islands like Flores near Southeast Asia around 850,000 years ago and the islands of the Mediterranean Sea around 300,000 years ago).

This tells us that we obviously had language, social structure, and the ability to plan for the future. I mean, seriously, you can't any of those above without all that.

But war with the Neanderthals forced us to go beyond those basics. Thus, long before Sun Tzu authored the *Art of War* or Hannibal conquered the Alps, our ancestors were pitted in a battle for survival. Rising to the occasion, we extended our trade and communication networks, effectively building coalitions against a common foe.

STONE AGE CLOTHING

Often, it is assumed that we didn't begin wearing clothes until recently. Yet there's evidence of clothing up to 500,000 years ago! Our ancestors wore leather, fur, and colorful woven linens. In colder areas, like Paleolithic Europe, we have examples of layered clothing embellished with ornate shellwork.

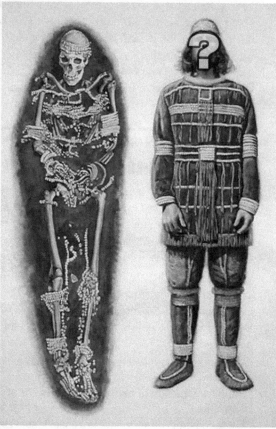

The reconstruction above was obviously drawn to look like a modern European, but it still provides a good example of what clothing looked like in Europe over 20,000 years ago. These three images come from Sungir, Russia, circa 26,000 BC. The layout of shells in the burials gave artists a hint as to how the clothing was designed.

Bottom left: A sewing needle from 17,000 BC.
Below: Examples of pendants worn then.

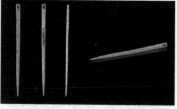

Another development that occurred when we traveled north into Europe was the invention of cold-weather clothing.

Of course, there's evidence of clothing long before this, but we'd never needed to wear layers in Africa. Venturing into Europe introduced us to the coldest place we'd ever been to. It's tough to survive in that environment without adapting your diet and your attire. We hunted more game than ever before and wore clothing sewn from fur, flax, and leather, with bird bone needles and thread made from animal sinew or plant fibers. (For more, see "The Origins of Style" in *Black People Invented Everything*)

THE ORIGINS OF LONG-DISTANCE TRADE

The jewelry and other artifacts that were carried across long distances show us that our trade networks had grown considerably. Before 200,000 years ago, we typically only find items transported (or traded) across short distances. By 80,000 years ago, the average "zone" of trade was about 20 miles. By 40,000 years ago, this had grown to 500 miles!

Unless we want to think one person walked that far to do trade, we have to assume that there was a serious network or economic system in place. This sort of information-sharing also explains why Upper Paleolithic sites across Europe and the Near East share so many cultural features, even when separated by great distances. Even the artwork is pretty consistent. This is because there was a common culture among the humans who ended the Neanderthal reign. This culture would go on to take over the world.

The humans who populated the globe after the Neanderthal onslaught were the smartest, fittest, and most ingenious folks humanity had to offer. Not only that, but this struggle forced disparate bands to come together as a cohesive whole to fight and survive. If there really was, as some anthropologists claim, a "spurt" in brain development during this period, it wasn't the result of us venturing into Europe, but the result of us coming together as one.

And we're not simply referring to the Original People of Africa and the Near East. There's evidence to suggest that the campaign against the Neanderthals brought together diverse groups of Original People from as far east as India and Central Asia. In other words, this period required Africoid and Australoid people coming together. We'll explore this history in our chapter on Europe.

MASTERING NATURE

While Neanderthals wrestled with the whims of nature and its many predators, our ancestors had a mastery of the natural world. Although we could precisely time the migration of game animals such as wild horses and deer to plan our hunts, we realized we needed more protection for our settlements and help with hunting, since the cold tundra of Eurasia wasn't exactly full of nutritious natural foods. So we made dogs.

WE MADE DOGS

Yes, we made dogs. To be technical, we bred wolves from the wild into domesticated dogs, but that was no lightweight accomplishment. Can you imagine breeding wild wolves to have all the features you'd desire in a guard dog today?

For starters, wolves will eat you. Haven't you seen *The Grey*? You have to know what you're doing if you plan on doing *anything* involving wolves. Second, wolves will eat you. In case that wasn't clear the first time.

Third, if you DO somehow get into the business of breeding wolves, you will learn that wolves don't bark. We bred out their ability to bark (to signal danger). Think about that. How would you take a non-barking animal and make an animal that barks? That's pretty serious. Especially if you're working with an animal that wants to eat you. We also bred these dogs to be the only animals that can respond to our eye movements. Experienced dog trainers know that you can tell a dog where to go, with just your eyes.

There's no other animal going for that. None, not even with modern breeding techniques. But that's how thorough we were, selectively breeding wolves over several generations to become man's best friend, over 30,000 years ago. There's a possibility this wasn't our first time using this knowledge, as evidence from canine DNA collected by Robert K. Wayne suggests that we originally domesticated dogs on a smaller scale around 100,000 years ago or earlier.[152] As we'll see in Volume Four, this wouldn't be our last time either.

Oh, and these dogs weren't no little punk dogs either. In 2008, fossil material excavated from a Paleolithic site at Goyet Cave in Belgium turned up evidence of a 36,000-year-old dog, a large and powerful animal who ate reindeer, musk oxen and horses.[153] Yeah, we bred dogs that ate horses.[154] In 2010, the remains of a 33,000-year-old dog were found in the Altai Mountains of southern Siberia,[155] and in 2011, the skeleton of a 27,000-year-old dog were found in the Czech Republic. It was buried with a mammoth bone in its mouth.[156] You might have a blue nose pitbull with a head the size of a watermelon, but I'm pretty sure even THAT dog can't handle a mammoth bone.

ADVANCED WEAPONRY

The first long-range missiles were hand-thrown projectiles. 25,000 years before the Greeks stole the idea of the javelin from indigenous people, we were bangin on our enemies with wooden spears. According to a November 2008 article in New Scientist magazine, "human aerial bombardments might have pushed Neanderthals to extinction." This theory is based on the bone shapes of human arms from the period, compared to those of their Neanderthal enemies.

You see, in professional baseball players, frequent overhand throwing from an early age permanently rotates the shoulder-end of the humerus toward an athlete's back, compared to people who haven't spent much time hurling. Jill Rhodes, a biological anthropologist, studied the arm bones of prehistoric remains, and found evidence for projectile use in male humans living in Europe around 26,000 to 28,000 years ago – around the time we were at the height of competition with the Neanderthals. Changes in bone shape left by a life of overhand throwing hint that Stone Age humans regularly threw heavy objects, such as spears, while Neanderthals did not. Neanderthals typically fought and hunted their prey with melee weapons like clubs and hand-held spears. It was our Aurignacian ancestors who perfected the art of projectile aerodynamics to outhunt and conquer their Neanderthal foes from a safe distance.

Of course, this science goes back further than our occupation of Europe. Stone points resembling the tips of spears were used in Africa over 60,000 years ago, as was the bow and arrow. In fact, there's even some speculation that the Acheulean hand ax, which remains a fixed feature in the Homo erectus tool kit for over 1 million years, may have been aerodynamically suited for use as a projectile.[157]

"DEATH RAYS FROM OUTER SPACE"

Then what happened? Would you believe that we summoned the forces of Nature to help eliminate our enemies? Well, I don't know if we conjured anything up ourselves, but we know that something of celestial proportions did happen. In a theory anthropologist John Hawks calls "Death Rays from Outer Space," researchers Jean-Pierre Valet and Hélène Valladas propose that geomagnetic excursions at 40,000 and 32,000 years ago weakened the ozone layer, thereby irradiating the Neanderthals with extra ultraviolet light from the Sun, weakening their health considerably.[158] Considering the possibility Neanderthals may have been light-skinned, this makes sense.

Meanwhile, the Elbrus volcanic eruption (c. 38,000 BC) had negative effects on the health of Neanderthals living in the caves of the Caucasus Mountains in southeastern Europe.[159] But they apparently recovered, making more weapons and increasing their activity, until a second, larger eruption (c. 30,000 BC) finally killed off Neanderthal populations from the Caucasus to Central Europe.[160]

This cleared the way for us to forge forward and take them off the planet. The "robust," big-headed Neanderthals were weak now, barely able to get enough food to survive, as not only had the climate changed considerably, but Neanderthals' large brains and body structures required more energy (and thus more calories per day) than ours.[161] With the playing field leveled considerably, we could compete with the remaining Neanderthals for resources, which finally led to Neanderthal extinction.[162] Though, of course, there's also evidence we straight up killed them off, sometimes removing jawbones from their bodies and wearing strings of their teeth as necklaces.[163]

NEANDERTHAL CULTURE, OR THE LACK THEREOF

Oh cut it out. Don't feel sorry for them. They fought to kill. And the remains suggest that these creeps ate us whenever they could. While we could've ate the Neanderthals we killed, it doesn't look we did that. Even in the same environment, we never adapted the lifestyle of our enemies.

The Neanderthals however, copied us quite a bit. Most of their rituals were copied directly from ours. They still failed to develop much of a symbolic or artistic culture, but they did pick up a few things. Fortunately for us, they didn't learn everything.

Our warriors used projectile weapons, such as bows firing arrows tipped with poison, so they could kill from a safe distance. The Neanderthals mostly attacked with melee weapons like clubs and spears.[164] By at least 50,000 years ago, we were killing Neanderthals with what scientists call "advanced projectile weapons." One Neanderthal body, impaled by a flying spear, may be the earliest evidence of a modern human using a weapon against a member of another hominid species.[165]

And we kept developing newer, better technology. Areas where humans and Neanderthals crossed paths present some of the earliest examples of the net (c. 27,000 BC),[166] the bola,[167] the spear thrower (c. 28,000 BC), and the bow and arrow (c. 28,000 BC).[168]

Finally, 28,000 years ago – after thousands of years of war – the Neanderthals were themselves trapped in their final holdout, the Iberian Peninsula (now home to Spain, Portugal, and Gibraltar). Human populations from Central Europe and Northern African converged, forcing the Neanderthals into their "last stand," facing settlements of Black warriors to the South and the East, and – on the other sides – the Atlantic Ocean. And Neanderthals couldn't sail. They were doomed. There are cave paintings in Spain dating back to this time period depicting some of the earliest battles ever recorded by man. Unlike the Moors 1300 years ago, when we took Iberia from the Neanderthals, we left none living to rise up again.[169]

But is "extinction" the right word? After all, I don't mean a total disappearance, since modern Europeans (and some Asians) have 1-4% Neanderthal DNA.[170] Why? How? We'll get into that story in Volume Four. For now, if you consider yourself Black, it's more reasonable to consider the Neanderthals the enemy of your ancestors than to consider them your ancestors.

WHERE WOULD WE BE WITHOUT THE NEANDERTHALS?

Still…no matter which way you slice the genetic record, the Neanderthals were critical to human history. I'll explain why. Scientists are still debating what exactly led to the "rapid" development of humans in the years leading up to the "Out-of-Africa" migration. Some say that humans didn't become "advanced" until they reached Europe, where we've dug most of the evidence of prehistoric artwork and whatnot.

That racist theory has finally been disproven by recent discoveries of even older artifacts in Africa, where modern archaeology has barely begun digging seriously. Other scientists have credited our "rise" to the invention of language, which is also flawed. Language has been useful, but we were doing a great deal before there's evidence we used written or spoken language of any kind.* Still others have looked at the "invention" of fire or stone blades,[171] which they say gave us some sort of competitive advantage over the animal kingdom.

Again, there's clear evidence we had those things LONG before 50,000 years ago. And there's evidence that we didn't need or depend on those things in the way many anthropologist think. In fact, some societies gave "inventions" like the bow and arrow a shot (no pun intended) thousands of years before they later caught on. Obviously, we only used inventions when the demand arose on a widespread level in our societies, not the other way around (the idea that we "discovered" an invention and it changed the way our whole society worked).

So if it wasn't language, fire, blades, or the magic land of Europe, what spurred our rapid development from a people who lived almost too simply to measure for over 5 million years…into a people that settled the globe and built urban civilizations everywhere in less than 50,000 years? The Neanderthals. They forced us to come together again. And that's when all our greatness became even greater. Lesson!

---

* For details, see "The Origins of Language" in *Black People Invented Everything*.

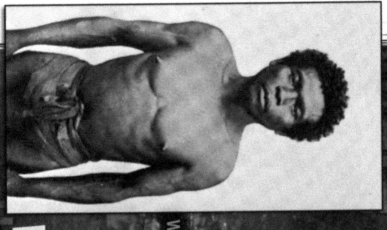

Where Are They From?

WWW.WHENTHEWORLDWASBLACK.COM

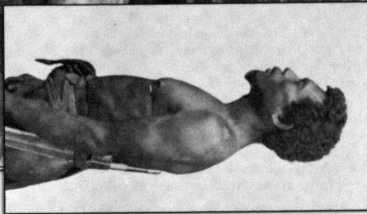

THE ORIGINAL PEOPLE

THE SURVIVORS

*"The Pygmy was the first Homo [sapien]...From
Africa these little men spread all over the world,
North, East, South and West, until not only Africa
but Europe, Asia, North and South America and
Oceania were populated by them." – Albert
Churchward*

As devastating as the events of the previous chapter may have been,
there were people who had left the Nubian Complex more than
75,000 years ago, but somehow survived these threats and remained
settled in Asia, Europe, and other parts of the world. Of course,
millions of others went on with their lives as usual in Africa.

Of those who left Africa over 100,000 years ago, very few of these
communities have survived into the modern day. Some were later
absorbed into more recent populations, such as the Australoid
populations who swept through Asia after recovering from the Toba
event, or the Mongoloid populations who spread through the same
regions much later on. Others were wiped out in recent years.

Wherever we find these people (or their traces), they have been
marginalized and pushed to the fringes of their old homelands. They
live in the forests or mountains. They have the darkest skin and the
woolliest hair of any ethnic group in that area, and they often speak
languages unrelated to any language that came into the area within
the past 10,000 years. They have their own customs and traditions,
and they avoid unnecessary contact with most other people,
especially Westerners.

For many, their community's continued survival is seriously
threatened by the expansion of those who now live in their
homelands. With their isolation, it's clear that their distinctly African
culture could not have come from outside influences. These are the
world's oldest people. And throughout the world – even in Africa –
these people tend to be as small as children. But why?

WHAT YOU'LL LEARN IN THIS CHAPTER

❑ How and when we began expanding out of the Nubian Complex.

❑ How almost all of the people who left this area before 75,000 years ago were killed off.

❑ What killed off most of our ancestors who took the southern route across Asia.

❑ What killed off those of us who attempted to travel north into Europe and Central Asia.

❑ The incredible scientific and cultural advances we made in response to these threats (such as "making" dogs from wolves!).

THE WORLD'S OLDEST PEOPLE?

In the chapter on Africa, we discussed the short-statured Mbuti and Mbenga people of Africa, and how they carry one of the world's oldest genetic lineages. There are people with similar features in Australia, Thailand, Malaysia, the Andaman Islands, Indonesia, the Philippines, New Guinea, and – in ancient times – pretty much anywhere the world's first settlers went. All of these people tend to carry the oldest genetic lineages.

They all look Black...but there's something unique about them. They're small. Adults are almost never taller than five feet. Some are only three feet tall. Because of their size, they're commonly known as pygmies, and sometimes as "Negritos" (meaning "little Blacks") in Asia, and (less often) as "Negrilloes" in Africa. While the word "pygmy" isn't meant to be offensive on its own, it can make these people seem to be something "other" than man, when in fact they are the Original People!

Albert Churchward called them "seed people," meaning they were the "seeds" of all humanity. Eminent historians like Yoseph ben Jochannan and Basil Davidson referred to them collectively as the *Twa*, the ethnic name for one of the oldest and largest pygmy populations in Central Africa. Non-Twa people such as the Aka and Mbuti would naturally object to this term, however.

Aka-speaking people in Central Africa use the term Ba Aka (the plural of Aka) to refer to themselves (one of the rare cases of an ethnic group being known by a name it didn't get from someone else), and this name is sometimes used in the Central African Republic to refer to all "pygmy" people.

In fact, the name "Akka" has even been found in ancient Egypt, North Africa, and Moorish Spain, always to describe people who match the description of the Central African Ba Aka people.* Still, Ba Aka (or just Aka) are insufficient, because not all "pygmy" people have Ba Aka features in common.

This is because – despite what white people have said – all Black people don't look alike! The Negritos of Southeast Asia have many features that distinguish them from the Hadzabe of Tanzania. Yet they're both over 100,000-year-old human communities!

So what do they have in common? Two things, above all: They're diminutive, which is simply a technical way of saying short-statured. And they're Black. Wherever we find them – even if their hair isn't entirely wooly (and it often is), their skin is dark. These are clues to their origins and their history. Dark skin reveals their origins because we know the first humans were Black and they came from East Africa.

Their short stature reveals their history because these people didn't start out so short. We'll explain that in a minute. For now, let's agree to use a term that covers all "pygmy" people throughout the world. We propose the use of Diminutive Black People, or the DBP people,† to refer to the diverse array of human communities who fit the "pygmy" profile across the world. Everywhere you find DBP people, **you're looking at quite possibly the oldest human communities in that region.**

We know that the Original People traveled east of Arabia, settling all of southern Asia and beyond. Wherever they went, they came to be known by over 300 different names, such as the Khyeng of Pakistan, the Jarawa and Onge of the Andaman Islands (near India), the Aeta of the Philippines, the Skraelings of Greenland, and so on. All of these names refer to Diminutive Black People, who are regarded as the "first" people of those regions.

And those are just the cultural names recognized by anthropologists; the names used in mythological and oral traditions would raise this

---

* There are also Asian names that may somehow be cognates of Aka. For example, the Aeta (or Agta) of the Philippines. And all Greater Andaman tribal names contain the prefix Aka-, Akar-, A- or Oko-. In the various tribal languages, these roughly mean "language." A member of the Aka-Bea tribe, therefore, was someone coming from the tribe speaking the Bea language.

† And yes, I know the use of "DBP People" is redundant (the "P" already stands for people!). But I like this fact, as it is important to constantly keep in mind that we are talking about "people" and not simply historical events. After all, many of the human communities we describe in this text still exist today. You can actually meet them, should you be prepared to make those kinds of travels.

number to over 1,000! Naturally, these people developed variations in language and culture over the past 50,000 years, but you'd be surprised by how much they remained alike.

One thing is for sure: wherever they settled, they survived for tens of thousands of years. This is why there are accounts of the DBP in ancient Greece, India, China, the Americas, and just about everywhere in between, from ancient times until now. For as long as there's been written history, people have been writing about these "little Black people."

They are recorded as being respected (or feared) by everyone from Hercules, to the Moors of Spain, to the early European storytellers who made them into the subject of myth and legend. And many of the descendants of the DBP have survived into the present day – although their continued existence is under daily threat. Nowhere is this more the case than in the Andaman Islands, where the oldest surviving DBP population – with an occupation history of over 50,000 years and genetic record to prove it – are at risk of extinction due to Western "intervention."

EARLY ACCOUNTS OF THE DBP

Bas-relief images of little Black people are sculpted on the tombs at Sakkara, from the 5th Dynasty of Egypt (3366 BC). The important gods Bes and Ptah are also depicted as DBP, for reasons that Gerald Massey attempts to explain in *Ancient Egypt: The Light of the World.** Egyptian king Pepi II (c. 2278 BC) sent an expedition into central Africa and it returned with a dancing "dwarf" known as Akka.

Small Black people are also depicted on Greek vases with Black skin, curly hair, broad noses, and sometimes armed with lances. The Greeks have had a long fascination with them, but, then again, so did everyone who encountered them. In the Greek epic *Iliad*, Homer makes the first use of the word "pygmy" to describe a race of tiny folk dwelling in a far southern land where cranes fly when cold winters hit the northern shores.

Later writers usually place them near the sources of the Nile, where the cranes were said to migrate every year to take over the pygmies' fields. Hecataeus said they cut down grain with axes, also suggesting they practiced some type of plant cultivation. Aristotle and Pliny described DBP who inhabited the marshes of Upper Egypt towards the sources of the Nile, who lived in caves and had exceedingly small

---

* You'll find the full excerpt from Massey in *Black God*.

horses, suggesting they practiced animal domestication as well.

Herodotus reports how a party of Black explorers, while journeying through the African desert, were gathering fruit when they were seized by a group of pygmies who led them across forest marshes to their town, near a great river which flowed from west to east containing crocodiles. This was probably the Niger, and the people described were most likely the ancestors of the Ba Aka that still live in central Africa. During his 6th century AD voyage through the Red Sea, the Roman writer Nonnosus reported seeing them on the last of the Farasan islands, which are situated between Ethiopia and Arabia. He described them as...

> ...very short, black-skinned, their bodies entirely covered with hair. The men were accompanied by women of the same appearance, and by boys still shorter. All were naked, women as well as men, except for a short apron of skin round their loins. There was nothing wild or savage about them. Their speech was human, but their language was unintelligible even to their neighbors, and still more so to Nonnosos and his companions. They live on shell-fish and fish cast up on the shore. According to Nonnosus, they were very timid, and when they saw him and his companions, they shrank from them as we do from monstrous wild beasts.

Wild beasts, you say? It's only later Europeans who described the DBP and other Blacks as savages. Most ancient writers saw them as civilized and highly ethical people. While some noted that the DBP avoided white people like the plague, others suggested this was not due to fear. A strong example can be found in Philostratus the Elder's account of Hercules (considered by the Greeks to be the strongest man in the world) venturing into Africa, where he is nearly vanquished by an alliance of tall and short Black people. (See Volume Four for more on THAT story.)

Although the Egyptians and Greeks offer us some of the oldest recorded accounts of the DBP, there are records of them nearly anywhere people have settled on the planet. If man has been there, they were there first. Artistic renderings and oral accounts can be found in India, China, Australia, Northern Europe, the Americas, and nearly everywhere the Original People settled.

Classic texts like David MacRitchie's *Fians, Fairies, and Picts* describe their presence in such unexpected places as ancient Britain. There are many others. In 1897, R.G. Halliburton published details on how even the Moors respected and revered the pygmies of North Africa and Spain, considering them holier (and more powerful) than themselves, and keeping them a secret from outsiders.[172]

Other works include *The Tasmanians* by James Bonwick (describing DBP in and around Australia), *The Negritos of Zambales* by William Allen Reed (describing DBP in the Pacific), *The Pygmies* by Armand de Quatrefages (describing evidence of DBP nearly everywhere in the world), and *The Distribution of the Negritos in the Philippine Islands and Elsewhere* by A. B. Meyer (self-explanatory).

Most of these works are hard to get your hands on nowadays (and you can probably see why), so – through Two Horizons Press – we're republishing all of them. We'll cite more accounts of the DBP and their unique presence in the world's civilizations as we discuss individual regions in the pages that follow.

THE GREAT MIGRATION

When the Original People first left the Nubian Complex, they spread from southern Arabia into Pakistan, India, China, and Southeast Asia, then to Australia and the islands of the Pacific (all of them!), ultimately sailing all the way into South America. We know this because there are still traces of them in these regions, and – wherever they still survive – DNA confirms they were the oldest people there.

Throughout Africa the people who carry the oldest DNA lineages (like Y-DNA haplogroups A and B) are sometimes tall (like the Nilotic people of the Sudan or the Beta Israel of Ethiopia), but many of them (especially in Central Africa) are much smaller than their neighbors, so they are called "pygmies." Throughout the rest of the world, people with the oldest lineages (like mtDNA haplogroups M and N) are often the smallest people of that area. Both in Africa and beyond, they are almost a mysterious people, because we know so little about them, particularly their prehistoric past.

WHAT DON'T ALL DBP PEOPLE LOOK ALIKE? (WARNING! TECHNICAL STUFF AHEAD!)

As we've already discussed, DPB populations are typically the recent descendants of the world's oldest people. DBP adults are short-statured but otherwise, their body proportions closely resemble those of African people. In fact, as the DBP people are descendants of the world's first human settlers, it's natural to assume they'd look distinctly Africoid. And if, by "Africoid," you simply mean "like Black people," well then you're right on target. However, if you want to get specific – as many scientists do – there are some distinctions that can be made.

You see, if it were up to me, I'd say there were all Black people, locally evolved to carry small variations in their physical type. But modern anthropologists would call me clueless. You see, they make sharp distinctions between the DBP of Africa and the DBP of Asia. This is why they were called "Negrillos" in Africa and "Negritos" in Asia. Anthropologists also make sharp distinctions between the Africoid (or "Negroid" or "Congoid") people and Australoid people who look like taller versions of these same people.*

We know two things that help make sense of this mess. First, DBP people weren't always short-statured. We'll explain that in a minute. For now, let's just say that DBP are the local descendants of the world's oldest people. And the world's oldest people didn't look "strongly" like African people or Australian people, but more like a blend of the two. And these people were highly diverse! These people had all the features where today's races come from.

The fact that all of the Original People didn't look alike, and may not have looked (as a group) like any one particular race – together with about 75,000 years of localized evolution (especially after Toba) – provides a sufficient explanation for why all of their DBP descendants don't look alike today.

It should be noted, of course, that some DBP look like their neighbors because of generations of mixture. This can be seen among the Aetas of the Philippines and the "little Black people" found in ancient Chinese artwork. You can actually look at old pictures of the Aetas or any other DBP population in Asia and see people who look "pure" alongside those who look more mixed. Very few pure people are still around in these areas.

There's also a third scenario for the diversity in DBP people: Some populations who arrived long after the first southern migration were ALSO pushed into the forests, where they developed the same small stature as the original DBP people. This can be seen in the pygmy people of South America. This is known as convergent evolution, which simply refers to when two populations independently acquire the same development or feature because they're in similar circumstances. Kinda like if you move to Alaska and your friend moves to Antarctica. You're both going to evolve into people who wear coats all the time. Still seems complicated? Don't worry, I'm about to explain everything.

---

* That is, DBP in Asia often (but not always) look somewhat Australoid, while DBP in Africa look more Africoid than the DBP in Asia.

WHY WERE THE DBP SO SHORT?

Scientists are still undecided as to why the world's oldest populations tend to be pygmies. Early historians believed that was simply how we started out. For example, Albert Churchward, in his 1912 *Origin and Evolution of Primitive Man*, writes:

> The Pygmy was the first Homo [sapien]…From Africa these little men spread all over the world, North, East, South and West, until not only Africa but Europe, Asia, North and South America and Oceania were populated by them.[173]

But were they? The earliest *Homo sapiens* skeletons aren't diminutive. They're a little shorter than we are now, but they're still within the range of "regular" people, not "pygmies." And there are plenty of people in Africa with DNA lineages that are over 100,000 years ago, and they're as tall as any of us.[*]

Yet, throughout the world, many of the oldest human communities are startlingly small. Why? In recent years, scientists have proposed that they became smaller over thousands years of living in harsh conditions. Some of those theories blame malnutrition, others blame living in constricted environments of tropical forest, and still others suggest that diminutive size allowed us to reproduce earlier, which was necessary given higher mortality rates among marginalized people. But DBP people are not always malnutritioned,[174] and nobody has shown that they are able to have children faster than other people.

Recent studies suggest that environmental factors, particularly living in dense forests, are what produced the change in stature. One study found that after 60,000 years of separation from the people who became the taller Africans (who typically don't live in forest areas), the ancestors of the African pygmies became small. Historian John Iliffe, in his *Africans: The History of a Continent*, suggests:

---

[*] Examples include the Nilotic people of the Sudan and the Beta Israel of Ethiopia.

> The Pygmies who now occupy the equatorial forests are possibly a
> Negroid sub-group, specialized to an extreme environment and
> showing great genetic diversity between one isolated local group and
> another.[175]

Iliffe is saying that there's no universal, homogenous DBP
population. Genetically, there is no evidence that pygmies are entirely
different from other Africans. That is, there's no "pygmy marker"
that is common to all African pygmies and exclusive of all other
Africans.[176] And he's right. There are tall people in Africa who also
have that original L1 or A haplotype. There are also some "pygmy"
people whose genetic lineages aren't as old as others. What this
suggests is the following theory:

DBP people – wherever they are in the world – have been nearly
pushed to the brink of extinction by the people who came after
them. It hasn't always been outright war and domination, but
competition for land and resources has been tough on the world's
first settlers. So, throughout the world, these people moved into
jungles and heavily forested mountain areas, where some are not able
to get the nutrition they need, and their mortality rates are high.

Migliano and colleagues have proposed a theory that their short
stature is a result of generations of choosing mates who can have
children younger. Their research fails to prove that DBP people have
children earlier, but they provide us with a theoretical model that
suggests the ancestors of the DBP could have consciously selected
(or bred themselves, so to speak) for increasingly smaller stature.

But why? All I know is that being pushed into the jungles would
have created the necessary cramped conditions to promote the
development of increasingly smaller body size. This happens both in
nature among animals isolated on islands (as in pygmy animals), and
through manmade mechanisms like animal domestication (as in
massive wolves being bred into tiny dogs). However it happened,
these changes could have occurred within the past 60,000 years.

This makes sense, as the examples of pre-human survivals in
Southeast Asia and Southwest Africa show that the way for archaic
humans to survive is by "living unobtrusively" and "becoming
essentially invisible to the new arrivals."[177] But – as with any working
theory – I could be wrong. Yet the historical (and genetic) record is
crystal clear that the DBP – despite being nearly forced into hiding –
represent the descendants of the Original People, the first humans to
settle Asia, Europe, Australia, and the Americas. The ancestors of
the DBP populated the entire globe, from its hottest locales to its

coldest outposts. There doesn't seem to be a place where they didn't go. In most places, the traces of their occupation are minimal, so our understanding of the "Original Culture" may be limited.

Some things, however, are fairly obvious. For example, we know they were hunter-gatherers, living off the land. They didn't practice farming, but they cultivated and tended to wild plants. They also taught other people how to farm, which suggests they knew how to do it. Yet they didn't! Their way of life may have been as natural as it got. If they were, indeed, the first stewards of the Earth, the populations who displaced them made a grave mistake. You'd have to understand their culture to know just how important these Original People were.

In so many ways, these were a people without vices. They didn't lie, cheat, or steal. They didn't even tolerate egos and boasting. They had no leaders, no property. The laws were natural. The culture was ethical. They lived symbiotically with their environments, meaning they lived off the land without disturbing the balance of nature. Yet they had all the knowledge! As we'll explain in Volume Three, these were the people who truly paved the way for all the world's cultures and civilizations, even when they didn't adopt all of the traditions or transitions they introduced to the world. Perhaps this is why so many of the indigenous communities who settled areas after them would regard them as gods or at least "semi-divine beings."

Who should be included in the cultural community we call the "Original People"? When we look at indigenous communities and we ask, "Are these people Original People?" it's easy to look at external features like dark skin and woolly hair texture, but there's so much more to the picture. Before white people made us so self-conscious of our Blackness and our other physical features, we determined who was "the Original People" by how closely a community (or individual) observed the cultural fundamentals that have defined Original People for at least the past two million years (and much longer if you consider the arguments we make in *The Science of Self, Volume One*, where we trace the above principles back to the origins of life and the universe itself).

These principles can be associated with the world's oldest communities and cultures. This is what other scholars have called a "natural way of life," a way that many of us are struggling to return to today. These are the principles we explore in Volume Three of this series.

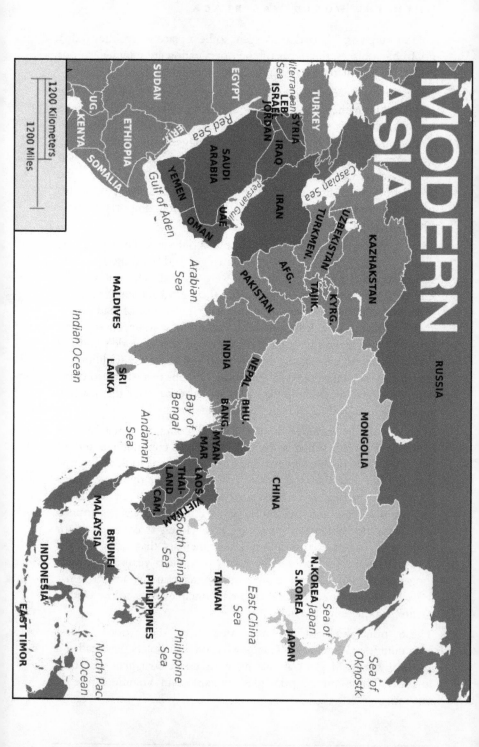

ABORIGINAL PEOPLE OF INDIA

YENADIES

BEDUR OR VEDDAR

YENADIES

KHONDS/GONDS

INDIA

THE INDUS VALLEY

"There can be little doubt that the "pre-Dravidian" tribes…have a preponderating element of Negro blood." – Sir Harry Hamilton Johnston

Who were the Original People of India? There are many different communities in India. Some look nearly white, many are various shades of brown, and some are as black-skinned as the people of the Sudan. Actually not some, but MANY.

India today has over a billion residents, so there's actually a LOT of Black people there. In fact, all things considered, India has the largest Black population in the world outside Africa. But what does this mean? What makes these people Black? Who were the first Black people in India? And what did they accomplish?

WHO WERE THE DRAVIDIANS?

For those of us who have come across this topic before, we've probably heard that the original Black people of India are known as the Dravidians. This isn't all wrong, but it's not exactly accurate either.

For starters, Dravidian is a language family, not a race or "tribe." You don't have to be Black to speak Dravidian. There are over 200 million Dravidian speakers, most of them living in southern India. Others are scattered across central India, Sri Lanka, Bangladesh, Nepal, and Pakistan.* The largest Dravidian-speaking groups are the Telugus, Tamils, Kannadigas, Malayalis, Tuluvas, Gonds and Brahui. If you look at pictures of them, you'll see the Black genes.

But these people don't all look exactly alike. They look different and

---

* For this chapter, we'll include the entire region that was once known as India, before the British came. This includes India, Bangladesh, Pakistan, and several neighboring areas, all of which were carved into pieces when the British took over. Until this time, the empire now known as India was the richest nation in the world.

there are unique variations in each of their languages, some of which is a result of them having different ancestral groups. This is because the Dravidians weren't the first Black settlers in India, or the last.

People – especially those of us in the business of explaining such things to others – tend to reduce things to the simplest possible understanding. As a result, some of us associate all the indigenous Black people of India with the Dravidians, but there's more to the story than that. You see, most Dravidian people (like the Tamil) look Australoid, while some (like the Gond) look more Africoid. Why the difference? This is because there was more than one migration of Black people settling in India.

THE FIRST BLACK PEOPLE IN INDIA

In his *Short History of Civilization,* Professor Lynn Thorndike described the ancient people of India as "short black men with almost Negro noses."[178] There is considerable agreement, even among Indian historians, that the first settlers of India could be associated with "little Black people" or Negritos. As Vidya Prakash Tyagi explains in the excellent *Martial Races of Undivided India*:

> The aboriginal habitants of India belonged to an ancient population of unsure origins who mainly populated the jungle environments of the subcontinent, **much like the modern day Pygmies of Africa and the Negritos of Southeast Asia.** We can only presume that the morphological features shared by these last two geographically diverse populations, such as very small-stature, dark skin, woolly hair, scant body hair and occasional steatopygia, must also have characterised the ancient Indian homunculi [little people].[179]

Over 2000 years ago, Greek historian Pliny knew of "dwarf races" throughout both Africa and Asia, while his colleague Megasthenes placed these people in the center of India.[180] Several other Greek writers mentioned Indian pygmies living underground, east of the river Ganges.[181] Around 400 BC, Ctesias reported:

> In the middle of India there are black men, called Pygmaioi (Pygmies), who speak the same language as the other inhabitants of the country. They are very short, the tallest being only two cubits in height, most of them only one and a half…They are snubnosed and ugly. Their sheep are no bigger than lambs, their oxen, asses, horses, mules, and other beasts of burden about the size of rams [suggesting, again, that they knew how to breed animals].
>
> Being very skilful archers, 3000 of them attend on the king of India. They are very just and have the same laws as the Indians. They hunt the hare and the fox, not with dogs, but with ravens, kites, crows, and eagles.[182]

Is this picture from West Africa? East Africa? Or...

Neither? These folk dancers belong to the aboriginal Gond people of
India. They're descendants of India's first settlers. India has the largest
Black population outside Africa. What else haven't we been told?

The KURUMBAR

The Kurumbar are descendants of the indigenous Dravidian people that once reigned across all of India. They now live primarily in Southern India, where they herd cattle, but remnants of their original population are seen in other areas as well. When you look at the above examples, note the diversity innate within this population. Looking at people like the Kurumbar, it is easy to see how all races could have come from one ancestral Black population.

In other words, these little Black people had a rich and dynamic culture. They stuck around as a distinct population long enough for the ancient Greek records to be full of references to "little Black people," and for more recent European and Chinese accounts to cite a "Negrito" presence in India's forests. According to George Weber, at least eight DBP populations are still living in India.

These were all "pre-Dravidian" people, or Black people in India before the Dravidians came. In *The Negro in the New World*, Sir Harry Hamilton Johnston writes:

...there can be little doubt that the "pre-Dravidian" tribes of the Nilgiri Hills (the Kota, Kurumba, Irula, and Badaga) and of the forests south-west of Madras and of Maisur, Cochin, and Travancore (the Kader, Paniyan, Pulaya, Puliyar, and Kaniyan) have a preponderating element of negro blood. Many of these people are dark-coloured, with kinky or curly hair, are prognathous and flat-nosed, with thick, everted lips.[183]

Then what happened? According to R. Thapar's textbook, *A History of India*:

Ethnological studies have revealed six main races in the Indian sub-continent. The earliest was apparently the Negrito and this was followed by the Proto-Australoid, the Mongoloid, the Mediterranean, and later those associated with Aryan culture.

There is evidence of the Proto-Australoid, the Mediterranean, Alpine, and Mongoloid in the skeletal remains at Harappan sites. Presumably by this time (~1500BC) the first five of the races mentioned above were well settled in India.

The Proto-Australoid were the basic element in the Indian population and their speech was of the Austric linguistic group, a specimen of which survives in the Munda speech of certain primitive tribes.

The Mediterranean race is generally associated with Dravidian culture. The concentration of the Mongoloid people was in the north-eastern and northern fringes of the sub-continent, and their speech conforms to the Sino-Tibetan group.

The last to come were the people commonly referred to as the Aryans. Aryan is in fact a linguistic term indicating a speech-group of Indo-European origin, and is not an ethnic term.[185]

In other words, most anthropologists recognize Africoid people as the Original People of India. These people eventually became the DBP, through processes we explained in a previous chapter. These Original People were followed by Australoid people. Then there was a later influx of "Mediterranean people" (probably the Anu, who we discuss in Part Two), Mongoloid people, and, lastly, the so-called Aryans (who we discuss in Volume Four). In other words, everybody was Black and dark brown until the Aryans came.

THE ANDAMAN ISLANDS

Where are the "Negritos" of India found? Some may still live in the forests of central or southern India, but these people are best survived in a group of islands between India's east coast and the western shores of Southeast Asia. According to anthropologist J.H. Hutton:

> [T]he Negritoes were the oldest inhabitants of India, but have left virtually no trace on the main land of the subcontinent. Some of the representatives of the Negritoes are found in Andaman and Nicobar Islands and among some of the Nagas.[186]

In his 1937 work, *Environment, Race, and Migration*, distinguished anthropologist Thomas Griffith Taylor identifies a group of "dwarf folk in the rugged hills in the extreme south of India" with the people of the Andaman Islands.

B.S. Guha, former director of the Anthropological Survey of India, used physical measurements carried out during the census of 1931 to devise a racial classification that is "considered as the most authentic." According to Guha's findings:

> Most probably, the Negritoes were the earliest arrivals in India…Their representatives are the Andamanese, Nicobaris, and the Irulas, Kadars, Kanikkars, Muthaiwans, Paniyans, Puliyans, Uralis living in the hills of Tamil Nadu, Kerala, and Karnataka… Their arrival in the Andaman and Nicobar Islands (Jarawa, Onge, Sentinelese, Shompen, etc.) is believed to be from the Peninsula of Malaysia. In appearance, culture, and traditions, they are very close to the Semangs and Sakais tribes of Malaysian Peninsula.[187]

In other words, these Black people are descendants of the Original People to settle India.

WHERE DID THEY COME FROM?

Guha says Southeast Asia, and we agree, for reasons we explain in a little later. But ultimately, these people came from Africa. A 1999

Scientific American article entitled "Out of Africa, Into Asia" opens with the byline "Controversial DNA studies link Asian hunter-gatherers to African pygmies." It reports on recent studies that reveal how the earliest populations of Southeast Asia, including India and China, were Black people most closely related to the indigenous people of the Andaman Islands.

WHO ARE THE ANDAMAN ISLANDERS?

They're a nearly jet black-skinned DBP people living on the strip of islands situated in the Bay of Bengal, about midway between India (on the west) and Burma (on the east).. They look just like African DBP, peppercorn hair and all.

If you didn't know how tall they were, you'd think you were looking at some brothers from right around the corner and up the block. But the Andaman people are the oldest unmixed Black population in Asia, having lived in those islands for over 50,000 years without interruption! Well, at least until recently.

THE ANDAMANESE GENOCIDE

When Europeans "discovered" them in the late 1700s, they made it their business to "study" them. One report on the Andamanese, found in Frederick Starr's 1901 text *Strange Peoples*, alleges: "The Mincopies [Andaman Islanders] are true savages, living entirely on wild food."

Starr follows this vile labeling with an odd disclaimer: "[But] they are gentle and non-savage in disposition…Although savages, these little people know how to build good houses."

So you mean to tell me, these people are total animals, but they know how to build good houses? Starr adds:

> In the houses of the Mincopies fires are kept burning. It is said that these people do not know how to kindle fire; if this is true, they are almost the only people who are ignorant of this important knowledge. They are careful of the fires they have and feed them well.

Think about that. Do you really think a people could be too ignorant to know how to start a fire, yet smart enough to know how to keep a few dozen fires burning year-round, inside thatched huts, in all types of weather – including *monsoon season*? I mean, could YOU do that?

As we noted in *The Science of Self, Volume One*, the Andamanese were people who upheld traditions that were thousands of years old.[188] They refused to accept fire-making tools from Westerners. In fact, they refused almost everything white people offered them. But some

THE ANDAMAN ISLANDERS

Between the coasts of India and SE Asia live the Andaman Islanders. Carrying the oldest genetic lineages in Asia, they reveal what the first Asians looked like.

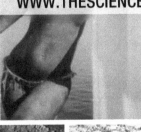

TRIBAL MARKS JARAWA

communities allowed whites to come and study their ways.

Before long, entire communities were dying off, thanks to Western diseases, something like the smallpox epidemics that killed off many Native Americans and East African Maasai. Those islands that were most receptive to foreigners (which later included Indians under British rule), were the quickest to die off.

As of 1858, there were 13 different "tribes" comprising several thousand Andaman Islanders. Now, there are only three:

❑ Jarawa – 250 to 400 people
❑ Onge – less than 100 people
❑ Sentinelese – 100 to 200 people

Disease did much of the dirty work, but the rest was accomplished through a government relocation program that moved the Andamanese to reservations while the government drained their islands' natural resources. Sound familiar?

People like the Onge are now confined to two small reservations on their island, while the Jangil, who originally lived on Rutland Island, were extinct by 1931. The only ones still living free are the Sentinelese on North Sentinel Island. Why is no one bothering them? Because – as their name suggests – they are NOT playin any games with you.

THE SENTINELESE WILL CUT YOU INTO PIECES

The Sentinelese never accepted European interest. Among the neighboring Onge and Jarawa, foreigners could make some headway by bringing Western "treats" and "trinkets." The Sentinelese weren't interested. It was almost impossible even to get a picture of one of them, even from a distant ship. **They wouldn't come out of the jungle.**

When boats or helicopters came too close, even with food, the Sentinelese shot poison-tipped arrows with deadly accuracy. And if any European "explorer" was foolish enough to actually step foot on their island, they would make an example out of him by cutting off his arms and legs, then propping his torso up on the beach and setting him on fire, for all passing ships to see!

Yet the West remained undeterred. In 1974, a European film crew (along with an Indian anthropologist) attempted friendly contact by leaving a tethered pig, some pots and pans, some fruit and toys on the beach at North Sentinel Island. They filmed from a boat, expecting a glimpse of the Sentinelese. Instead, one of the unseen islanders shot the film director with an arrow. The following year, another batch of European visitors were sent back to their mommas with a flurry of deadly arrows.

On August 2, 1981, the ship Primrose grounded on the North Sentinel Island reef. They'd been stuck there for a few days when crewmen on the ship observed that "small Black men" were carrying spears and building boats on the beach. The captain immediately radioed for help (an airdrop of guns, actually). The Sentinelese were simply waiting for the seas to calm down before making their move, but the crew of the Primrose was rescued by an Indian navy helicopter before that could happen.

As recently as 2006, Sentinelese archers killed two fishermen who were fishing illegally within range of the island. When a helicopter came to retrieve the bodies, the archers hit the helicopter with so many arrows that they flew away like they were under machinegun fire. To this date, the bodies remain unrecovered.

Clearly, they are NOT trying to join the white world and die. In one of the first, and only, photographs of a Sentinelese, we see a well-built Black man looking up at the helicopter that takes his picture. He is grabbing his nuts, sending a clear message that says, "Get the f*** outta here!"

Yet it seemed like all of the Andaman Islanders, even the Sentinelese were doomed to extinction when the tsunami of 2004 struck. They even disappeared for a while after the waters had receded. But later they reemerged. People like the Onge had actually refused to get help when they heard the tsunami was coming, saying their people knew about such things and were prepared. Again, they *wouldn't come out of the jungle*. Now, it's one thing to see Original People all over the world refuse to live in Western-style homes even when they are provided for free – preferring instead to live in their traditional homes – but this seemed extreme. *To refuse shelter when a tsunami is coming?*

Yet somehow, most of them survived. They were so in tune with the way nature worked that they knew what was coming and what to do. This may tell us something about how some people in the area survived the effects of the Toba eruption.

Yet, while the Onge and Jarawa continue to struggle against Western disease (and now Western diet and culture), the steadfast Sentinelese have lost so much of their natural food sources that they've been forced to begin accepting coconuts and other familiar foods floated to them from foreign ships. In recent years, some foreigners have even brought the highly-prized coconuts on land.

DOESN'T IT MAKE YOU WONDER?

It should make you wonder why it is so important to Europeans to engage these people, when they know they will die after contact. I think it's clear that it's not out of some sincere desire to "help" a people who have survived just fine for over 50,000 years (with no malnutrition or crime!). With the passing of Boa Senior, the oldest surviving Bo woman, we have lost *yet another* ancient Black language and the culture that comes with it. It may be only a matter of time before the Onge, Jarawa, and even the Sentinelese, are gone too.

BEFORE THE ANDAMAN ISLANDERS?

You'd think that the Andaman Islanders – with genetic lineages over 50,000 years old – are representative of the very FIRST humans to pass through India. Recent studies are starting to suggest that Black people were here even before them. Beware: We're talking genetics ahead!

Geneticists have found that one of the oldest mtDNA lineages, Haplogroup M, is at least 74,000 years old in East Asia, but seems younger in India (60,000 years old or later), which is odd, because it looks like the M lineage started in the East and traveled backwards. That's unlikely, because there is plenty of evidence for M originating in Africa. So these people came from Africa, traveled all the way into Southeast Asia (and beyond), and then began traveling BACK into India?

This means M left Africa (with sister lineage N) and expanded into India, East Asia, and Oceania BEFORE the Toba explosion, which killed off most of the M people in India, but left survivors further east. Later generations of M must have "re-settled" in India and the Andaman Islands in the millennia that followed. This suggests that even the oldest genetic lineages in India (M, N, and R) are descendants of a "re-population" movement that settled in places previously settled by even earlier Black settlers.[189] These people include the Andaman Islanders. This explains why they are so genetically distant from African people, and gives credence to Guha's theory that they came from somewhere near Malaysia, where they resemble DBP populations like the Semang.

In 1937, Thomas Griffith Taylor concurred with other writers of his time that "India shares with Africa Proto-negroid beginnings...and with southeast Asia the superimposition on them of Proto-Australoid elements." He explains:

> There are now no negroes or negritoes on the mainland except in Perak (and perhaps in the tip of India). But there are millions of Australoids (the so-called Pre-Dravidian tribes) in the eastern hills of the Deccan in India and in Ceylon...Fewer went to the southeast and so ultimately gained Papua and Melanesia. The Semang of Perak and possibly some tribes in Assam support this hypothesis.[190]

These people may have started rebuilding from the East, progressing westwards until they reached Africa again. In 1921, Carlton Coon identified an ancient Australoid presence in Arabia, similar to the Veddoid people still inhabiting parts of India. In 1929, anthropologist Grafton Elliot Smith identified a prehistoric colony of Australoid people in North Africa.[191]

According to Dr. Victor Grauer:

> Toba would not only explain the discontinuity between India and points east, so evident on the genetic maps, but also the gap I've been stressing, involving cultural practices found in both Africa and greater Southeast Asia, but almost completely absent from the Middle East, Pakistan and India. African-related cultural survivals can indeed be found in exactly those areas to the east and northeast of Toba that would have been upwind from the eruption and thus relatively unaffected.[192]

This would explain why the cultural traditions of Paleolithic India – both before and after Toba – resemble Paleolithic Africa. As the authors of a recent study have noted, the artifacts found in Indian sites that date before Toba and after Toba both resemble "African Middle Stone Age traditions (such as Howiesons Poort)."[193]

It seems clear now that the people who built the Nubian Complex 130,000 years ago went into South Africa 70,000 years ago to establish the Howiesons Poort and Still Bay cultures, while others went East to establish the same traditions in India. Later, these cultural traditions are brought into Paleolithic Europe.

FROM INDIA TO THE NEAR EAST

Thomas Griffith Taylor said the Black people from India were later found throughout the Near East:

> We find much the same order in the zones of folk in Arabia, Mesopotamia, Persia, and Turkestan. All round the borders of the

Indian Ocean there seem to be relics of a negroid or negrito stratum. Husing (1916) suggests a race of negritoes as the most ancient population of the coasts between India and the Persian Gulf. He thinks that elements of a Dravidian population are found in the interior of Persia. Dieulafoy found negrito or negro people near Susa in southwest Persia. While no negroes survive in Syria, there are many skulls...being found in the caves hereabouts, which may well indicate the presence of an early negroid zone. Ruggeri suggests that the brakeph [meaning broad-headed] Arabs of Yemen differ from the Arabs of Muscat owing to some of this negrito blood, which is also shown by their lower stature and curly hair.[194]

One of the first destinations of this new movement was the Fertile Crescent. There, they came together with other indigenous populations to build the first civilizations in the Ancient Near East.

AUSTRALOID PEOPLE IN INDIA

Who came after the earliest Black populations? Scholars on the subject have called them Australoid, Proto-Australoid, and Veddoid.[195] In other words, they were Australoid people. These people may have come from the east after the Toba event. B.S. Guha agrees:

> After the Negritoes, the Proto-Australoids entered the Subcontinent of India, most probably from Australia. Their representatives are found among the Bhils, Chenchus, Hos, Kurumbas, Mundas, Sandials, and Yeruvas. Their common physical traits are dark brown to black-brown complexion, broad nose, wavy to curly hair, short stature, and thick everted lips.[196]

Thomas Griffith Taylor says that India's original Africoid settlers were followed by Australoid people, who are sometimes called Veddahs or Veddoid people:

> Next, come the Veddahs, just where one would expect them, in the tropical jungles of the Island of Ceylon...They are fairly closely allied to the Australian aborigines...Many other fragments of tribes in India are allied to the Veddahs, such as the Santals, Mundas, Kols, etc., all of whom...have all been classed as Pre-Dravidians (i.e. Australoids).[197]

J.H. Hutton says Australoid people followed the DBP into India. Hutton says they came in large numbers and spread throughout the country, leaving modern day representatives in the various aboriginal peoples of India. At some point in our campaign against the Neanderthals in Europe, many Australoid people traveled west to join forces with communities from Africa.

THE EXTENT OF AURIGNACIAN CULTURE

In our chapter on Europe, we'll explore the African roots of the Aurignacian people. Black people from across Asia also constituted a significant part of the occupation campaign that eliminated the Neanderthals in Europe. In turn, Aurignacian culture can be found as far east as Siberia and possibly China. According to James Brunson:

> Skeletal remains from Neolithic period peoples similar to Austric Veddoid-types were found at Anau (Turkestan), submerged regions along the northern Black Sea, the Caspian Sea, and the Sea of Azov. These Aurignacian Blacks eventually occupied a vast area extending beyond the Ural Mountains [which "separates" Europe from Asia] to Lake Baikal [in Siberia]...The art of the Paleolithic period connects Europe to Asia as far as Siberia, presenting an overall "uniformity of pattern" which is an indisputable fact. A direct offshoot of a highly developed and distinctive Paleo-African tradition, steatopygous figurines bear testimony to the artistic as well as physical characteristics of their creators.

<table>
<tr><td>

DID YOU KNOW?
It took nearly 20,000 years (from 47,000 to 28,000 years ago) for Europe to be fully colonized, and for the Neanderthals to be fully "displaced." Consider it prehistoric gentrification.
And like gentrification, where residents of the hood, who have been there for generations, are used to those conditions and better adapted – while newcomers have to struggle to adapt – the same happened in Aurignacian Europe. The Neanderthals had been living in the cold for 200,000 years. They were adapted.
Tropically-adapted Blacks from Africa and Asia had to quickly develop new strategies, like layered clothing, to survive in this environment. Those who came from Siberia may have provided some of this knowledge.

</td></tr>
</table>

ALL THE WAY INTO SIBERIA?

The founders of the Aurignacian culture went everywhere the Neanderthals were. That meant traveling deep into Siberia. This explains why Upper Paleolithic sites in Siberia (40-25,000 years old) are like those in Aurignacian Europe. You can find the same flutes made from delicate bones, the same kinds of Venus figurines, and even the same genetic signatures in some of the surviving populations.

As Nicholas Wade reports, genetic marker M173, which identifies some of the men who introduced the Aurignacian culture to Europe, "is a brother to the M3 lineage that is found in some Siberian populations and many American lineages."

Wade notes that these two lineages originated from the same source, perhaps in India, which suggests that India was a dispersal point for many prehistoric population movements.

"In India there was a historic parting of the ways," Wade explains. Some of the Australoid population continued to expand and settle along Asia's southern coasts. Others, however, "pushed inland in a northerly direction, through the lands that are now Iran and Turkey, and began the long contest with the Neanderthals for the possession of Europe. Both paths tested the power of the new modern people to innovate, survive in hostile surroundings, and overcome daunting obstacles." Those who went into Europe carried the R1b DNA lineage first associated with the ancestors of the Anu people (beginning 18,000 years ago), and much later with modern Europeans (beginning 6,000 years ago).

Yet another branch of India's Australoid population found their way into the Americas. They brought with the same kinds of dogs they had domesticated to beat the Neanderthals in Aurignacian Europe. Despite all these movements out of India, there's no clear predecessor to Aurignacian culture in India.

The genetic evidence suggests a migration came from there, but the cultural evidence points elsewhere, suggesting that the "brains" of this operation came directly from the root of civilization (Northeast Africa/Arabia), while physical reinforcements came from India and other areas, possibly as far as east as China.

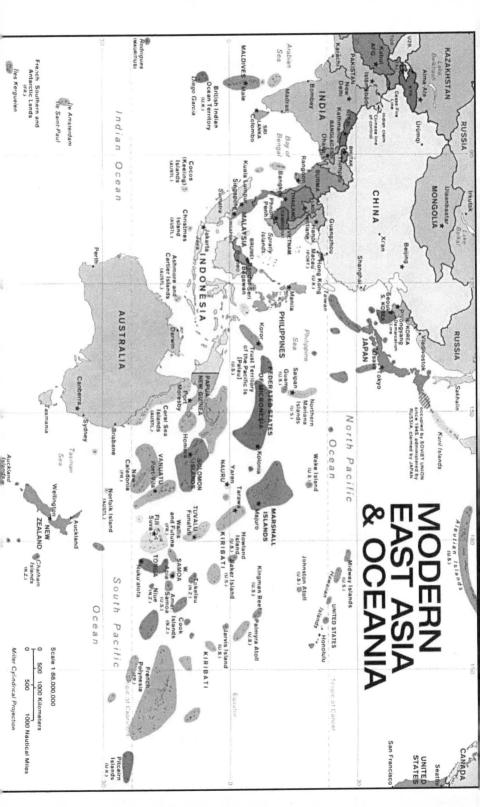

MODERN EAST ASIA & OCEANIA

Scale 1:88,000,000

Miller Cylindrical Projection

TIMOR

SOUTHEAST ASIA

FROM VIETNAM TO INDONESIA

"But we have seen that in the Orient everything suggests that the Negritos have preceded, on the soil were we find them, the races which have oppressed, dispersed, and almost annihilated them." – Armand de Quatrefages, The Pygmies[198]

For thousands of years, Southeast Asia has served as a home and, in many ways, a place of refuge, to those few Black populations to survive the Caucasian invasions from the west.

Southeast Asia consists of the countries southeast of China, including Cambodia, Laos, Burma (or *Myanmar*), Thailand, Vietnam, Malaysia, Brunei, East Timor, Indonesia, the Philippines, and Singapore.

In 1910, Sir Harry Hamilton Johnson reported on the "black belt" that reached its final point (on the Eurasian mainland) in Southeast Asia:

> The Negroid element in Burma and Annam is, therefore, easily to be explained by supposing that in ancient times Southern Asia had a Negro population ranging from the Persian Gulf to Indo-China and the Malay Archipelago.[199]

This "black belt" – a massive stretch of settlements and civilizations spanning from Southern Spain and Northwest Africa all the way to East Asia – was real. In fact, pockets of it have survived into modern times. Some of the Blackest people in East Asia can STILL be found in Southeast Asia. These people are the original people of this region, and have been there for thousands of years. In Malaysia, for example, there are small Black people commonly known as the *Orang Asli*, which means the "Original People." Because of the protection offered by its "jungles," many of these people have survived without being wiped out or absorbed, as has happened in so many other places. Yet this region also presents us with a number of intriguing questions, which we hope to answer in this chapter.

THE WORLD'S FIRST
BLACK PEOPLE SOUTHEAST OF INDIA

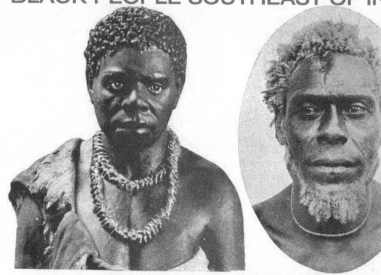

A Tasmanian Female, "Truganika."
From the bust in the Museum.

A Melanesian (New Britain Group), exhibiting the Negro frizzly hair.
From a photograph in the Museum.

AETA WOMAN FROM PHILIPPINES

ABORIGINAL AUSTRALIAN

PAPOU MAN FROM NEW GUINEA

VANUATU BOY FROM MELANESIA

THE DBP IN SOUTHEAST ASIA

Armand de Quatrefages, author of *The Pygmies,* has documented an ancestral "Negrito" presence preceding the tall Black populations that followed them everywhere in Southeast Asia. Rene Verneau, the famed French paleoanthroplogist who reconstructed the "Negroid" Grimaldi remains, also noted Black features among the oldest remains of Southeast Asia.[200]

In southeast Asia, the DBP survive in the jungles, rural areas, and remote regions in sizable numbers. As George Weber documents on his *Lonely Islands* website, there are literally hundreds of "Negrito" tribes scattered throughout southeast Asia who descend from the original DBP people. Weber devotes a chapter to "The Negrito Race," wherein he documents 53 populations of two types:

❐ Negrito and Negritoid [corresponding to the "dwarf" or "pygmy" populations], and

❐ Vedda and Veddoid [corresponding to taller, usually coarse-haired, "Negroid" populations].

Weber notes that although he thought the Negritos to be the earliest human inhabitants of southeast Asia (dating back to at least 50,000 years ago), they were, in most parts, superseded by waves of the Australoid and Melanesian types during the later Paleolithic, who were themselves followed, still later, by Austro-Asiatic peoples. The Mongoloid type was the last to make its way across southeast Asia.[201]

CAMBODIA, LAOS, AND VIETNAM

Want to see some Black Asians for yourself? Visit Indochina. Where's that? It doesn't exist anymore. At least not politically. When the French were in control of Southeast Asia, they named the region Indochina. "Indochina" roughly covers modern Cambodia, Laos, and Vietnam. G. Coedes, in his *Making of South East Asia,* says:

> Indochina was from the earliest times inhabited by a variety of peoples, some of whom were related to the Negritos and the Veddas, some to the Australians and the Melanesian Papuans, and others again to the Indonesians. The Mongoloid strain...seems to be of much later origin.[202]

George Weber has observed that archaeological traces of populations with "Negrito-Papuan-Austro-Melanesian affiliations" have been found all over the ancient and prehistoric strata of Indochina and southern China.[203]

And if you visit Cambodia, Laos, and Vietnam, you'll still find plenty of Black Asians. They've been there so long, it makes me wonder if

SOUTHEAST ASIA

Who were the first people of Southeast Asia? When we look at the aboriginal people of these regions, it's not hard to see that they were once Black.

JAVA

BURMA

SINGAPORE

1

2

3

AETA OF ZAMBALES, PHILLIPINES

MODERN AETA WOMAN

'PURE' AND MIXED AETA WOMEN

JULIET CHAVEZ
BEAUTY CONTEST
WINNER, PHILLIPINES

the U.S. was bombing that area just to wipe them out.

Francis Allen, in a paper presented before the Anthropological Institute of Great Britain and Ireland, spoke of the woolly-haired *Moy* people inhabiting the region between South Vietnam, Laos and Cambodia. Allen believed these little Black people were driven into the mountains by the Kings of Tonquin in the 15th century. He quoted the report of Charles Chapman, an officer of the East India Company sent to the region in 1778:

> The aborigines of Cochin China [South Vietnam*] are called Moys, and are the people which inhabit the chain of mountains which separate it from Cambodia. To these strongholds they were driven when the present possessors invaded the country. They are a savage race of people, very black, and resemble in their features the Caffrees.[204] [*Kaffirs*, that is, the Dutch slur for Africans]

A.R. Colquhoun also described Black pygmies in the area (calling them *Tra*) in his *Amongst the Shans*:

> At the outset of their relations with the natives, the Chinese became acquainted in their new country with tattooing populations, and with two races the characteristics of which are still peculiar enough to still be wondered at by modern travelers. One was a race of pygmies, the Tiao, who are still represented by the a) Tra, now located east of Bienhoa, in Cochin-China, almost the shortest of men; b) the Hotha Shan, in southwest Yunna; c) the Mincopies of the Andaman Islands; d) the Simangs of the Malay Peninsula and e) one of the races of Formosa, all diversified representations of one Negrito race.[205]

According to Allen, the Tra may have been the same people as the Moy, as the DBP have been called by literally hundreds of names throughout the world. Sometimes the names used are similar enough to make inferences. Allen also drew connections between the Moy of southeast Asia and the Chinese *Mai*. He mentions, reluctantly it seems, "Negroid" features among the Mai, and possible connections between them, Negroid depictions of the Buddha (as well as several Hindu idols), and the traditions of the Chinese "respecting the earlier inhabitants of their country."[206]

MALAYSIA

There are some dark-skinned folks in Malaysia, the predominantly Muslim country situated just south of Thailand, right before you can island hop into Indonesia. This is because Malaysia has strong Black

---

* During French control, the area now known as South Vietnam was called Cochin China. North Vietnam was known as Tonkin, where Rene Verneau also found "Negrito" and Australoid remains across the Paleolithic and Neolithic strata.

roots that survived well into the modern day. And these roots don't come from the Arabs and Africans who brought Islam to the country centuries ago.

The foundations of Malaysia can be found among the Orang Asli, the generic Malaysian term for the indigenous people of Malaysia. Orang Asli literally means "Original People." Officially, there are 18 Orang Asli "tribes," categorized it three groups according to their different languages and customs:

❐ Semang (or Negrito), generally confined to the northern portion of the peninsula

❐ Senoi, residing in the central region

❐ Proto-Malay (or Aboriginal Malay), in the southern region

All of these populations have survived – to some extent or another – into the modern day.

In anthropologist George Weber's comprehensive online documentation on the Andaman people and other DBP populations, he provides some background on these groups, noting that Malaysia was first settled by a "Negrito" population known as the Semang people, who may be closely related to the Andaman Islanders. Later there came "Veddoid groups with Negritoid admixtures as well as remnant proto-Malay tribes." We've referred to these people as Australoid and Paleo-Mongoloid people, respectively.

Weber continues:

> It also has some very ancient archaeological sites. At least one site at Bukit Jawa in Kelantan State goes back more than 50,000 years. At that time, sea levels were much lower and much of what is now sea between the Sunda islands was dry land. Beach and other prehistoric sites, therefore, are now deep underwater and next to impossible to find and excavate. The stone tool technology called Hoabinhian (so known from its North Vietnamese site) is known from all over mainland Southeast Asia. It has tentatively been linked to Negritos but this has not been definitively confirmed and remains an open question.[207]

Indeed, the hunting-and-gathering Hoabinhian Cultures of 10,000 years ago were most likely the work of the Original People who first settled Malaysia and later became today's Semang, a DBP (or "Negrito") people. According to historian Peter Bellwood, these people had a "trade network along which travelled shells, stone resources, forest products and social information. There is no confirmed evidence that the population grew rice or practiced systematic agriculture, but encouragement of plant resources most probably took place."[208] This refers to the "soft management"

THE SEMANG
OF MALAYSIA

practices we discussed earlier.

During the Peninsular Neolithic (c. 4,500-2,500 years ago), the ancestors of the Senoi introduced field agriculture involving rice and foxtail millet.[209] These traditions came down from Thailand, but most likely originated among the Anu people of India and China.

INDONESIA

South of Malaysia, Indonesia is another predominantly Muslim country in Southeast Asia. It is known for the natural beauty of its islands (like Bali) and for Lake Toba, the ancient site of the Toba Supervolcano. Indonesia also has an interesting mix of folks.

Scholars have presented several theories about how Indonesia was settled:

❏ Birdsell suggested three waves of migration through the west Pacific to Australia: (1) the Negrito, (2) the Murrayian (Australo-Melanesoid) and (3) the Carpentarian (Veddoid).[210]

❏ Hooton saw five successive layers occupying Indonesia: the Proto-Australoid and Negrito, the Indonesian, the Proto-Malay, and the Malay. Hooton groups these into (1) the Negrito-Australoid, (2) the Indonesian, and (3) the Malay.[211]

❏ Von Eickstedt presents six successive migrations: (1) the Australid, (2) the Palae-Melanesid, (3) the Neo-Melanesid, (4) the Weddid (Veddoid?), (5) the Polynesid, and (6) the Palae-Mongolid.[212]

❏ And de Zwaan proposes four layers of populations: (1) the Negrito, (2) the Wedda-Austromelanesian, (3) the Proto-Malay, and (4) the Deutero-Malay. Von Eickstedt grouped these last two into a single Palae-Mongolid race.[213]

After reviewing these theories, Indonesian paleoanthropologist Teuku Jacob concluded:

> Taking into account all of the above we are inclined to agree with Snell that there are only two main racial elements to consider in Indonesia's racial history, the Austromelanesian and the Malay. Before other convincing evidences are put forward, only these two elements are important in any racial differential diagnosis of archeological skeletons in Indonesia. Multiple synonyms, too much emphasis on slight variations, and the ever present urge to create new terms, merely complicate the approach and obscure the problem.[214]

We call these two types Australoid and Paleo-Mongoloid. They were the foundational populations of Indonesia.

What about the "Negritos"? In *The Pygmies*, Armand de Quatrefages writes:

> I have remarked that in this maritime world Sumatra and Java are

the only large islands where they (Negritos) have left no other traces than some doubtful mixed breeds and the remains of an industry which appears not to have passed beyond the age of stone. It is in Java that the destruction has probably been the most sudden and complete.[215]

It's quite possible that there were people here before Australoid people settled, but there are no "Negrito" remains in Indonesia. Also, recent studies suggest that many (but not all) of the DBP populations in Southeast Asia descend from Australoid people who experienced the "pygmization" process during the Neolithic, possibly after being displaced by Paleo-Mongoloid people. This could explain why many of the DBP in Southeast Asia resemble their Australoid neighbors further south.

THE PHILIPPINES

The people of the Philippines tend to be some of the darkest-complexioned East Asians you'll encounter. In fact, that's why they don't even consider themselves East Asians. They categorize themselves with Pacific Islanders, a group that includes Samoans, Melanesians, and other near-Black people living in the islands to the west of the U.S. And it's not just a superficial thing. Most Filipino people know that the original people of their island, their ancestors, are Black.

These people are most commonly known as the Aetas.* They have been around since the dawn of Filipino history. In *The Pygmies*, Armand de Quatrefages describes the small people of the ancient Philippines and Java:

> When the Spaniards began to settle the Philippines they met, in the interior of Luzon, by the side of the Tagals of Malay origin, dark men of whom some had smooth hair, while others possessed the woolly headcovering of the African Negroes. These last alone were true blacks, whom the conquerors called *Negritos del monte* (little Negroes of the mountain) on account of their remarkably little stature and their habitat. The local name of Aigtas or Inagtas, which seems to mean blacks, and from which is derived that of Aetas, is generally adopted.[216]

In the beginning of the 13th century, Chinese author Chao Fu-Kua described a tribe of DBP dwelling in the valleys of the Philippine Islands, calling them *Hai-tan*, which most likely comes from *Aeta*.

---

* They are also known as Ati, Aeta, Agta, Arta, Atta, Alta and Ita, among other names. The word appears to be not their own name for themselves but a name given by surrounding Filipinos. In Austronesian languages, *ita* often means "black".

In the 19th century, several European authors dedicated entire texts to the DBP presence in these islands. In addition to the foundational *The Pygmies* by Armand de Quatrefages, there are *The Negritos of Zambales* by William Allen Reed and *The Distribution of the Negritos in the Philippine Islands and Elsewhere* by A. B. Meyer.

The Aetas aren't simply an ancient presence on the Philippine Islands; they're the foundational people. Modern Filipino people are a mix of Aeta (or DBP), East Asian (Mongoloid), and Spaniard, with the Black element being both foundational and dominant. And they're still around. There are between 32,000 and 120,000 living DBP people in the Philippine Islands today. However, many of them are mixed and none speak their original languages. They now speak Austronesian languages that came from Southeast Asia around 5,000 years ago. Just as many of them are now mixed, there are also many Filipinos who carry strong Black traits from this ancient DBP presence.

And they know where these traits come from. In fact, just as the Saisiyat do in Taiwan, the people of Luzon hold a regular festival in honor of the "Negritos" of the Philippines.

AUSTRALOID PEOPLE IN SOUTHEAST ASIA

From India, the Australoid people appear to have traveled into Southeast Asia before many of them returned to India. Others remained, where they survive in small populations across Indonesia, Malaysia and other parts of Southeast Asia, all areas that George Weber says they "formerly inhabited at large."[217]

Still others used outrigger rafts or other vessels to navigate the oceans, settling in Australia and various islands along Southeast Asia. It wasn't long before they went deeper into the Pacific, settling New Guinea, and other islands along the Pacific.

According to G. Coedes, there were three successive waves of migration into southeast Asia, all originating somewhere in the south of China. Coedes believes the first wave was of the Australoid type, followed by Melanesians, whom he associates with pygmy types (linking them to the DBP). More recent research suggests that the Melanesian people were a composite society, resulting from mergers between an older DBP migration and the Australoid people who came after.

The 1962 finding of the Tabon Man remains in the island of Palawan confirmed that Australoid people had reached the

Philippines by 22,000 BC. This was amazing enough, but findings from the cave where Tabon Man was discovered revealed that he actually belonged to a later group of inhabitants, and was preceded by people who populated the area as early as 50,000 years ago.[218] These must have been the Original People.

In Java, the Wadjak Man (dated to around 8,500 BC) represents the Australoid presence in Indonesia. The Wadjak 1 skull is described as "proto-Australoid," looking like the stage between prehistoric Australians (and Paleolithic Chinese) and modern Australian aborigines. A companion skull, Wadjak 2, had prognathism like that of an African. The oldest skulls from Thailand – Tabon, Niah, Gua Gunung – all look like Australian Aborigines or Melanesians.[219]

In Vietnam, it's the same way until about 1200 BC when Mongoloid types start dominating.[220] In Malaysia, a well-preserved skeleton dated to 12,200 BC has been described as "a late representative of a non-specialized morphology, similar to Australian Aborigines."[221] Archaeologist Peter Bellwood claims that the vast majority of people in Southeast Asia, the region he calls the "clinal Mongoloid-Australoid zone," are simply Southern Mongoloids with a high degree of Australoid admixture.[222]

Australoid people certainly passed through southeast Asia, but for some reason, they seem to have left the area to the DBP and others. Some appear to have set sail for Australia and New Guinea. Others headed for the Americas. Still others returned to India. What made them leave the area? We simply don't have enough evidence to know.

EPILOGUE: THE EVOLUTION OF LIGHT SKIN IN THAILAND

When I visited Thailand in 2001, I was surprised by two things:

First, several Thai people were brown-skinned and had curly hair or other Black features, but most of them were people that lived outside the big cities. I also saw that there were "tribal" people who wore rings around their neck like some African groups, others who had giant earrings and stretched-out earlobes, and – perhaps most notably – they had more statues of the Buddha as a Black man than Atlanta had statues of Jesus as a white man. These were clear signs as to what the Original People of Thailand looked like.

At the same time, I also noticed that many of the people living in the big cities, like Bangkok, were considerably lighter-complexioned, with less of the features I noted above. Then I dug into the history. Turns out Bangkok was becoming overwhelming Chinese. Not only were Chinese people the majority of its residents, there was an ongoing campaign to promote "light skin" as beautiful and desirable. As a result, the Thai people – even those who weren't Chinese – were "making themselves light." This happened through two mechanisms:

❒ The cosmetics industry thriving on skin-lightening creams, while the media promotes light-skinned people, and

❒ A process I called "subconscious eugenics," which refers to how a dark-skinned population can become light over several generations because they choose lighter mates over darker mates.

These two processes have happened all over the world. As we explained in *The Hood Health Handbook, Volume Two*, skin-lightening creams are a billion-dollar industry throughout India, East Asia, Africa, Latin America, the Caribbean, and among Black communities in the U.S.! Meanwhile, all of these communities tend to have a "color complex" about what complexion is most beautiful, resulting in subconscious eugenics.

SOUTHEAST ASIANS IN INDIA

Throughout Eastern India, many indigenous people have traits that suggest a mix of Africoid (or Australoid) and Mongoloid ancestry. For example, some Orissa people look just like Africans, while others look more like Cambodians. One of the most well-known of these populations are the Nagas.

WHO WERE THE NAGAS OF INDIA?

The Nagas of East India and the Shompen people of the Nicobar Islands are predominantly Mongoloid. Hutton said some of them have traits suggesting Negrito ancestry, and Guha said, "The Angfuni-Nagas have also been considered as having some of the traits of the Negritoes."

The Nagas may have once been an Africoid people, but there's very little evidence to suggest this, except perhaps that they tattoo their faces black, perhaps in reverence to Black ancestors or cultural leaders that had significant influence on this community. What's likely is that the bulk of the Nagas and Shompen people came from further east within the last 5,000 years.

BLACK EAST ASIANS HEADED BACK TO INDIA?

India is incredibly diverse. Some Indian populations have been identified with the Munda languages, which are unrelated to either the Indo-European or Dravidian languages. The Munda languages, as part of the larger Austro-Asiatic language family, are thought to have

CAMBODIA

come into India from the east, possibly from the area that is now southwestern China.

In other words, Munda-speaking people in India may descend from people who worked their way into Southeast Asia, and then back westwards into India (while other members of their group traveled further into Oceania, the Pacific Islands, and eventually the Americas). These people could have been Australoid, but there are strong indications that the first Munda speakers were Paleo-Mongoloid, or a mix of the two.[223] Perhaps now is a good time to explain who and what we mean by "Paleo-Mongoloid."

WHAT DOES MONGOLOID MEAN?

Mongoloid is one of the three essential "identity types" or "races" that anthropologists use to classify present-day people and historical remains, based on anthropometric traits. At one point, there were five or more such classifications, including Negroid, Caucasoid, Mongoloid, Australoid, and others, many of which were used to further subdivide Black classifications (such as Negritoid, Capoid, Khoisanoid, etc.).

Since then, anthropologists trimmed these distinctions down to the first three: Negroid, Mongoloid, and Caucasoid.* None of them sound pleasant. In fact, Mongoloid is offensive anywhere outside of an anthropological context, because its early use derived from calling people "Mongols" because they had features that white people associated with Down's Syndrome (known as "Mongolism").†

But, as we'll explain, the origin of the Mongoloid complex of features begins with Australoid people. In other words, the "East Asian" look is just one of the major variations of the features found among the Original Black people of Asia.

But it seems like a stretch doesn't it? To say that Chinese or Korean people come from Black roots...it seems counterintuitive because

---

* More recently, many anthropologists have abandoned these classifications altogether, for reasons we discussed earlier. But these classifications aren't useless. They can give us hints into who went where, based on the remains we find.

† There are few words that are respectful to east Asian people as a specific population. "Oriental" is meant to describe objects, such as art, not human beings. (Same with "Negro," Spanish for a black object) "Asiatic" has a checkered past, and even when the 5% reclaim its usage, it's not specific to east Asians. "Yellow people" gets a mixed reception because of the negative connotations of being yellow, as in cowardly.

the features are SO different. The problem is that we associate "Mongoloid" with a very stereotypical or extreme set of features, ignoring the fact that all Mongoloid people do not look alike (despite what the uninformed may think).

Anthropologists generally agree that typical Mongoloid traits include bracycephalism (or round-headedness instead of a long skull), sinodonty (or shovel-shaped incisor teeth), an epicanthic fold (the way East Asian eyelids tend to be shaped), coarse straight hair, and light, often yellowish, skin. But do all East Asians have these traits?

TWO TYPES OF MONGOLOID

As early as 1900, Joseph Deniker recognized that there was a sharp division among Mongoloid people. Noting the strong differences between different populations, he said the "Mongol race admits two varieties or subraces: Tungese or Northern Mongolian...and Southern Mongolian."[224] Northern Mongolian would include the indigenous people of Siberia, the Manchu of China, and others who have the typical Mongoloid look.

The Southern group looked, well, a little more like Black people. Their skin was darker, their lips fuller, their jaws stuck out more (known as *prognathism*), their noses broader (known as *platyrhinny*), their heads longer (known as *dolichocephalism*), their hair coarser, and their eyes lacked that familiar feature (known as an *epicanthic fold*).

But why? Was the southern group simply a more "mixed" group of Mongoloid people? Or were they representative of the Original Mongoloid population? The evidence suggests the latter.

Akazawa Takeru, Professor of Anthropology at the International Research Center for Japanese Studies in Kyoto, also splits the population in two. Neo-Mongoloids, or "new Mongoloids" have "extreme Mongoloid, cold-adapted features." Examples include the Chinese, Buryats, Eskimo and Chukchi of Siberia. On the other hand, Paleo-Mongoloids look less Mongoloid because they are less cold-adapted. Examples include the Burmese, Filipinos, Polynesians, Jōmon and the indigenous peoples of the Americas.[225]

Paleoanthropologist Peter Brown of the University of New England has concluded that the "Mongoloid" look doesn't show up in China until 5500 to 7000 years ago. The light complexion of many East Asians may not have come until thousands of years later, when the foreign Zhou conquered the Black Shang dynasty.

Roland B. Dixon, in his 1923 *Racial History of Man*, says the predominance of platyrrhine (flat-nosed) and dolichocephalic (long-

BLACK CHINESE?

Are East Asians as different from Africans as we think? In some ways, the distinctions are clear. But not always. For example, there are many African people, like the San, who carry the physical traits found among East Asian (or "Mongoloid") people. Is it common origin or convergent evolution?

THE !KUNG SAN

The Nakhi of southern China were once described as a Black people. But today, the Nakhi look like other Chinese. Old photos reveal they didn't always.

THE NAKHI

THE HEI MIAO

Most of the "Black Chinese" we discuss in this book are no longer (visibly) much different from other people in the area. This is true for many ancient Black communities. After all, there have been centuries of subjugation and "mixing" since those reports were first made. Sometimes, old photos can help us work backwards. Occasionally, even older paintings are even more helpful. To the left is a rare 18th century painting of the renowned Hei Miao when they were still a Black community.

headed) factors among otherwise "Mongoloid" populations suggests the "remnants of an earlier Proto-Australoid and Proto-Negroid type."[226] For example, the skulls of Tibeto-Burman speaking *Shan* people were, in the earliest period, both dolichocephalic and platyrrhine. In other words, the faces of Asia changed over time, through various processes of "small regional evolution."[227]

To be fair, some of these traits may have come directly from Black ancestors, without any regional evolution. For example, some typical "Mongoloid" features can be found in the diversity of Africa's oldest people. In *Before the Dawn*, Nicholas Wade notes that the Khoisan of Africa look so similar to Asian populations that "both lineages may have inherited these features from the ancestral human population." He explains:

> Many Khoisan speakers have yellow skin, the epicanthic folds above the eyes that give some Asian eyes their characteristic shape, shovel-shaped incisors (front teeth hollowed out on the tongue side of the mouth, found commonly in Asians and Native Americans), and mongoloid spots – a bluish mark on the lower back of young infants. The !Kung San themselves apparently recognize this similarity since they assign Asians to the category of Real People like themselves, as distinct from !ohm, the category of non-San Africans and Europeans.[228]

Historian James Brunson adds the Madi, Nuba, Nyanja, Yao, Ngoni, Tong, and Wemba to the list of African populations with some Mongoloid features.[229]

THE EVOLUTION OF MONGOLOID FEATURES

However, it is more likely that the bulk of Mongoloid morphology came about after a long-term resettlement of Australoid people. That is, Mongoloid people are simply descendants of Australoid people who are much more cold-adapted because of generations of settlement in colder, wind-swept climates. The more their features adapted to this environment, the more Mongoloid (and less Australoid) their features.

This is why many Paleo-Mongoloid people – particularly people who didn't stay in this climate as long – retain Black features. And this is why J. Lawrence Angel reported that the "eastern Asiatic proto-Mongoloid norm" looked JUST like the Black Australoid people who settled Palestine 45,000 years ago, JUST like the Black Australoid people who first settled the Americas, and JUST like Black Australoid people elsewhere throughout the world.[230]

Where and when did these traits emerge? Evidence from genetics, linguistics, and physical anthropology suggest a large community of Australoid people – associated with lineages like Y-DNA Haplogroup Q – left India around 16,000 years ago. They traveled north, settling in Central Asia. Some may have gone west into Europe, but most remained settled in the area now known as northwest China and Mongolia. Here, they could have easily evolved the set of traits identified with Paleo-Mongoloid people by 10,000 years ago.*

Some of these people left and headed west. Between the northern fringes of Eastern Europe and Central Asia, there is evidence of Mongoloid migrations between 10,000 and 5,000 years ago.[231] Some of these people became a part of Paleolithic Europe, enduring many of the changes of the Neolithic, and surviving into modern times as the indigenous Saami people (also known as the Lapps) of Scandinavia.†

Another branch of these Paleo-Mongoloid people took the coastal route across China's eastern shore before settling in Southeast Asia. At this point, the movement of some genetic lineages and languages like the Munda suggest that some Paleo-Mongoloid people went back to India, where they became the ancestors of the Assam, Nagas, and Nicobarese.

Meanwhile, others took to the waters, traveling via the Pacific Ocean to the earliest Polynesian sites. For example, the Samoans and Maori are considered good representatives of Paleo-Mongoloid (or "Proto-Mongoloid") types. In fact, the Maori tell of fleeing a war with Black-skinned people in India before arriving in New Zealand. Some of the Mongoloid seafarers ultimately arrived on the western shores of South America.

While all this was happening, some of the Paleo-Mongoloid population in Central Asia had moved further north into Siberia. Here, they developed the Yeniseian languages which ultimately found their way into the Americas. They also developed a more cold-adapted set of features, which Takeru calls the Neo-Mongoloid

---

* This, of course, doesn't include all of the features associated with Neo-Mongoloid people, who carry a set of features that developed more recently. Cheikh Anta Diop proposed that the epicanthic eyelid developed as a result of people migrating to Mongolia where the eyelid fold evolved to protect against high winds. Light skin and especially straight hair (as opposed to the wavier texture of Paleo-Mongoloid people) appear to be a more recent development, influenced in great part by an ancient influx of whites.

† Scandinavia consists of Finland, Norway, and Sweden.

complex. These features are found in skeletal remains throughout Siberia, Beringia, and the Americas.

In other words, another branch of Mongoloid people had taken the land route into the Americas. Some communities would remain settled at the northern extremes of Siberia for thousands of years before they ventured across the Bering Strait into Canada. Yet not all of the Neo-Mongoloid people went north. Some went south, traveling through Mongolia into Northwest China, Japan, and Korea. This is when the first "true" Mongoloid remains show up in China, long after the Australoid remains that typified the earliest human settlements.

These two waves of Mongoloid migration were confirmed by Indian anthropologist B.S. Guha, who identified a long-headed, brown-skinned Paleo-Mongoloid people entering India in the ancient past.[232] These people are followed by a later Mongoloid people having a "light yellow colour" and "flat face."[233]

QUESTIONS TO CONSIDER

Elijah Muhammad taught that the ancestors of the Indians of the Americas were "exiled" from India 16,000 years ago. We may never know exactly why so many people left India, but it does seem that the ancestors of Mongoloid people in the Americas did leave India, settling in Central Asia (either the deserts of Mongolia or the tundra of Siberia) before arriving in the Americas (via sea and land). The Maori people are explicit that they crossed the Pacific after being exiled from India. In fact, the Maori say they started out in the Near East, which happens to be where Haplogroup Q may have originated. So were the ancestors of these people forced to leave India? And, if so, why?

If so, it wasn't a Mongoloid population who was sent out of India. Before they developed these traits in Central Asia, they were Australoid people. So were Australoid people somehow compelled to relocate to the Americas? We should note that there wasn't just one such migration. Beginning about 16,000 years ago, there were several population movements that ultimately arrived in the Americas, many of which can ultimately be traced back to India or the Near East.

Some Australoid people went directly to the Americas via the Pacific Ocean, while others – mostly those who had first settled in Central Asia and developed the Mongoloid complex – appear to have arrived much later. Some went northeast via Beringia, others went northwest into Europe and then across the Atlantic, and others traveled across the Pacific Islands.

As an interesting piece of this puzzle, Fard Muhammad taught that exiled people were often accompanied by escorts. This was noted in regards to early whites being led through Europe, but the data suggests that Mongoloid people were either preceded or trailed by Australoid people making accompanying migrations.

There's no other plausible theory to explain why the Mongoloid people who traveled by land from Siberia, across Beringia, and then into North America…were accompanied by a coastal migration of Australoid people who sailed from Japan, along Beringia's southern shores, to Northwest Canada (where they settled as the Haida), and ultimately to the western shores of Baja, California…nor why the Polynesians were "followed" by a migration of Black seafarers, all the way into the Americas. Why would two groups of people seem to walk hand-in-hand…yet remain distinct culturally and genetically?

In any case, even if the ancestors of Mongoloid people were somehow "exiled" from a prehistoric Black settlement in the distant past, this would be just one of many periods where our ancestors have developed historical rifts, only to reunite at some point in the future. In fact, the earliest rifts go back to the Rift Valley, where the first humans separated into dozens of tiny bands scattered across East Africa, until environmental change forced them to come together to survive. Thus it is not surprising that the past 2,000 years have witnessed several phases of reunification between "Black and Yellow people." We'll cover some of these episodes (as well as the early conflicts) in our discussions of North America and the Pacific Islands in Part Two.

INDONESIA

THE FAR EAST

CHINA, TAIWAN, JAPAN, AND KOREA

"The Eastern blacks are found mainly in the archipelagoes lying between the Asiatic land-mass and Australia. They are the Oriental survivors of the black belt which in very ancient times stretched uninterruptedly from Africa across southern Asia to the Pacific Ocean." – Lothrop Stoddard, 1920

WHAT DOES IT MEAN TO BE "CHINESE"?

What does it mean to be "Chinese"? Li Chi, in his *Formation of the Chinese People*, offers the following definition:

> [The Chinese are those] who are found in, or whose origin is traceable to, the land called China proper, and who acknowledge their association with the making of Chinese history from the beginning.[234]

So when was the beginning? Who originated there? And who were the first authors of Chinese history? In this chapter, you'll learn why even China is rich with Black history.

China may look homogenous to some outsiders. That is, everyone looks the same. You may think everyone shares the same shade of skin and similar facial features. Now, to be honest, China may be more homogenous than many other nations, but there's quite a lot you may not be seeing.

China today, with over one billion inhabitants, is the product of several thousand years of semi-continuous history wherein several groups have contributed, at one time or another, to its development into what it is now. Today, 92% of the people of China are descendants of the Han, which is why so many of the people share similar features.[235]

However, in the "beginning" the Han peoples, or their type, were not so much the majority as they are today. Instead, China – in its earliest stages – was driven by populations that have now been pushed into the fringes. The original authors of Chinese history are either displaced from the continental mainland, isolated atop lonely hill and mountain stretches, entirely extinct or vanished, or absorbed into the dominant population, but ignored by their descendants.

Kenneth Scott Latourette, Professor of Oriental History at Yale University, dedicates a chapter of his two-volume work *The Chinese: Their History and Culture* to the subject of "Racial Composition." He begins the chapter clearly enough, declaring: "Racially the Chinese are a mixed people. That much we know."

Latourette claims no certainty about who contributed to this mixture, or how, but asserts that any observer who has actually traveled through China would know that there is a racial difference among the people there. Latourette finds the greatest evidence for this racial difference between the people of southern China and northern China. The people of the south, he notes, are generally darker, shorter, with broader noses, and a less conservative disposition.[236] He also sees "the sharp division between commoners and aristocrats in ancient times" as evidence of a racial difference.*

When we want to research a question that hasn't yet been properly explored, it's almost as if we're following clues like breadcrumbs on a trail. We follow leads and see where they lead us. We then assess everything we've found to arrive at a working theory. Then we compare the theory against any evidence that could support or, more importantly, refute, our theory. So let's start by looking at some of these "different" people – the "dark" people of China.

THE DARK PEOPLE OF CHINA

There are dozens of ethnic groups in China, both past and present, who don't fit the stereotypical look associated with modern Chinese people. In Part Two, we'll discuss the Black people who were responsible for founding ancient China's first dynasties and essentially establishing Chinese civilization. In this book, we'll discuss some of the ethnic groups who were settled in China before the Xia

---

* Certainly the same stratification may be said to exist throughout the world today, where Europeans, or fair-skinned peoples borne from miscegenation with Europeans invaders (or "colonizers"), rule over darker, native populations. This is the case in nearly every non-white nation or society where Europeans have had some kind of impact, the major exceptions primarily being those where figureheads are selected from the native populace to act as tools for the Europeans interests concerned.

and Shang dynasties were founded.

As early as the Shang dynasty (the first dynasty from which we have written records), there are people known as the Miao. The Miao of southern China were also called *Man*, which some scholars say meant "barbarian" (as in foreigner). Other say *Man* was simply a generic term for southern ethnic groups,[237] but some of the *Man* populations mentioned in the early sources were located towards the east.[238]

This would suggest that calling someone *Man* was like calling someone "African." In other words, it wasn't about where you were at, but where you were from. These were the pre-Chinese people of China.

The Miao may have originally been settled in southeast Asia, where they are known as the Hmong. Tripitaka, a Chinese monk who surveyed southern China and southeast Asia, observed that "the Cambodians remind me of the *Man*, our southern Chinese barbarians; they are coarse featured and very dark."[239]

Scholars think the *Miao, Moi (Moy), Mai, Mon, Min, Meng, Hmong* and *Muong* may have all derived from one parent-group, which originally fell under the *Man* designation.[240] Chai Chen Kang suggested these people were related to the dark-skinned aborigines of Taiwan, whom he proposes may have come from a mix of the Miao and the Malayans.[241]

Thus it makes sense that the modern-day Hmong (descendants of the Miao, or Man people) are one of the darkest-complexioned, and most socially-repressed, ethnic groups in every country in which they live. But the Hmong fare better than many of their kin. There are still thousands of "non-Chinese" peoples living in the hills and mountains of China as a result of the conquering Chinese driving them out. They often represent some of the last surviving vestiges of China's indigenous people. Latourette has said of these peoples:

> They are divided into numerous tribes, such as the Chung Chia, the Miao, Miao Tzu, or Miao Chia (made up of several groups, among whom are the Hei Miao, or "Black Miao," presumably so-called because of their dark-colored clothes, and the Hua or "Flowery" Miao), the Kachins, the Kah-lao, the Loi (on Hainan), the Lo-lo, the Yao, the No-so, and the Man Tzu or Man Chia...The Chinese have exploited them, have driven them out of desirable lands, and have held them in contempt.[242]

Almost all the people named above were once Black, and many remain dark-skinned and coarse-haired to this day. LaTourette's silly claim that such "Black" designations referred to "dark-colored clothes," makes sense if you look up the Black Miao and see pictures of them looking like "regular" Chinese people wearing dark turbans. But the lie falls apart when you dig up (as I did) a Chinese artist's 18th century painting of the Hei Miao, wherein they are clearly not wearing much of anything dark, except their skin. They have every feature you'd expect to find in a Black population, including the woolly hair texture.

THE BLACK COMMUNITIES OF CHINA

As you'll see, many of these ethnic groups were originally described as "Black." Many of these people are the "Black" minorities of an already small minority group.

For example, as with the Black Miao, there is also a "Black" subgroup of the *Lo-lo* (the *Hei Lo-lo*)[243], as well as a "Black" *Tai.*[244] The *Lipo* tribe of He Lisu, or "Black Lisu" is a minority in east Yunnan. Their language is very different from the rest of the *Lisu* group to whom they belong. They also use a different script. The name of the *Lisu* themselves, who are also known simply as *Li*, derives from *Li tzu* (or "black son").[245]

Russian-born Peter Goullart lived among the Nakhi people and became immersed in their culture. In his classic memoir, *The Forgotten Kingdom*, Goullart connects these groups with the Nakhi:

> The Nakhi, Burmese and Black Lolos, along with the Tibetans, belong to a racial subdivision called the Burmo-Tibetan stock. They do resemble each other to a degree, their languages and dialects have a common root...[246]

According to a 1933 study by Dr. Joseph Rock, *The Ancient Nakhi Kingdom of Southwest China*, the Nakhi people of China were once an unmixed "Negro" population, numbering over 200,000, who inhabited the region for several millennia. According to Frank LeBar's *Ethnic Groups of Mainland Southeast Asia*, the name Nakhi means "Black man" (*no*: black; *khi*: man) and was given to these people because of their dark complexions.[247] The Nakhi still retain a hieroglyphic-like style of writing, known as *dongba*, which is primarily used by the shamans who preserve their oldest traditions.

In *The Forgotten Kingdom*, Goullart describes similar traditions among the Black Lolo [no relation to Shawty Lo], such as their secret libraries of manuscripts written in a hieroglyphic script made of "circles, half-moons, swastikas and rhombs [diamonds]." The Black Lolo rarely let outsiders gain similar access to their culture. Thus, Goullart's notes as especially enlightening. He writes:

> The Black Lolo always means the Noble Lolo or, as they call

themselves in Chinese, Hei Kuto (the Black Bone). Actually the word Lolo is derogatory and should never be used to their face. It is best to refer to them in conversation as Hei Yi (the Black Yi), for an unwary choice of the word may mean instant death. I prefer to call them the Noble Lolos because they were, as a whole tribe, **the most noble-looking people I have seen in my life.** They are very tall and are of regal bearing. Their complexion is in no wise black but, **like certain mulattoes, of a chocolate and cream tint.** Their eyes are large and liquid, with a fire always burning in them, and their features are aquiline and almost Roman. Their hair is black, slightly wavy and very soft; and its arrangement is a distinctive feature of all Lolos. It is gathered through a hole at the top of their dark blue or black turbans and hangs as a limp tail or, more often, springs up like a miniature palm-tree, supported by a sheath of black strings. The hair of the Lolo is sacred and no one is supposed to touch it under the pain of death. They believe that the Divine Spirit communicates with man through the exposed lock of his hair which, like upstanding antenna or the aerial of a wireless set, conveys the spiritual impulses, like waves to a receiver, to the brain.

Goullart goes on to describe how the Black Lolo (or Hei Yi) love nothing more than to engage in guerrilla warfare against the ruling Chinese, luring their soldiers into ambushes. No battle against the Black Lolo, Goullart says, has been a decisive victory. He continues:

Even at the present time, it is reported, the Lolos still remain unconquered. The new Chinese regime has demanded the surrender of their arms and their submission to the new government. Instead, the Black Lolos have arranged the withdrawal of all their clansmen and their families who lived on the outer, exposed mountain slopes, to the main ranges of the Taliangshan. At a great conclave a king was elected to lead them, a drastic and almost unprecedented measure which is **only resorted to in a very grave emergency, when the existence of the whole race is at stake.**

This sounds a lot like some of the cultural changes we'll cover in Part Two. These people observe a strict social code and place great emphasis on chivalry, righteousness, honor, and etiquette. Goullart adds:

The **White Lolos are not related racially to the Black Lolos.** Originally they were of Chinese and other tribal stock, captured and enslaved by the Lolos...No Black Lolo might marry a White Lolo, and did so only under pain of death. Romances between the castes were strictly taboo, because **the purity of the Black Bone had to be zealously guarded.** Punishment for disloyalty, and even for a breach of discipline, was swift and just, irrespective of caste.

In other words, the "Black" and "White" labels weren't based on clothing colors or artistic conventions, but actual racial distinctions that have mostly faded with time and intermarriage. People like the

Black Lolo were able to remain "chocolate" colored as late as the 1950s because of their strict marriage laws.

WHERE DID THESE DARK PEOPLE COME FROM?

We began this section by talking about the "racial differences" found between the light and dark people of China. So how do we explain the origins of this difference? Some of these people, like the Nakhi and Black Lolo, have cultural traditions and features that make them seem related to the Anu, the Black travelers we'll discuss in Part Two. Other clues suggest that these communities are rooted in the ancestral Black populations that first settled all of Asia.

Geomorphologist George F. Carter once proposed:

> Chinese history is that of the Mongoloid people from the northwest of China pushing out the Negrito people of southeast Asia, who as late as the early centuries A.D. were still the dominant people of south China. Indeed in a real sense they are still there, for the short, dark south Chinese are pretty clearly the result of the mixture of the Mongols with the smaller, darker folk who had long been there. [248]

In other words, foreigners came from the northwest and took over, changing the face of China forever. Yet these outsiders, who the ancient Chinese called "Western barbarians" weren't the authors of Chinese civilization. Instead, it was the dark people of China who should be associated, as Li Chi says, "with the making of Chinese history from the beginning." So let's go back to the beginning.

THE ORIGINAL PEOPLE OF CHINA

China has been settled for quite a long time. There are Paleolithic sites in China dating back to at least 20,000 years ago. But man must have been there long before if he made it to the islands of New Guinea over 100,000 years ago.

I think it's pretty clear by now who was making these kinds of moves during this time period. But for a place like China, which has taken great pride in its historical continuity and homogeneity – to the point of some Chinese scientists trying to prove that the Chinese do not descend from Africa – I think it's important to flesh it all the way out.

What do we know about the oldest human presence in ancient China? We know that the early record says very little, but the little that we have says a lot. Carl Whiting Bishop, in discussing the scanty evidence of the very early human occupancy at China has stated:

> We have evidence that the southern and coastal portions of China

were once inhabited by Negritos akin to those still found in the Malay Peninsula and certain of the East Indian islands. The last remnants of these "black dwarfs," as an old Chinese record calls them, disappeared during the early centuries of our Era; but unmistakable traces of their blood still persist in the present mountain folk of southern and western China.[249]

In other words, the DBP were descendants of the first people to settle China. G. Coedes, in his *Making of South East Asia*, attests to the fossil evidence:

> Along the coast of the China Sea...the skeletons and skulls belong to a race of pygmies similar to the Negritos of the Andaman islands and to certain Papuans of Melanesia.[250]

These DBP were the descendants of the original "Black belt" of Original People that settled the world around 100,000 years ago. These people survived and became the DBP, but also blended into many later populations.

Even the premier white supremacist author of the early 1900s, Lothrop Stoddard, was bold enough to admit in his magnum opus *The Rising Tide of Color Against White World Supremacy*:

> Besides its African nucleus the black race has two distant outposts: the one in Australasia, the other in the Americas. The Eastern blacks are found mainly in the archipelagoes lying between the Asiatic land-mass and Australia. They are the Oriental survivors of the black belt which in very ancient times stretched uninterruptedly from Africa across southern Asia to the Pacific Ocean. The Asiatic blacks were overwhelmed by other races ages ago, and only a few wild tribes like the "Negritos" of the Philippines and the jungle-dwellers of Indo-China and southern India survive as genuine Negroid stocks. All the peoples of southern Asia, however, are darkened by this ancient Negroid strain.[251]

According to Professor Chang Hsing-lang, the *Jiu Tang Shu (Old Dynastic History of Tang)* makes mention of a people living to the south of the region of Linyi, who "have woolly hair and black skin."[252] In his *Les Negritos de la Chine*, published in Hanoi in 1928, French anthropologist H. Imbert wrote:

> The Negroid races peopled at some time all the South of India, Indo-China, and China...In the first epochs of Chinese history, the Negrito type peopled all the south of this country and even in the island of Hai-Nan, as we have attempted to prove in our study on these Negritos, or Black Men of this island. Skulls of these Negroes have been found in the island of Formosa and traces of this Negroid element in the islands of Liu-Kiu to the south of Japan. In the earliest Chinese history several texts in classic books spoke of these diminutive blacks; thus the *Tcheu-Li* composed under the dynasty of Tcheu (1129-249 BC) gives a description of the

inhabitants with black and oily skin...[253]

THE DBP IN LATER CHINESE HISTORY

Anthropologist Li Chi notes a reference to "blackish-colored dwarfs" in the *Official History of the Liang Dynasty* (502–556 AD),[254] but comes up short for other references to the DBP in early Chinese literature. I'm not sure how he missed it, but the Chinese actually have a rich literary and artistic tradition centered on the DBP.

For starters, *Kunlun Nu* ("The Negrito Slave") is a popular Chinese romance written during the Tang Dynasty around 880 AD. The hero of the tale is a Negrito slave named *Mo-lê*, who has "supernatural" physical abilities. After Mo-lê saves his master's lover (who has now fallen for him), he finally escapes with his dagger (apparently his only possession) and flies over the city walls to escape apprehension. He is seen over ten years later selling medicine in the city, not having aged a single day.

Later Taoist commentary says that Mo-lê's gravity defying abilities and agelessness suggest he was a Chinese Immortal (a myth popular in early Taoism and modern Kung fu movies).[255] In fact, it appears that the "Immortals" of Chinese tradition were inspired by stories of these "magical" Blacks, much as the stories of the mythical beings of Europe's "enchanted forests" were based on the ancient Black presence there.

In his *Formation of the Chinese People*, anthropologist Li Chi documented, among the Yunnan tribes, a people known as *Hala*, which means "the black." Li wrote:

> The description of the Hala given by the [Chinese] Encyclopedia, brief as it is, corresponds almost exactly to that of the modern Sakai as given by Skeat and Blagden. If they do have any affiliation, it would be more appropriate to call them Negroid rather than Negrito. Modern writers on Szechuan and Kansu have found traces of both the Negroid and the Negrito in China. None, however, has found any pure type.[256]

The modern-day *Hlai* inhabit the mountains (and some tropical forest areas) in central and south central Hainan province in southern China. They are an official Chinese minority known as *Li* (which means "black"), and are also known by smaller tribal affiliations such as *Li, Dai, Lai, La, Loi,* and *Le*. While they are traditionally hunters, and still polytheistic, many are now farmers.

One of their five major divisions is known as *Ha Li*, which may have derived from Hala.[257] It is interesting, especially in regards to ancient Chinese religion, to note that among the Malayan Negritos, who originally occupied China, the shaman was known by the name *Hala*.[258] This takes us back to the connection between the Black people of China and conceptions of the divine, a theme we'll explore in Volume Three.

THE DBP IN CHINESE ART

In early Chinese art, depictions of Black people are everywhere. Some are more stylized than others, but many are so clear in representing Black features that scholars have jumped through all sorts of intellectual hoops to try to explain them away. For example, one bronze wine vessel from the Shang dynasty clearly depicts a DBP male embracing a large tiger.[259] This has been described as a "tiger eating a Negro baby" as if that was a typical occurrence in ancient China!

In reality, the tiger probably represents the Black male's "alter ego" as the male himself is a shaman. In fact, the very origins of Chinese religion begin with the "shamanism" characteristic of aboriginal Black cultures elsewhere in the world, especially among DBP people.*

In fact, early Chinese art is replete with motifs that represent the original Black people of China. From the wide-eyed, full-lipped faces on the ritual mask and stone cong used by Chinese shamans, to the jade sculptures of "squatting barbarians" **there are literally hundreds of representations of Black people,** most of them DBP people, in ancient Chinese art.

George Weber accounts for at least 53 distinct "Negrito" populations throughout southeast Asia. Four of these groups can be found in or very near China. Six other nearby locales (including Hainan and Taiwan) retain local legends or other evidence about extinct populations with Black traits.[260] Weber adds:

> [S]o many cross-connections and similarities between the Negritos, Veddoids, Papuans, Melanesians, Australians and Tasmanians have been noted that at the very least a long period of common residence in tropical Asia if not a common origin must by assumed. Which brings us to the second school of thought which holds that all these groups share a common ancestral origin somewhere in southeast Asia or southern China...
>
> [T]he hypothetical ancestral race of Negritos, Veddoids, Papuans, Australians, Tasmanians and Melanesians once occupied, perhaps as much as 100,000 years ago...ranged from India through Indo-China

---

* To be clear, what anthropologists call shamanism, we can call by other names that are more illustrative of the science behind the symbolism used. We'll get into that in Volume Three.

to Indonesia and from southern China through Taiwan to the Philippines, with New Guinea, Australia and Tasmania settled later by the same people.[261]

THE AUSTRALOID PEOPLE OF CHINA

According to Carl Whiting Bishop, a second wave of people "supplanted the Negritos" in China. These people may have been Australoid. When did they come? It's not entirely clear when they first arrived, but there is evidence of their presence as early as 20,000 years ago. Because of the coastal route we typically took, most of the earliest settlements can be found in the south.[262]

Even notoriously Eurocentric historian Carleton Coon detected an ancient Australoid colony in southern China. But, as noted earlier, many of the earliest southern settlements have been swept away by rising sea levels. Fortunately, there is also a decent amount of evidence left behind by our excursions inland.

One of the earliest sites of human occupation in China, Yuchanyan Cave in Hunan, yielded shards of ceramic vessels and other artifacts which were dated to be 17,500 to 18,300 years old. That would make these the oldest known examples of pottery.[263] Who were the people of Yuchanyan? A clue can be found further north. Skeletal remains at the site of Zhoukoudian, known as the Upper Cave, date back to about 20,000 years ago, and can tell us quite a lot about the early Chinese.

Why? They're Australoid. Meaning they looked like the (Black) Australian aborigines. Meaning the prehistoric Chinese came from the same ancestral population as the people of Australia. Not only do the oldest skulls tell this story, but there are shell beads and other artifacts that are nearly identical between Zhoukoudian Cave, China and Devil's Lair Cave, Australia (c. 20,000 BC).[264]

SO WHEN DID THINGS CHANGE?

Regarding the racial transition in ancient China, K.C. Chang theorized:

> [B]y the beginning of the Recent (Holocene) period the population in North China and that in the southwest and in Indochina had become sufficiently differentiated to be designated as Mongoloid and Oceanic Negroid races respectively, even though both of them may have evolved out of a common Upper Pleistocene substratum as represented by the Tzu-yang and the Liu-chang skulls.[265]

In other words, within the past 10,000 years, the expanding populations of China may have differentiated enough for some to look more Mongoloid and others to look more Negroid. But they all came from the same ancestral population, as represented by the "much older" Tzu-yang and Liu-chang skulls.

Chinese scholars assert that, while the Liu-chang skull may have been the origin for populations south of China, the Tzu-yang skull looks Mongoloid and was likely the origin of Mongoloid features among the Chinese. In other words, Chinese people always looked this way. But is this true?

It doesn't look like it. The "ancestral" Tzu-yang skull doesn't support the claim that the Chinese didn't start out Black. For starters, the Tzu-yang skull may have more of a Mongoloid appearance, but it isn't as old as they thought. It only goes back to about 5,000 BC. Not so much of an "ancestor" as they'd like.

On the other hand, the Liu-chang (or Liujiang) skull is at least 60,000 years old (possibly more), so it may be a better representation of the Original People of China. And guess what? **It looks Black.** Scholars have often described it as Australoid, connecting it to the Australoid skulls found at Zhoukoudian,[266] the skulls of early Neolithic China,[267] and later skulls from the Shang dynasty.[268]

In other words, Black people were the foremost presence at every major step of Chinese cultural development. The Liu-chang skull has also been compared to the earliest skulls found in the Americas, which reminds of what Walter Neves said about those remains.[269]

And these people didn't disappear. They survived in China all the way into the Neolithic. Wolfram Eberhard's *History of China* documents the presence of a Neolithic culture in southern and coastal China at least as early as 4000 BC. These were the people, he clarified, who formed the "original stock of the Australian aborigines," adding:

> They survived in India as the Munda tribes, in Indo-China as the Mon-Khmer, and also remained in pockets on the islands of Indonesia and especially Melanesia. All these peoples had migrated from southern China.

Many of these people were influential in the founding of the first Chinese dynasties. This is the story we'll cover in Part Two.

PHILIPPINES

THE ORIGINAL PEOPLE OF TAIWAN

You probably own a few things that say they're "Made in Taiwan," but do you know where Taiwan is? It's an island off east coast of China, not too far from its shores. You can imagine that it was probably settled by the same people who first settled China. But unlike China, the island was mainly inhabited by Taiwanese aborigines until the Dutch took over in the early 1600s and mainland Chinese began immigrating to the island. That's when they called it "Formosa." Needless to say, it wasn't pretty the way they did the aboriginal people to make their rule easy.

And Taiwan's aborigines are quite an interesting people. Oh, you didn't know? Have you seen *Warriors of the Rainbow*? It's a pretty incredible film, the most expensive film made in Taiwanese history. It's the story of Taiwan's aborigines and their fight against imperialist Japan in 1930. Long story short, it's like the Taiwanese *Braveheart*. But there's more to this story. The aborigines of Taiwan are – as you'd expect – darker-skinned than the people of China or Japan. They tend to have "Blacker features" overall. But were they the first people of Taiwan?

THE DBP IN TAIWAN

Several isolated Chinese populations have oral traditions suggesting an ancient Black presence that has, with time and the disappearance of the Blacks themselves, lent itself to the realm of legends and rumors. Today, that presence is quite possibly best remembered by those tribal populations least affected by the integration and assimilation of the Chinese mainland, that is, those of the neighboring islands. Foremost among these is Taiwan. There, a rumor from the Saisiyat tribe persists. It states:

> [B]ack many years ago there used to be a population of small-body sized people with very dark skin color living in the mountain area. People usually called them 'little black man.' They were good-natured fellows, good swimmers and liked to play jokes…These people disappeared not too long ago.[270]

Chai Chen Kang declares in his conclusion to *Taiwan Aborigines: A Genetic Study of Tribal Variations*:

> The widespread presence of Negritos in the South Pacific Islands support the theory that they may have been the earliest inhabitants of Taiwan. Kroeber referred to them as an ancient and primitive people, who may have inhabited wide stretches of Africa, Asia, and Oceania before its invasion by Mongoloids and Caucasoids from the north…Our study provides what also may be biologic evidence of

genetic infiltration from this vanished race [the Negritos], in the short stature and dark skin of the western tribes, especially the Bununs and Paiwans, who also have the broad head and nose and short, wide face typical of the Negritos.[271]

Every year, the Saisiyat tribe of Hsinchu and Miaoli* commemorate the "little Black people" they unknowingly exterminated. As Jules Quartly reports in the *Taipei Times*:

> For the past 100 years or so, the Saisiyat tribe has performed the songs and rites of the festival to bring good harvests, ward off bad luck and keep alive the spirit of a race of people who are said to have preceded all others in Taiwan.
>
> In fact, the short, black men the festival celebrates are one of the most ancient types of modern humans on this planet and their kin still survive in Asia today. They are said to be diminutive Africoids and are variously called Pygmies, Negritos and Aeta. They are found in the Philippines, northern Malaysia, Thailand, Sumatra in Indonesia and other places.
>
> Chinese historians called them "black dwarfs" in the Three Kingdoms period (AD 220 to AD 280) and they were still to be found in China during the Qing dynasty (1644 to 1911). In Taiwan they were called the "Little Black People" and, apart from being diminutive, they were also said to be broad-nosed and dark-skinned with curly hair.
>
> After the Little Black People – and well before waves of Han migrations after 1600 – came the Aboriginal tribes, who are part of the Austronesian race…Gradually the Little Black People became scarcer, until a point about 100 years ago, when there was just a small group living near the Saisiyat tribe.
>
> The story goes that the Little Black People taught the Saisiyat to farm by providing seeds and they used to party together.[272]

This is when things go downhill. Their community had dwindled down to the point where there no available females to bear children and create a next generation. They attempted to take some of the aboriginal community's women, and that didn't go over well. Quartly tells what happened next:

> So, the Saisiyat took revenge and killed them off by cutting a bridge over which they were all crossing. Just two Little Black People survived. Before departing eastward, they taught the Saisiyat about their culture and passed down some of their songs, saying if they did not remember their people they would be cursed and their crops would fail.[273]

That's heavy. Did you catch the part about how the DBP taught the aboriginal people of Taiwan how to farm *and* how to have fun? That

---

* What does Miao-li mean? Look back and think about it.

says a lot about what the DBP taught the people who followed them, especially considering that the DBP themselves were typically not farmers. The Saisiyat tribe's oral tradition is one of the few surviving records of how important the DBP were to the world's civilizations. I cannot help but wonder if the "Little Black People" of Taiwan consciously foretold the destruction of Taiwan's aboriginal people by the Japanese. When you watch *Warriors of the Rainbow*, don't miss the scene on the bridge.

AN INTRODUCTION TO JAPAN

I'll be honest. When I went to Japan in 2003, I had a moment of American ignorance. There were so many people with a similar complexion, similar nose shape, similar eyes, and similar hair texture that it did seem a little homogeneous at first. In other words, I was starting to think everyone looked the same. So yes, I was one of those "uninformed" people I mentioned in the last chapter.

Fortunately, I stayed for three weeks, which gave me ample time to learn some of the language, culture, and history. For starters, modern Japan is home to several waves of immigrants from Korea and China, who don't actually look the same. However, modern Japanese, Koreans, and Chinese all share some traits in common – like hair texture – which are, in fact, quite different from the features of their oldest ancestors.

Outside Tokyo, I encountered a wider variety of "ethnic" features among the people. I also visited a few temples where Black gods like Bishamon were still celebrated by the local people.[274] I got a chance to hear a traditional form of music known as Taiko drumming, where African rhythms had clearly been preserved.

I learned that Japan had been a strong supporter of the Black Nationalism movements of the early 20th century U.S. Most importantly, I learned about the Ainu and the Jōmon people, two of the biggest clues into who the Original People of Japan were.

THE LITTLE BLACK PEOPLE OF JAPAN

In a 1903 study of the racial elements of Japanese history, Karl Kiyoshi Kawakami wrote:

> The first inhabitants of Japan were probably Pigmies, who lived in hill-sides and vaults along the coast of the Pacific Ocean and the Sea of Japan. This thesis, maintained by Professors Koganei and Tsuboye, of Tokio Imperial University is based upon the results of

excavations and upon traditions compiled in the Kojiki* and other records. How many years ago and whence this small race came to our land is a matter of conjecture. They were the race of the neolithic or, perhaps, of the palaeolithic stage.[275]

In his groundbreaking 1895 work *The Pygmies*, Armand de Quatrefages, Professor of Anthropology at the Museum of Natural History of Paris, says of the original people of Japan and other adjacent islands:

> On the north, Formosa is the last place where the race of which we speak has preserved all its characteristics; but it reveals its ancient existence beyond this island by the traces it has left among the present populations. In the little archipelago of Loo-Choo [Ryukyu], Basil Hall Chamberlain found at certain points 'some men very black by the side of others who were almost white.' Ancient traditions in Japan speak of formidable black savages who were subdued and driven away only with great difficulty…

Quatrefages adds that human remains confirm his theory:

> Kempfer and Siebold have reported the differences in color and hair which certain classes of the population present, and the latter mentions particularly the black color and the more or less crinkly hair of the inhabitants of the southeast coast. Long since, I mentioned these characters as confirming the opinion first propounded by Pichard relative to the intervention of a black element in Japan, and this element can only be referred to the Negrito race. The examination of a Japanese skull from the Broca collection has fully confirmed these conclusions. Studied by Hamy and myself, it has presented a mixture of features, of which the most characteristic clearly betray this ethnic origin. The details given by Dr. Maget have fully confirmed these conclusions. He has discovered and described veritable *Negrito metis* [mixed-bloods] living in the midst of Japanese populations.[276]

Kawakami continues:

> [I]t seems almost certain that Pigmies of some sort or other peopled the islands of Japan at a time long before the dawn of the historic age. Notwithstanding de Quatrefages' remark that these Negritos of the North were not exterminated as in Java, we are not able today to perceive so much as a trace of this primitive stock so far as the people of Japan proper are concerned. In Riu-Kiu and Formosa, our new territories, we may perhaps recognize to a greater

---

* According to Kawakami: "At the beginning of the eight century of the Christian era, a book entitled *Kojiki*, or *Book of Ancient Traditions*, was compiled. It is the oldest record now extant, and contains many mythological traditions concerning the primitive state of the aborigines. From this and traditional records written subsequently, and from various articles lately excavated in different districts, it is inferred that the Japanese race was the outgrowth of a mixing of various stocks."

or less degree a certain relation to those early peoples, as the prominent French anthropologist has pointed out. That the races who first peopled Japan were extraordinarily short in stature has been shown by the smallness of the vaults recently found and alleged by scholars to have been the habitations of the prehistoric folk, as well as by the evidences handed down through folk-lore...

These DBP may have been called by names such as *Koshito, Koropokguru,* or *Aoshima.* Later Japanese myths describe "little black demons" inhabiting the mountains and forests, which – as such myths go in Europe – may also describe the DBP. What happened to the DBP of Japan? Kawakami concludes:

For how long a period this short-statured race had existed in Japanese islands before stronger savages came to subjugate them, is not definitely known. Whence they came, where they went, how they disappeared, are questions no less obscure...Professor Koganei, of Tokyo University, insists that these Pygmies, attacked by a superior race now called Ainu, gradually retired to the North, and finally crossed over to Siberia and America by the way of Yezo, Saghalin, and other islands. He is bold enough to say that they were the ancestors of the present Esquimos.

This could explain why the history of human habitation in Japan predates the appearance of the Jōmon, who are considered its founding population.

BLACK SAMURAIS AND THE AINU

In his *History of China,* Wolfram Eberhard notes a Neolithic culture in northeastern China, who he connects to the Papuan people of Melanesia. He says they came from southern China, as did a southeastern culture of Blacks who went on to settle Australia. In Eberhard's analysis, "Both groups influenced the ancient Japanese culture." In other words, Japan was once a diverse array of Black people, most of them of the Australoid type. Today, we'd have a hard time tracking down the descendants of those early populations. Yet there is one indigenous population in Japan that has maintained some of its unique heritage by *remaining distinct.* They are known as the Ainu.

WHO WERE THE AINU?

The Ainu don't look like most Japanese. Today they can best be described as a pale-skinned people who look somewhat Caucasian. On closer examination, we can identify Australoid traits, such as heavy body hair, brow-ridges, and wide noses.

Indeed the pale-skinned Ainu, along with Australoid remains in

Paleolithic Europe, suggested to many historians that the origins of the white race may have laid in the depigmentation of Australoid people. For more on that story, see Volume Four.

But **the Ainu were not always pale.** They were originally Black like their cousins in Australia and New Guinea. If you follow the trail provided by photographs from the early 1900s and work your way backwards to watercolor paintings from the late 18th century, you'll see the gradual color change among the Ainu.

According to Albert Churchward, in *Signs and Symbols of Primordial Man*, "These Ainu are of the same original race and type as the Australian Aborigines." In 1937, Thomas Griffith Taylor also noted a connection between the Ainu and the Australoid people of India:

> A very interesting tribe is the Toda people of the Nilgiri hills. They are characterized by their hairy appearance, thus resembling the Ainu and the Australian. Indeed, they may be akin to an early form of the Nordic race.[277]

The Ainu are also genetically linked to the Australoid people who came into the Americas 16,000 years ago. A 1994 genetic study revealed that the ancestors of the Ainu people migrated into the Americas in the Paleolithic.[278] Some of these people may have become the Native Americans of North America's eastern seaboard.[279]

THE ANCESTORS OF THE BLACK SAMURAIS

James Brunson writes in *African Presence in Early Asia*:

> An ancient tradition points to the conquest of Japan from the southeast by a race of warriors of black or near black origin. These invaders were probably the ancestors of the Black Samurai, and later Shogun, Sakanouye Tamuramaro. Sakanouye's father and uncle were members of the warrior class "Azumbabito" or "Men of the East." The Azumbabito, who had praises sung of them in early Japanese literature, are probably the subject of the proverb, "for a samurai to be brave, he must have a bit of black blood."[280]

And there is, indeed, a connection between the Black blood of the Ainu and the Black blood of the samurai. Genetic studies have confirmed that the Ainu made "a recognizable contribution to the warrior class – the Samurai – of feudal Japan."[281]

WHERE DID THE AINU COME FROM?

Kawakami says the DBP were part of the Ainu's ancestry:

> [I]t will be safe to admit that in some cases there was an intermingling of the blood of the Pigmies and the Ainus. If the Pigmies played any role in the characterization of the Japanese

The Ainu are the aboriginal people of Japan. They've been there for thousands of years. Historians say the Ainu look like Caucasians. At first, it seems possible.

But if you dig further back in time...

...it gets clearer...

Ainu Elder c.1900

The first Japanese were the same Black people who settled Australia.

THE AINU OF JAPAN

It's no coincidence that Japan's aboriginal people, the Ainu, were once painted much darker (and with coarser hair) than other Japanese. Old photographs reveal their Black roots. Also note the practice of tattooing thick black lips on women as beautification (particularly among lighter women).

AINU MAN, JAPAN

COMPARE WITH
AUSTRALIAN ABORIGINAL
TRACKER AND EXPLORER,
TOMMY WINDICH...

THE ANCIENT JŌMON OF JAPAN

JŌMON VILLAGE RECONSTRUCTIONS

The Jōmon period of Japan begins roughly 13,000 BC, when hunter-gatherers arrived in Japan from Central Asia. Jōmon villages resembled those in many other parts of the world, including those of Mesolithic Europe. Their art also resembles that of other ancient cultures, and often celebrates features normally associated with Black people.

Recent reconstructions of Jomon faces (see right) have sought to differentiate them from modern Japanese with wider faces, wider eyes, broader noses, and full lips.

"THINKER" OF HAMANGIA
ROMANIA, C. 5500 BC

JŌMON DOGU
C. 2000 BC

TAINO FIGURINE
DOMINICAN REPUBLIC

nation, it could have been only through the Ainus who in turn gave
way before other conquering tribes of Aryans and Mongolians...

Thus, it is asserted that the Japanese nation is of no single origin. It
is the outcome of the intermingling of entirely different ethnic
stocks. The blood of the Mongolians, the Aryans, and the Ainus,
together with some tinge of the blood of the Pygmies, is mingled
together in the veins of the Japanese people.

Beyond this, Kawakami says, "As to the original abode of the Ainus,
the scholars are, however, still in darkness." If previous chapters
have shed any light, we know that Australoid people were survivors
of the Toba extinction and probably repopulated East Asia from
somewhere in the southeast.

THE JOMON CULTURE

The Ainu are quite possibly the strongest survival of Japan's Original
People, but there's more to the picture. Human habitation of Japan
goes back at least 35,000 years, when early settlers mined stone from
Mount Takaharayama to produce obsidian tools like those found at
African sites.[282] Such mining practices continued into the Jōmon
Period, which lasted from 13,000 to 2,500 years ago. The Jōmon
culture was made up of the Original People of Japan. Some of these
people later became the Ainu.

In addition to extensive mining, the Jōmon also:

❏ Had an extensive pottery tradition.
❏ Fished, foraged, and hunted for their food, only occasionally planting
   hemp or other non-native crops.
❏ Built large, stable villages that reflect a sedentary (not nomadic)
   population.
❏ May have sailed the Pacific coasts to eventually become part of the
   early Native American population.

Mark J. Hudson, Professor of Anthropology at Nishikyushu
University in Japan, said the country was settled by a "Proto-
Mongoloid" people in the prehistoric past. These people became the
Jōmon and their features can be seen in the Ainu and Okinawan
people. Proto-Mongoloid (or Paleo-Mongoloid) people, as we noted
earlier, descended from Australoid ancestors.

This is why Jōmon remains don't look exactly like modern East
Asians. In many ways, they resemble Australian Aborigines more
than modern Asian people.[283] According to Jared Diamond, they had
wide-set eyes and "strikingly raised browridges, noses, and nose
bridges," traits found in Australoid populations.[284] Other studies have
established that the Jōmon's limb proportions were those of a *tropical*

people.[285] As we've noted elsewhere, "tropical" means dark-skinned.

SO HOW DID THE JOMON BECOME THE JAPANESE?

The Original People of Japan maintained their culture, and their independence, for thousands of years. A recent study suggests these people actually *avoided* the people who attempted to introduce agriculture:

> [T]he hunter–gatherer population, which settled in Japan around 12,000–30,000 BP, managed to fend off the farmers for thousands of years until being abolished suddenly and dramatically with the arrival of proto-Japonic-speaking farmers around 2400 [years ago]…During all this transition outside, the hunter–gatherers of Japan continued to prosper by using simple stone tools and without adopting full-scale agriculture, despite knowledge of cultivation of many crops.[286]

So who introduced the racial, linguistic, and cultural change that shifted Japan away from its Black roots? A later group, known in Japan as the Yayoi, came into Japan about 2400 years ago. The Yayoi brought the science of wet rice agriculture and a military tradition, quickly displaced their Jōmon predecessors. The Yayoi were not tropically adapted but cold-adapted.

What does this mean? According to Hudson, this is when "Neo-Mongoloid" people entered Japan, quickly becoming the dominant population.[287] In other words, most Japanese descend from a mix of the original Australoid Jōmon people and the Neo-Mongoloid Yayoi people, who came much later.

The genetic legacy of the Jōmon is best preserved among the Ainu. Anthropologist Umehara Takeshi believes the Ainu and Ryukyuans preserve the "Proto-Mongoloid" traits of the Jōmon era.[288] So the Ainu look the most like the original Jōmon, while most Japanese look more like the Yayoi. Modern Japanese ancestry is about 60% Yayoi and 40% Jōmon. Modern Koreans share the same roots.

THEN WHAT HAPPENED?

As recently as the 1940s, Japan was working to bring the Black and brown people of the world together. Along with India and some Middle Eastern nations, Japan was sending delegates to build alliances with Black Nationalist organizations in the U.S.

In an excellent article titled "When Japan was Champion of the Darker Races," Black historian Ernest Allen, Jr. reports on the Asian activists sent to Black communities in the early 20th century, all with the intentions of dismantling white supremacist rule.

A notable figure from this period is Satokata Takahashi, a Japanese general who worked to build revolutionary relationships with Black people in America. In one speech, delivered to a Black working-class audience, Takahashi asserted:

> Three-fourths of the world are black people and one-fourth is white, and it is not in accordance with God's will for one-fourth of the world to rule the three-fourths, which are black. Now that Japan has gained rightful recognition in the world, she is willing to help other dark races.
>
> We know that the black people of the United States are citizens thereof, and can not help Japan directly in case of war, but there are other things that can be done. If the white man knew that you sympathized with Japan, he would not allow you to shoulder arms or go near an ammunition plant in case of war...Japan is making overtures to you. If she fails you fail. This is the last chance of the dark races of America to overcome white supremacy and to throw the white tyrants off your backs.

In another speech, he declared:

> You are clinging to an era of Caucasian civilization and psychology because you are afraid to leave the sinking ship. I say the sinking ship because western prestige is doomed. It is pursuing its inevitable course to the graveyard of obscure history. Here is the Negro's chance to freedom in life. Leave the sinking ship.[289]

By all accounts from those who knew him, Takahashi was sincere in his pleas. He worked with people representing the Moorish Science Temple, the United Negro Improvement Association, the AME Church, and the Nation of Islam. Thanks to Takahashi and others like him, pro-Japan sentiment was growing rapidly in Black communities across the U.S. By 1942, the government had serious concerns about Black support for Japan conquering the U.S. in war.

CAN'T HAVE THAT...

In August of 1945, the United States became the first and only country to drop atom bombs on another country, leaving the Japanese cities of Hiroshima and Nagasaki in a state of such obliterated carnage that the people of Japan continue to wear masks to this day because of the residual fallout.

After Japan surrendered, the U.S. began rebuilding the country, this time according to a new set of rules. It wasn't long before baseball replaces sumo wrestling as Japan's national pastime, nor was it long before Japanese culture absorbed the sort of Western-style racism that continues to permeate today.

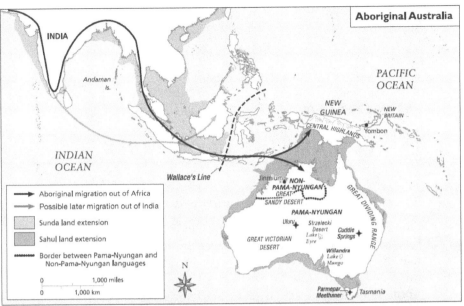

Aboriginal Australia

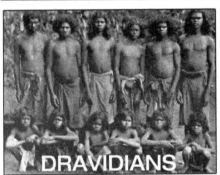

DRAVIDIANS

AUSTRALIANS

MODERN AUSTRALIAN PEOPLE

MODERN PAPUANS (NEW GUINEA)

AUSTRALIA

THE BLACKFELLAS DOWN UNDER

"We know we cannot live in the past but the past lives in us." – Charles Perkins, Aboriginal activist

One thing you will draw away from this book is that the same things have happened to Black people **all over the world**. In Australia, we find the same tragic story that happened to the Original People of the Americas, Africa, and Asia. That story can be summed up in one word: annihilation.

The Aboriginal people of Australia were subjected to a true genocide, including the theft of their land and natural resources, being forced to live on desert reservations, being hunted down and shot like dogs, and even lynchings in the same fashion as in colonial America. While films like *Rabbit-Proof Fence* and *The Tracker* tell some of this story, there is no film – to my knowledge – that captures the way our people in Australia were killed off and violently repressed.

In fact, many of the aboriginal populations of the area – such as the Tasmanians – are now gone forever. Meanwhile, the survivors have been left to witness the theft and co-opting of their cultural traditions and knowledge. White folks might like boomerangs and didgeridoos, but nobody wants to talk about what happened to the people they belong to.

And, indeed, Australia has much to teach us, so long as we do not look through the deceptive lenses of culture bandits like Marlo Morgan (who we'll soon discuss). After all, these are a people whose way of life worked for over 60,000 years! By comparison, it would seem that our own society is near-collapse after only five centuries.

"The Australian native can withstand all the reverses of nature, fiendish droughts and sweeping floods, horrors of thirst and enforced starvation - but he cannot withstand [Western] civilisation."
– Daisy May Bates, Australian activist

So why don't we hear about Australia when we talk of ancient Black civilizations? Because – given the limited scope provided by the Western model for civilization, which we discussed earlier – the Black people of Australia never had "civilization." They never congregated into large urban centers and built big stone buildings surrounded by farmland.

But who's to say they weren't advanced? Even though they maintained relatively the same way of life since the time they settled there, they didn't have many problems (until Europeans came). All the anthropological accounts of the Aborigines, as well as James Bonwick's 1870 account, *Daily Life and Origin of the Tasmanians*, describe a way of life that made perfect sense, given the population density and environment.

"Our culture is something that has sustained us for thousands and thousands of years and will continue to do so in generations to come." – Hetti Perkins

That is, the aborigines didn't NEED urban centers, because they had plenty of room to spread out, and plenty of natural food sources to live comfortably. They had so much free time that they preserved a rich, complex culture involving several layers of cosmologies and hundreds of traditions to go along with them. And when a need arose, they met it with a surprising (to modern researchers, at least) degree of intelligence and ingenuity. For example, the recent discovery of a 35,000 year-old stone axe in Arnhem Land, Australia is much more advanced than was expected. Archaeologist Adam Brumm noted:

Aboriginal material culture was regarded by early European observers as the most primitive technology on earth...Yet at the same time that early European hunters were using stone arrowheads to bring down large and dangerous Ice Age animals, the ancestors of modern-day Aboriginal people employed an equally if not more sophisticated type of stone tool in order to gain access to vital foods.

In other words, "Australia was at the forefront of technical innovation 35,000 years ago."[291]

"This painting is not from today. We've got a story. And we've got laws. We not only believe of land, we believe of even river or creek or saltwater. That's our own law there. Our own law and story. "
– Gawarrin Gumana

Before Europeans pushed the Australians into the desert fringes of their old homelands, they had easy access to thousands of plants and animals, which they knew well.

Before Europeans came, aborigines had few physical ailments, and few (if any) mental health issues or addictions. Early accounts note Aborigines being repulsed by the thought of drinking the white man's *grog*, but before long these people were plagued by alcoholism.[292]

In fact, in the initiation process of Euahlayi boys, they were told that their shamans could see in their "sacred crystals" images of the future. They saw the Black color of their people growing "paler and paler, until at last only the white faces of the Wundah, or spirits of the dead, and white devils were seen, as if it should mean that some day no more blacks should be on this earth." The account continues:

> The reason of this must surely be that the tribes fell away from the Boorah rites, and in his wrath Byamee [the "All Father"] stirred from his crystal seat in Bullimah. He had said that as long as the blacks kept his sacred laws, so long should he stay in his crystal seat, and the blacks live on earth; but if they failed to keep up the Boorah rites as he had taught them, then he would move and their end would come, and only Wundah, or white devils, be in their country.[293]

THE ORIGINAL PEOPLE

"This is the land of dreamings, a land of wide horizons and secret places. The first people, our ancestors, created this country in the culture that binds us to it." – Hetti Perkins

Scientists have confirmed that Australian Aborigines have "one of the oldest continuous population histories outside sub-Saharan Africa today."[294] But they've also established that the Aboriginal population is not monolithic.

Before the Europeans came, there were about 600 communities (or "tribes"), each consisting of 500-1000 people and speaking its own dialect. There are hundreds of unique ethnic (and linguistic) groups in Australia for a reason.

Recent research reveals there is a ton of genetic diversity in the aboriginal population, including representatives of most of the world's haplogroups. The genetic research has also determined that the Australian aborigines look genetically related to a diverse array of the world's oldest people, including hunger-gatherers from Nepal and the Philippines, the Great Andamanese and Onge from the Andaman Islands, the Highlands people of Papua, New Guinea, and certain "aboriginal" people from India. This could mean that Australia was populated in several waves or that it represents a generalized population that predated many of the human splits that occurred over the past 50,000 years.

How did these waves of migration come in? As we've noted elsewhere, it took sailing to populate Australia and New Guinea more than 50,000 years ago. Some scientists claim there were land bridges connecting everything, but plenty of areas had nothing connecting but several miles of water. As we noted earlier in this book, Australasia (or the Sunda and Sahul) was one of those areas.

So yes, boats. Or canoes. Or some pretty serious rafts. But some sort of watercraft was necessary. And it couldn't have been a few small fishing boats that were simply shipwrecked after getting carried away by an unexpected tradewind or ocean current. We know that these maritime migrations were deliberate because there are computer simulations that factor in normal fertility rates and the genetic diversity of modern populations. These studies tell us that it would have required more than "just a boatload or two of colonists" to establish the kind of aboriginal populations we see today.

BEFORE THE ABORIGINES?

We know that Australia, because of its location, was one the "final destinations" of migrations out of Africa. And until recently, the aboriginal people of Australia didn't have too many visitors. As a result, Australia constitutes one of the oldest continuous sites of settlement by an ancestral population of Black people (outside of Africa and the Andaman Islands) as well as an "outpost" of the Black presence across Asia.

Scientists have traditionally thought that Australia was first settled by the migration that left Africa over 75,000 years ago, arriving there about 70,000 years ago. Thus people assume that the tall "Australoid" aborigines living there today are remnants of the first people in that area. But the aborigines themselves have a rich historical tradition that – in the guise of "myth" – encodes over 50,000 years of community history, including a "Dreamtime" state that may represent a more distant ancestral past.

A critical piece of their historical recollection is the memory of an older population who settled Australia before the present-day aborigines. The folklore of the indigenous people of northern Australia tells of fairy-like beings known as Mimis. They are described as having extremely thin and elongated bodies, so thin as to be in danger of breaking in case of a high wind. To avoid this, they usually spend most of their time living in rock crevices. This is reminiscent of European, Native American, and Chinese myths about the "thief in the night" manner of DBP people, who disappear into the earth and are described with fanciful imagery that emphasizes their diminutive size.

These Mimis are said to have taught the aborigines of Australia how to hunt, prepare kangaroo meat and use fire. They are said to be like humans but they live in a different dimension, perhaps Dreamtime.[295] This reminds us of the click-language Damin, which is said to have been taught by ancestral beings from Dreamtime. Could Damin have come from the Original People who first inhabited Australia?

You might say that we're assuming quite a lot, if all the evidence we have for the DBP in Australia is aborigine myth, huh? As we've said elsewhere, "myth" is just a European word for our version of history and science. And the older the "myth," the closer it is to the truth.

Fortunately, there's scientific evidence to corroborate these histories. The work of anthropologists Keith Windschuttle and Tim Gillin reveals that not only did dark-skinned, "wooly-haired" pygmies inhabit Australia (until relatively recent times), but that the presence of these people was deliberately hidden by most early historians. The Australian DBP, who appear to have survived over 50,000 years, were then systematically destroyed by the colonists (like the extinct Tasmanians).[296]

The archaeological evidence suggests the Original People made it to Australia quite a long time ago. In an alluvial deposit in Western Australia, Mance Lofgren and John Clarke discovered more than 30 stone tools dating back more than 100,000 years

So who pushed the world's first settlers into the margins of existence? Much as taller Bantu people displaced older populations across Africa, the same thing happened throughout the rest of the world. In Australia – long before the Europeans came – the ancestors of today's Aborigines displaced the people who had come before them.

In his 1937 work *Environment, Race, and Migration,* Thomas Griffith Taylor remarks:

> Perhaps we may assume a negrito migration during an early glacial period, when it was easy to get into Papua and also into Melanesia and Australia. Then the Papuan hordes moved to the south after Australia was shut off by the drowning of the Sunda region. They entered Papua at a time when we may imagine extensive deserts in northern Australia for reasons given earlier. They drove the Tapiro into the hill-jungles. Later the first horde of Australians arrived during an Ice Age, when the Sunda and Sahul areas were dry land. They moved down the central rivers to the south-east. They mixed with the negritoes in the south to some extent, producing the Tasmanian type. The next migration drove the Tasmanian further south, and was in turn driven into the thick forested regions of New South Wales by the latest migrations.[297]

These Australians may not have been much taller than the people they displaced, but they settled in such massive numbers that they pushed their predecessors into Tasmania, the island at the southernmost tip of Australia. This may have been what began the "pygmization" process.* Not long after this displacement, Australia soon became heavily desertified.

Considering the ecological knowledge of our earliest ancestors, I wouldn't be surprised if the Original People – who became Australia's DBP – had been the ones keeping Australia's ecosystem compatible with human habitation…until they were removed from their land. Sound familiar?

Genetic studies of surviving populations reveal that at least two distinct groups of ancient people settled Australia after the DBP, one a "more robust" type very early in the continent's history, the other a "more gracile" type much later on. We'll talk about this second population in Part Two.[298]

---

* It seems that the longer the original settlers remained on the fringes, the shorter they became. The Tasmanian "pygmies" were no more than 4 feet, 6 inches tall when anthropologists came to examine them in the 1800s. And once the Europeans arrived, it wasn't long before the Tasmanians – who were virtually cornered – became extinct.

AN INTRODUCTION TO ASTRONOMY

ROBERT BAILEY

Astronomy is the science that studies celestial objects (like stars, planets and galaxies) and other phenomena that occurs in outer space. More specifically, astronomy is concerned with the evolution, motion, physics, classification, nature and meteorology of these celestial objects and cosmology. Astronomy used to be viewed as the same as astrology. According to the book *History of the Inductive Sciences: from the Earliest to the Present Time Vol. 1*, when mysticism was introduced into Greek philosophy, their physical sciences became magic and astronomy gave birth to astrology.[299]

Astronomers obtain their data through ground and space based observations, use computers to make models and simulations, then go on to analyze and record their findings. It isn't a hard science to put into practice, nearly anyone can do it. In fact, amateur astronomy (which is astronomy done by laypeople) has contributed many important discoveries to the field as a whole. After all, Clyde Tombaugh discovered Pluto before he went to college. Bernabe Cobo has written:

"The movements of the heavenly bodies are an admirable thing, well-known and manifest to all peoples. There are no people, no matter how barbaric and primitive, that do not raise up their eyes, take note, and observe with some care and admiration the continuous and uniform course of the heavenly bodies."

From our early beginnings, humans have been looking up and observing the heavens, making astronomy the oldest science. Even with all of today's "advancements," people still look to the skies, lost, searching for answers. Not to say that this is solely always the reason for observation. Practicing astronomy aided farmers and hunters by giving indication of coming seasons and helped numerous people with calendric and navigational purposes.[300] Studies show that Australian aborigines (who've been integrating astronomical information into their oral traditions and daily lives for more than 50,000 years) could be the world's oldest known astronomers.[301] Numerous other indigenous tribes (like the Maori people or the Skidi Band of the Pawnee tribe, for example) have been found to have proficient astronomical knowledge. Moving forward, civilizations such as Ancient Egypt, Greece, China, Mesopotamia, India, Mesoamerica and the Islamic world helped to advance the science. The invention of the telescope helped bring about modern astronomy, in which women were allowed to play a greater role. But you know...WE didn't need telescopes.

PALEOLITHIC ASTRONOMY

In the November 2010 issue of *the Journal for Astronomical History & Heritage*, Hamacher and Frew present evidence that the Boorong people of northwestern Victoria practiced what UniverseToday.com called "astronomy without a telescope." The Boorong – a people who have been in Australia since the Paleolithic – have an oral tradition surrounding Eta Carinae, a massive binary star system – of which the dominant member is an eruptive blue variable star. The system's last significant "eruption" – also known as the 'great outburst' – made Eta Carinae briefly the second brightest star system in the night sky after Sirius (from 1837 to 1845), and then it faded again.

This great outburst left behind the Homunculus Nebula, which – like the Swan nebula – figures into aboriginal mythology. But the Boorong also recorded the eruption of Eta Carinae itself and incorporated the event into their oral traditions, which have basically outlived the prominence of the star system![302]

SIRIUS KNOWLEDGE AMONG THE DOGON

These details remind me of another indigenous people who recorded the patterns of a binary star system into their oral tradition. French anthropologists Marcel Griaule and Germaine Dieterlin, in their 1965 work *The Pale Fox* reported that the Dogon of Mali were well aware of Sirius A as well as its partner Sirius B, despite the fact that Sirius B is not visible to the naked eye.

In an article titled "African Observers of the Universe: the Sirius Question," renowned scientist Hunter Adams remarks:

> Their extensive celestial knowledge, particularly that concerning this invisible star (Sirius B), is a mystery that has sent shock waves around the scientific world.

But this shocking information didn't really hit the mainstream until 1977, when Robert Temple published *The Sirius Mystery*. Temple *seriously* claimed that mysterious spacemen from the Sirius star system must have brought this astronomical knowledge down to the Dogon people (which were never mentioned in *The Pale Fox*).

This is a prime example of why we must consult PRIMARY sources, not simply the second-party and third-party interpretations. You see, Griaule and Dieterlin never claimed to have an explanation for the Dogon's knowledge, saying, "The problem of knowing how, with no

> **Did You Know?**
> As Robert Bailey notes in the 2012 *365 Days of Real Black History Calendar*: "Blacks started astronomy. Ruins of a 300 BC astronomical observatory were found at Namoratunga in Kenya. A stone observatory over 5,000 years old was found west of Egypt."

instruments at their disposal, men could know the movements and certain characteristics of virtually invisible stars has not been settled, nor even posed.[303]

What made it so bad was that Temple wasn't your run-of-the-mill amateur historian with a kooky idea. He was an established member of the Royal Astronomical Society of Great Britain, concocting sheer stupidity just to deny that Africans could generate their own astronomical knowledge!

Science writer Ian Ridpath and astronomer Carl Sagan quickly responded to Temple's ridiculous theory. These scholars offered an equally ridiculous theory: that the Dogon's knowledge must have come from "highly knowledgeable" explorers from Europe or America who came to discuss astronomy with their priests.

But James Oberg, in "debunking" the alien origins of Dogon knowledge, concludes that the "Europeans taught them" theory is just as baseless as the "Aliens taught them" theory:

> The obviously advanced astronomical knowledge must have come from somewhere, but is it an ancient bequest or a modern graft? Although Temple fails to prove its antiquity, the evidence for the recent acquisition of the information is still entirely circumstantial.[304]

In recent years, critics have attempted to dismiss Griaule because he only relied on one Dogon elder and one translator for his information (definitely not the best way to go about such important research), while others, like Temple and Sagan, celebrated his findings only to pervert them for their own agendas.

Now, with this recent evidence from the Boorong in Australia – who recorded similar information about a binary system that was even harder to observe than Sirius – perhaps scientists can agree that the Dogon knew what they were talking about.

And here's the real nail-in-the-coffin. The Dogon spoke of another star in the Sirius system, Emme Ya, or a star "larger than Sirius B but lighter and dim in magnitude." This was before a third star was theorized in the 1950s. Years later, when there was still no evidence of any such star, Robert Temple said, "If a Sirius-C is ever discovered and found to be a red dwarf, I will conclude that the Dogon information has been fully validated." In 1995, gravitational studies confirmed the possibility of a brown dwarf star orbiting around Sirius (a Sirius-C).[305]

THE PRESERVATION OF ASTRONOMICAL KNOWLEDGE

The Dogon created iron artifacts representing the movements of Sirius. Presumably, some of the artifacts of the Boorong could communicate their astronomical knowledge as well. But these wouldn't be iron; they'd most likely be wood (and thus unlikely to last thousands of years).

We do, however, have the Lebombo Bone, the Ishango Bone, the Thaïs Bone, the Abri Blanchard Bone, and the Wolf Bone to confirm that we recorded lunar cycles. Archaeological evidence from the Dordogne region of France suggests that we used a lunar calendar (c. 30,000 BC) and there's other evidence even older than that.[306]

Archaeologists Brian Hayden and Suzanne Villeneuve argue that the techniques for using such tools allowed the holders of this knowledge – most likely the shamans – to develop a 'secret society' of people with astronomical knowledge. Shamans may have also embedded these devices into cupules and other rock art, as well as the cave paintings of the time.

Many Paleolithic caves themselves appear to have been chosen for their orientation to the nighttime sky or daytime stars. Hayden and Villeneuve also suggest natural alignments like trees and posts were used to monitor celestial phenomena, but this practice left few archaeological traces.[307] The tradition of orienting structures on land with structures in the stars is one that the Black builders of civilization carried over into the Neolithic period. We'll discuss this in greater depth in Part Two.

A survey of 26 modern hunter-gather groups revealed that Orion was known to 16 groups, Venus to 15, the Pleiades to 12 and the Milky Way and Ursa Major to 10. Many other constellations and star nebulae enjoyed local fame. But throughout the indigenous world, the consistency is amazing.

For example, the Pleiades are known everywhere as a group of women, and Ursa Major is seen around the world as a bear. What's thought-provoking is that the Ursa Major constellation doesn't even look like a bear! So there must be a common source, which has to at least date back to the Palaeolithic.

This is why we can find similar evidence among other indigenous societies who maintain Paleolithic traditions. Hayden and Villeneuve examined hundreds of indigenous ethnographies and found almost all peoples had a concept of the extreme limits of the Sun and the solstices. They also tied lunar cycles to environmental events, like the appearance of first fruits, or the migration patterns of local wildlife, useful knowledge for people who subsist on hunting and gathering.

Our Paleolithic ancestors used astronomy to schedule social activity, around these ecological events. They developed mythological oral traditions that symbolized this science so future generations could easily preserve the practice. And – at these seasonal celebrations – we ate GOOD.

In fact, this is the era in which competitive feasting emerges. Not competitive EATING (as in who can eat the most), but FEASTING, as in who can provide the most food for their group.[308] Let's talk about THAT for a minute, and maybe we'll see some of what we're missing today.

THE STRUGGLE IN AUSTRALIA

"How can it be, in an egalitarian society, that injustice to the marginalized creates scarcely a ripple? The answer I think is found at the threshold: most Australians do not recognize the original inhabitants, the stolen generations, the faceless asylum seekers, as people: at least, not in the same sense that we are people. Their humanity is of a different order..." – Julian Burnside, On Privilege

Runoko Rashidi has shared the following words on the plight of the Original People of Australia:

Australia was settled at least 60,000 years ago by people usually referred to as the Australian Aborigines. Physically, they are distinguished by straight to wavy hair textures, and dark to near black complexions. In January 1788, when Britain began using Australia as a prison colony, an estimated 300,000 indigenous people were spread across the continent in about six-hundred small-scale societies. Each of these communities maintained social, religious, and trade connections with its neighbors.

The dumping of British convicts into Australia proved catastrophic for the Blacks. Victims of deliberate poisonings, calculated and systematic slaughters; decimated by tuberculosis and syphilis; swept away by infectious epidemics; their community structures and moral fibers shredded, by the 1930's the Aboriginal Australians had been reduced to a pathetic remnant of about 30,000 people, and perhaps twice that number of mixed descent.

When the continent was invaded by Europeans in the nineteenth century, the white historians who wrote about Australia invariably included a section on the Blacks, and acknowledged that the original inhabitants of the continent had had an historical role. After 1850, however, few writers referred to the Blacks at all. The Blacks were thought of as a "dying race." By 1950 general histories of the continent by European-Australians almost never referenced the indigenous people. During this period--the indigenous people--whether part or full blood, were excluded from all major European-Australian institutions, including schools, hospitals and labor unions. They could not vote. Their movements were restricted. They were outcasts in white Australia.

Today, the Blacks of Australia are terribly oppressed, and they remain in a desperate struggle for survival. Recent demographic surveys, for example, show that the Black infant mortality rate is the highest in Australia. Aborigines have the shoddiest housing and the poorest schools. Their life expectancy is twenty years less than Europeans. Their unemployment rate is six times higher than the national average. Aborigines did not obtain the right to vote in federal elections until 1961, nor the right to consume alcoholic beverages until 1964. They were not officially counted as Australian citizens until after a constitutional amendment in 1967. Today, the indigenous people constitute less than three per cent of the total Australian population.

"My view is that the Australian Constitution has served 97 per cent of the nation well. It has not worked, and does not work, for 3 per cent: my people, indigenous Australians. It is broke and was broke for the 3 per cent from the beginning in 1901." – Noel Pearson

To conclude this chapter, I'd like to quote Australian journalist Xavier Herbert, who wrote in 1983:

> Until we give back to the Blackman just a bit of the land that was his and give it back without provisos, without strings to snatch it back, without anything but complete generosity of spirit in concession for the evil we have done him - until we do that, we shall remain what we have always been so far, a people without integrity; not a nation but a community of thieves.[309]

THE PACIFIC ISLANDS

REPRESENTATIVE FACES OF MODERN PACIFIC ISLANDERS

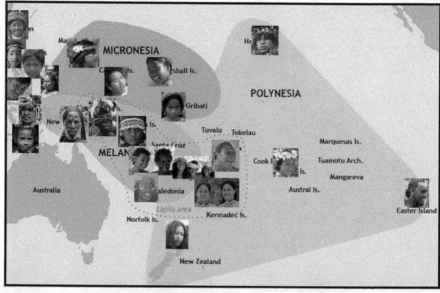

PEOPLE OF THE PACIFIC

The people of the Pacific Ocean clearly have Black roots. The following examples come from Fiji, Papua (New Guinea), and Hawaii.

WWW.WHENTHEWORLDWASBLACK.COM

Their woolly hair suggests that many of these people descend from the migration of Original People that left Africa and spread across the world before the Toba volcano erupted 74,000 years ago. Later Australoid people settled these regions, followed by Mongoloid people associated with modern Polynesians.

THE PACIFIC ISLANDS

THE BLACK AND BROWN ISLANDS

"I have remarked that in this maritime world (the Pacific Islands), Sumatra and Java are the only large islands where they (Negritos) have left no other traces than some doubtful mixed breeds..." – Armand de Quatrefages, The Pygmies

The Pacific Islands are a visual paradise. Their beautiful, pristine natural landscapes are so awe-inspiring that they've provided the backdrops for just about any feature film that takes place in a "land before time" kinda setting.* There are the islands everyone knows about, like New Zealand, Hawaii, and Fiji, but those are really only the tip of the iceberg. In fact, those islands only carry about 2% of the history of the Pacific Islands – partly because their history doesn't go back as far, but also because there are simply so many other islands to consider.

In fact, there are so many islands in the Pacific that people normally discuss them in groups, like Melanesia, Micronesia, and Polynesia. Polynesia alone consists of over 1,000 islands, all settled and resettled by different waves of Original People. Almost all of them were ultimately taken over by Europeans through colonization or conquest. All of these stories, some more tragic than others, begin based upon a Black foundation.

These islands – over 10,000 in all – were originally settled by members of the ancestral human population who became the DBP. Many were later settled by Australoid people, and many more were even later settled by Mongoloid people. Some of these people ultimately traveled from the Pacific Islands into the Americas.

In *The Negro in the New World*, Sir Harry Hamilton Johnston writes:

> To this day dwarf negro people survive in the Far East – the

---

* For example, *The Lord of the Rings* trilogy and *The Chronicles of Narnia* were filmed in New Zealand. *Jurassic Park* was filmed in Hawaii.

Samang in the forests of the Malay Peninsula and the Aeta in the Philippine Islands. There are traces of the passage of a negroid people through Sumatra and Borneo, in the island of Timor, and markedly so in New Guinea, though here they have mingled with the Australoid and have produced the well-marked Papuan race.

The existing populations of the Solomon Islands, of New Ireland, and of the New Hebrides are much more negro-like in physical characteristics; in fact, perhaps the people of New Ireland are the most nearly akin to the African negro of all the Asiatic or Australasian peoples.

Asiatic negroes also seem to have entered Australia from New Guinea and to have passed down the eastern part of that continent till they reached the then peninsula of Tasmania, not, of course, without mingling with the Australoids.

There is a negroid (Melanesian) element in Fiji, and as far west as the Hawaii Archipelago and among the Maoris of New Zealand; in a much less degree, also, in Burma, Annam, Hainan, Formosa, the Riu-Kiu Islands, and Southern Japan.[310]

MELANESIA

The Original People ventured far beyond the islands of Southeast Asia. They continued east, becoming the first to settle the Pacific islands. Their first destination may have been the islands of Melanesia. Well-known parts of Melanesia include: New Guinea, Fiji, the Solomon Islands, the Torres Strait Islands, the Trobriand Islands, and Vanuatu.*

The Pacific Islands are unique because anthropologists say the Black people living there were, like many Australian Aborigines, still living in the Stone Age! We've already shown that "Stone Age" culture can be entirely sufficient for meeting a people's needs, but the story of the Pacific Islands can take us even deeper. Without calling their culture "primitive" as others have done, historian Nicholas Wade credits this fact to the tribalization of places like New Guinea, where 1200 different languages occupy a region about the size of Texas.

But were the people of the Pacific Islands in a state of "stunted growth?" Digging into this question makes us revisit the idea of "change vs. progress" and the meaning of civilization. What does progress really mean? If it ain't broke, do we need to fix it? Just

---

* A more complete list includes Amphlett Islands, Bismarck Archipelago, d'Entrecasteaux Islands, Louisiade Archipelago, Maluku Islands, New Caledonia, Norfolk Island, Raja Ampat Islands, Schouten Islands, Santa Cruz Islands, and Woodlark Island.

something to consider as we discuss the history of the world's cultures and civilizations.

NEW GUINEA

In 1526, Portuguese explorers come across a land that had not yet been conquered by any European nation. Jorge de Meneses, the first Portuguese governor of the Moluccas, named the island *Ilhas dos Papuas* based on the Malay name for its people *Orang papuwah*, which means "frizzy-haired people." These people, later known as the Papuans, represent what Lothrop Stoddard called the eastern end of the "black belt" that once "stretched uninterruptedly from Africa across southern Asia to the Pacific Ocean."

The Papuans know of this belt. In the 1970s, Ben Tanggahma, Foreign Minister of Papua New Guinea announced:

> Africa is our motherland. All of the Black populations which settled in Asia over the hundreds of thousands of years, came undoubtedly from the African continent. In fact, the entire world was populated from Africa. Hence, we the Blacks in Asia and the Pacific today descend from proto-African peoples. We were linked to Africa in the past. We are linked to Africa in the present. We will be linked to Africa in the future.[311]

As early as 49,000 BC, Blacks were living in the highlands of New Guinea, using stone axes with wooden handles to remove trees, which scientists see as evidence "that the early inhabitants cleared forest patches to promote the growth of useful plants."[312] Anthropologist John Hawks observed:

> The "Highland" aspect is more interesting, suggesting a fairly quick adaptability of early humans to a novel ecology. People had found the local plant foods in a unique ecology, they were exploiting a range of altitudes in their foraging activities, and possibly were altering their landscapes by forest clearing.[313]

This is, as noted elsewhere in this book, an early example of our agricultural knowledge, before the widespread use of agriculture.

But how do we know the DBP were here? In *The Times* of June 3, 1910, an expedition organized by the British Ornithologists' Union reported a tribe of little Black people still living in the snow mountains of New Guinea, at an altitude of about 2,000 feet above sea level.[314] Guess what? After thousands of years of occupation in these colder regions, they were still Black.

What were they doing in these mountains? The first humans in New Guinea may have been remnants of the Original People who left the Nubian Complex long before 75,000 years ago. I'll explain.

There are two large language families in Melanesia: Austronesian and "Papuan." Austronesian originated somewhere in southern China or Southeast Asia and began expanding into Melanesia and Polynesia within the last 4,000 years. Most of these newer populations settled in places that were already settled by older people speaking incredibly old languages known as Papuan.* In other words, the Papuans are the original people of the area. They were there long before Austronesian people came with the science of planting crops and stonemasonry.

HOW LONG HAVE THEY BEEN THERE?

Genetic studies suggest that 84% of the Papuan people of New Guinea descend from lineages that go back to between 80,000 and 122,000 years ago, suggesting they could be survivors of a pre-Toba migration out of the Nubian Complex.[315]

Dr. Victor Grauer has theorized that these Blacks were once settled in Australia, but encroaching waves of Australoid people sent them fleeing. Some went south into Tasmania, others sought refuge in the tropical forests of Northeast Queensland (which was, according to Birdsell's research, once home to small groups of Pygmies), and still others went north into New Guinea. According to Grauer:

> If the newcomers had arrived while New Guinea was still attached to Australia, the refugees could have made their way north by land, but if the sea had already separated the two regions, they could have retreated in boats or rafts, at least while the distance was not too great. The Australoid invaders would have followed them, and at that time taken over the New Guinea coast, while the natives retreated into the highlands.

When Mongoloid people speaking Austronesian languages migrated into Melanesia between around 5,000 years ago, they, in turn, displaced these Australoid people. Grauer says:

> Their only recourse would have been a retreat into the highlands, which would therefore have come to harbor a mixed population, partly of "Negrito" and partly of Australoid origin. Since these groups would have formerly been bitter enemies, it's not difficult to see how the endemic warfare we now see in the New Guinea highlands could have originated at this point, although many of these populations seem ultimately to have merged, both physically and culturally.[316]

---

* The so-called "Papuan" languages are actually a large group of unrelated language families – along with several languages regarded as unaffiliated "isolates" – spoken by people living, for the most part, in the interior highlands.

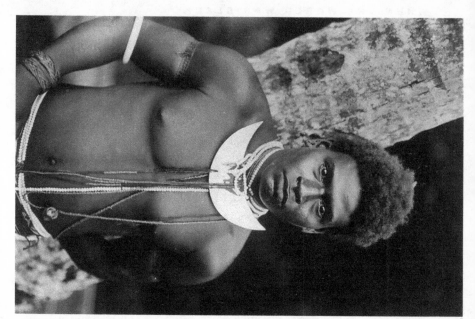

THE SOLOMON-ISLANDS

BLACK POLYNESIANS?

Fiji is the easternmost island of Melanesia. Most of us don't associate Fiji with Black people, and assume it is mostly Polynesian. Not so. Others assume that, beyond Fiji, Black people didn't settle the Polynesian Islands. Also not true.

INDIGENOUS MEN OF FIJI

(YES, THAT'S AN AFRO PICK)

New Zealand is a similar story. Few of us know how deep its Black history is.

Members of the Black Power "street gang" circa 1979

This isn't from the U.S. This is New Zealand. Members were Maori and Polynesian.

NINETEENTH CENTURY IMAGES OF THE MAORI

The story doesn't stop there.

Samoans also have Black roots.

On every Polynesian island, even Hawaii, you can find traces of a Black presence.

Sounds like a troubled past. Yet within the past 300 years, the Black people of New Guinea have suffered more threats to their existence than in the preceding 50,000 years combined. First the Spanish came in 1545, introducing deadly diseases and escalating local conflicts into wars. Then the Dutch took over, making things worse. In 1963, the United Nations passed control of half the island to Indonesia (who had already been colonized and "rewired"). The eastern half of the island remained independent, known today as Papua, New Guinea, while the western half became Irian Jaya, commonly known just as Papua.

There, Indonesian rule has been as oppressive as those of their Dutch predecessors. This is why the Free Papua Movement (OPM) was formed. The Republic of Senegal promptly offered the Papuans an international base for a movement known as the Revolutionary Provisional Government of West Papua, New Guinea.[317] Today, many Papuans identify with the Black Nationalism and Black Liberation movements of the U.S.

FIJI

Fiji is an island nation in the South Pacific, comprising over 300 islands in Melanesia. Its largest island is Viti Levu (or "Great Fiji"), where most Fijians live today.

According to the oral tradition of the indigenous people of Fiji, legendary warrior chief Lutanasobasoba led his people across the seas to the new land of Fiji. From where? One textbook on Fiji reports, "Most authorities agree that people came into the Pacific from East Africa or South East Asia via Indonesia."[318]

The legend of Chief Lutanasobasoba is more specific. The Fijians say he sailed from Lake Tanganyika in East Africa, via the Rufiji River that crosses Tanzania. They arrived on the west coast of Viti Levu, the chief was immortalized as *Degei*, the Supreme God of Fiji, and his people moved inland into the mountains.

Today, the Fijian government recognizes this origin story as historical fact, and most Fijians trace themselves back to their African ancestor Lutanasobasoba.[319]

In one of his many commentaries on the global Black Diaspora, historian Runoko Rashidi describes his experience in Fiji:

> I found Fiji to be a tropical paradise and the Fijians turned out to be some of the most beautiful Black people that I've ever encountered. In fact, much to my delight, the brothers and sisters in Fiji, dark-skinned Black people who wore big natural-type hairstyles, didn't merely identify themselves as Black but said that they came from

Africa and said it with great pride! What a refreshing revelation. In Fiji, needless to point out, I felt right at home. These Black folk were just my kind of people.

What Rashidi says next is of incredible value to all of us who want to travel abroad:

As a matter of fact, the brothers and sisters in Fiji that I met seemed as interested in me as I was in them. Believe me when I say that if there is one thing that I excel in it is in asking questions and I asked the Fijians all kinds of questions about exactly what part of Africa they came from, when they got to Fiji, how they got there, what their present living conditions were like, what was their relationship with the recently arrived Indian population, how did they feel about White people, the nature of their oral traditions, myths and religious beliefs, male-female relationships, diet, health, other Pacific islanders, general projections about the future and just about everything that I could think of. They never got tired of answering my questions and had quite a few for me also. They told me that the two most well known African-Americans were Rev. Martin Luther King and Muhammad Ali. Of course, they knew about Michael Jordan and Magic Johnson and most of the major African-American sport figures. One Fijian brother, a businessman that I met in the lobby of a luxury hotel, told me how proud he was of the brothers and sisters in America and how much African-Americans had advanced the cause of Black people around the world.

I asked the Fijians how often they encountered Black people from the United States. They replied that African-Americans frequently came to Fiji for holiday vacations but that I was different in that I spent a lot of time with them and wanted to know all about them...The Fijians always referred to me as "brother" and singled me out for special treatment. We drank kava together (an extremely important Fijian tradition) and really bonded, and I met people who looked like all the Black folks that I have ever known. In fact, one village chief physically seemed to be almost a twin brother of Dr. John Henrik Clarke! When I told him of the resemblance he seemed to be extremely pleased and insisted that I come and sit next to him![320]

THE SOLOMON ISLANDS

The Solomon Islands are important to our discussion of the Black presence in the Pacific Islands because they reveal to us yet another case of the startling diversity found among indigenous Black populations. You see, many of the people of the Solomon Islands look just like Black people elsewhere in the world...except they have blonde hair! For centuries, it was thought that early European sailors (like Captain Cook's crew) must have "contributed their genes" (ahem) to the island's native women, and that's where all this blonde hair came from. But recent genetic studies have revealed that the blonde hair genes of Solomon Islanders is different from the blonde hair genes found in white Europeans. Of course, the Black version of the gene is older, but it's totally unrelated to the white version, showing us that they were separate developments. This is just one of many instances where we find every imaginable trait found in the world...among Black people.

MICRONESIA

Micronesia isn't all well-known as its more popular siblings, Melanesia and Polynesia. Well-known parts of Micronesia include Guam and the Marshall Islands. The Micronesian culture was one of the last native cultures to develop in the Pacific. It is the byproduct of a mixture of Melanesians, Polynesians, and Filipinos. Because of this mixed heritage, many of the ethnicities of Micronesia feel closer to some groups in Melanesia, Polynesia or the Philippines.

POLYNESIA

So who are the Polynesians? Well-known parts of Polynesia include: Hawaii, New Zealand, Samoa, the Cook Islands, and Easter Island.* Historians argue that the Polynesian Islands were settled no more than 5,000 years ago, and Melanesian or Australians never sailed that far.

There really isn't strong archaeological evidence for settlements more than 5,000 years old, but how did Australian-looking people arrive in the Americas over 20,000 years ago if they didn't pass through the Polynesian Islands? It's a question worth investigating. In *Ethiopia and the Origin of Civilization*, John G. Jackson says, "These Asiatic black men were not confined to the mainland," and quotes Sir Harry Hamilton Johnston, who wrote:

> In former times this Asiatic Negro spread, we can scarcely explain how, unless the land connections of those days were more extended, through Eastern Australia to Tasmania, and from the Solomon Island to New Caledonia and even New Zealand, to Fiji and Hawaii.[321]

Here's what we know so far. Recent linguistic studies suggest that the most recent waves of Black migration into Polynesia (hailing from

---

* A more complete list includes French Polynesia, Niue, Norfolk Island, Pitcairn Islands, Rotuma, Tokelau, Tonga, Tuvalu, Wallis, and Futuna.

South China and Vietnam) encountered "mixed communities" already there. These communities were a mix of Austro-Asiatic/Austronesian speakers from Taiwan and non-Austronesian (possibly "Papuan") speakers from Melanesia.[322] In other words, the linguistic evidence ALSO suggests that the Original People made it past Melanesia into Polynesia.

In 1870, Thomas Huxley observed:

> As linguistic evidence leaves no doubt that Polynesia has been peopled from the west, and therefore, possibly, from Indonesia, it becomes an interesting problem how far the Polynesians may be the product of a cross between the Dyak-Malay and the Negrito elements of the population of that region. I am inclined to think that the differences which have been over and over again noted between the elements of the population in Polynesia, and notably in New Zealand, may be due to such a mixed origin of the Polynesians.[323]

According to Alfred R. Wallace, the "brown Polynesians" were "much more nearly related to the Papuans than to the Malays, and should therefore be classed as Negroid instead of Mongoloid." Wallace found the Polynesians to carry themselves like Africans and "Negroid" Papuans, with great energy and humor, as opposed to the more somber demeanor of Australoid people. Wallace maintained "that the typical Polynesians were fundamentally Negroid with a considerable Mongoloid intermixture, and not originally Mongoloid with a Negroid intermixture."[324] Others have argued that the "Negroid" element came later, an issue we'll discuss in Part Two.

SAMOA

Earlier in this book, we discussed "Paleo-Mongoloid" people. One example of a Paleo-Mongoloid people still living today may be the Samoans. Physical anthropologist Louis R. Sullivan considers Samoans Mongoloid but says their features represent a "slightly different evolution since the time of their separation and isolation from their parental stock." Sullivan notes the retention of features, like wavy and woolly hair, that have been lost in other Mongoloid types.[325]

In other words, Samoans still have the original Black traits their ancestors had, minus the "Neo-Mongoloid" traits found among other population. Perhaps this explains why Samoans share genes with Australian Aborigines.[326]

These Black genes may also help explain why Samoans are one of the most maligned populations among Polynesians. Samoans are

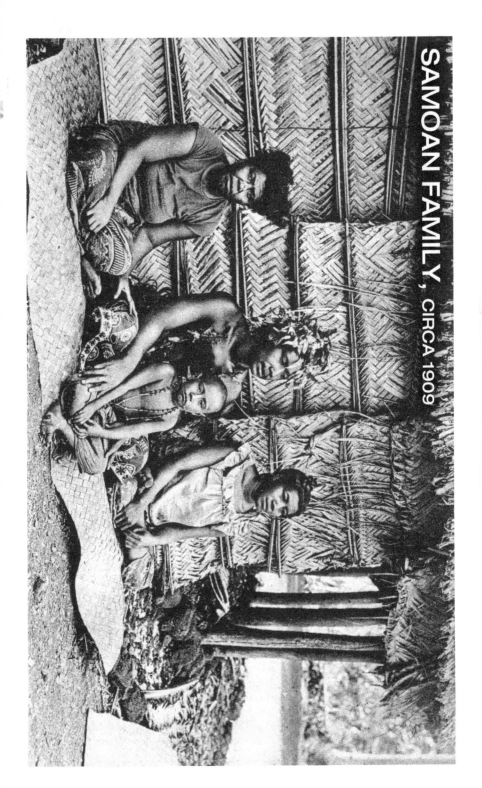

SAMOAN FAMILY, CIRCA 1909

seen as warriors, criminals, and a ton of other bad things. When we consider how much they look like Black people, it makes sense. And if you think the Samoans have it bad, wait til you hear the story of the Maori.

THE MAORI OF NEW ZEALAND

The Maori are the indigenous people of New Zealand. Where did the Maori people come from? Their oral history goes all the way back to mainland Asia. But that's where you've gotta sift through the lies.

Some online sources claim that Maori elders told veteran anthropologist Elsdon Best that they migrated from India 161 generations ago (approximately 1500 BC), after a "disastrous war with a dark-skinned folk, in which great numbers were slain." When I encountered this reference, I thought to myself, "But the Maori are dark-skinned (and were even more so in the past), so why would they point out the dark skin of the people they were at war with?"

When I dug up the original sources, I found that the Maori have quite a different story of their migration. In "The Origin of the Maori," Elsdon Best actually reported the following:

> The East Coast natives of our North Island have preserved the following tradition of the original homeland. In remote times the ancestors of the Maori dwelt in the lands of Uru and of Irihia, two distinct regions of, apparently, an extensive land. A state of war in the land of Uru led to the migration of a certain people under a chief named Puhi-rangirangi (given as Ngana-te-ariki in another version). These migrants proceeded eastward because one Tu-te-rangiatea had informed them that away to the east of the mainland (or interior lands) of Uru lay a goodly land called Irihia. That land of Irihia was inhabited by a dark skinned, spare built folk, whose food supplies were fish, and ari, and kata, and porokakata, and tahuwaero, and koropiri. A leading chief of these folk of Irihia was one Kopura, a person of great mana, whose followers were so numerous that a local saying was:—"Tena te ngaoko na me te onepu moana." ("Yonder they move like unto sands of the ocean.") Upwards of seven hundred and fifty chiefs were under his sway.
>
> The names applied to these people by the immigrants from Uru are terms betokening their dark skin colour. It is said they had peculiar side glancing eyes. Some of the tribes of Irihia were folk of low culture, who lived wandering lives in the forests. War seems to have raged between the immigrants and the people of Irihia, the former suffering severely, hence eventually they, or some of them, left the land of Irihia in seven vessels and sailed away to the eastward in search of a new home. These were the ancestors of the Polynesians who wandered from isle to isle until their descendants reached,

explored and settled the innumerable isles of Polynesia. Probably this was not the only party of migrants that left the land of Irihia to seek new homes across the sea.[327]

Where was Irihia? The name comes from Vrihia, an ancient name for India. And Uru? That may have been Ur or Uruk, two of ancient Mesopotamia's oldest cities. Is there any merit to this story? Well, Elsdon Best – unlike many anthropologists of his era – was not known for altering the stories he recorded (or making up his own stories). And the Maori could not have known about the rugged tribal people who lived in the forests of India (pushed there by the Aryan invasion) without some sort of firsthand knowledge.

If their oral tradition is true, they arrived at New Zealand after settling a long stretch of islands. Their oral tradition also describes their ancestors settling Hawaii and Fiji. This is when I realized that not all Maori are dark-skinned. There are Maori who are distinctly more Polynesian in looks and ancestry. The migration myth above was the story of the ancestors of the Polynesians being expelled from India. In *Polynesian Voyagers*, Best reports:

> The cause of the exodus from the homeland, which is said to have been a great country, was a disastrous war with a darkskinned folk, in which great numbers were slain. It is possible that the scattered colonies of Polynesians found occupying islands in Melanesia and Micronesia are descendants of settlers left at such places during the eastward movement, or such colonies may have been an ethnic backwash of later centuries – some assuredly were.
>
> Again, who were the negroid-like people of Maori tradition spoken of as dwelling on various isles of eastern Polynesia thirty generations ago?...If Melanesian, were they a remnant of an original population of those isles, or were they new-comers? If the latter, how is it that we see nothing in tradition pointing to Melanesian navigation of wide seas at that period?
>
> Cook remarked that the natives of Ra'iatea (Rangiatea) seemed in 'general smaller and blacker than those of the neighbouring islands...The natives of the Bay of Plenty district have preserved a tradition of a vessel having reached Whakatane many generations ago the crew of which was composed of a very-dark-skinned people. These immigrants, probably castaways from a drift voyage, are said to have settled at Omeheu, on the Rangitaiki River.[328]

DID BLACK PEOPLE COME FIRST OR LATER?

Various studies of the Maori people cite them having "Australoid (Tasmanoid) and Polynesian components" as well as Melanesian blood.[329] But when did these people come? As we mentioned earlier, this is a subject of debate, with some sources saying Black people came first, while others say Black people came later.

According to T.H. Mollison, the Maori is a mixed group, mainly Polynesian with an "Australoid-Melanesian" element in its past, possibly related to the "dark pre-Polynesian population in New Zealand."[330] H.L. Shapiro says, "The mixture of this aboriginal population with the invading Polynesians varied according to locality, thus producing the present tribal differentiation among the Maori."[331]

In other words, the Maori, like the Samoans, like most other Pacific Islanders and Southeast Asian, are **a mix of "aboriginal" Black people and Mongoloid people who came later.**

THE MODERN MAORI QUAGMIRE

The Maori have a long history of being brave warriors. They observed a strict honor code and were skilled on the battlefield – but when the Europeans came in the late 1700s, bringing a battery of diseases (including, measles, influenza, typhoid, and cholera) – they quickly lost battles they never had the resources to fight. Their populations fell from at least 200,000 in 1769, when Captain Cook arrived, to less than 56,000 in 1858. Along with their personal cache of deadly germs, the Europeans also brought loaded muskets.

Between the 1820 and 1830s, many Maori warriors died in the musket wars, while their kin died at home from disease. Meanwhile, the missionaries campaigned as hard as always. By the 1840s, a majority of the Maoris were Christian converts, having lost much of their traditional culture in this tragic period. In 1840, however, New Zealand was annexed by Great Britain. The British government feared continued resistance (or an extinct labor force), so they promised the Maori land rights and civil rights in exchange for their sovereignty. This agreement became known as the Treaty of Waitangi, New Zealand's founding document.

In recent times, the Māori protest movement has resurfaced as an indigenous rights movement in New Zealand. Through the tireless efforts of movement organizers and mobilized Maori people, they've established the Waitangi Tribunal,* won the return of some Māori land, made the Māori language an official language of New Zealand, and popularized campaigns against racism. Their movement is part of a broader Māori Renaissance.

---

* An official process by which Maori can raise and investigate breaches of the promises made to the Maori in the Treaty of Waitangi, which established British rule of New Zealand, by a coalition of Maori chiefs under considerable pressure.

The first act of the Māori protest movement was when a handful of elders boycotted Waitangi Day* in 1968 in protest over the Māori Affairs Amendment Act. A small protest was also held at parliament, but neither event made much impact. In 1971, a youth movement known as the Ngā Tamatoa (the "Young Warriors") tried a different approach, disrupting the Waitangi Day celebrations by chanting and performing *haka* (the traditional war cry and dance) during speeches, not to mention attempting to destroy the flag! Needless to say, it was THIS event that led to the explosive growth of the Māori protest movement, and protest has been a feature of Waitangi Day *ever since*.

But being characterized as rebellious warriors comes with its downsides. In 2006, Dr. Rod Lea, a genetic epidemiologist, told the International Conference of Human Genetics in Brisbane that Maori men were born with a "warrior gene." That is, Maori were twice as likely as Europeans to bear a gene connected with risk-taking behavior like smoking, gambling, and criminal activity. He said the discovery went "a long way to explaining some of the problems" Maoris had in New Zealand.

Maori people were outraged. Tariana Turia, a co-leader of the Maori party, said the findings were incredible. "I have never felt criminally inclined," he said. "And I'm very pleased to say that the majority of Maori people don't feel criminally inclined." Brian Dickson, a respected Maori elder, said: "I could wrap all his words up in one – colonization."

In New Zealand, Maoris are convicted of more than 65% of all offenses, despite making up only 15% of the population. Sound familiar? But New Zealand's white population (which includes a sizable number of skinheads and Neo-Nazis) doesn't entirely hate/fear the Maoris. New Zealand's most popular sport is rugby. Rugby teams are dominated by Maoris. In fact, New Zealand's national team is named the 'All Blacks.' Sound familiar again? This struggle is a global one, and I can't wait to explain its origins and pathology in Volume Four of this series.

---

* A holiday celebrating the signing of the Treaty of Waitangi.

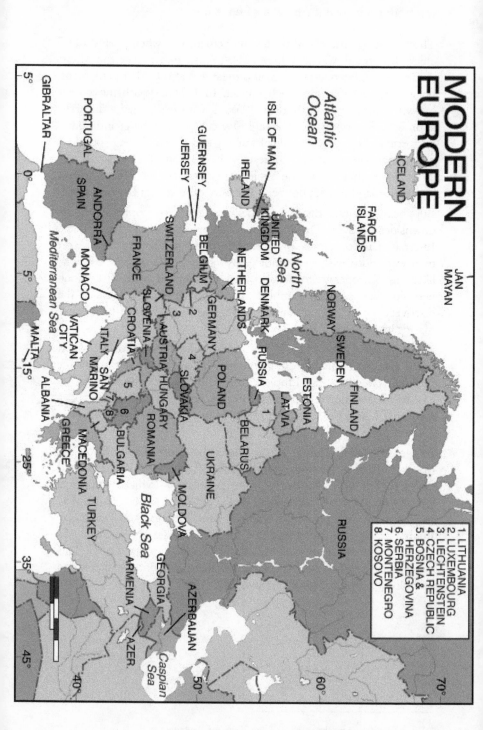

MODERN EUROPE

Atlantic
Ocean

JAN
MAYAN

ICELAND

FAROE
ISLANDS

ISLE OF MAN

IRELAND

GUERNSEY

JERSEY

UNITED
KINGDOM

North
Sea

NORWAY

SWEDEN

FINLAND

GIBRALTAR

PORTUGAL

SPAIN

ANDORRA

MONACO

VATICAN
CITY

FRANCE

SWITZERLAND

BELGIUM

NETHERLANDS

DENMARK

GERMANY

RUSSIA

ESTONIA

LATVIA

Mediterranean Sea

MALTA

ITALY

SAN
MARINO

SLOVENIA

CROATIA

AUSTRIA

HUNGARY

SLOVAKIA

POLAND

BELARUS

ALBANIA

GREECE

MACEDONIA

TURKEY

BULGARIA

ROMANIA

UKRAINE

MOLDOVA

Black Sea

RUSSIA

GEORGIA

AZERBAIJAN

ARMENIA

AZER.

Caspian
Sea

2
3
4
5
6
7
8

1. LITHUANIA
2. LUXEMBOURG
3. LIECHTENSTEIN
4. CZECH REPUBLIC
5. BOSNIA &
   HERZEGOVINA
6. SERBIA
7. MONTENEGRO
8. KOSOVO

5°
0°
5°
15°
25°
35°
45°
40°
50°
60°
70°

THE FIRST EUROPEANS

There's more to the Black foundations of Europe than the Grimaldi remains. In fact, even with the diversity of early human faces, the oldest European remains all carry features that would make them look "Black" in any American setting.

SUNGIR RECONSTRUCTIONS

SUNGIR MAN, RUSSIA
26,000 BC

Note the diversity in the three faces in this family. Clearly, all Black people don't look alike!

CRO-MAGNON MAN

RUSSIAN RECONSTRUCTION   **AMERICAN VERSION**

SUNGIR BOY, RUSSIA
26,000 BC

Below: One of the most important (and recent) reconstructions.

"THE FACE OF THE FIRST EUROPEAN"

Different artists can reconstruct the same skull in different ways. For example, above, there are two reconstructions of the same "Cro-Magnon" skull. Notice that the American version looks less "Negroid."

ROMANIA
34,000 BC

KOSTENKI MAN, RUSSIA
30,000 BC

EUROPE

BEFORE WHITE PEOPLE

"The discoveries of abundant prehistoric remains all over Europe, particularly France – these with one accord tended to show that European aborigines of the Stone Age were not Mongoloid like the Lapps, after all but the exact opposite. In every detail they resembled rather the dolichocephalic Negroes of Africa." – William Z. Ripley, The Races of Europe

WHO WAS THE FIRST EUROPEAN?

On May 4th, 2009, one of Britain's biggest national newspapers, *The Independent*, published an article on its website titled "Revealed: The Face of the First European." The byline below the title read "35,000-year-old skull fragments found in Romania are made flesh by scientists." Sounded interesting.

There was a large picture beside the article's text. You'd think it would be the face of the...um...first European, right? It was Tom Hanks. And, at the date of this writing, it's still Tom Hanks.[332] You don't get to see the face of this first European until you click to the second page. This would seem odd, until you see the picture. Then it all makes sense. The reconstructed face is undeniably a Black man.

You're already pretty familiar with the story of the Black campaign against the Neanderthals, so it shouldn't come as that much of a surprise to you that the first humans in Europe were Black. But for white historians and archaeologists, it's been a tough pill to swallow. And they've been swallowing it long before 2009. You just might not have known that they knew.

EUROPE IS WHERE THE ARCHAEOLOGISTS WENT

Archaeologists have only recently begun digging into Africa (outside Egypt), Asia (outside the Near East), Australia, South America, and the Pacific Islands. And we all know why. But as Europeans have excavated all over Europe in search of the white man's prehistoric past, their discoveries have been bittersweet. While the earliest sites of settlement provide fantastic evidence of "advanced" culture and technology, often more than 25,000 years ago, the evidence also suggests something disturbing for many European academics. The most consistent thing about all these sites? Everything looks like Black people.

THE FIRST REPRESENTATIONS OF HUMANS IN EUROPE

Ever heard of the Venus figurines? Long before the Roman sculptures of the goddess Venus, prehistoric artists were making their own three-dimensional tributes to the feminine form. Although the Roman Venus was based on the Egyptian *Hathor*, she was sculpted with typical European features. The prehistoric Venus figurines, on the other hand, looked very much like Black women.

Archaeologist Edouard Piette, who discovered some of the oldest Paleolithic figurines over 100 years ago, cited their "unusual condition of steatopygia"* as proof of "the Negroid race of Europe."[333] He was perplexed by the "racial differences within the collection of figurines and the resemblance of some of them to African populations,"[334] but remained adamant that "they should be read literally as realistic depictions of human anatomy"[335] since the people of the period were "profound realists" who "represented themselves in engraving and sculpture."[336] In other words, he was saying, **"These were definitely Black people."**†

Many early historians believed that the Paleolithic in Europe extended to North Africa, and theorized that the Khoisan (or their prehistoric ancestors) were responsible for prehistoric European art. As Sir Arthur Evans noted in 1901:

> The negroid contributions at least in the southern zone of this late Quaternary field must not be underestimated The early steatopygous images – such as some of these of the Balzi Rossi caves – may safely be regarded as due to this ethnic type which is

---

* "Steatopygia" technically means an accumulation of fat in the posterior (which juts out from the lower back at a pronounced angle). In laymen's terms, it simply means "big booty." As it occurs naturally, it is unique to Black women.

† However, the African-presence theory proposed by Piette quickly lost ground after the 1920s and was replaced by new theories that maintained the idea of realistic body portrayal yet somehow removed any mention of Black people. The new non-racial theories proposed that these figurines had large hips and butts because they represented a "mother goddess" – even though these figurines were often found accompanied by sculptures of males, and almost never with an actual child.

also pictorially represented in some of the Spanish rock paintings...Once more, we must never lose sight of the fact that from the early Aurignacian period onward a Negroid element in the broadest sense of the word shared in this artistic culture as seen on both sides of the Pyrenees.[337]

These Venus figurines are found far and wide throughout the ancient world. And they most definitely represented Black women. Not just the "steatopygia," but the face and hair texture (when included) are giveaways, as is the black or dark brown color of the stones most preferred.

These figurines may have been celebrations of the woman, but we don't know much for sure beyond that about their significance. We know that archaeologists like James Mellaart fabricated the "Mother Goddess" myth by neglecting to mention the male figurines that were found alongside the females. We also know that they were part of an artistic tradition dating back over 500,000 years in Africa.*

We also know that they continued to be crafted up to about 2,000 BC in ancient Crete, Libya, and Egypt, and until much more recently in other parts of the world. British archaeologist John Pendlebury thought their original home was in North Africa.[338] In fact, Piette saw the figurines of Paleolithic Europe as so similar to Egyptian models that he called them "uncontestably Egyptian in nature."[339]

Steatopygous figurines are found in Neolithic strata nearly everywhere the "Mediterranean race" is said to have been. In ancient Crete, for example, the majority of female figurines are short and stout with what excavator Sir Arthur Evans called an "extraordinary development of the rump, which is often even more prominent than that of the modern Bushman women."[340] Italian physiologist Angelo Mosso compared the Cretan figurines to similar models from pre-Dynastic Egypt, and noted:

> The theory [of their origins] is complicated by the presence of steatopygous women in the interior of Africa, and by the preference for fat women shown by men in the East. We shall see that the present inclination of the African populations for fat women already existed in the Neolithic age, and this atavism deserves to be recorded in the psychology of the peoples.

---

* The two earliest examples are the Venus of Berekhat Ram, found in present-day Syria, and dated to at least 230,000 years ago; and the Venus of Tan-Tan, found in Morocco, and dated to between 300,000 and 500,000 years ago. The use of red ochre on this figurine to simulate reddish-brown skin, as is the case with many Venus figurines, suggest that the Tan-Tan statuette is the earliest Venus figurine, and possibly the earliest representation of the human form.

THE VENUS FIGURINES OF EUROPE

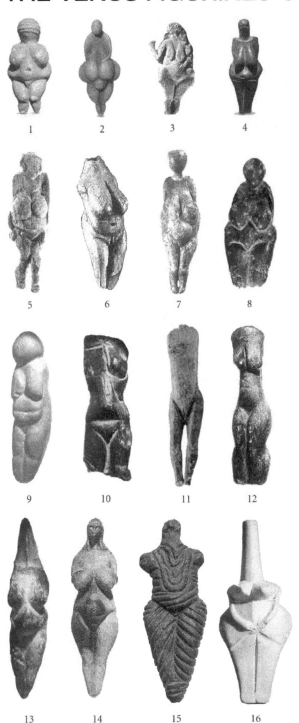

(1) Venus of Willendorf (Rhine/Danube)

(2) Lespugue Venus (Pyrenees/Aquitaine)

(3) Laussel Venus (Pyrenees/Aquitaine)

(4) Dolní Věstonice Venus (Rhine/Danube)

(5) Gagarino Venus (Russia)

(6) Moravany Venus (Rhine/Danube)

(7) Kostenki Statuette no. 3 (Russia)

(8) Grimaldi Venus (Italy)

(9) Chiozza di Scandiano Venus (Italy)

(10) Petrkovice Venus (Rhine/Danube)

(11) Venus Impudique (France)

(12) Eleesivitchi Venus (Russia)

(13) Savignano Venus (Italy)

(14) Brassempouy Venus (Pyrenees/Aquitaine)

(15) Venus Roumanie (Romania)

(16) Golovita Figurine (Romania)

What do these figurines have in common? They're obviously all women. Some are slim, while some are either obese or pregnant. Few have faces or hair. What do they share? They're all built like Black women. You'll need to turn them around to see.

A CLOSE-UP OF VENUS

Rarely does a Venus have hair or facial features. When they do, both are unmistakeably Black. Black stone is preferred to portray faces.

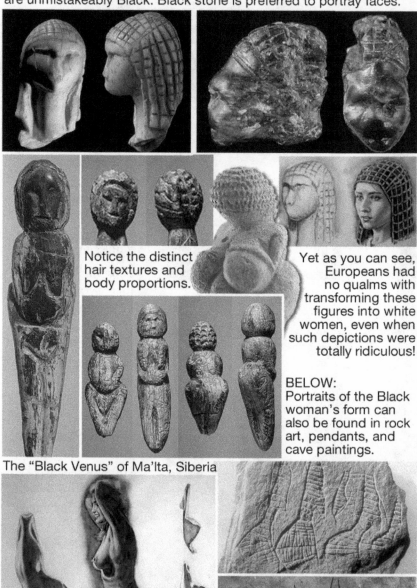

Notice the distinct hair textures and body proportions.

Yet as you can see, Europeans had no qualms with transforming these figures into white women, even when such depictions were totally ridiculous!

BELOW: Portraits of the Black woman's form can also be found in rock art, pendants, and cave paintings.

The "Black Venus" of Ma'lta, Siberia

The "White Venus" of some European artist's imagination.

THE OTHER SIDE OF VENUS

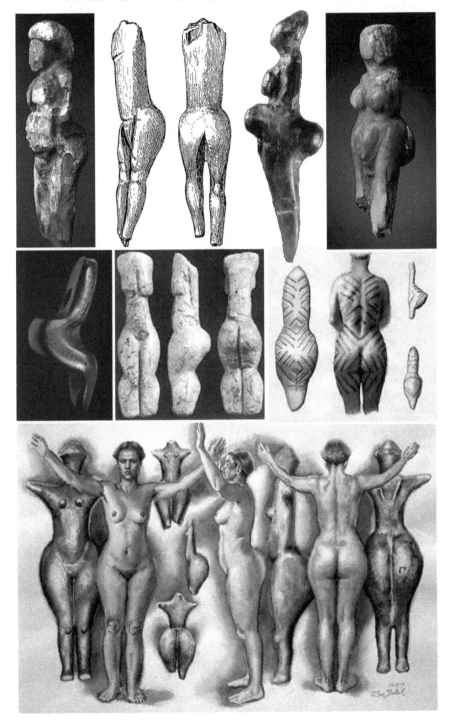

BLACK VENUS

For the first forty years after the Venus figurines of Paleolithic Europe were discovered, white historians said the women they depicted and the artists who created them, were Black people. In later years, they recanted.

ABOVE: Carved into a cave wall in southern France, the 25,000-year-old Venus of Laussel is not only an early Venus, but a depiction of one of the first calendars, made by a woman keeping track of her menstrual cycles by carving marks onto a horn.

TOP RIGHT: Louis Mascare's 1914 clay sculpture of prehistorian Aime Rutot's vision of the Venus of Laussel. On its base an inscription reads *"Negroide de Laussel, Drodogne."*

BOTTOM RIGHT: Part of the frieze sculpted by Constant Roux on the façade of the *Institut de Paleontologie Humaine* in Paris, erected in 1923. It depicts an African San man sculpting the Venus of Laussel.

> It is known that in South Africa and at the Cape of Good Hope the Bushman and Hottentot women present a great development of the posterior part...[These forms] exactly resemble in profile the Neolithic idol which I found in Crete and the Egyptian female figures.[341]

Mosso then says this same "peculiarity" is also found in other parts of Africa, including among the Kaffirs, Somalis, and Berbers.[342] He cites Reinach, Morgan and other scholars of his time regarding the "steatopygous race" in Europe during the Neolithic. He notes Virchow's theory that this race entered France from Africa during prehistoric times.[343]

Today, we know that the people who crafted these figurines weren't all Egyptians, but they were most certainly Black people. One clue to this fact is that the earliest figurines are found at sites where "Negroid" skeletons are also found. This connection does, as Virchow proposes, go back as far as prehistoric times. Thomas Griffith Taylor notes "small statues and rock paintings (found in Spain and France chiefly) which certainly point to a race akin to the Bushmen [Khoisan]" alongside skeletons bearing matching traits. He continues:

> At Willendorf (near Vienna) a statuette of a nude woman is steatopygic and has hair apparently of the peppercorn type. Similar negritoid figures come from Brassempouy and Lespugues in the south of France, and perhaps indicate a former widespread negrito stratum.

In Europe, the most notable of these sites is in France, where the famous Grimaldi man was discovered.[344]

WHO WAS THE GRIMALDI MAN?

On the groundbreaking song "Nature of the Threat" Ras Kass raps:

> Savage Neanderthals until the late Paleolithic age/ That's when the Black Grimaldi man came/ With the symbol of the dragon, fire and art/ Check cave paintings in France and Spain to the Venus of Willendorf

And with these words, Ras Kass introduced many of us to the idea of Black presence in prehistoric Europe, long before the Moors' conquest of Spain, before Hannibal's conquest of Rome, and even before the Black Builders of Stonehenge (we'll get back to that one!). Ras Kass may have been translating some of what he'd learned from Cheikh Anta Diop, who wrote extensively in *Civilization or Barbarism* about the "Grimaldi Negroids" of prehistoric Europe.

In 1901, the Grimaldi remains were discovered in the *Grotte dei Balzi*

Rossi, a cave situated on the border of northwestern Italy. They consist of two skeletons, dated to between 25,000 and 35,000 years ago. When they were found, they turned the world of European archaeology upside down. Here was conclusive proof that the first humans in Europe were in no way Caucasian.

These skeletons were accompanied by hundreds of "Venus figurines" depicting physical features only found among Black women. Perhaps this was the reason they instituted a 50-year moratorium on excavations at one of the most important archaeological sites for this time period. What did they have to hide?[345]

Sir Arthur Keith, one of the early scholars who described the Grimaldi Man as "Negroid" almost sacrificed his career for this remark, and later recanted his statement. (We'll discuss his new "theory" a little later). Others suffered similar fates. In later years, the name "Grimaldi" itself was virtually *erased* from texts on the subject.

Scientists now lump them with other "early modern humans" and only identify the Grimaldi man by his local culture, the "Aurignacian" culture. No more "Grimaldi Man." Now they say "Aurignacian" and the memories of "Negroid" Europeans are magically erased! Ain't it amazing how easy it is to rewrite history?

Either way, the Black bearers of this Aurignacian culture did indeed – as Ras Kass rapped – introduce art to Europe, from the "cave paintings in France and Spain to the Venus of Willendorf," all of which resembled the prehistoric artwork we find everywhere the Aurignacian people went. These first humans in Europe were the ones who took the Neanderthals to war.

BLACK EUROPEANS, CIRCA 50,000 BC

Until the coming of modern humans, Europe and Palestine were Neanderthal territory. The earliest evidence of humans in this area dates back to about 48,000 years ago, when a warm period ushered in the end of a massive Ice Age. In other words, as soon as it got warm enough to head north, some of us veered off our southern coastal settlement pattern and took the fight with the Neanderthals onto their home turf. As Nicholas Wade notes in *Before the Dawn*:

[T]he Neanderthals may have had light skin and their conquerors black. Early Europeans, including the great artists of the Chauvet cave in France, may have retained the dark skin and other badges of their African origin for many thousands of years.[346]

THE GRIMALDI WEREN'T THE FIRST OR LAST

Despite the importance of the Grimaldi remains, we've gotta be clear that the Grimaldi "presence" was not an isolated case. Some authors have proposed that the people who came before and after the Grimaldi man were NOT Black, and the Grimaldi were special because they were a Black presence in Europe. This is a lie that advances the idea of a white prehistoric Europe.

In fact, at the time Grimaldi man was found, racist historians like Arthur de Gobineau were busy arguing that Europeans were the original (and superior) race, the progenitors of humankind. This meant the people of Africa and Asia had to come from European ancestors. In other words, the original white Europeans gave birth to the Grimaldi Europeans, who gave birth to Black Africans.*

So, for some historians, Grimaldi was celebrated as a "Negro cousin of the Hottentots and Bushmen of South Africa" because it satisfied a political agenda of promoting a European origin for Black people. The truth, as we now know, is that the first Europeans were all Black.

But the Grimaldi remains are important because there aren't too many human remains older than those in Europe. Yet we know that humans were there long before and after Grimaldi, because we left tools and other evidence behind at various sites. These sites are grouped together based on common culture, and each cultural phase, or "industry" is given a name.

THE CULTURES OF PALEOLITHIC EUROPE

The first Black humans in Europe introduced a culture known as the Aurignacian. This culture, in turn, was followed by several other cultures. Here's a quick review of the Upper Paleolithic in Europe:

❒ The Aurignacian culture (47-27 kya) represents the first modern humans in Europe, sometimes called the Grimaldi people. They

---

* Yes, many historians taught that Black and brown people had white origins! So the Grimaldi finds gave them what they were looking for. Grimaldi man was made out to be the ancestor of all Black people, and a skull from Chancelade – with it's more "Asiatic" features – was made out to be the ancestor of the "yellow" races of Asia. And of course, it was assumed that these European "ancestors" of ours sprang from a white ancestor themselves. After all, they WERE in Europe, right?

defeated the Neanderthals and introduced Europe to cave paintings and stone Venus figurines. The culture extended from Spain on the west to Ukraine in the east and to Palestine in the South. They were Black.

❏ The Gravettian culture (28-22 kya) made the first ceramic Venus figurines. The culture extended from central Europe to Ukraine. They were Black.

❏ The Solutrean culture (22-17 kya) didn't make as much art, but made many new tools. The culture extended from Spain to central Europe, and may have reached North America (Clovis culture) either by seafaring west across the Atlantic or the eastern land route via Beringia.* They were Black.

❏ The Magdalenian culture (18-10 kya) is known for its amazing cave paintings, detailed sculptures, and innovative tools and weapons. The culture extended from Portugal in the west to Poland in the east. This period was once known as the Reindeer Age because we hunted large quantities of reindeer. By 14 kya, we were breeding and domesticating them.[347]

❏ The Azilian culture (c. 12 kya) marks the last lingering survivals of the Paleolithic in Europe. They too were Black. Yet, because of environmental issues, innovation and cultural sophistication appear to have finally waned off, until another group of Original People introduced the Neolithic.

Of all these periods, the most notable is the one that laid the foundation: The Aurignacian. These were the people who built the house that Europe became.

WHAT DID AURIGNACIAN PEOPLE LOOK LIKE?

What else do we know about the amazing people of the Aurignacian? They were us. Well, us over 40,000 years ago. The Black people who built the Aurignacian culture, wiped out the Neanderthals, and became the first modern humans in Europe were physically not too different from most Black people in America

---

* There is some genetic evidence that a group of people carrying the X haplogroup, could have left northern Europe after building the Solutrean culture, then sailed to Greenland (where they were found and called "Skraelings" by later writers), and then settled in northeastern Canada, where Solutrean artifacts are found again. The only other explanation for this connection is that the builders of the Solutrean culture left Europe and traveled east across Siberia into the Americas.

today.[349]

The tricky part is that – without skin and cartilage – we are stuck letting anthropologists tell us which skulls had "Negroid" traits, and those aren't the best ways to tell who was Black and who wasn't. Not to mention that remains can be interpreted differently based on what you're looking for. You can even see how scientists are able to play with skeletal remains by comparing different reconstructions of the same skull.

Another source of confusion is the fact that all Black people don't look alike. This is obvious when you compare the Black people of Australia, those of West Africa, and those of East Africa. Not all of the people of Paleolithic could easily be classified into one physical "type." The further back you go, the less you see different "races" and the more you just see diverse populations of Black people. The Grimaldi are a prime example.

WERE THE GRIMALDI AFRICOID, AUSTRALOID, OR WHAT?

Since the discovery of the Grimaldi remains, at least five different theories have been proposed regarding their racial origin:

❐ (a) The Grimaldi were Negroid (Boule, 1903; Verneau, 1906).

❐ (b) The Grimaldi were an intermediate race with Negroid features (Keith, 1911; Osborn, 1915).

❐ (c) The Grimaldi were Australoid (Smith, 1927; Abbie 1951).

❐ (d) The Grimaldi were Capoid or "Bushmen" (Sollas, 1913; Hrdlička, 1930; Breuil, 1930).

❐ (e) The Grimaldi were simply "Cro-Magnon" (Keith, 1931; Bean, 1932).

The earliest commentators on the Grimaldi (the discoverers actually) described the skeletons as Negroid. In the years that followed, there were many revisions and retractions of this assessment. For example, in 1911, Sir Arthur Keith – notorious for this kind of backpedaling – proposed that the Grimaldi were an "intermediate" race between Black and white with "Negroid features."

In *The Negro in the New World*, Sir Harry Hamilton Johnston details the physical features that make the Grimaldi remains "Black" people, yet also distinct from modern African populations. He connects the Grimaldi people to several different Black populations – including "Nilotic Negroes," the Khoisan, Australoid Blacks, and "modern Negroes" – suggesting that the Black people of Paleolithic Europe could simply have possessed "generalized" features that were not yet specific to a distinct population.[350]

In other words, there could have been a "prototypical" population so old, and so ancestral, that they had diversity in their features – which only later became homogenized into different racial types through genetic drift. In other words, they all looked kinda different but still kinda similar, until thousands of years of mixing had different population looking more alike.

THE DIVERSITY OF AURIGNACIAN EUROPE

Another way to look at the problem of diversity among Paleolithic European remains is to consider multiple migrations into Europe. Thomas Griffith Taylor believed that Europe was first occupied by Neanderthals, and then by several waves of Black people.

First, he said, there were Negritos (or DBP), then Negroid people, and then Black Australoid people. He says of the Australoid stratum:

> The fourth stratum, which is almost world-wide, and which probably extends to America, is the Australoid. It is, of course, universal through Australia, Indonesia, south-east Asia, and South India. Types akin to the Australian were common in early Palaeolithic times in Europe. It is, however, difficult to decide whether some early peoples were more like Australians or Africans (Negro).[351]

Taylor's last comment is especially important. Many European anthropologists called early remains Australoid, but that only means they looked like Black people. It doesn't always mean that they looked specifically more like modern Australians than modern Africans (as Walter Neves has noted in recent studies).

In 1923, Roland Burrage Dixon traced the prehistoric Australoid presence across the Mediterranean and as deep into Europe as modern Switzerland.[352] This explains why so many of the oldest European remains have been described as Australoid. It also explains the similarities between the rock art of Paleolithic Europe and Australia.

And it certainly explains the 30,000 year-old boomerang they found in Poland, made from pure woolly mammoth tusk![353] And that boomerang was no crude throwing-stick either. They tested it and found that it could kill at a distance of over 600 feet!

WHERE DID THESE PEOPLE COME FROM?

There is strong evidence that the strongest cultural influences for Aurignacian culture came from North Africa via the Near East. In 1937, Thomas Griffith Taylor connected the Aurignacian culture to Algeria:

> In Upper Tonkin seventeen skulls of Australoids akin to those found in the Aurignacian in Europe are mentioned by von Eickstedt. Many of the people living in Western Europe about 20,000 BC were very like the Australoids; and Sir Harry Johnston draws attention to the Australoid appearance of the Ushtettas still living in the mountains of Algeria.[354]

Grafton Elliot Smith also said Australoid people were prehistorically settled in North Africa.[355] But does it all begin in North Africa?

In *The Origin and Evolution of Primitive Man*, Albert Churchward traces the tall Black people of prehistoric Europe back to the Nile Valley:

> The tall race of Europe, who came up from Egypt, were an exodus of the Turkana. These Nilotic Negroes are still found in Africa, a fine race of men, some of them over seven feet in height, very muscular and powerful, have high foreheads, large eyes, rather high cheek-bones, mouths not very large and well shaped, lips rather full. He was followed by another race from Egypt, of shorter stature, like the Ipswich man, and, after, the Galley Hill man.[356]

Churchward may have been referring to the later entrance of the Anu People, who took the same routes as their Aurignacian ancestors.

CONNECTING THE DOTS PAST NORTH AFRICA

"There was once an "uninterrupted belt" of Negro culture from Central Europe to South Africa."
– W.E.B. Du Bois, The World and Africa

Archaeologists have found 48,000 year old artifact sites in south-central and eastern Europe, similar to those of the Emirian culture in Palestine.[357] Soon after, Proto-Aurignacian sites show up in Europe, resembling the Ahmarian culture of the Near East. Connecting these dots, we can see that these European sites were settlements of Black people moving from the Near East into Europe. These people birthed the Aurignacian culture around 47,000 years ago.[358]

We can easily connect the dots in Europe back to sites resembling Aurignacian culture in the Near East (near Israel) and North Africa (near Morocco and Tunisia). These sites are anywhere from 30,000 to 50,000 years older than comparable sites in Europe. Clearly, we should know where Aurignacian culture originated.

But scientists act as if they can't connect the dots between one culture in Europe and an older version in the Near East, and an even older version in Africa. To anyone who can see objectively, it is quite obvious that the African cultures of 100-50,000 years ago were clearly the sources for "Upper Paleolithic" cultures in Europe.

For example, we can find similar cultures at Howiesons Poort in southern Africa over 60,000 years ago, predating the Aurignacian in Europe by almost 20,000 years. We know that the people of Howiesons Poort basically "disappeared," so perhaps some of them went to Europe? Many of their innovations could also be found at prehistoric North African sites. On the other hand, perhaps the reason why Howiesons Poort has been connected with the L3 haplogroup reflects the fact that they migrated south from Northeast Africa.

Thomas Griffith Taylor saw a connection between the Aurignacian people and the Khoisan people of South Africa:

> In their culture the Bushmen [Khoisan]…resemble in so many ways some of the Aurignacian folk of Western Europe that Sollas and others have little doubt of their being of the same race. Customs, weapons, steatopygy, small stature, and especially the artistic work of the two groups, are exceedingly alike…It is suggested that the similarity in the pictures found at Cogul (Spain), in the present Bushmen territory in South Africa, and at Raigarh (340 miles west of Calcutta) is due to their common origin. We may imagine these negrito people spreading from a cradle-land (between the three regions mentioned) and carrying the culture independently to Spain, South Africa, and India.[359]

This could explain why some Aurignacian remains were described as Khoisanoid (like the south African Khoisan) or Capoid (like the Africans of the southern Cape), while others were simply described as Negroid, and still others as Australoid (like some of the remains from North Africa).

Why so many different descriptions? It would seem that – between 40,000 and 15,000 years ago – several infusions of Black people joined up with the rebel alliance in Eurasia. The tropically-adapted body proportions of all these people, including later people who are just described as "Cro-Magnon," suggest that – despite variations in the shape of their nose or brow – these were all Black people who originated in the motherland. However, many of these people joined the Aurignacians after embarking from settled in the Near East, India, and Central Asia.

In the chapter on India, we explore the expansive reach of Aurignacian culture and related traditions, as well as the likelihood that Blacks from Northeast Africa were joined by Blacks from across Asia.

BLACK PEOPLE EVERYWHERE

As Taylor notes, Black people were found in India, South Africa, and Spain at their most prehistoric dates of human occupation. He identifies these Blacks as "the earliest races, as we may deduce from their invariable position in the inland inaccessible portions, or in the marginal islands, of the territory which they share with other folk." In other words, these people were the Earth's first humans, but became marginalized and forced to live on the fringes of their old territories by new arrivals.

Taylor continues:

> Their artefacts and drawings have been found in an uninterrupted belt from Europe to southernmost Africa. Drawings of a similar nature are also found at Raigarh in Central India. In the map they are seen to be the sole people to have reached Tasmania; they are the lowest stratum all through the East Indies and Melanesia, and also in India...

These people are almost never discussed by modern historians. In the September 1896 issue of the *Arena*, Professor Willis Boughton of Ohio University wrote about how historians had already begun ignoring these Black foundations:

> The black race has a history. In fact, all history is full of traces of the black element. It is now usually recognized as the oldest race of which we have any knowledge. The wanderings of these people, since prehistoric history began, have not been confined to the African continent. In Paleolithic times the black man roamed at will over all the fairest portions of the Old World. Europe, as well as Asia and Africa, acknowledges his sway. No white man had as yet appeared to dispute his authority in the vine-clad valleys of France or Germany, or upon the classic hills of Greece or Rome. The black man preceded all others, and carried Paleolithic culture to its very height. But the history of all lands has been only a record of succeeding races.[360]

Verneau found so much evidence of a Black presence in later periods of European history that he credited them to Grimaldi ancestors:

> That we may still find at the present day so many traces of a racial type having characters recalling those which I have observed in the Grimaldi race must of necessity have been due to the fact that this race was formerly represented in our country by a whole group...We must therefore admit that an almost Negroe element lived in South-Western Europe towards the Mid Quaternary

Era...[361]

Thomas Griffith Taylor believed that Europe was settled by **Blacks who extended from Switzerland to Siberia**:

> [Negroid] people must have been quite abundant in Europe towards the close of the Palaeolithic. Boule quotes their skeletons from Brittany, Switzerland, Liguria, Lombardy, Illyria, and Bulgaria. They are universal through Africa and through Melanesia, while the Botocudo and the Lagoa Santa skulls of East Brazil show where similar folk penetrated to the New World. A Mousterian station near Krasnoiarsk in Siberia, associated with the mammoth, probably shows the presence of this Neanderthal-Negro-Australoid type in North Asia.

In *Civilization or Barbarism*, Cheikh Anta Diop observed that the Black presence in prehistoric Europe was so widespread it extended into East Asia:

> The Grimaldi Negroids have left their numerous traces all over Europe and Asia, from the Iberian Peninsula* to Lake Baykal in Siberia [just north of Mongolia], passing through France, Austria, the Crimea, and the Basin of Don, etc.[362]

Between 40,000 and 15,000 years ago, delegations of these people may have joined the occupation campaign against the Neanderthals in Europe. This explains why there is such great diversity in the features of Paleolithic Europeans. Yet, even with this diversity, it's hard to deny that all of these people were Black.

The remains at Combe-Capelle (found in Dordogne, France and dated to 28,000 years ago) have also been described as Negroid, as have the remains from Sunghir (found near Moscow, Russia and dated to 30,000 years ago). And these are just the ones that are undeniably "Negroid." As far east as China, the 20,000-year-old remains at Zhoukoudian are Black. And there are hundreds of other skulls bearing "Black" features, but scholars won't commit to calling them "Negroid" or "Africoid" or anything close.

Yet these Original People – at least during the Aurignacian period – weren't much different from us. They weren't pygmies and they weren't giants either. The Grimaldi skeletons were over five feet tall, which lends support to the theory that the world's oldest people weren't always as small as they are nowadays. However, after new waves of people came into Europe, many of the aboriginal Black settlers were displaced. These people may have become Europe's

---

* The Iberian Peninsula is the western end of Europe, comprising Spain and Portugal. The span between Portugal and Lake Baykal is almost 6000 miles.

DBP.

THE "LITTLE BLACK PEOPLE" OF EUROPE

In Europe, there are thousands of ancient accounts describing DBP populations. Today, it's highly unlikely you'll find any "little Black people" as you would in the Philippines, but plenty of evidence suggests that the DBP survived in Europe until quite recently. The 1911 *Encyclopedia Britannica* reported that:

> Relics of a pygmy race are supposed to exist now in Sicily and Sardinia, i.e. along the high road between Pleistocene Africa and Europe. Near Schaffhausen [Switzerland], Dr. Kollman found skeletal remains of small human beings, which have been regarded by some authorities as belonging to the European pygmies of the Neolithic period. Some anthropologists of authority…believe that a dwarf negroid race at one time existed in northern Europe, and may have given rise to the traditional tales of elves, goblins, gnomes and fairies.[363]

One of the most prominent of these authorities was British historian David MacRitchie, who wrote several works on the Black presence in ancient (and modern) Europe, and how these little Black people living underground became regarded as supernatural beings of immense power. These reports later became stories of myth, coming down to us now as tales of little fairies, trolls, gnomes, elves, and leprechauns. Yes, that's all about US. Because it sounds so far-fetched, we're republishing MacRitchie's books and letting him speak for himself.

WHO WERE THE CRO-MAGNONS?

Remember Sir Arthur Keith? The guy who said the Grimaldi man was Black? An eminent archaeologist with much to lose, Keith endured quite a bit of criticism when he said this in 1911. In 1931, he retracted his statement and said he now considered the Grimaldi to be just a "morphological variation" of "Cro-Magnon" man. In other words, they weren't Black…they were just a "Black-looking" variant of non-Black prehistoric Europeans.

WHAT'S RACE GOT TO DO WITH IT?

What does Cro-Magnon really mean? For starters, it's a very broad category. Cro-Magnon quickly became the racial type for just about any human remains found in Paleolithic Europe, regardless of their facial features. This sort of racial redaction became common from the 1930s onward, but became the norm after the emergence of the

> **DID YOU KNOW?**
> The Qafzeh and Skhul remains from Israel are examples of human remains outside Africa more than 75,000 years ago. They are 80,000 to 130,000 years old, and have African-like, or "tropically adapted," body proportions.[366] The remains named Skhul 5 and Skhul 9 (dated to 119,000 years old) are especially "Negroid" in appearance, while others are more generalized. The people of the Skhul site wore the same jewelry (necklaces made of *Nassarius shell beads)* that were found in eastern Morocco, where they dated back to 82,000 years ago. They also shared other cultural traditions with people living in northern Africa at the time.

"no such thing as race" school of anthropology in the 1960s.

To be fair, Paleolithic Europe was composed of different cultures and different genetic groups, and some of these populations had very different facial features. Yet scientists employ a very NARROW set of criteria in deciding who and what was Black.

Sometimes, when there's no way around it, they'll say the find was unimportant. Later, once they've sterilized race out of the discussion, they'll come back and use racial arguments to subtly promote that these people were actually pretty great…and white.

Case in point: Once it became passé to speak of the Grimaldi as "Negroid," a new generation of paleoanthropologists began grouping a wider variety of human remains together into broader categories. Finds as distant as the Qafzeh remains of Israel, the Combe-Capelle remains of France, Minatogawa Man in Japan, the Kabwe skull of Zambia, and several Paleo-Indian finds (Stone Age remains from the Americas) were lumped together as Cro-Magnons,[364] and eventually the term Cro-Magnon was expanded to encompass all early "anatomically modern humans," including the Grimaldi remains.[365] Yet *ALL of these remains* represent Black people.

We know this new labeling system was promoted to minimize the emphasis on race, but let's not forget that anthropologists only cared about minimizing this emphasis once racial analysis suggested "Black" features. When they thought the fossils were white folks, it was all about race. **Race was important THEN!**

But when the fossils turned out to be Black, it was time to dismantle the concept of race altogether! And this happened in EVERY branch of science. As soon as medical science found that Blacks were actually dominant in every sense, race was deemphasized and considered "an outdated concept" in medicine and genetics.

When archaeologists were busy talking about white Egypt and white Mesopotamia, race was worthy of discussion. Once the evidence suggested that the founders of the world's ancient civilizations were Black, race became an "outdated concept" in the archaeological community. C'mon son! Anyone with half a brain can see how it went down. Fortunately, there are books like this to tell the side of the story that's not being told anymore.

WEREN'T THE CRO-MAGNONS THE FIRST WHITE PEOPLE?

Nope, not them either. Just as the Grimaldi man was Black, so too were the people who came after him. Although Cheikh Anta Diop believed that the Cro-Magnon people who came after Grimaldi man were the first "white people," based on their morphology (shape of facial features like nose and cheekbones), recent evidence (unavailable to Diop at the time he wrote) suggests that the Cro-Magnon people were not pale-skinned.

French anthropologist Rene Verneau compared the Grimaldi man's remains with those of later remains classified as Cro-Magnon, and concluded that "there is no reason why they should not have had some ties of kinship." Verneau even adds that the Grimaldi Negroids "may have been the ancestors" of these later Europeans.[367]

In their 1998 text, *African Exodus: The Origins of Modern Humanity*, Christopher Stringer and Robin McKie confirm this early observation, noting:

> Early Europeans still resembled modern tropical peoples – some resemble modern Australians and Africans more than modern Europeans. Nor does the picture get any clearer when we move on to the Cro-Magnons, the presumed ancestors of modern Europeans. Some were more like present-day Australians or Africans, judged by objective anatomical categorizations, as is the case with some early modern skulls from the Upper Cave at Zhoukoudian in China.[368]

Beyond looking at skull shape, skin color, nose shape, and prognathism, scientists can tell if people come from tropical climates by looking at their body proportions. For example, Neanderthal limb proportions were cold-adapted, but prehistoric Eurasians **were not**. Erik Trinkhaus explains:

> Their distinct limb proportions are instead indicative of an equatorial ancestry and better culturally based thermal protection...The limb proportions of the Eurasian early modern samples are retentions of the African ancestral morphology of long limbs with long distal segments...[369]

In other words, these folks look like Africans. Roger Lewin supported this notion, stating:

> Cro-Magnon skeletons exhibit a warm-adapted body stature, not the cold-adapted formula seen in Neanderthals. This character may be taken as strong evidence of the replacement of Neanderthals and

DID YOU KNOW?
Recent studies of genetics, blood types and cranial morphology indicate that, as Diop proposed, the Basque people of Spain may be the descendents of the original Cro-Magnon population. But scientists have also agreed that the Basque people are the closest thing to Black that you will find among "unmixed" populations in Europe, genetically and phenotypically (yet that's a story we'll have to explore in a future volume).

supports the single African origin hypothesis.[370]

The next time we see "cold-adapted" bodies like the Neanderthals is among modern white Europeans, but not among early Europeans like the Grimaldi Man or Cro-Magnons. So, although some Cro-Magnon people had facial structures resembling that of many Europeans, we should be well aware that indigenous Black people can have a WIDE variety of features, including narrow noses and flat faces.

As C.L. Brace has said, "The oft-repeated European feeling that the Cro-Magnons are "us" is more a product of anthropological folklore than the result of the metric data available from the skeletal remains."[371] In other words, **white people are not the "original people" of Europe**. Since the ONE feature we can *consistently associate with white people* is "whiteness," it's *not enough* to note that the Cro-Magnons might have had relatively "straight" noses, or even coarse, straight hair.*

And here's the best part: In recent years, "Cro-Magnon" too has fallen out of use among anthropologists. Why? Because they've been forced to realize that these people weren't different, in any definable way, from other human populations of the time. Which is exactly what I could've told them if they'd asked me before they came up with this Cro-Magnon mess.

SO WHEN DID THE FACE OF EUROPE CHANGE?

By now, you might be wondering to yourself, "If the first humans in Europe were Black, and the Cro-Magnons were Black, and the Europeans who came after them were Black, when did Europe become white? And how?

Well, that's quite a complicated question. And to date, no one has fully documented the true story, at least not using the standards of evidence we're sharing with you in this series. This is why we're

---

* As suggested by the straight hair found among many Australoid people and the hair shown on small ivory bust of a man found at Dolní Věstonice and dated to 26,000 years ago, though the later Venus of Brassempouy suggests curly hair or braids and dozens of others figurines show woolly-textured or peppercorn hair.

dedicating an entire volume of this series to that topic – the origins of white Europeans and the white cultural complex.

And, in researching that text, we've come to appreciate WHY such a book hasn't been written yet. For starters, it's an unpopular subject! Nobody wants to touch it. And if you're one of the brave few who do, the research is mind-bogglingly difficult, because so few have attempted to approach the subject honestly and comprehensively in laymen's terms.

Not to mention that much of the data has been ignored, buried, or altered! Fortunately, recent years have provided a wealth of journal-published studies that tell bits and pieces of the untold story. They say modern Europeans are mostly the byproduct of a population wave that swept in during the Neolithic, over 40,000 years after the first Black humans came into the region.[372]

Here's an example of one of those studies, in laymen's terms:

Journal Text	Laymen's Translation
"Body proportions are under strong climatic selection and evince remarkable stability within regional lineages.	The length of different parts of your body says a lot about where you're from, and they stay the same even when other things change.
As such, they offer a viable and robust alternative to cranio-facial data in assessing hypothesised continuity and replacement with the transition to agro-pastoralism in central Europe.	So these lengths can tell us a lot more than facial features about who came into Europe when they started farming and who was there before them.
Humero-clavicular, brachial and crural indices in a large sample (n=75) of Linienbandkeramik (LBK), Late Neolithic and Early Bronze Age specimens from the middle Elbe-Saale-Werra valley (MESV) were compared with Eurasian and African terminal Pleistocene, European Mesolithic and geographically disparate recent human specimens.	We looked at the bones of many skeletons from Europe around 4000 to 2000 BC, and compared them with much older skeletons from Africa and Europe, as well as with skeletons of modern people from around the world.
Mesolithic Europeans display considerable variation in humero-clavicular and brachial indices yet none approach the extreme "hyper-polar" morphology of LBK humans from the MESV.	The old European skeletons from 10,000 years ago had a lot of diversity, but none had the "extreme white" features of Europeans of the LBK culture, which spread throughout central Europe after 5000 BC.
In contrast, Late Neolithic and Early Bronze Age peoples display elongated brachial and crural indices	On the other hand, people in other parts of Europe between 4000 and 2000 BC looked like the oldest

reminiscent of terminal Pleistocene and "tropically adapted" recent humans.	African skeletons as well as modern Black people elsewhere in the world.
These marked morphological changes likely reflect exogenous immigration during the terminal Fourth millennium cal BC."	This suggests that there was some kind of foreign migration of white people coming into Europe around 3000 BC.
Gallagher et al. (Mar 2009). "Population continuity, demic diffusion and Neolithic origins in central-southern Germany: the evidence from body proportions." Homo 60(2):95-126.	In March of 2009, the anthropological journal *Homo* (meaning "Man") published this study by Gallagher and colleagues on pages 95 to 126 of Volume 60, Issue Number 2.

QUESTIONS TO CONSIDER

Where did this new population come from? How did they take over so quickly? What was their relationship like with the Original People of Europe? How different was their cultural complex from those that came before them? And how did these people go on to conquer so much of the ancient world? No way we could do those questions justice in a chapter or less. And thus, Volume Four of this series.

Understandably, some readers will be furious, because you're "sure" that white skin is a product of the cold climate of Europe and "must have" emerged long before 6,000 years ago. And we've just got to tell you, sorry, but you've been misinformed on both counts. As we noted, we WILL dig deep into the topic in Volume Four and explain everything, but for now, just consider this quote from W. C. Boyd's 1956 text, *Genetics and the Races of Man*:

> The aborigines of the New World, though not by any means identical, agree in having on the whole considerable skin pigmentation. If pigmentation is adaptive, and conforms to climate, why are not the Eskimo and the inhabitants of Tierra del Fuego as light as Europeans?[373]

Apparently, most Inuit people – living in areas that are as cold as it gets – are still brown-skinned enough to warrant such a question. And this was after centuries of white explorers coming among them and marrying into their families! This fact adds special relevance to what Bory De Saint Vincent said about the same population in 1839:

> Whatever the reason, both sexes, more tanned than people in Europe and Central Asia, darker than any other Americans, are even blacker the farther north one goes; an additional proof that it is not, as generally believed, the heat of the sun that causes black skin-color in certain intertropical regions. It is not rare to find Eskimos, Greenlanders, and Samoyeds at 70 degrees latitude who, darker than Hottentots at the opposite extreme of the old continent, are almost

as black as Wolof or Kaffirs on the Equator.[374]

THE "SPARK" OF HUMAN DEVELOPMENT?

"Wherever Homo arose, and Africa is at present the most likely continent, he soon dispersed, in a very primitive form, throughout the warm regions of the Old World...If Africa was the cradle of mankind, it was only an indifferent kindergarten. Europe and Asia were our principal schools." – Carleton S. Coon, 1962

Some scholars assert that humans only became true "modern humans" when they entered Europe. Why? They explain that the amazing developments in human ability that are seen in the Aurignacian culture of Europe are evidence of a profound brain "jump." Meaning evolutionary development was given a nitro boost around this time...but more so, around this *place*. All the while, ignoring the Aurignacian culture's precedents in Africa over 30,000 years prior.

The idea that humans only became behaviorally modern within the past 40,000 years (coincident with our migration into Europe) is reminiscent of similar (but more openly racist) theories from the 19th century, which asserted Europe as both the birthplace of civilization and humanity itself.

The modern version of this theory is championed by paleoanthropologist Richard Klein, who says Aurignacian Europe of 40,000 years ago is the first time and place we see such a "spark" in human development. Fortunately, Klein's argument is not universally accepted.

Two critics, Sally McBrearty of the University of Connecticut and Alison S. Brooks of George Washington University, argue that modern behavior didn't experience the "dramatic shift" Klein claims. They write:

> As a whole the African archaeological record shows that the transition to fully modern behavior was not the result of a biological or cultural revolution, but the fitful expansion of a shared body of knowledge, and the application of novel solutions on an 'as needed' basis.

But Klein remains steadfast in arguing that there was no modern behavior in Africa prior to 50,000 years ago. For example, the eight barbed harpoon points made of bone, from the 100,000 year old fishing site in Zaire? Klein believes that the bone points are less than 12,000 years old. And so it goes, anything African and old must be recent. Same story line of thinking the white supremacists of the 19th century proposed, only updated for modern audiences.

THE "BLACK BREEDS" OF EUROPE?

This is a page from William Ripley's _ *Races of Europe*. According to Ripley, these photos represent the last survivals of the Black Australoid people who first settled Europe. Compare the top photo to one of a native Australian and judge for yourself.

103.   "OLD BLACK BREED" TYPE.   104.

105.   "OLD BLACK BREED" TYPE.   106.

107.   A TEUTONIC-BLACK BREED CROSS.   108.

SHETLAND ISLANDS.

-VAPORE-
-MARICOPA-

THE AMERICAS

WAAAY BEFORE COLUMBUS CAME

"It seems on the whole probable that the Proto-Austroloid must have been one of the earliest, if not the earliest, type to spread into the North American continent." – Roland Dixon, 1923

WHO WERE THE FIRST AMERICANS?

When you think "Native American," who do you think of? If you know some history, you might think of Tecumseh, Geronimo, Crazy Horse, Sitting Bull, and some of the other resistance leaders that attempted to stop Europeans from taking over their homelands. If you don't know much about history, you might think of Pocahontas, Sacagawea, and some of the other people white folks like to celebrate for having helped them accomplish this same goal.

What you probably won't think of is Black people. Yet the first Americans were Black. Every modern anthropologist knows this. We don't. We learned that there was a land migration across some "ice bridge" known as the Bering Strait, which connects Siberia (in Asia) and Alaska. This is said to have happened 16,000 to 13,000 years ago, and the people who came looked, talked, and acted just like modern Native American people.

And that's it. Nobody questions if there was more than one migration across this little land bridge, or if there was any other way to get to the Americas. Or if all Native Americans – throughout North and South America – really descend from this one small group of migrants.

Yet when they tell the history of Egypt, they want to tell you about every single group of foreigners that ever stepped foot in the direction of the Nile Valley. And they'll be quick to tell you that everybody looked different and that it wasn't such a simple story.

Turns out that American history is, as usual, all wrong. The evidence suggests that migrations into the Americas came from many different directions, over the course of at least 40,000 years. In this chapter, we'll explore all of the earliest migrations into the Americas.

THE TRAGIC FATE OF THE PERICÚES

In 1533, Spanish navigator Fortún Jiménez became the first European to set foot in Baja, California. Never being the one to break tradition, Jiménez and his crew murdered a few Pericú men, including an elder, and raped their women. Typical European stuff. But the Pericú were not pleased. They captured Jiménez, beat him to a pulp, and killed him, quickly establishing they were not to be played with.

In 1697, Jesuit missionaries from Spain began setting up missions in the Baja peninsula. But it took over 30 years before they were brave enough to set up camp at the southern tip where the Pericú reigned. The Spanish Jesuits – who were there to establish control of the people before the colonists could come – knew the Pericú did not fear them enough...yet.

In 1730, Jesuit priest Nicholas Tamaral founded a mission in Baja, where he began baptizing Pericú Indians, typically with promises of prosperity to follow. Seeking to establish power, Tamaral and company identified an important Pericú leader, a shaman named Botón, and charged him with "licentious" behavior because he had more than one wife.* They declared that Botón was not fit to lead, and that he had been stripped of his leadership role, hoping to establish a show of dominance.

They weren't ready for what would come next. Botón quickly mobilized a rebel alliance of Pericú and Guaycura Indians to oust the Jesuits from Pericú land. Their plan was multifold. First, they would kill the native soldiers (Indians who now fought for the Spaniards) one by one, and then the missionaries and converts, before finally sweeping the missions themselves.

And they actually followed through! They stormed the Santiago mission, creeping in while the soldiers were out, slaying the priest in charge with a hail of arrows. When a native convert in the mission couldn't stop crying over the dead priest, they killed him too. When the soldiers came back, they killed them too. They took all the bodies, threw them in a pile, and set them on fire, along with all the

---

* The Pericú were polygamists, but not oppressive, as women were known to hold leadership positions and were treated as peers, not property.

Bibles and religious items. Next, they killed Tamaral, burnt down his mission, and drug him through the streets as a true show of dominance.[375]

By 1737, the Jesuits had been forced to abandon several missions. It almost looked as if the Spaniards would lose control of the Baja region to the Indians. For them, that wasn't an option.

In 1742, King Felipe V sent in boatloads of royal funds to pay for additional military assistance to suppress the revolt. The same year, a typhus epidemic "somehow" spread through the area, killing off entire tribes. Soldiers attacked the survivors mercilessly. By the end of the 1700s, most of the indigenous people of the Baja area, including the Pericú, were extinct. [376]

Soon after, King Charles III of Spain expelled the Jesuits from America, possibly because they'd "allowed" such a rebellion to take place. He quickly replaced them with the Franciscan Order, showing that it's really not at all about religion – but power.

THE PREHISTORY OF THE PERICÚ

Who were the Pericú? Where did they come from? How long had they been there before they met Europeans? The Pericú society possessed sophisticated maritime technology, making use of wooden rafts and double-bladed paddles. And studies of their skulls suggest they were veteran divers. The evidence suggests that the ancestors of the Pericú came to the Baja peninsula by boat over 10,000 years ago.[377] This would explain why the Pericú were quite different from their neighbors. How different? They were Australoid.

Mexican geologist Dr. Silvia Gonzalez theorizes that the Pericú people were related to a set of human remains known as Peñon woman, found by an ancient lake bed near Mexico City.[378] At over 10,700 years old, she is one the oldest remains in America. Gonzalez, who dated the skulls, was also the first to declare that "Peñon Woman was originally an Australian."[379]

In fact, prehistoric skulls from the Baja region are hyperdolichocephalic (extremely long-headed), like those of the first remains along coastal South America...and unlike those of most Native American people today. Besides their skulls, the ancestors of the Pericú also left behind thousands of cave paintings to tell us

THE CALIFORNIA INDIANS

THE INDIANS OF CALIFORNIA

Below you'll find various 19th century depictions of indigenous people from California, where some of the first people to reach the Americas settled.

Figure 3.—Yu' rok Woman.

In identifying people with so-called "Negroid" features among indigenous populations, we're not saying all indigenous people looked this way.

To Original People who don't consider them-selves Black, we're simply saying, "Look, your people look like this too. Across the world, we're one people." To everyone else, we're saying, "See how Black are wherever you look."

about themselves. They painted themselves in only two colors, black and red. To be specific, many of the human figures are black, many more are half-black and half-red (split down the middle), and a small minority are only red.[381] What does this mean? It could mean many things, both symbolic and literal. Taken literally, they speak volumes on the history of the Americas.

THEY CAME WAAAY BEFORE COLUMBUS

In the December 1986 issue of the *Journal of African Civilizations* Runoko Rashidi and Legrand H. Clegg II discuss the Black history of the Americas in a period that few other scholars have touched. While many have focused on the pre-Columbian periods that gave birth to Olmec civilization and other more recent contacts with Africa, Rashidi and Clegg focus on the more distant past.

They address the pivotal work of anthropologists like Harold S. Gladwin, Roland B. Dixon, Earnest A. Hooton, Thomas Griffith Taylor, and Sir Arthur Keith, all prominent white scholars and scientists who fell into disfavor for their views about the first people to settle the Americas. Their crime? They said the first Americans were Black.

In his 1947 *Men Out of Asia* (now out of print), Henry Gladwin identified Australoid traits in skulls found at early sites along the path that the migration into the Americas is likely to have taken.[*] Regarding finds in southern California, southwestern Colorado, southern Arizona, the Texas Gulf coast, Punin and Paltacalo in Ecuador, and Lagao Santa in eastern Brazil, Gladwin remarked that all demonstrated...

> ...characteristics which link these various instances together and point to their wide distribution and common ancestry with other Australoid peoples, as do also certain vestigal traces in some modern people, such as the Pericú of Lower California, the Seri on nearby Tiburon Island, and various tribes in Central and South America...
>
> [P]eople of Australoid type were once widely distributed, and survivals of some of their features, customs and culture are still to be found in isolated localities.[382]

---

[*] This is because massive ice sheets were still covering a great portion of North America, leaving only the western extremities exposed. That glacial cover receded as one moves southwards into Central America, thus leaving groups of migrants free to move eastward.

THE PUNIN SKULL OF ECUADOR

Until 1975, the most conclusive evidence of this prehistoric Black migration was the Punin Skull, discovered in a small village in the Andean region of Ecuador, accompanied by the remains of an Andean horse, known to have been extinct for over 10,000 years. Runoko Rashidi calls it "the most well-documented single piece of evidence for the early presence of Australoids in the prehistoric Americas during the period of Gladwin's writing."[383] Indeed, the skull was heralded by the American Museum of Natural History of New York as the earliest evidence of humans in the Americas. At the same time, it was evidence of *Australoid* humans in America.

The "dean of English anatomists," Sir Arthur Keith, noting the similarities between the skull and those of indigenous Australians, declared, "The discovery at Punin does compel us to look in the possibility of a Pleistocene invasion of America by an Australoid people."[384]

On the other side of the Atlantic, Harvard anthropologist Earnest Hooton echoed Keith in stating that the skull was one "that any competent craniologist would identify as Australian in type." Yet he added much to the bigger picture by following:

> It is easier to find Australoid-looking dolichocephals [long-headed] in the more ancient burials in the New World than anything in the way of a skull that resembles a Mongoloid.[385]*

Another eminent Harvard anthropologist, Roland Dixon, also saw the Australoid characteristics of prehistoric skulls found throughout western North America:

> It seems on the whole probable that the Proto-Austroloid must have been one of the earliest, if not the earliest, type to spread into the North American continent. On the Pacific coast in California and Lower California it appears to constitute the oldest stratum, characterizing as it does the crania from the lower layers of the shell-heaps from the islands of Santa Catalina and San Clemente off the coast, and from the extinct Pericue, isolated in the southern tip of the peninsula of Lower California. It is moreover, prominent among the ancient basket-weavers of northern Arizona, who represent probably one of the earliest peoples in this whole area. In the northeast the type is of importance among the Iroquois and the southern Algonkian tribes, such as the Lenape.[386]

---

* Ironically enough, Keith originally became famous for promoting the fake skull known as Piltdown Man, which made whites appear to have an older, more widespread presence. But he became *infamous* for suggesting the same idea – *truthfully* this time – for Black people!

Where some scholars saw Australoid traits, others described them as Negroid. Thomas Griffith Taylor declared in his *Environment, Race and Migration* that surviving crania indicated "the presence in the far past of negroid peoples in the American continent."[387] Dixon also cited prehistoric crania of the "Negroid" type in Arizona, the Ohio Valley, Tennessee, New England and northern Mexico.[388] Needless to say, Dixon later regretted ever making these comments, and after enduring endless harassment from other academics, renounced most of these views and referred to his 1923 work *Racial History of Man* as "my crime."[389]

"America had often been discovered before Columbus, but it had always been hushed up." – Oscar Wilde

Gladwin, the only one of the above named to hold his ground, was also the one with the least at stake. Gladwin, like me, was not considered a "true" scientist by others in the archaeological community and other circles of academia. Gladwin was regarded as little more than amateur who had gained most of his knowledge and experience through actual fieldwork, as opposed to the indoctrination – ahem, instruction – of some prestigious university or institute. Yet this is probably why he could "think outside the box," come up with a new way to look at the data, and actually hold onto these convictions with little to lose.

Gladwin explained:

> It has been this negative attitude of mind, for instance, which has consistently refused to recognize the definite implications of the many references by physical anthropologists to such tribes as Australoid or Negroid in the makeup of various Indian tribes – even though veiled by such qualifications as Proto-Negroid or pseudo-Australoid. Terms such as these will be found only in technical papers on physical anthropology, but never in orthodox reconstructions of native American history. We have included them here because we think they cannot be fairly ignored, and, once you accept them as facts to be reckoned with, they turn out to be essential to an understanding of the problem since they show that Mongoloid people could not have reached North America before the time of Christ.[390]

Gladwin didn't have as much to lose as the others. These eminent scholars immediately caught hell for their ideas. Some sacrificed their entire careers as a result. They were outcast, along with their ideas.

In 1966, renowned anthropologist J. Lawrence Angel vindicated these early scholars, confirming that the first Americans were Australoid, and noting that his predecessors had already documented these connections:

Hooton, Count, Hrdlicka and many others have identified Paleo-Amerind individuals or even "types" which approximate Australoid or archaic White, and Negritoid or Melanesoid modes in East and Southeast Asia...This eastern Asiatic proto-Mongoloid norm does indeed show long-range resemblances to eastern Upper Paleolithics [from the Near East] and to Australoids (or Amurians and Negritoids), as well as to Palaeamericans...For example, the Liukiang South Chinese Paleolithic male skull, some Shang dynasty Chinese skulls and the female from Burial 5 at Tranquillity [in California] have low and broad noses, shallow malars, short faces and alveolar protrusion: a Negritoid (or Australoid?) trait complex.[391]

In other words, "Yup, they were right. These people were definitely Black."

Yet such conclusions were practically ignored. Even when Ivan Van Sertima republished these articles in the compilation *African Presence in Early America* in 1987, the idea that the first Native Americans were Black was considered yet another "Afrocentric myth." Few scholars took the idea seriously. Native American communities weren't too thrilled with the idea either.

Nearly a hundred years after Dixon published his *Racial History of Man*, it's becoming increasingly clear that the founding population of the Americas was, indeed, Black.

LUZIA AND FRIENDS

It was August 22, 1999. The heading in the UK *Sunday Times* declared boldly, "The first people to inhabit America were Australian Aborigines – not American Indians." Sarah Toyne reported on what the 12,000-year-old remains of a young girl unearthed in Brazil, told us about earliest human skeleton found in the Americas. This girl, whom scientists have named Luzia, has proven to be conclusive evidence that the first Americans were Blacks out of Asia. [392]

Walter Neves, professor of biological anthropology at the University of Sao Paolo, examined Luzia's skull for clues into the anthropological ancestry of the earliest Americans. Shocked by the results, he responded:

When we started seeing the results, it was amazing because we realized the statistics were not showing these people to be Mongoloid; they were showing that they were anything except Mongoloid... They are similar to modern-day Aborigines and Africans and show no similarities at all with Mongoloids from east Asia and modern-day Indians.[393]

Luzia's skull was then reconstructed by University of Manchester forensic artist Peter Neave, who echoed the remarks of Neves: "That to me is a negroid face. The proportions of the face do not say anything about it being Mongoloid."[394]

In the published study, the scientists reported:

In the first case, Lapa Vermelha IV Hominid 1 [also known as Luzia] exhibited an undisputed morphological affinity firstly with Africans and secondly with South Pacific populations. In the second comparison, the earliest known American skeleton had its closest similarities with early Australians, Zhoukoudian Upper Cave 103 [See the chapter on China], and Taforalt 18 [in prehistoric Morocco]. The results obtained clearly confirm the idea that the Americas were first colonized by a generalized Homo sapiens population which inhabited East Asia in the Late Pleistocene, before the definition of the classic Mongoloid morphology...[395]

In other words, Mongoloid Native Americans were a later wave, preceded by a wave with African or Australian features. But this was all based on one skull. Critics claimed Luzia could have been a "mutation" or "anomaly" and not representative of the norm.

By 2005, Neves had even more skulls to examine. In one of the most comprehensive reports on the first human skeletons in the Americas, the authors concluded:

Comparative morphological studies of the earliest human skeletons of the New World have shown that, whereas late prehistoric, recent, and present Native Americans tend to exhibit a cranial morphology similar to late and modern Northern Asians (short and wide neurocrania; high, orthognatic and broad faces; and relatively high and narrow orbits and noses), the earliest South Americans tend to be more similar to present Australians, Melanesians, and Sub-Saharan Africans (narrow and long neurocrania; prognathic, low faces; and relatively low and broad orbits and noses).[398]

In other words, most modern Native Americans may resemble Mongoloid people in Northeast Asia, but the earliest remains suggest the first Native Americans were Black people. Neves had found that the earliest remains – from southern Chile to coastal Florida to "Kennewick Man" in Washington – all looked Australoid and Africoid.[399]

In addition to Luzia, Peñon Woman, and Kennewick Man, other examples include the Wilson-Leonard remains from Texas (dated to 10,000 BP), the Santana do Riacho remains from Bahia, Brazil

(around 9,000 BP),[400] and the "Eve of Naharon" remains from an underwater cave in Mexico (13,600 BP).[401] By at least 14,000 years ago, the Australoid population had settled the Americas. By 10,000 years ago, Australoid people spanned the continents from end to end.

So we call the Australoid people the foundational people of the Americas because they laid the foundation for the modern Native American gene pool. Despite tons of admixture (first with Mongoloid people, then with centuries of European rapists and colonizers), there is still Australoid blood running through the veins of many Native Americans today.

BEFORE THE AUSTRALOIDS

Native American traditions recall mysterious "little people" who were not considered to be mortal men. There are dozens of accounts of these little people, who are held in high regard, often with fearful superstition of their semi-divine capabilities. Often they are not described as new arrivals, but the people who came first. Were they real? And if so, who were these people?

The ancestral human population (that is, the Black people who exited Africa 130,000 years ago) may have arrived in the Americas long before the Australoid wave. Unlike the Australoid wave, the ancestral human population may not have had many surviving descendants in the Americas.

As a result, we can't find any genetic traces of them in the Americas, but there are sites in Brazil that are 30-50,000 years old, and some sites that may be even older.[402] For most archaeologists, these represent the earliest evidence of human settlement. These could have been the Original People

They could have been the same people who became the Andaman Islanders, who never "make" their own fire, but instead carry naturally-struck fires from site to site. As we noted in *Volume One*, this isn't because they didn't know how to do so, but because they upheld a timeless tradition, shared only by the aboriginal DBP people of Tasmania. As Jean-Pierre Hallet notes in *Pygmy Kitabu*:

The Pygmies make and use artifacts that are far more complicated than friction firesticks. This is a fact that their stupid or bigoted critics somehow fail to realize. They preserve "perpetual fire" for religious reasons. Egyptians, Norsemen, American Indians, Greeks, Hindus, Persians, Hebrews, Christians, and many other people have zealously maintained perpetual altar fires, lamps, and candles. The Pygmies traditionally carry burning brands from one campsite to the next. The Greeks of early historic times brought fire to each new colony in identical style. The Pygmies supposedly marched through the blizzards of ice-age Siberia, Alaska, and Canada to accomplish their "Pygmoid visitation" to the Americas. This very chilly journey has been attributed to people who possessed no means of making artificial fire.

In other words, you're dumb if you think they were too dumb to master fire. They *had* mastered fire, but they'd also mastered the discipline required to survive in any environment without making their own fires. Which skill do you think is more impressive?

Still, we actually don't know what path they took, or when they came, but there's evidence they were here. In *Men Out of Asia*, Henry Gladwin wondered whether the Yahgans of Tierra del Fuego (who we'll discuss later) were of a Black "Pygmoid" extraction. He mentions "visitations" of small Black people before the Australoid wave, but they're never described as a large population movement.

Like everywhere else, few of these ancestral people would survive into the reign of the Australoid people. They were mostly likely pushed into the forest and mountains, where they eventually became the DBP. It's also possible that DBP populations from outside the Americas came into the Americas "already small."

Most traces of their presence can be found in myths and legends. Lewis and Clark, in their *Travels to the Source of the Missouri River*, said that the Sioux recalled a 'Mountain of Little People' near the Whitestone River, said to be inhabited by tiny humans, who were...

...armed with sharp arrows, and ever on the alert to kill mortals who should dare to invade their domain. So afraid were all the tribes of Red Men who lived near the mountain of these little spirits that no one of them could be induced to visit it.[406]

According to historian Donald A. Mackenzie, the Indians of California believed themselves to have been preceded by an earlier race that was "diminutive."[407]

The DBP of the Americas were the subject of nearly as much myth-making as the DBP of Europe and Asia. Native Americans held these diminutive Black, and later African people in general, to be exceptional healers and medicine men. For example, the Aztec god Ixtlilton, known as "the little negro," or "the black-faced," was the god of medicine and healing, and cured children of various diseases. He was also the god of feasting, dancing, and games.*

Occasionally, anthropologists uncover more concrete traces of the DBP. For example, pygmy burials were found near Cochocton, Ohio in 1937.[408] In Tennessee, similar graves were found, but the remains were dismissed as those of children. Virgilio R. Pilapil disagreed, using body measurements to argue that those graves were most definitely DBP burials. Because of their appearance, Pilapil theorized that they were Negritos who had arrived by boat from the Philippines, possibly related to today's Aetas. Pilapil also cited a Cherokee tradition that mentions the existence of "little people" in eastern North America, as well as a tradition among British Columbia Indians who recalled a very small people called the Et-nane.[409]

If the DBP were present in British Columbia, they may have indeed taken a land route. These may have been the people who Thomas Griffith Taylor said left "traces in America of aborigines akin to the Melanesians, and so ultimately to that great group of humanity to which the negroes belong."[410]

BLACK ESKIMOS?

We've been taught so wrong that we really believe there are Eskimos living in freezing-cold igloos on the ice in Alaska. For starters, they are known as the Inuit, and Eskimo is a name given to them by other people to insult them. It means "eaters of raw meat." Second, they don't live in igloos. Igloos are the temporary housing they construct when they go on hunting and fishing trips in frozen areas. And igloos

---

* For more on the Black gods of the Americas, see *Black God*, a forthcoming work from Supreme Design Publishing, to be released in the Summer of 2013.

might be made of ice, but they're warm inside, because their construction includes a special cold air trap that seals in warm arm, which is further heated with oil lamps. Guess what they build to live in? Houses. Yes, they used to build houses. That is, until the American and Canadian governments took over their lands and put them in cheap shacks. The point is, we're missing a lot of the story.

So don't be surprised when I say there's even a DBP presence in the history of the Inuit. The 12th century writer Eustathius tells of a little people in ancient Thule (Greenland), described as short-lived, small, and armed with spears that were like needles. The people of Greenland called them "Skraelings." In the 1911 book *Northern Mists: Arctic Exploration in Early Times*, Norwegian explorer Fridtjof Nansen writes:

> As the Skraelings of Greenland were dark, it was quite natural that they should become trolls...I have already stated that the Norse name 'Skraeling' for Eskimo must have originally been used as a designation of fairies or mythical creatures. Furthermore there is much that would imply that when the Icelanders first met with the Eskimo in Greenland they looked upon them as fairies; they, therefore, called them 'trolls,' an ancient common name for various sorts of supernatural beings. This view persisted more or less in after times. Every European who has suddenly encountered Eskimos in the ice-covered wastes of Greenland, without ever having seen them before, will easily understand that they must have made such an impression on people who had the slightest tendency toward superstition. Such an idea must, from the very beginning, have influenced the relations between the Norsemen and the natives, and is capable of explaining much that is curious in the mention of them, or rather the lack of mention of them, in the sagas, since they were supernatural beings of whom it was best to say nothing.

In Marshall B. Gardner's *A Journey to the Earth's Interior*, he explains:

> Nansen also notes that when Skraelings were mentioned in Latin writings the word was always translated "Pygmaei" and they were also described as living underground. 12th century Norse accounts even describe Skraelings bringing them into the fantastic world of their underground settlements. Nansen later explains that the present-day Eskimo is considerably different from the original "Skraeling" described by the Norse, due to Scandinavian intermixture after Norway cut off ties with the Greenland colonies in the 14th century, leaving the Norse to "mix" [ahem] with the indigenous people they once avoided. So, explains Nansen, "the Eskimo race as we know it today is not the same in physical appearance as the race that ordinarily came out of the interior of the earth."

In other words, many of the "dark" Skraelings eventually became light brown Inuit.

INUIT LEGENDS OF BLACK PEOPLE

Runoko Rashidi has written and published on the original Black population of the Americas, who were followed by a later Mongoloid migration that, over time, became the dominant population. Rashidi cites Henry Gladwin, who observed:

> The arrival of the Eskimo along the Arctic Coasts marked a fundamental transition in the anthropological history of North America. It was the last of a series of long-headed migrations, and the broad faces and slant eyes of the Eskimo marked the initial stage of a long period of Mongoloid domination in lands where Mongoloid people had therefore been unknown.

Rashidi adds:

> Mongoloid peoples, in fact, were soon coming to the Americas in such massive numbers, crossing the Bering Strait in boats rather than across the Beringia land bridge, that they eventually almost totally absorbed the New World's earlier arrivals. The resulting fusion of peoples constituted the native American populations at the time of the catastrophic European intrusions during the fifteenth and sixteenth centuries. The earlier arrived Blacks (the very first Americans) tended to fade away with increasing rapidity into the shadowy realms of fairy tales, myths and legends. Some native legends of the Americas abound with exploits of early Black people.

He cites an Inuit legend, describing an Inuit woman's encounter with a man who was "black all over, even his face." The Black man wanted to take the woman to live with him, but her father replied, "I won't have my daughter going away with a black man like you." The legend continues:

> The stranger became angry and made a step forward with his right foot. The whole house shook. Then the father said to his daughter, "My daughter, you'll have to go away with this man. This will go badly with us if you don't." She got ready and left the house, with the stranger behind her. Before leaving, he put his left foot down hard on the floor and the house shook again. He went out, put the girl on the sledge and shoved the sledge because it had no huskies. After a while they saw a house – the man's house. They stopped and entered. Everything inside was black, and his parents also were completely black.[411]

There are several myths and legends like this among the Inuit, the Tlingit, and many other native people in Northwestern Canada (as well as among the Iroquois and others further south). They don masks that look like Black people during their most important cultural ceremonies. Clearly, there is some remembrance of a Black people deep in their history.

But the Original Inuit people were not necessarily pale-skinned. Many of them, too, bear the traces of ancient Black roots. For example, many of them are not broad-headed, but long-headed. Their bodies are cold-adapted, but their skin is still brown. In fact, some sources (especially the older ones) have said that they were darker than any of the other indigenous people in North America, and – in some cases – they were "blacker" than any African! (See the chapter on Europe for the quotes.)

THE DBP IN SOUTH AMERICA

As far south as Brazil, there are legends of little-people, described variously as "leprechauns", "pygmies", and "dwarves," who are seen sporadically in the Amazon rainforest. When the Rio Negro River in Manaus, Brazil experienced an extreme drop in water levels, a fisherman noted some unusual markings on rocks that were now exposed above the water's surface.

Scientists visited the region and identified geometric shapes, spirals, and serpentine designs. Also found were a series of human characters, some with pygmy characteristics. Although rock carvings are hard to date (because of the lack of organic material), scientists have suggested the drawings may date back to about 7,000 years ago, when river levels were similarly low in the region.[412]

THE 500 NATIONS

If you haven't had a chance to check out the documentary (and book) *500 Nations*, it's definitely worth a look. And its title is no exaggeration. Within the geographic boundaries of the U.S. alone, there are more than 566 indigenous nations, speaking over 250 languages. When you factor in Central and South America, you've got at least 1,000 ethnic groups to consider. Many of these people are descendants of small clans that came into the Americas, had several thousand years to split up, go their separate ways, and become distinct nations on their own.[413] We can use genetics, linguistics, and anthropology to establish who may be related, and who came from who. As you look, however, the traces of the early Black presence may be difficult to find.

Obviously, most of the indigenous people of the Americas don't look Black today. You'll have to realize, of course, that there's been over 70,000 years of genetic drift and mutation since our brothers in the Americas left Africa. You can't expect them to look straight-up

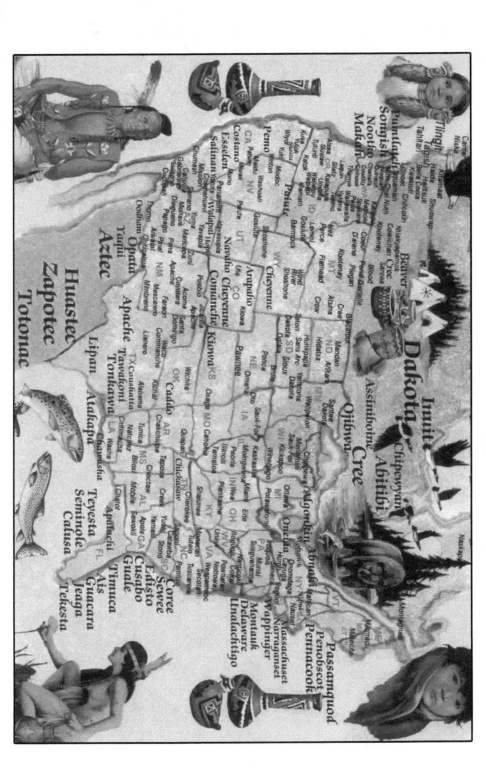

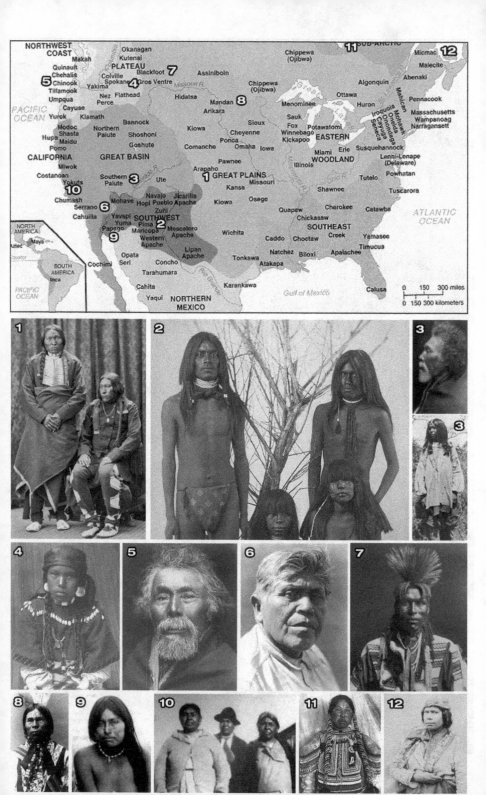

African or speak African languages. But you might be surprised how much is preserved. You can still find Australoid features among many Native American faces, such as those of the Pericú and the Fuegians of South America.

The further you go back into the photographic record, you will also see that the original Indians were much darker than they are now. Their hair was also much coarser. Many even wore dreadlocks. In fact, you can see that hundreds of Native American cultural traditions are near duplicates of those found in Africa. We'll get into that common culture in Volume Three.

After you've considered 70,000 years of regionalized evolution and genetic drift, you then have to remember the history of how European conquest works. They literally rape women everywhere they go. I'm not saying that to be extreme. That is what the historical record tells us.

Any "contacted tribe" of indigenous people ANYwhere in the world has experienced some degree of "miscegenation" thanks to the lust of European males. If they weren't simply *taking* women outright, they would *marry* as many as they could afford to, all the while writing back to Europe with reports on how they despised these ignorant savage people.

This history has quite a lot to do with the gradual lightening of the Native American complexion over the past 500 years of European domination. Not to mention that the past century has seen the growing popularity of "indigenous lifestyles." This has inspired thousands of whites to claim Native American ancestry, some simply for bragging rights, some to escape "whiteness," others for more insidious reasons. So the face of the Americas, again, has changed considerably within recent years.

But there is yet another element that contributed to the transition from an Australoid foundation to today's 500 Nations: another wave of ancient migrations.

How Many Migrations were There?

"The 'native' inhabitants of the Western Hemisphere are not all minor variants of the same people."
– Anthropologist C. Loring Brace

For as long as scholars have been studying the indigenous people of the Americas, they've observed that *they don't all look alike*. This has led to decades of speculation about how many groups of people actually settled the Americas, and who those people became.

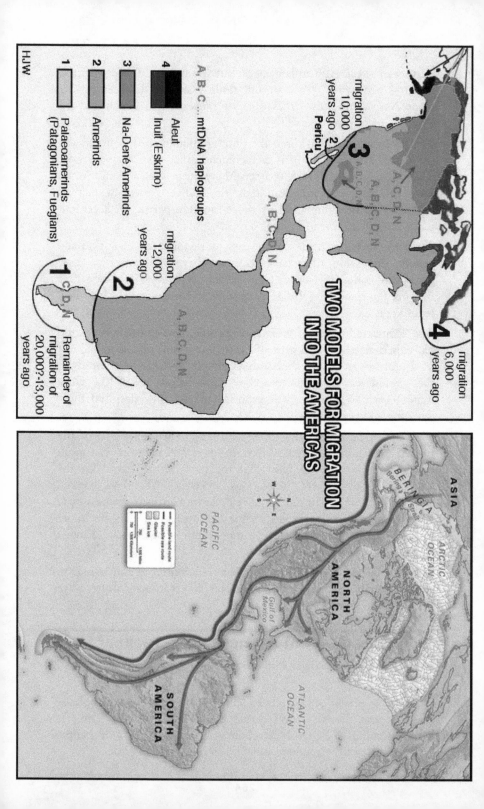

TWO MODELS FOR MIGRATION INTO THE AMERICAS

A, B, C ... mtDNA haplogroups

4 — Aleut Inuit (Eskimo)
3 — Na-Dené Amerinds
2 — Amerinds
1 — Palaeoamerinds (Patagonians, Fuegians)

migration 10,000 years ago

Pericu

migration 12,000 years ago

Remainder of migration of 20,000?-13,000 years ago

migration 6,000 years ago

HJW

Figuring out the "true story" of the prehistoric peopling of any part of the world is like assembling a puzzle. With the story of the Americas, there's a big chunk of the puzzle missing, and it's hard to put the picture together without it. You see, many indigenous nations of the United States aren't interested in being involved in DNA studies of human ancestry.* This means there's a lot we don't know about millions of indigenous people in North America.

Fortunately, we can figure out some of what's left unsaid by looking at what is being said. That is, studies of language can reveal a great deal about people and population movements.

In 1492, an estimated 30-40 million Native Americans spoke more than 1,000 different languages. Renowned linguist Joseph Greenberg proposed that all of these languages could be classified into three groups:

❏ The Na-Dene family: These languages are spoken from Asia to Alaska to northwestern America (with a few offshoots reaching as far as Mexico). The roots of Na-Dene may be in Siberia. They arrived between 6,000 and 10,000 years ago.[414†]

❏ The Eskimo-Aleut family: These languages are mostly spoken in Alaska, northern Canada, and Greenland, and include the languages of the Inuit people. They arrived between 3,000 and 6,000 years ago.

❏ The Amerind family: This is Greenberg's grouping for all the languages that don't fit in the other two groups, including isolated languages that don't seem connected to anything else, like the languages spoken by the people of Matto Grosso in Brazil. Some of these languages may derive from the original Australoid population of the Americas. Some are connected to languages found in Oceania. Other languages in the Amerind family appear to be related to the Afro-Asiatic language family. Others may have arrived with the first wave of Mongoloid migration into the Americas between 12,000 and 14,000 years ago.[415]

We certainly still don't know enough about the languages of the Americas. There remains considerable disagreement about how and when these language families arrived, and who introduced them. But on thing is clear. What these language families suggest is that that there were *at least* three waves of migration into the Americas.

---

* For example, in a 2012 study, the Genographic Project of the National Geographic Society wrote to all the federally recognized tribes in the U.S. asking for DNA samples, but only two agreed to give them. In their defense, there are old samples from many indigenous nations that can be consulted.

† For more on the Na-Dene languages, and their possible connection to Afrasiatic people, see "Unexpected Genes in Early America" in the Appendix of Part Two.

THE STORY IN THE SKULLS

Another way to dig into the evidence is by examining skeletal remains. Dr. C. Loring Brace, a professor of Anthropology at the University of Michigan, has analyzed over 1500 skulls from across North, Central and South America as well as their possible ancestors in Asia and Australia. Brace says the skulls suggest the people of the Americas came in at least three distinct waves, some of whom trace back to recent Asian ancestors, others to a Paleo-Mongoloid population that is no longer widespread in Asia, and still others to prehistoric Australoid people.[416]

HOW DID THEY GET THERE?

From the distribution of the earliest sites in the Americas, it appears that there were four routes by which people arrived:

- ❏ From Southeast Asia and Oceania across the Pacific Ocean, sailing east into the west coasts of the Americas.
- ❏ From Asia (India/Siberia/China/Japan) along the northern land route across northeast Asia into Alaska and then southward into North America.
- ❏ From Africa, sailing west across the Atlantic Ocean, into eastern Central and South America (Olmec Mexico and Brazil).
- ❏ From northwest Europe, island-hopping from Greenland into northeastern Canada.

ACROSS THE PACIFIC

Almost all of the oldest American remains are found along coastal sites, and none of them look like modern "Amerindians." They look like Australian Aborigines, Melanesians, Ainu, Papuans, and South Indians. In other words, Black people. Specifically, they most closely resemble Australoid people.

How did they get here? It appears the Australoid colonization of the Americas came by way of maritime convoy, rather than by land.[417] They obviously had the technology to navigate these waters, and the desire to do so. In August of 1999, *BBC News* reported on some of the evidence that supports this theory:

> [H]ow could the early Australians have travelled more than 13,500 kilometres (8,450 miles) at that time? The answer comes from more cave paintings, this time from the Kimberley, a region at the northern tip of Western Australia.
>
> Here, Grahame Walsh, an expert on Australian rock art, found the oldest painting of a boat anywhere in the world. The style of the art means it is at least 17,000 years old, but it could be up to 50,000

INDIANS OF THE PACIFIC NORTHWEST

INUIT HOUSE

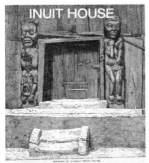

HAIDA WEDDING

Note the faces of the Haida men, and the statues at the doorway of both buildings. Compare with the Inuit tradition of Black sentries standing outside meeting houses.

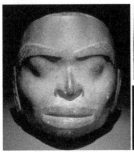

NORTHWESTERN NATIVE MASKS
(Eyak, Tlingit, Haida, & Tsimshian)

These masks - associated with shamans - appear to portray Black features (in varying degrees of exaggeration). Compare with the Iroquois "False Face Society."

LEFT: The only known photo of Haida shamans in their masks (c.1881). These masks clearly represent Black people. MIDDLE: A clearer image of Chief X'ana's tattoos. Tattooing is one of many traditions shared by the Ainu, some Pacific Islanders, and the Haida. RIGHT: A modern Haida male at a canoe dedication ceremony. Again, note the reverence for Black people, as seen in the mask.

years old. And the crucial detail is the high prow of the boat. This would have been unnecessary for boats used in calm, inland waters. The design suggests it was used on the open ocean.[418]

They could have come and settled anywhere their boats landed, expanding southwards and northwards along the western coasts before expanding inland. Because sea levels have risen 100 feet since that time, most of the sites where they first landed are probably buried underwater now. We're probably also missing a ton of evidence from the Asian side of things as well. Still, there's plenty of evidence of an Australoid presence up to 20,000 years old.

THE HAIDA OF NORTHWEST CANADA

In Japan, where Australoid people later founded the Jōmon culture, there is also evidence of boat use 20,000 years ago. This could explain why some Native American remains resemble Jōmon remains. It also connects East Asian maritime cultures to maritime cultures on the west coast of the Americas.

For example, we've already discussed the Pericú of Baja, California. Further north, the Haida of Northwest Canada are a sailing culture who resemble the Jōmon (and later Ainu) in many ways. For example, they practice tattooing, they have a bear cult, they practice shamanism, and look more like Australoid people than their neighbors. In fact, some of the masks worn by the oldest shamans are made to look just like African or Australian faces.

In the early 1900s, Dr. John Swanton of the Bureau of American Ethnology, reported that "the richest man among the Skidegate Haida is a Negro."[419] In his *Haida Texts and Myths*, Swanton retells a Haida story of young man who visits a house where shamans gathered. In front of the house stood two shamans "with big bellies and black skins." In another story, a young man's uncle asks him about a journey he took recently to the top of a mountain. He says:

> Did you see the one standing there with a black skin? He shoots down on those people below who treat each other badly. Then the land below is also full of smoke, and there is sickness every where...Be watchful. If one always watches, he, too, will live here. **The black man always keeps watch on those who are foolish.**[420]

WHEN DID THESE BLACK PEOPLE ARRIVE IN CANADA?

Or better yet, how? They certainly could have taken a boat route from northern Japan, along the shores of the Bering Strait, onto the coasts of Northwest Canada. But the majority of the evidence suggests that all of the earliest Americans did not come this way. Most of the dates point to an ocean migration from Southeast Asia

DID YOU KNOW?
According to a recent study of 1500 skulls from Asia and the Americas, the Blackfoot, Iroquois, and many other tribes along the eastern U.S. resemble the Jōmon, the prehistoric people of Japan! The Jōmon were a later branch of the Australoid people, who may have evolved regionally in east Asia. The Indians of the eastern seaboard would thus be descended from the Australoid people of East Asia, with some traits that may have evolved locally. The study suggests that the Inuit are an even later branch from that same Jōmon trunk.[421]

or Oceania, island-hopping across the Pacific Islands, before ultimately landing on the Pacific coast of Peru (and possibly Mexico).

This would explain why the sites and settlements get older when you go further south. In other words, Australoid people who landed in South America then traveled north to settle North America's shores. And here's the thing: Crossing the Pacific Ocean – a distance of over 8,000 miles – wouldn't have been as tough as it sounds. Just as there are ocean currents that will carry just about any sailing vessel from West Africa into eastern Brazil and Mexico, there are also ocean currents – like the Equatorial Countercurrent – that could carry Australasian canoes and rafts across the entire Pacific.

Ironically, one of these trans-Pacific ocean currents is known to the Japanese as the *Kuro Shiwa*, or "Black Stream." On November 30, 1980, six Japanese researchers arrived in Chile, six and a half months after leaving Shimoda, Japan in a 43-foot catamaran. They took the Kuro Shiwa Current east to the Northern Pacific Current, taking that to San Francisco, then sailing down the coast to Chile. In 1991, Gerard d'Aboville rowed a 26-foot boat from Japan to Washington State in just 134 days.[422] Again, these migrations are not unrealistic at ALL.

Not to mention that they'd have plenty of islands to stop at along the way! In 1978, a man named Webb Chiles left San Diego to circumnavigate the world in an 18-foot boat. He stopped at several islands along the Pacific as he made his way west. Two years later, he sailed into Cairns Harbor, 1250 miles north of Sydney, Australia.[423]

You mean to tell me that our ancestors couldn't do this? Of course they could. And you'll find this part of our journey described in our chapter on the Pacific Islands.

THE MONGOLOID MIGRATION

When did the face of the Americas change? Genetic evidence suggests that at least one wave of people migrated into the Americas via the Bering land bridge which once connected Siberia to Alaska. Thus, while one group took the luxury route, sailing ships into the west coasts of the Americas, another took the hard road, walking through thousands of miles of bitter cold tundra. The branch that took the land route left India about 16,000 years ago.

We don't know how long they remained in Siberia before they migrated into Alaska, but it's uncertain if they were in the Americas more than 10,000 years ago, as all of the old sites that are associated with the "first Americans" can no longer be attributed to this group of people. Not only that, but the oldest Mongoloid remains don't even seem to go back that far.

But there's no denying that a Mongoloid population DID come into the Americas, where they quickly began displacing and replacing the old Australoid populations. Same thing happened later in East Asia and even later in the Pacific Islands. Different anthropologists place the Mongoloid migration into the Americas at different times. Some say it dates back as far as 10,000 years ago, while other say it only happened within the past 3,000 years.

Compounding the confusion, it also appears that more than one wave of Mongoloid people came into the Americas.[425] The oldest waves were what we call Paleo-Mongoloid, while later waves from Siberia were Neo-Mongoloid, meaning they were closer in appearance to modern East Asians. Some of these people only made it as far south as Mexico. And an even later wave of "southern" Mongoloid people – related to the Polynesians – came by sea from the Pacific Islands, reaching the west coast of the Americas and then spreading outwards. We'll talk about some of these transitions in our chapter on the Pacific.

WHAT ABOUT WEST AFRICANS?

As far as the people who came from West Africa, these people were obviously Black. But there may have been multiple voyages, and it's hard to tell when the first voyage could have been. In *They Came Before Columbus* and *African Presence in Early America*, Ivan Van Sertima establishes mountains of data for pre-Columbian voyages from Africa over the past 3,000 years.

As early as 1922, Leo Weiner, in his two-volume text *Africa and the Discovery of America*, was making the same case. But could the 30,000-

year-old sites in Brazil have been populated from Africa? It's possible, but unproven. The Atlantic Ocean has a current that sweeps off the North West coast of Africa and across the Atlantic toward the Americas. This current, known as the Canaries Current, is so efficient that it could carry even a simple West African fishing boat (like the 8,000 year old Dufuna Canoe found in Nigeria) all the way to Brazil, Mexico, or the Caribbean Islands.

In 1988, Rudiger Nehberg sailed from Senegal to northern Brazil, in a small Fiberglass pedal-rowing boat, taking only 74 days. Two years prior, Alain Pichavant and Stephane Peyron took only 24 days to travel from Senegal to Guadeloupe (and then New York) in a small sailboat. In 1985, two men even made a transatlantic crossing by *surfboard* in only 39 days![426] So it wouldn't take complicated boats to make the journey – the current would have done most of the work.

James Guthrie notes that there is a sizable body of evidence supporting an early African migration into South America and the Caribbean:

> Some have argued for African influence between 8000 and 5700 B.C. on the basis of cultigens, including cotton, jackbeans, and the bottlegourd, which may have reached South and Central America from Africa before 5000 B.C. (Schwerin 1970; Simmonds 1976; Lathrap 1977). Wendel, Schnabel, and Seelanan (1995) have now established the identity, through DNA sequences, of a cotton variety grown both in Africa and in the Isthmus of Tehuantepec, presumably a result of early human activity.

> It remains to be seen whether a connection will be made between postulated early African voyaging and the very early pottery of the lower Amazon (8000-6000 B.C.) reported by Roosevelt et al. (1991) and Hoopes (1994). Hoeppli (1969) identified African parasitic diseases that were present in early America and was able to distinguish them from those brought later by the slave trade.

> Some South American populations, especially the Ge groups of eastern Brazil, possess some seemingly African traits, but it does not seem possible at present to make a conclusive case for extreme antiquity of sub-Saharan African traits. Africoid skeletons from Venezuela and Yucatán appear to demonstrate Atlantic travel from Africa to the Caribbean (Wiercinsky 1972), but they are from a later

period. Any early African colonists are likely to have been submerged beyond easy recognition by the more numerous Asians.[428]

In others, if these Africans had any descendants, they'll be tough to identify because any West African DNA in the area will be assumed to come from the slave trade.[429] However, we've pieced together much of this puzzle in Part Two, where we've covered a wide array of genetic data pointing to Black migrations within the past 5,000 years, as well as the civilizations they built.

REVIEW

In 1947, Henry Gladwin asserted that there were four successive waves of migrations to enter North America: (1) Australoid Blacks, (2) Asiatic Negroids, (3) Algonquians, and (4) Eskimos (Inuit). It was a revolutionary proposal, and far ahead of its time. Recent studies of Native DNA (outside the U.S.) have confirmed that at least three waves settled the Americas.[430] Based on my review of the available data, it is my theory that there were indeed dozens of migrations into the Americas before Columbus. We can group them into a few categories as follows:

❑ First came the Original People/DBP, either by foot, by sea, or both. They may have come anywhere between 30 and 100,000 years ago, and may never have been here in large numbers.

❑ Next came Australoid People, settling the west coast of the Americas by boat, beginning about 20,000 years ago, but possibly before then. They became the founding population of the Americas.

❑ Between 3,000 and 15,000 years ago a Paleo-Mongoloid people left Siberia by land. These people established a dominant presence in the Americas, absorbing many of their Australoid predecessors.

❑ Several more Mongoloid migrations followed, via both a northern route through Northeast Asia and a southern route along the Pacific Islands. These people became another dominant face in the Americas.

❑ Over the past 8,000 years, several voyages came from Africa, but they didn't displace or replace the native populations they enountered. They were, however, more influential than any European visitors before Columbus.

In Part Two, we'll cover the last wave of these migrations, particularly those coming from Africa and the Black civilizations of East Asia.

WHY IGNORE ALL THESE MIGRATIONS?

Why are the multiple migrations to the Americas ignored? Because

America – pre-white people – was held to be a nonentity in world affairs, and of no real significance. It lay outside the peripheral view of Western minds even after Columbus discovered it for them, and only gradually grew in relevance as Europeans increasingly found it useful (for resources to improve the conditions of those in Europe) and habitable (for those who had no place left to go in Europe). But Europeans continued to debate whether Indians were human for almost 100 years.

The issue of whether the "Indians" were human was debated for almost 100 years. It was addressed directly by Pope Paul III early on in the May 29, 1537 papal bull *Sublimus Dei* in which the pope declares the indigenous peoples of the Americas to be rational beings with souls, denouncing any idea to the contrary as directly inspired by Satan. He condemns Indian slavery and declares their right to liberty and property, concluding with a call for their evangelization.*

So why a New World? Cause the "Old World" revolved around Europe. Adam and Eve were white, and everything – including Black people – were thought to come from them.†

So the Americas, like Africa, spent quite a while sitting on the shelf, awaiting serious consideration by Europeans. It was during this time that the land bridge migration theory was first proposed by José de Acosta, S.J. in 1590 in *Historia Natural y Moral de las Indias*.

Over the next 200 years, the Americas became important, Indians became human, and the original migration theory was revised, updated, and amended with scientific data. It kept things simple: to think that the Americas was settled by one group of people at one point in time. Thinking of it this way preserved the simplicity of the Americas, which were still obviously not as relevant to the world as those places that experiences hundreds of population movements over thousands of years.[431]

---

* Yet Africans and Muslims were a different story. In 1452, when the Portuguese sought confirmation that they could enslave infidels seized in the Crusade, the Pope issued *Dum Diversus*, which allowed them to conquer and reduce to "perpetual slavery" all "Saracens and pagans and other infidels and enemies of Christ." Two years later, the Pope issued *Romanus Pontifex*, which granted the Portuguese a perpetual monopoly over Africa. For more, see *Black Rebellion: Eyewitness Accounts of Major Slave Revolts*, published by Two Horizons Press.

† It's true that some historians called Black people "Pre-Adamites," but this was typically used to say they were subhuman, while many others simply considered Blacks a cursed race descended from Noah's son Ham.

So, nobody has seriously entertained the idea of several waves of migration coming into (and possibly out of) the Americas because, well, that's the type of stuff that only happens in important places. It's a racist assumption, and it goes hand-in-hand with another racist assumption that we accept without question: that sailing across the Atlantic or Pacific Ocean was somehow outside the range of capabilities available to ancient Black and brown people before they met white people. Seriously, think about it. That's the assumption.

Never mind the fact that Black folks had to sail to Australia over 60,000 years ago (whatever land bridge they claim didn't connect it all the way – there were at least seven miles of water to cross even when there was a land bridge). And our ancestors certainly had to know how to sail to settle every last one of the damn Pacific Islands – and there's literally more than 10,000 of them – spanning across over 68,000,000 square miles of ocean!

You mean to tell me these folks could sail all the way up to the last island, right before you hit the west coast of the Americas…but they never made it into the Americas? Are the Americas some sort of magic land bottled up in an impenetrable casing – except at the very top corner where there's a small opening that opened once in the distant past?

It's the same type of thinking that has us thinking of a "Black Africa" (or "Sub-Saharan Africa") as if Africans could never get out of the bottom of a pot called the African continent…except through a little spout in the top corner that opened once in the distant past.

QUESTIONS TO CONSIDER

We have plausible theories, but we don't know exactly how or when Australoid people first arrived. All we know is that they were the first large population movement into the Americas. This leaves us with questions.

For example, if most of the oldest American skeletons are found along the coasts, and most of the coasts are now underwater, how far back does Australoid settlement go? Currently, the oldest skeleton, the Eve of Naharon, dates back to at least 13,600 years ago, and was found in an underwater cave near Mexico.[432] But how many more are there to be found?

Further, how many Original People (before the Australoid migration) came into the Americas and how did they come? If we're trying to figure out how they got there, it'll be tough. We don't know when the first humans arrived, but it could have been more than 30,000 years ago. The problem is that there simply aren't enough remains and none of the remains have been reliably dated. All we know is that SOMEBODY was here before the time period when all the Australoid remains show up along the coast.

How far did these early humans spread? Were they all displaced by Australoid people, and does that explain accounts of DBP people in the Americas? Did any of these DBP people survive, perhaps in the remote forest regions of the Amazon where there are "uncontacted tribes" we know very little about?

And why do Australoid skeletons appear all along the west coasts of the Americas, but also on the eastern coasts of Mexico, near the Caribbean? K.R. Fladmark says they could have traveled the entire length of America's west coasts in ten years' time.[433] During their initial colonization did they travel to the east coast by land (across Central America) or did they sail across some prehistoric water channel in the Isthmus of Panama? Or did they take the longer water journey around the southern tip of South America?

> *"[S]ome scientists are of the opinion that the South American Indians are the present representatives of Paleolithic man, who dwelt in Africa before the evolution of the Black race."*
> *– J. Fitzgerald Lee, Great Migration, 1932*

And what about the African routes into the Americas? Genetic evidence suggests that African sailors were in South America by 8,000 years ago, but did anyone come from African before this? We know West Africa wasn't heavily populated before 8,000 BC, but could Saharans have sailed down the Niger River and made this journey 20,000 years ago? As Willard P. Leutze writes in "The First Americans – Red or Black?":

> [T]here were two different groups of early man in the western hemisphere, and that the group advancing from the south to north was earlier than the Asiatic migration by a substantial margin. If men entered the Americas through South America, they probably originated in Africa.

If so, which prehistoric skeletons in the Americas look more Africoid than Australoid? Or were some prehistoric Africans, like the 36,000 year old Hofmeyr skull from South Africa, more Australoid? Or is Walter Neves correct in describing populations this old as looking so much like either branch that they should be described as resembling both African AND Australoid people instead of being associated with only one of the two?

THE WORLD'S TONAL LANGUAGES

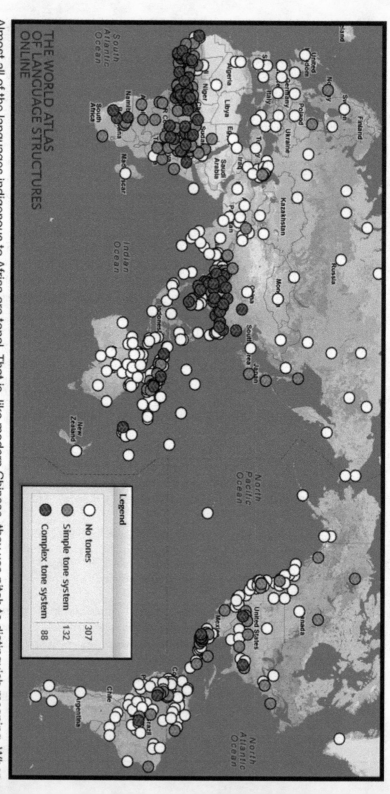

THE WORLD ATLAS
OF LANGUAGE STRUCTURES
ONLINE

Legend

○	No tones	307
◐	Simple tone system	132
●	Complex tone system	88

Almost all of the languages indigenous to Africa are tonal. That is, like modern Chinese, they use pitch to distinguish meaning. When we look at places where tonal languages occur in isolation, are we looking at places where Africans introduced their style of speaking? Other forms of linguistic evidence, along with the genetic evidence, suggest these connections are as real as they sound.

AN EXERCISE IN CORROBORATING DATA

LOOK AT THE FREQUENCY OF TYPE O BLOOD AMONG INDIGENOUS PEOPLE

Grupo O

25-45%
45-70%
70-100 %

NOTICE AFRICA, AUSTRALIA, AND THE AMERICAS

COMPARE WITH THE GLOBAL DISTRIBUTION OF TONAL LANGUAGES

CROSS-CHECK AGAINST THE DARKEST INDIGENOUS PEOPLE IN THE AMERICAS

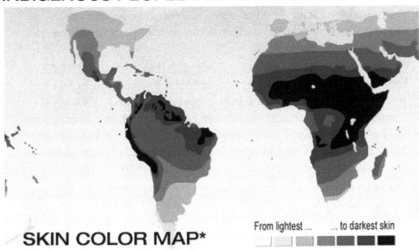

SKIN COLOR MAP*

From lightest ...   ... to darkest skin

Source: Chaplin G.©, *Geographic Distribution of Environmental Factors Influencing Human Skin Coloration*, American Journal of Physical Anthropology 125:292–302, 2004; map updated in 2007.

AT THE EXTREME END OF SOUTH AMERICA
WHO WERE THE FUEGIANS?

"In Tierra del [Fuego] I first saw bona fide savages; & they are as savage as the most curious person would desire. – A wild man is indeed a miserable animal, but one well worth seeing." – Charles Darwin

The Black people of South America didn't disappear. One of the strongest pockets of survival appears to be in Tierra del Fuego, which is found at the southernmost tip of South America. It is the southernmost inhabited land in the world, and the closest to Antarctica. The region is notorious for its treacherous rocks, violent winds and mountainous waves. There are few days without rain, sleet, hail, or snow. Living marginalized at the extreme end of the Americas, the Fuegian people are one of the oldest people on the planet, and most likely the oldest people of the Americas.

The Fuegians are physically, culturally and linguistically distinct from other Native Americans. According to Walter Neves, the Fuegians may be the descendants of the original Australoid people who settled the Americas, mixed with later people from East Asia. Therefore the Fuegians are **the last surviving remnants of the original people of the Americas.**

Anthropologists guessed at this long ago, because many Fuegian people practiced body painting and rock art that looked just like the kind you'd find in Australia. Several linguists have compared the Fuegian languages to those of Australia.[434] Erich Von Hornbostel likened Fuegian songs to those of Australia, Ceylon, and the Andaman Islands.[435]

Later studies have found that many Fuegian remains were Australoid.[436] Recent studies have described Fuegians skulls as aligning "with Africans and Australians, instead of with Asians and modern Amerindians."[437]

So who were the people of Tierra del Fuego? Joseph McCabe believed that the migration that brought the Fuegians from Asia into the Americas came before a later migration of "Red Indians" who "pushed the crude earlier population south, or into the forests, just as the arrivals from Europe displaced the Indian."[438] Later studies have confirmed that the people of Tierra del Fuego may be descendants of the oldest surviving population in the Americas.

For several thousand years, they've maintained a thriving lifestyle in a harsh and unforgiving environment, with no worries, and little evidence of strife or struggle. They lived in the frigid cold and biting wind, wearing almost nothing, even swimming naked in the freezing water! Remember, this is the southernmost tip of South America, not far from Antarctica! Though the Fuegians make fires and build domed shelters, European anthropologists reported that they often slept in the open, completely unsheltered, while the Europeans shivered under their blankets.

Old photographs of the Fuegian people reveal them to be darker than many of the indigenous people further north. Some look Mongoloid (from a later migration), but others are dark-skinned and have kept their Australoid features.* When Charles Darwin – who was supposedly "not a racist" – reported on his visit to the Fuegians, he said:

> I could not have believed how wide was the difference between savage and civilised man: it is greater than between a wild and domesticated animal, inasmuch as in man there is a greater power of improvement...Their skin is of a dirty coppery red colour...The party altogether closely resembled the devils which come on the stage in plays like Der Freischutz.[439]

In other words, these were some dark-skinned people. For many Europeans, this alone was enough to be considered savages and devils.

THE FUEGIAN GENOCIDE

Like the Andamanese, the Aetas, and the San, they are one of the oldest surviving remnants of the Original People who settled the four corners of the Earth. And like those people, the Fuegians are being exterminated.

Why? Joseph McCabe thought the Fuegians were among the best examples of how indigenous people with the longest histories still live today. He grouped them with the Veddahs of India, the

---

* Dark-skinned? After 13,000-20,000 years of cold? How did they survive in this environment, for thousands of years, without their skin turning white? Simple. Cold climates don't produce white skin. What does? We'll explain the "secret" to the origins of whiteness in Volume Four.

> **DID YOU KNOW?**
> DBP people aren't the only subjects of European myth and legend. It is now known that the legendary stories told by early European explorers about the Patagones, a race of giants in South America, are actually based on the Tehuelches, a Fuegian people who are taller than most Europeans. When European explorers described these people, who average about 6 feet tall, they called them giants and said they were 12 to 15 feet tall. Early maps of the New World afterwards would sometimes attach the label "Land of Giants") to the area. "Patagonian" became synonymous with "giant" in European folklore.

Tasmanians, the Andamanese, the Khoisan of South Africa, the Aetas of the Philippine Islands, and "a few less known fragments of the human family" as some of the most marginalized people of today. Yet he contends:

> These peoples at the lowest level have no moral rules or ideas, yet they rarely steal, lie, or murder. They are kindly to the widow and aged. They live peacefully. They observe the decalogue [Ten Commandments] better than more advanced tribes, but they have no decalogue.[440]

These people also have lower instances of mental illness, disease, and other issues...until European contact. These groups have never – in thousands of years of oral tradition – had an instance of suicide....until they met Europeans.[441] These groups had ways of life that worked for tens of thousands of years without interruption, but were stopped almost immediately and driven to near extinction when they met Europeans. The Fuegians are yet another case study of how this happens.

WHO'S THE BEST MAN?

When whites met the Fuegians, they were civilized and strong. One of the first missionaries/explorers to encounter the Fuegians, Captain Robert Fitzoy of the HMS Beagle "forbade his sailors to wrestle with the natives, who, **being the stronger would learn to despise the white man.**"[442] Stop. Just let that marinate for a minute.

Charles Darwin, who traveled with Fitzoy, remarked on the mental acuteness of the Fuegians:

> They are excellent mimics: as often as we coughed or yawned, or made any odd motion, they immediately imitated us. Some of our party began to squint and look awry; but one of the young Fuegians (whose whole face was painted black, excepting a white band across his eyes) succeeded in making far more hideous grimaces. They could repeat with perfect correctness each word in any sentence we addressed them, and they remembered such words for some time.
>
> Yet we Europeans all know how difficult it is to distinguish apart the sounds in a foreign language. Which of us, for instance, could follow an American Indian through a sentence of more than three words?

All savages appear to possess, to an uncommon degree, this power of mimicry. I was told, almost in the same words, of the same ludicrous habit among the Caffres; the Australians, likewise, have long been notorious for being able to imitate and describe the gait of any man, so that he may be recognized.

How can this faculty be explained? Is it a consequence of the more practiced habits of perception and keener senses, common to all men in a savage state, as compared with those long civilized?[443]

Isn't that ironic? "Savage" people can remember any word they learn from a foreigner, but "civilized" whites can't process three words from a savage? It's not like these European really *believed* they were advanced, however. **They just made it their image.** By 1850, British explorer W.P. Snow was reporting back to his countrymen:

In their rude state wild men often fancy themselves our superiors in many things, and to rightly deal with them we must show that we can hunt, fish, sing, talk, dance, and endure hardship as well as they.[444]

If you believe that any European to visit Tierra del Fuego (or anywhere else indigenous people are found) was actually able to *compete* in fishing, hunting, singing, or any damn thing, you're kidding yourselves. So what did they do? What do you *think* they did?

IF YOU CAN'T BEAT EM, KILL EM

Before long, whites began destroying the Fuegian people. How? As we'll explore in Volume Four, it's almost as if they had a script everywhere they went. Here's how it went in Tierra del Fuego:

❏ The first to come were missionaries, who introduced - along with culturally incompatible ideologies* - European diseases like smallpox and measles. Thus began the genocide.

❏ The missionaries also forced the Fuegians to wear clothes, which caused more problems. The grease the Indians put on their bodies protected them from rain and ocean spray, but their new clothes were perpetually damp. So outbreaks of pneumonia, influenza, and tuberculosis soon became common.[445]

❏ Not long after they set up camp, Europeans began taking Fuegians hostage and assimilating them, only to use them to later take better advantage of the native people and land.

❏ Soon, Spanish sheep ranchers and gold miners launched a campaign of extermination against the indigenous peoples of Tierra del Fuego. They literally began hunting and killing them like animals.

❏ Before long, the surviving Fuegians found themselves starving

---

* Fuegians practice the same kind of Shamanism found among the oldest people of Asia, Africa, Australia, and the rest of the Americas.

because European and American ships were eliminating their natural food supply by overfishing the region.

As it goes everywhere else they did this, the combined effects were devastating. The Fuegians were reduced from tens of thousands pre-European contact, to over 6,000 when Europeans set up a permanent camp in 1871, to a few hundred by 1902…to only one woman as of 2004. You can take a guess how many there are now.

As Charles Darwin wrote in his 1871 *Descent of Man:*

> At some future period, not very distant as measured by centuries, the civilised races of man will almost certainly exterminate and replace throughout the world the savage races.

BLACK, BROWN, AND YELLOW

Hinton Rowan Helper was a prominent North Carolina abolitionist. He saw slavery as a barbaric practice so unsustainable it would cripple the country. After abolition, he sided with movements to repatriate Africans to the land of their ancestors. But in 1869, he was quoted in a published critique of the "true intentions" of white philanthropists, activists, and abolitionists:

> We should so far yield to the evident designs and purposes of Providence, as to be both willing and anxious to see the negroes, like the Indians and all other effete and dingy-hued races, gradually exterminated from the face of the whole earth.

In other words, *all Black, brown, and yellow people have got to go. And some of us are gonna look like the bad guys, while some of us look like the good guys, but all of us need to be in it together.* That was the mission and the vision.

Does this help you put things in perspective? Do you understand what you're up against? There's a reason why we are "all Original People." It's not because – despite our overwhelming diversity – we somehow all decided that we were one people. It's because, historically, until the coming of Europeans, *we never decided that we weren't.* We come together instead of seeking to racially annihilate one another. We would rather unify, absorb, merge, and synthesize than wipe each other off the planet.

But it's not always easy. Whenever you have different groups of people living in close proximity to each other, you're gonna have conflict. Petty disputes grow into long-term rivalries. Minor distinctions evolve into big differences. Trivial things can get out of hand quick. This is something you'll see today in urban complexes throughout the world, including our own.

This goes back to the ridiculous conflicts that exist between different groups of Original People today. Most of them were instigated and escalated by Europeans, often by putting us in proximity to each other while only allowing us a limited number of resources to compete over – all while highlighting what makes us different to the point where that's all we know about each other. This book exists to change that. We hope to teach the Original People of the planet about their history, and show them the tree we all branch off from. In doing so, we can bring Black, brown, and yellow together.

Fortunately, we already have a model for this process. It definitely happened in the early 1900s, when Black, Asian, and Latino communities were coming together to overthrow white supremacy, but it also happened long before then.

I'm referring to the dawn of urban civilization, when thousands of people from diverse cultural backgrounds came together to become a metropolitan society. This couldn't have happened without an effective leadership ushering in the needed changes. Otherwise, growing populations and limited available resources have spelled chaos. It took a small number of men and women to keep that from happening. Those Black men and women – and the civilizations they built – are the subject of the second part of this book.

PHILIPPINES

THEN WHAT HAPPENED?

THE CYCLES OF HISTORY

In *The Science of Self, Volume One*, we explored the history of man, beginning with the origins of life itself. You may have noted how the development of man followed the same mathematical process that we find in the evolution of life and in the development of the material world (the physical universe) itself.

For humanity, this process (1) began with the foundation of the first man, who then (2) diverged, spread, and attempted whatever was in its capacity, and then (3) came to realizations about what worked and what didn't. This led to (4) humans developing institutions, cultures, and traditions based on what was effective, as well as social groups that engaged in the same patterns of behavior. Many of these bands of people (5) grew considerably in size and industry due to their consolidation and shared culture, and developed into (6) egalitarian societies with an equal distribution of labor, ownership, prestige, and responsibility. However, this eventually gave way to (7) the rise of leadership and privilege, with some individuals esteemed over others, and therefore possessing more property, knowledge, and/or rank in the society. When this occurs, it leads to (8) a natural process of accumulation and loss, progress and problems, advance and sacrifice, power and poverty. In essence, the rise must come with a fall. This is all part of the natural order though, and even massive extinctions of entire population groups can sometimes be the necessary consequence of the trajectory of this course. That is the nature of how all processes are brought to (9) completion, so that another cycle can begin.

Thus, as "advanced" as our early ancestors may have been, they didn't begin their presence on this planet as a socially cohesive community of like-minded individuals, working cooperatively to achieve outstanding results with the least amount of time and effort! Anyone who would claim that our first human ancestors were flying around in hovercrafts and beaming lasers out of their eyes…well, you just shouldn't listen to those kinds of people. In reality, our ancestors were not "primitive savages" but they certainly "evolved" into their mastery of the world we inhabit. Robert Greene talks about this briefly in his latest book Mastery, and we'll explore this topic again in Volume Three of The Science of Self series.

As we conclude this half of Volume Two, however, we're left with several questions. As you've seen, between 200,000 and 20,000 years ago, our ancestors settled nearly all of the planet, learning and eventually mastering every climate and environment they encountered. They conquered just about everyone obstacle imaginable. They maintained symbiosis (or balance) with their natural environments, in ways we're struggling to do today. And they became "fruitful" and multiplied, growing from an ancestral population of a few thousand to several hundred communities, each containing hundreds of men, women, and children.

But what happens when these communities are all vying for the same resources? Sure, they can go their separate ways and start new communities (and new genetic lineages). But what if these people – far removed the "root" from which their ancestors dispersed – lose some of the ancestral knowledge that allowed them to maintain a perfect balance with nature and its resources? Both because of the way that Earth is "designed" to transition through cycles (like Ice Ages) and because many of our ancestors overconsumed their region's resources (like cutting down too many trees), some communities were finding it a bit harder to survive.

And when resources get low, anyone living in an urban community knows what comes next. Conflicts are coming. Warfare is coming. Things will get worse. These diverse communities had come together before, particularly in their battle against the Neanderthals. But the Neanderthals were long gone. Our ancestors had – once again – gone their separate ways.

Who would introduce the knowledge needed to transition our ancestors into a new phase of culture – one that would address the difficulties of the changing climate? Who could bring these diverse communities together in order to institutionalize and propagate these systemic changes? What would these cultural leaders have to teach, and how would they teach it? And where would they come from? Where would they go? How would a small community of change-makers reach *all of the people who had settled the world before them*?

These are the questions we answer in Part Two. Part Two is the story of when "modern civilization" was introduced to the world. In its birth, these traditions and practices were associated with the changes needed to keep things going and moving forward. We'll explore who they were, where they went, and what they did. Because their contributions were so important, not only to the ancient world but to the modern world, I'll make sure to (again) dedicate considerable time and space to demonstrating one of the most important things we should know about these people: **They were Black.**

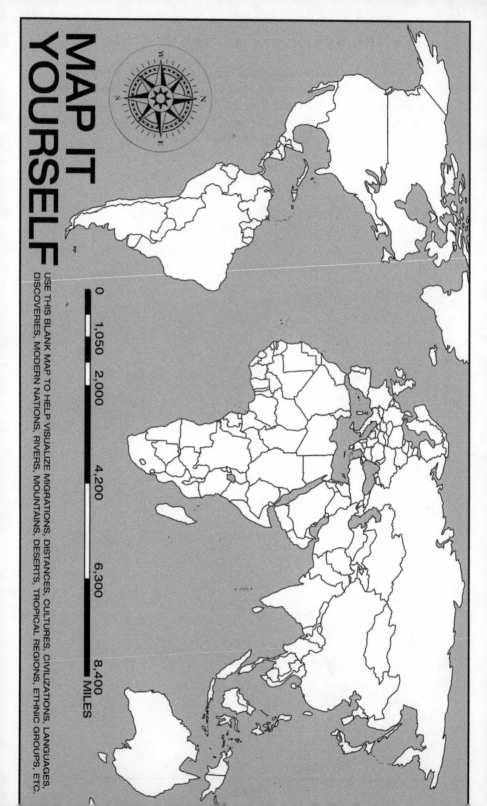

APPENDIX

ALL THE STUFF THAT DIDN'T FIT

In this section, you'll find all kinds of resources to help you make sense of the content in this book and others like it. I've decided to start this section with a list of questions frequently asked by people who reviewed this book before publication, followed by a guide to making sense of historical information.

FREQUENTLY ASKED QUESTIONS

1. Why use BC and AD instead of B.C.E. and C.E.?

Throughout this book, I've done my best to present very difficult information in the clearest and simplest way possible – without compromising the academic integrity of this work. It hasn't been easy striking that balance. Some parts may be smoother than others. In cases where I could avoid unnecessary confusion by using a common or colloquial term, I did. For example, many people have heard of BC before. But some people haven't! And how many actually "get" the concept?

So there's no way I'm going to try to teach people about BCE and CE when so many people don't even understand BC and AD! Similarly, I know the part of the Earth known as Africa was never known to its people as Africa – but that's how most people today know this part of the Earth. In other words, I'm just doing my best to keep things simple wherever I can.

2. Why use so many quotes?

It's one thing for you to read me, a guy named "Supreme Understanding" saying these things – and it might help that I actually have solid academic credentials and a good reputation – but it makes it easier for me to SHOW you this stuff is real when I can let some white professor or scientist tell you himself.

3. But why quote all these *old* books?

As we explained earlier in this book, the historical documentation on Black people in the ancient world is much harder to find nowadays.

If you find it, its shrouded in technical language lacking any whisper of the word "Negroid" or "black-skinned." Back when Europeans wrote openly about race, they put out books that establish many of the points I'm making in this book. Some of these books are unknown and out-of-print nowadays. I'm bringing them back out. And not only am I quoting Sir Fuddyduddy the Third to show you how the Mayans loved Black people, I'm going to add some modern sources to the mix (you know, the ones that never use the word "Black") to support my case.

4. Where can I find your sources?

You think I'm making this stuff up? C'mon, I'm not like the other guys, I promise. I've provided literally more than 1,000 endnotes citing the sources for the claims I'm making in this text. And these are reputable sources! There are at least 500 other sources which I've consulted over the past several years, but – as I wrote and edited – those are the ones I didn't get a chance to cite. If you'd like to follow up on any of those sources, you can dig them up at any library, or at Google Books, and research for yourself. In fact, it is my hope that you do just that. If you ever find a claim or statement where I didn't think to cite my sources specifically, just look up what I'm talking about on Google Books and you'll find plenty. I don't make things up, I promise.

5. Where's all the information on woman? What about them?

What do you mean? Don't think, because I'm not mentioning women by name, that I'm not including them in this history somehow. Everything you read about "Original People," you're reading about men and women. That's a given.

There are many instances where males dominated (but more so within the context of the Anu People, who we discuss in Part Two), but there are many instances where women were at the helm. The fact that migrations were often led by males does nothing to discount the importance of women. Just as men shouldn't be threatened by the fact that our earliest systems for mathematical notation may have been systems to keep track of a woman's cycle.

Anytime you see Y-DNA in this book, we're talking about men, but anytime you see mtDNA, those are maternal lineages. In other words, everywhere the men went, women were there…or else that was the end of them! Plain and simple! For a richer discussion of the roles played by males and females within the historical communities of Original People, check out Volume Three.

6. What does indigenous mean?

Indigenous is a tricky word. I use it in this book because it's a common word for what we call "Original" throughout this book. However, you have to understand what it means, and what it doesn't. Unless you're in east Africa where the first humans emerged, no one is really "indigenous" in the sense of originating someplace else on Earth. The idea of being "aboriginal" or "indigenous" is more so about claiming the original land rights as the first population to settle someplace and call it home. Keep in mind, I'm talking about communities who evolved into distinct populations in these new environments.

Thus, the "indigenous" people of the Americas are not a group of humans who "came from" the Americas, but a group descended from the Australoid and Mongoloid people who settled this region and made it home. Australoid people evolved in Australasia, Mongoloid people in central Asia, West African people in West Africa, and so on. But all these people can ultimately be traced back to the root – the Original People.

7. What does "ancestor" mean?

Sometimes, people think of their "ancestors" as a group of people who contributed *directly* to their lineage. As in their parents, parents' parents, and so on. But think about your great uncle. Wouldn't you consider him one of your ancestors? He was certainly kin to your great granddad, so why not? When I use the word "ancestor," I'm using it in the indigenous sense that appropriates one's entire family tree as one's ancestors. So, while you're thinking about it that way, consider how all the Original People we discuss in this book (and Part Two) are essentially *your* ancestors.

It may seem odd to call the people of the Indus Valley your ancestors if your family is from South Africa, but if you think about how much some of those ancient progenitors traveled, you'll realize that some Black brother from India really could have been in South Africa 6,000 years ago – or vice versa.

No exaggeration. They really traveled this much, especially in the period of the Anu people, who we discuss in Part Two. Perhaps this is why the "elites," the people in the statues, tend to look like familiar faces we've seen in statues from another civilization thousands of miles away. When you look at the statues, figurines, and effigy pots in Part Two, you'll see tons of lookalikes. You might also see some of your own features! When you do, ask yourself – who and where do I come from? Then…find out.

8. You mention a lot of indigenous populations that are, or were, "under attack." How do I help them?

You're right, and we'll discuss many more in Volume Three. Sadly, this is the state of affairs for much of the indigenous world, especially so the closer these people are to the oldest human lineages on the planet – that is, the Original People. So when we talk about the crusade against Black people worldwide, don't ever think that Europeans simply "hate us" for the "color of our skin." That's not it. It's about who survives, and who doesn't. If that doesn't make sense, it will become clearer in Volume Four.

As for the indigenous communities that are being destroyed as we speak, there are stories like this everywhere we look. There's a map from the Indigenous Peoples' Project at www.ifg.org that lists hundreds of aboriginal ethnic groups and the specific threats they face in this age of globalization. That should lead you to at least some ways that you can help these communities.

At the same time, never forget that "charity begins at home." Meaning, you might be able to make a long-distance donation to the Bagyeli people of Cameroon in their fight against Chevron, ExxonMobil, Petronas, Thanry, Bollore, Coron, Alpi, IMF, and the World Bank...or you may be able to raise some awareness by talking about their plight with others who would care...and you SHOULD...but don't forget that our own communities are full of the SAME kinds of people facing the SAME threat: eventual annihilation.

Of course, the tragedies experienced by people living in other countries are often greater than ours. We shouldn't lose sight of that fact, but our risk of being wiped off the planet is the same. We are ALL in bad shape. Just don't allow yourself to think we're in such bad shape because of some internal defect. It's not as if we wreaked all this havoc on ourselves. Partially, yes – but totally?

Just think. Many of us believe that we're a mess because alcohol and drug abuse is through the roof in urban communities. But aboriginal people *everywhere* in the world are now alcoholics. I'm not exaggerating. Find me ONE indigenous community that hasn't been set into "self-destruct" mode under European rule and I'll be surprised.

What we see in our communities are the long-term results of the SAME process we describe throughout this book. So what can we do? We can start by loving our own, coming together wherever and however we can, building more bonds than we break, teaching more youth than we condemn, and finding our common grounds with the people most tragically affected by the threats we all face.

SCIENCE VS. PSEUDOSCIENCE

What's science, and what's not? With all the information and misinformation raining down on us nowadays, it's often hard to tell what's real from what's false. In *The Science of Self, Volume One*, we dedicated one chapter to helping our readers better understand what science is really about. Here's a quick review of what you can expect to find when someone is employing "real science":

❑ Skepticism of unsupported claims
❑ Combination of an open mind with critical thinking
❑ Attempts to repeat experimental results.
❑ Requirements of testability
❑ Seeking out falsifying data that would disprove a hypothesis
❑ Use of descriptive language
❑ Performing controlled experiments
❑ Theories that are self-correcting
❑ A reliance on evidence and reason
❑ No claims for absolute or certain knowledge
❑ The production of useful knowledge

Science was not "invented by white people," but it was certainly used by them when advantageous to their goals. Why not us? For us, science can play a vital role in reconstructing a real sense of identity and history, leading to further solutions for our problems. These solutions, because they are based on scientific study, are more likely to be successful than ideas that aren't.

Far too many of our ideas are based on claims made by people who don't employ honest scientific inquiry. How do we tell which is which? As William D. Gray explains in *Thinking Critically About New Age Ideas*, pseudoscience (and religious thinking) have some of the following features:

❑ Has a negative attitude to skepticism
❑ Does not require critical thinking
❑ Does not require experimental repeatability
❑ Does not require tests
❑ Does not accept falsifying data that would disprove a hypothesis
❑ Uses vague language
❑ Relies on anecdotal evidence
❑ No self-correction

❏ Relies on belief and faith
❏ Makes absolute claims
❏ Produces no useful knowledge

Pseudoscience wasn't invented by white people either, but it was also used by them when advantageous. It has played a vital role in constructing a *false* sense of identity and history, leading to further problems and a lack of solutions.

HOW TO ANALYZE HISTORICAL INFORMATION

DEVELOPING THE ABILITY TO ANALYZE HISTORICAL AND CONTEMPORARY INFORMATION

❏ Apply understanding & knowledge of past events to new situations
❏ Identify cause and effect relationships
❏ Practice problem solving through the use of analogies

SYNTHESIZING INFORMATION

Synthesis is creating something new from a number of different sources. Synthesizing information is a process of examining and inferring relationships among sources and then making those relationships explicit. Synthesis is also a process of combining information and ideas to create or develop a new idea, focus, or perspective. An effective way to integrate and synthesize information is to recognize and use four particular thought patterns. These include:

Cause-effect – expresses a relationship between two or more actions, events, or occurrences that are connected in time.

Comparison-contrast – the comparison pattern is used to emphasize or discuss similarities between or among ideas, theories, concepts, or events, while the contrast pattern emphasizes differences.

Problem-solution – defines a problem and conducts research to test possible solutions.

Classification – organize information into broad types or categories.

USING ANALOGIES

The use of analogies to understand and interpret situations is another method for analyzing information. Using analogies requires one to identify similar problems or situations and compare them with the problem at hand. The use of analogies enables one to learn from the experiences of others. Some guidelines to follow are:

- ❏ How are the situations alike?
- ❏ How are they different?
- ❏ How well does the analogy apply to your situation?
- ❏ What does it suggest that you do?

RECOGNIZE & VALUE VARIOUS VIEWPOINTS

It's also important to factor in our viewpoints and those of others when we consider arguments. You can:

- ❏ Identify an individual's values and biases (including your own)
- ❏ Explore issues from multiple perspectives & understand multiple perspectives
- ❏ Examine your existing beliefs, attitudes, and opinions. Why do you think so? What evidence do you have to support that opinion?

Evaluating differing viewpoints is an essential critical thinking skill because it enables you to pull together divergent ideas and integrate differing, even contradictory, sources. The skill is valuable as you research papers, examine social and political issues, and resolve controversy.

SUGGESTIONS

- ❏ Deliberately put aside or suspend temporarily what you already believe about a particular issue.
- ❏ Discover what similarities and differences exist among the various viewpoints.
- ❏ Identify the assumptions on which each view is based.
- ❏ Look for and evaluate evidence that suggests the viewpoint is well thought out.
- ❏ To overcome the natural tendency to pay more attention to points of view with which you agree and treat opposing viewpoints superficially, deliberately spend more time reading, thinking about, and examining ideas that differ from your own.
- ❏ To analyze particularly complex, difficult, or very similar viewpoints, write a summary of each. Through the process of writing, you will be forced to discover the essence of each view.

For more on the science of thinking critically, check out *A Sucker Born Every Minute*, our guide to scams, cons, frauds, hoaxes, and how to avoid them.

WHAT DO WE CALL THEM?
NAMES, IDENTITY, AND CULTURAL CONFUSION

The Olmecs didn't call themselves Olmec. The Papuans didn't give themselves that name. The Aetas either. The list goes on: Yoruba, San, Moor, Ainu, Hottentot, Berber, Iroquois, Egyptian, Nubian, Ethiopian, Twa. All of these names were given to these people by other groups.

Very few of the names we have for the world's indigenous people actually came from those people themselves. Typically, they were descriptions given by others. Sometimes they were meant to be demeaning (e.g. Eskimo, which means, "eater of raw meat"), but many were simply descriptive names that meant "first people" or "Black people."

What did they call themselves? Well, the idea of "Black people" only becomes relevant when you're differentiating a group from people who are not Black. Thus names like *Nakhi* and *Hei Miao* in China (both translate to "Black people") differentiated them from other Chinese who weren't as dark. Same with the *saĝ gíg-ga* ("black heads") in ancient Sumer, one of the first civilizations to be overrun with whites.

But in situations where there's no color differential (or nobody cares about color), Original People distinguished their unique clan or cultural identity by their language group. For example, an Andaman Islander may say, "I'm a Bea man, and she's a Boro woman. Those are languages spoken by the people of the Andaman Islands.

Original People also used clan names that represent a common lineage, usually based on some sort of totemic animal that became considered a legendary ancestor. For example, in the nineteenth century the San of southern Africa lived in groups with names like The Giraffes, The Big Talkers, The Scorpions, and even The Lice.[446] Aren't these the same types of "clan names" used by the street gangs of the 50s and 60s? Sure are. It's also where the makers of Western sports got the idea of team names and mascots.

As you can see, our ancestors were not some monolithic, unified people. Every time a large group split into smaller groups, those groups were known by different clan names. Sometimes they identified with a totem, at other times with their dialect. Our history, not simply as the human species – but the history of life itself – is a steady succession of cycles: splitting and rejoining, dividing and reuniting, diverging and merging. It's simply the way life works. It's the mathematical nature of the way things went in the past and – as we'll explain in Volume Five – it's the way things will go in the future.

So it's not often that we'll find a "collective" identity for our prehistoric ancestors. Typically, they simply considered themselves "people" or "humans" until they encountered something distinctly "other" than themselves, either physically or culturally. For example, the Black people of the Andaman Islands have many clan names, but – as a group – they call themselves *Ang* (or *en-nge* or *Ya-eng-nga*), which simply means "human being."[447] The San people of southern Africa call themselves Ju│'hoansi, which means "Real People."* Yet they call Europeans *!ohm*, a category that includes predators and other wild beasts.[448]

So what do we call them? All things considered, "Original People" works well as a global group name for the planet's indigenous people. So does "Black people." Yes, even though few people actually have skin the color of coal, we can call Original People "Black." I'll explain.

For starters, some people don't think "Black" is a "real identity." "Black," they say, "is not a geographic identity or nationality." Fair enough, but it shouldn't be, because Black people are not bound to any one place on the Earth. "Africa" is where humanity was born, but – as we've seen in this book – these same Black people were the first people everywhere else as well. So the WORLD was once Black. Calling Black people "African" is not a bad thing, but we should not think of Africa as a special little box where Black people belong. The planet Earth belongs to the Original Man.

Second, Blackness is not simply a marker for the pigmentation of our skin, because all Original People aren't jet-black in complexion (though some are). Instead, the idea of being "Black" refers to an identity that is timeless and nonlocal. As we explained in *The Science of Self, Volume One*:

> Black is the life-giver, and life-taker, it is the absence and the presence, it is the source and the destination, it is everything and it is nothing. Because of this, Blackness is – on every level, including the human presence on Earth – both the origin and final destination of all things…This "Blackness" – at its deepest level – may be the consciousness that informs all of the above, from dark energy to

---

* Many people think they call themselves San, but San is a Khoi word for "original settlers" popularized by the Dutch. Even !Kung (as in !Kung San) is a name popularized by German missionaries, which simply means "they" in the Angola !Kung dialect.

electromagnetic energy, from dark matter to black matter, from the womb of the Earth to the mind of modern man.[449]

In other words, we are Black because "blackness" is where everything begins. We are both Original and the "Origin of All." Our Blackness did not begin with the first Homo sapiens, but with life and matter themselves.

Thus, it's no coincidence that the Original People of the planet are so dark-skinned. Melanin, the chemical that makes us rich in complexion is the key ingredient in much of life's formulas. It is known to the scientific community as an "organizing molecule," fundamental to the growth, order, and direction of life and its evolution. As we explained in *The Science of Self*, it's found in the depths of space and the center of our brains.[450]

Finally, those among us who think that "Black means death" or that "Black means evil" have allowed the wrong people to define things for us. Before the social orders of the world were turned upside-down, European explorers reported back to their governments that the people of Asia and Africa portrayed all their gods as Black and their demons as white. The darkest man among them was the most handsome, and – in India – they would rub their newborn babies in sesame oil to make their skin darker.

We've come a long way from the time when the world was Black, and many of us are quite confused about who and what we are. It is my hope that this book helps redefine our worldview, allowing us, ultimately, to usher in an era when the world is Black again, and the Original People of the planet prevail.

"THOSE FOREIGNERS"

Are you tired of foreigners? Sick of other ethnic groups who don't like you? Over the years, I've heard just about any complaint you can imagine regarding the presence of Arabs, Asians, and Latinos in Black communities. Whether it's the Vietnamese nail shop, the Pakistani gas station, or the Mexican construction workers, the overall impression seems to be "They don't like us or respect us, yet they want to take our money. We need to take back our communities." But this is actually not a "them vs. us" issue.

You see, there's a lot we don't understand about immigrants to the U.S. For starters, we need to be honest and consider the fact that Africans who move to the U.S. tend to have the same attitudes towards American blacks. So it's not just an "Arab/Asian/Mexican" thing. It's not a perspective specific to one or two groups of people. It's something widespread, and we need to research why.

Next, we should question how long these people have felt this way. We can look at history to see that the Black and brown world was once very unified. Even as recently as the 1940s, the rest of the world – from India to Japan to Mexico to Iran – were all trying to align with Black America. But then things changed.

So we have to look at the historical and social dynamics that led to the conditions we're seeing today. For starters, the majority of people who can afford to immigrate to the U.S. are not the poor people of their nations. They're a little better off, which might mean that they were connected to a politically conservative family who holds pro-American values.

At the very least, they believe in the American Dream. Once they get here, they end up establishing a business where they can afford to: in the poorest communities. Who gives them the loans? White people. White people are the ones who say, "We wouldn't give this loan to a Black American, but we have no problem giving it to you."

So when we look at the obvious disparity in the ownership of businesses in the Black community, we have to look at WHO makes that possible. We've got to stop looking at things at the surface level and dig deeper. Going back to when they first got to this country, you should also know that most immigrants, including Africans, are told to avoid Blacks and Hispanics. I'm not making this up. They WILL hear it from someone at some point in their naturalization process.

And when these kinds of things are seeded in their mind, together with the images they're force-fed by the American media, it creates those negative perspectives. But don't get it twisted. Everybody doesn't like everybody back in their homeland. But when immigrants from any country come to the U.S., they pool together with others from their ethnic group and collaborate in circles of trust and support – which allows them to thrive financially. They're able to share a car, a house, an apartment, anything, because they're still in the collectivist mindsets their people have back home. This is what it takes to keep a business alive. It takes coming together, which is hard to do if you're not part of that culture.

But don't think that – just because a few Kenyans and Ugandans can go half on a cargo shipment of designer handbags – that those people would get along just as well back in Africa. You see, America forces people to work together or they fail. This is why they look at

Black America as such a puzzle. Immigrants can't understand why a people who needs so desperately to come together, instead continues to squabble and bicker over the pettiest of differences, often killing each other over these issues. If only THEY knew the history of what White America did to Black America to make things this way.

The bottom line is not to misinterpret these historical dynamics, and walk away thinking that everyone hates you and you should hate them too. It's deeper than that, especially when you consider how many Black Americans have the same negative perception of Black America. This is the byproduct of miseducation and purposeful division. We've been turned against each other to their benefit. Because if you talk to enough immigrants, particularly the ones who came from less conservative backgrounds – and you just randomly say, "White people make me sick" – you'll see that many of them have plenty to say on that subject. Talk to the dark-skinned Indian store owners and ask them if they're Black. You might be surprised. Some will be scared to say yes, others will do so proudly. And once you know the history, and I mean the DEEP history – including how all the Black, brown, and yellow people of the world were done the EXACT same way by the exact same people – you'll have quite a LOT to talk and build about. So keep building with people from other countries, even if things don't click right away, and learn about their cultures. In turn, perhaps you can teach them what they missed in their miseducation process. You might be the one who closes the gap.

And when that's done, anything is possible.

GENETICS GLOSSARY

Allele: One of multiple alternative forms of a single gene. Different alleles can result in different phenotypic or genotypic traits.

Autosomal DNA: In humans, there are 23 pairs of chromosomes, 22 of which are autosomes. The 23rd determines gender: female (XX) or male (XY). The first 22 determine other traits. These traits can be dominant or recessive, making them more likely or less likely to be passed on to your descendants based on who you have children with (and their autosomal DNA).

DNA sequence: This is a "sentence" of information that directs the functions of an organism, also known as a gene or genetic sequence.

Founder Effect: The loss of genetic variation that occurs when a new population is established by a very small number of individuals from a larger population.

Gene: A DNA sequence or genetic sequence that can be inherited.

Different variations of a gene are known as alleles.

Genetic Drift: Genetic drift describes random variations in a group's genetic makeup. Small populations are especially prone to the phenomenon, because the genes of a single individual play a proportionately larger role in successive generations. Genetic drift can cause one individual's genes to predominate, or for another gene to be eliminated entirely.

Genome: The total package of genetic sequences possessed by an organism.

Genotype: The entire set of alleles present in an individual's genome. This is what produces the individual's phenotype.

Haplogroups: A group of similar haplotypes that share a common ancestor with the same SNP mutation. Different lines of Y-DNA and mtDNA can't combine back together again, so a haplotype can change only by mutation. These mutations are known by genetic markers, which can be traced to identify where a population has been, and for how long.

Haplotype: A haplotype is a combination of various alleles or SNPs that are associated. It's a "complex" of genetic traits, useful for identifying groups that share genes and ancestry.

mtDNA: Mitochondrial DNA is passed down the matrilineal line, from mother to child (no matter what gender).

Mutations: When DNA makes copies, sometimes there are errors in the copy. These errors become mutations. Many evolutionary biologists believe such mutations are random, but some say beneficial mutations are "pre-adaptive" and emerge to allow a species to thrive in new circumstances.

Phenotype: The visible physical (and behavioral) traits of an organism. This is basically whatever is manifested externally, and is determine by one's genotype.

Population Bottleneck: An evolutionary event in which a population descends from a reduced parent group, either because part of the parent group is killed or prevented from reproducing, or when a small group becomes separated from the main population. Over time, bottlenecks can increase genetic drift toward homogeneity. (Also see "Founder Effect")

Selection: Selection simply means the process by which the members of the next generation are chosen. "Natural Selection" is when the members with the features best adapted to their natural circumstances are the ones most likely to live and reproduce. The ones who aren't a good fit with nature will die off. "Direct Selection" is when members of a species choose which features they prefer. This also happens when animals or plants are domesticated, being bred to produce the most desired features, while other varieties die off.

SNP: An SNP (single-nucleotide polymorphism) is a DNA sequence variation found when one chemical in the sequence is different between members of the same species.

Survival Advantage: A member of a species has a reproductive advantage when their traits are better adapted to the needs of their environment than those of other members. (Remember, "survival" is about how long your genetic lineage survives, not how long you personally live.) This is what they mean by "survival of the fittest."

Y-DNA: Because only males carry the Y chromosome, Y-chromosome DNA is DNA passed solely along the patrilineal line, from father to son.

THE GENETICS OF ORIGINAL PEOPLE

One branch of the Original People carried Y-DNA haplotype DE, while another branch carried Y-DNA haplotype CF. The split between these two branches happened near India, sometime after the Toba eruption 74,000 years ago. The split between these two lineages produced what anthropologists now regard as the two oldest branches of the world's Original People: Africans and Australians.

THE AFRICOID LINEAGES

We can track some of the migrations of the world's first settlers using human genetics. The two oldest male (Y-DNA) lineages are Haplogroup A and B. Haplogroup A is the African macro-haplogroup from which all modern haplogroups descend. BT is a subclade, or descendant lineage, of Haplogroup A. BT has two major lineages, Haplogroups B and CT. If none of this makes any sense, see "A Re-Introduction to Genetics" and come back.

Haplogroup A (identified by genetic marker M91) is typically only found in Africa, especially among the Khoisan, many Ethiopians (especially the Beta Israel), Nilotic people,* and small groups of people in West Africa. Outside Africa, traces of Haplogroup A have been found in Yemen, Palestine, Jordan, Oman, England, coastal Turkey and several of the Aegean Islands.

Haplogroup B (Genetic marker M60) is also typically only found in Africa, especially among Central African pygmies, East African Hadzabe, and (again) Nilotic people. Outside Africa, traces of Haplogroup B have been found in Saudi Arabia, Qatar, Southern Iran, Pakistan, and India.

Could earlier migrations carrying Haplogroup A or B have made it out of Africa? Absolutely. In fact, there are a few people carrying those lineages outside Africa today, but we don't know enough to say

---

* Nilotic people are the Black-skinned people who speak Nilotic languages (a large subgroup of the Nilo-Saharan language family) along the Nile Valley, near the East African Great Lakes, and in southwestern Ethiopia. These include the Kalenjin, Luo, Dinka, Nuer, Shilluk, Ateker and the Maa-speaking peoples.

anything conclusive. All we know is that – if earlier human migrations did expand beyond Arabia (and they probably did) – they were effectively wiped out around 74,000 years ago, due to the explosion of the Toba supervolcano. In other words, just before the ancestral wave of Original People began their expansions, the Earth had basically hit the 'reset' button.

Outside Africa, the oldest human lineages are associated with Y-DNA Haplogroup D, which descended from Haplogroup DE around 65,000 years ago. Haplogroup DE came from the root of civilization, but we're not sure where it split into the D and E lineages. DE has been found in Nigeria and Tibet, suggesting the split could have happened anywhere in between. The split may have happened in East Africa, as Haplogroup E seems indigenous to the region. Today, most modern Africans carry E lineages.*

Meanwhile, Haplogroup D is found among the oldest people of India, the Ainu of Japan, the Miao-Yao and Nakhi of China, and several other minority groups in East Asia, particularly those speaking Tibeto-Burman languages. These people represent the oldest settlers of these regions.

Carriers of D may have made it into the Americas, but they didn't leave surviving lineages. In India, the distribution of D ranges from 0-65%, representing the people who originally settled the Indus Valley over 50,000 years ago. Everywhere we find Haplogroup D, Diminutive Black People are found. In fact, the short-statured Black-skinned people of the Andaman Islands are almost exclusively D, showing us what at least some of the original people of the DE Haplogroup may have looked like.

Studies of mtDNA confirm what the Y-DNA suggests. The Orang Asli (a DBP population of Malaysia) and the Andaman Islanders belong to mtDNA haplogroups M, N, and R, the oldest descendants of the L3 Haplogroup that began the human exodus from Africa.[451]

THE AUSTRALOID LINEAGES

The East African Haplogroup CT† gave birth to CF somewhere in

---

* E began a rapid expansion westward around 50,000 years ago. E is found almost exclusively in Africa, with traces in Europe and the Near East, wherever these Africans settled in ancient times. In Africa, DBP people only belong to the oldest E lineages, and are more often descendants of Haplogroups A and B. In other words, DBP are simply representatives of the oldest Y-DNA lineages everywhere.

† The T in CT comes from the fact this haplogroup was ancestral to all haplogroups from C up to T. The only haplogroups to come before it were A and B.

the Near East (possibly Palestine) about 50-60,000 years ago, a little after its older sibling Haplogroup DE. The ancestors of CF may have taken the northern route out of Africa, up the Nile Valley and through Sinai, before crossing the Levant, where C and F go their separate ways.

C begins the second wave of human expansion into Asia (Haplogroup D went first), in a coastal migration along Southern Asia, into India, then into Southeast Asia.* Some go south into Australia, some sail east into the Pacific,† and some travel up the Asian coast, into the Americas.‡

Meanwhile, the other branch of CF, haplogroup F, spreads from the Near East into Asia, Europe, and back into Africa. Both groups settled wherever we later find Australoid people or their traces. In other words, the descendants of Haplogroup DE continued the Africoid lineage found in A and B, while the earliest descendants of CF became Australoid people. After several thousand years, many of these lineages have merged and converged, but we can still trace them back to where they came from because DNA doesn't recombine in such a way that we lose our roots.

THE BIBLE AS HISTORY?

As we've said throughout this book, we can't rely on scriptures alone as a source of historical fact. Not only have these traditions been subjected to numerous revisions, outside influences, and outright tampering and alteration, they are also coded in the language of allegory and myth. In other words, people should not take these stories literally. At the same time, if we can appreciate that these traditions come from a diverse array of intelligent people from the Near East and North Africa, we can consider their accounts in an appropriate historical context.

---

* Haplogroup C is found at high frequency among the Australian aborigines, Polynesians, Vietnamese, Kazakhs, Mongolians, Ainu, Koreans, and indigenous inhabitants of the Russian Far East, and at moderate frequencies elsewhere throughout Asia and Oceania, including India and Southeast Asia.

† The Lani and Dani people of New Guinea are almost exclusively C, showing us what the original people of the C Haplogroup looked like. These people are also diminutive, another piece of evidence to suggest the DBP were not always small.

‡ Haplogroup C traveled with the Australoid migration into the Americas where it now occurs from the Athabaskan peoples of Alaska and western Canada all the way down to the Wayuu people of South America, with the highest frequency among the Na-Dené people.

CAN WE READ THE BIBLE SCIENTIFICALLY?

Is there a scientific way to approach the content of the Bible (or any scripture)? Absolutely. But you've gotta take faith and acceptance out of the equation and read things fresh while consulting plenty of outside sources. I'll explain. I took a few college courses in the study of religion. I learned that there are several methods of making sense of scripture. Two of the most prominent are known as exegesis and esegesis. Exegesis means "out of the text" and refers to religious scholars digging for meaning in the scripture by comparing it with evidence from outside sources. An example would be looking at archaeological evidence for the enslavement of the Hebrews (there's none).

Esegesis means "reading into the text" and refers to the act of coming up with meanings based solely on what's in the scripture itself. An example would be looking for proof of angels by looking for Bible verses that talk about angels. For many of us who don't want to "question the Word," this is commonplace. Perhaps that's why "esegesis" sounds just like "Easy Jesus."

It's really easy to skip the questioning and fast-forward to just believing. But you'll be missing most of the picture if you look at things that way. For example, most Biblical scholars accept that 70-80% of the words attributed to Jesus in the New Testament could not have been his, that books like Genesis were compiled from multiple source documents from different traditions, and that there are hundreds of places where one scripture contradicts another, or is simply inaccurate. And you can figure that out JUST by looking at the Bible itself. Imagine how much you could find if you look at the history of the Bible's compilation (like all the books that were left out and why), or the way that scribes and translators purposely altered its words.

Despite all this, you certainly can read the Bible and find some history in there, but it'll be tough to distinguish the actual historical records from the mythical traditions, allegories, contradicting claims, translator's alterations, and so on. The question then is, why do you want to?

BLACK PEOPLE CAME BEFORE ADAM?

In the 1800s, a theological argument known as Pre-Adamism regained prominence. Pre-Adamism is the theological view that there were humans on Earth before Adam. Typically the descendants of

Adam, known as Adamites, are understood to be white people, while the Original People of the Earth (the "Black, brown, and yellow races") are considered Pre-Adamites.

Pre-Adamism emerged because it was difficult for European theologians to reconcile the genealogy of Adam (which only goes back 6,000 years) with the evidence that other people – typically dark-skinned people outside of Europe – had been around, evolving and building civilizations, long before this time. Many of these theologians were attempting to find a logical way to address the findings of scientists and historians. This is how the idea of Pre-Adamism came to be.

One of the most popular advocates for Pre-Adamism was Alexander Winchell. Although he denied civilization and humanity to the "inferior Negro," Alexander Winchell could not deny that the Black man was the Original Man. Over 40 years before Louis Leakey began digging up human remains in Africa, Winchell knew such a day was coming. In his 1878 tract, *Adamites and Pre-Adamites*, he wrote:

> The search for the antiquity of the human species is, therefore, a search for the antiquity of the Black races. That search must be instituted in the regions which the Black races have occupied – Africa, Australia and obliterated continental lands. These races have left no records, no monuments; and hence the search must become a purely geological one. This task is one which has never been undertaken; but it is one from which science will not shrink; and I anticipate that somewhere in the caverns of Abyssinia [Ethiopia], or south Africa, or Australia, or in some of the stratified formations of those countries, we shall discover evidences of the existence of man at a date prior to the general glaciation of Europe and the United States.

Without the archaeological evidence that would be discovered in the 1920s, Winchell was still able to confidently conclude that the Black race came first. Pre-Adamism went hand in hand with the idea that Adam's creation goes back to only 6,000 years ago, and that Pre-Adamites built all of the world's cultures and civilizations before this time. Often, it was assumed that the Adamic race, or white race, must have somehow come from the Black race. Winchell wrote:

> The first white man may have descended from a remote progenitor of black color; but the first black man could not have descended from a white progenitor…Preadamitism means simply that Adam is descended from a Black race, not the Black races from Adam.

Later, Winchell added, "It is said to have been a dark race which fell, but if the white race sprang from the dark, it would inherit the moral taint, which entered the blood of the original offender." In Volume

Four, we'll explore Pre-Adamism, its history, and the significance of this quote.

GOING BACK TO AFRICA – 50,000 YEARS AGO

About 130,000 years ago, the ancestral African population expanded from Africa into southern Arabia. There, the Nubian Complex ran the world (at least as much of the world as humans knew then) until the migrations into Asia and Europe. The earliest outpost of this human expansion appears to have been India.

How do we know? Through genetics, we can track the people who left Arabia and see where they went. One of our ancestral groups carried the mtDNA haplogroup M1 (and the Y-DNA haplogroup DE) into India, where they established one of the earliest Black colonies outside Africa and Arabia. Then, offshoots of that M1 lineage, ventured furthered into Asia, and eventually beyond.

Around 74,000 years ago the Toba supervolcano blew, killing most of the M1 population in India. After Toba, the M1 people who survived in East Asia began a westward migration, eventually resettling India. They considered west into Arabia, and then back into Africa, around 50,000 years ago. Some of the people who came back to Africa may have been Australoid survivors of Toba. Grafton Elliot Smith said a prehistoric colony of Australoid people could be found in North Africa.[452] Albert Churchward Later studies involving some of the oldest human skulls in Africa have indicated proto-Australoid features.

This was when M1 and DE made their way back into Africa, effectively renewing the human history of Africa, and giving birth to a new population. Later, M, D, and E lineages again migrated out of Africa.

Basically, it appears that the same people who left Africa 130,000 years ago later came BACK to Africa about 50,000 years ago and mixed it up with the descendants of their ancestors. And there are no "pure" lineages in Africa that are without these elements. In a 2008 genetic study of Khoisan DNA, Behar and colleagues found that even the Khoisan, one of oldest genetic lineages in Africa, received an influx of "additional lineages" 40,000 years ago.[453] The BBC reported on the study:

> "Once this population reached southern Africa, it was cut off from the eastern African population by these drought events which were on the route between them." Modern humans are often presumed to have originated in East Africa and then spread out to populate

other areas. But the data could equally support an origin in southern Africa followed by a migration to East and West Africa. The genetic data show that populations came back together as a single, pan-African population about 40,000 years ago. This renewed contact appears to coincide with the development of more advanced stone tool technology and may have been helped by more favourable environmental conditions. "[The mixing] was two-way to a certain extent, but the majority of mitochondrial lineages seem to have come from north-eastern Africa down to the south," said Spencer Wells.[454]

If you find the idea of a "back migration" strange, why should it be? If Africa is the lush, tropical, resource-rich environment we know it is, why wouldn't the people who left when it desertified want to come back when things looked greener?

Actually, prehistoric back migrations *into* Africa were almost as common as migrations *out of* Africa.[455] So the back-migration 50,000 years ago was just one of many, but it was especially important because it may have set off a significant chain of events within Africa.

We know that these people spread as deep as southern Africa, and contributed genetically to every living population in Africa today. We also know that at least one branch of these people, those carrying Y-DNA lineage E, contributed heavily to the migration that settled West Africa and became the ancestors of most Black Americans today.

AFRICAN PHYSICAL DIVERSITY

In Africa, everyone doesn't look alike. In fact, Africa is the most diverse place on Earth. Considering that NO ONE on the planet looks the same as their ancestors did two billion years ago (unless you're still a squiggly little single-celled organism), you can imagine that we've also changed considerably from the appearance of our ancestors two million years ago, two hundred thousand years ago, and even two thousand years ago. Seriously, we've all changed. It's not just you. That's just kind of the way nature works.

Understanding that there is not a single African "look" can help you understand how all the world's people came from Black people. And when they say the Egyptians weren't Black, it's because they're saying there's only one way to look Black.

THE WEST AFRICAN LOOK

As we noted in "Who and What is Black?" (See Part One) there's a lot of confusion that arises from the misconception that only those fitting the West African profile are "true Africans." Effectively, this de-Africanizes many of the native populations of Africa itself, not to mention the billions of Black people who inhabit regions outside of continental Africa.

As noted earlier, this works well for Eurocentrists, who want to isolate a "true Negroid" type and then use these criteria to say that the people who founded the world's ancient civilizations might have painted pictures of themselves with Black skin, but they weren't really Black nor African. Notice that they never set such standards for what constitutes a "true" Caucasian, and will include just about anyone they want!

This is why African anthropologist S.O.Y. Keita has gone to great pains to scientifically establish the profound diversity of African physical types. In *History in Africa*, he explains, "The extreme Negroid variant is just that, a variant, and not a "founding" or the "original" type."[456] Yet, because West African Bantu people expanded across so much of Africa in the past 5,000 years, you would think that all Africans look like this. But the Bantu look is not the only look indigenous to Africa. In fact, the earliest African remains possessing "Bantu-type" features are found in Sudan at Tushka and Jebel Sahaba. Tushka dates back to about 14,500 years ago and Sahaba dates back to about 13,700 years ago. The oldest remains of this type in West Africa are the 11,000 year old Iwo Eleru skullcap from Nigeria and the 6,400 year old skeleton from Asselar, eastern Mali.[457] Before that time, Africans were certainly Black people, but they didn't look as much like modern Bantu people in West Africa.[458] Some of the earliest African skulls, the 36,000 year old Hofmeyr skull from South Africa, clustered with the Aurignacian people of Paleolithic Europe, who were Australoid.[459] In other words, these are ALL Black people, but they didn't have this "one" African look. In fact, if you've every traveled throughout Africa, you know there is still an incredible amount of diversity in its in indigenous people. Nowhere is this more so the case than in the place where humanity began: East Africa.

THE EAST AFRICAN LOOK

Despite any controversy from the Eurocentrists, the evidence clearly shows us that the ancient Badarians, Somalians, Ethiopians, and Egyptians were ALL Black, African people, but they didn't all look like West Africans. They looked like East Africans. East Africans are very diverse, but many of them, like the Samburu of Kenya, have straight, narrow noses and sharp cheekbones, but jet Black skin. Why do they look so different from West Africans? Was it Europeans or Arabs who got into the mix?

Let's look at the DNA. As we noted early, Y-DNA Haplogroup DE began its back-migration into Africa around 50,000 years ago, after recovering from the wake of Toba in East Asia. This is why the only two documented samples of DE are found in Tibet and Nigeria. By the time DE made it back to Nigeria, new branches had diverged from the DE lineage. D separated from DE somewhere in Asia, while E was African-born. E gave birth to many new lineages as it also traveled west towards Nigeria. The most common of these lineages is E1b1b, the primary genotype of most East and West Africans today. East Africans who carry E1b1b, such as the Oromo and Borana, don't show signs of genetic mixture with Europeans or Middle Easterners. E1b1b originated in Africa, is largely confined there and is rare outside Africa.[460] In other words, that "East African" look doesn't come from whites or Arabs. It's a product of the motherland, and a testament to the diversity of the Original People.

Jean Hiernaux agreed, suggesting that the East African ancestors of the ancient Egyptians had the features we find in many of the modern indigenous people of East Africa, who are "very dark-skinned and differ greatly from Europeans in a number of body proportions…" In other words, they're not the descendants of Arabs or Caucasians. Describing the oldest remains of East Africa, Hiernaux continues:

> There is every reason to believe that they are ancestral to the living 'Elongated East Africans'…Neither of these populations, fossil and modern, should be considered to be closely related to the populations of Europe and western Asia…[461]

FROM EAST TO WEST

So what brought out the features that distinguish West Africans from East Africans? Simple: people change! To be specific as to how and why, several factors have played a role. Primary factors include: A change in environment, the advent of agriculture, an increase in polygamy, and mixing with the indigenous people they encountered along their migrations.

As Jean Hiernaux explains regarding the features of East Africans:

> [I]t is clear that where the size and body shape of the human body are concerned, climate has played an important role in the genetic differentiation of the populations of sub-Saharan Africa. In light of

this knowledge, we are now in a position to explain, in terms of genetic adaptation, the external characteristics of the populations... such as the Masai of Kenya, the Tutsi of Rwanda and Burundi, and the Ful (or Fulani) of West Africa...It has been stated that they owe much of their constitution to a peculiar evolution in the semi-arid or arid crescent which caps sub-Saharan Africa to the north and northeast. We may now say that their most conspicuous features – the elongated body, the especially long legs (which are very efficient cooling radiators owing to their diameter), the narrow shoulders and thorax, the leanness, the narrow head and face, and the high and narrow nose – are all represent genetic adaptations to dry heat. **There is no need to postulate an extra-African 'Caucasoid' element in their genepool for explaining such a characteristic as the narrow nose.**[462]

Dr. Keita has added that the humid regions of West Africa demanded a different set of features:

> An important function of the nose is to warm and moisten inspired air. When air is exhaled, some heat and moisture are lost to the surroundings. The longer the nasal passage, the more efficient the nose is for warming and moistening incoming air and also the less heat and moisture are lost on exhalation. A narrow, high nose gives a longer nasal passage than a low, broad nose. Therefore, in cold or dry conditions, a high, narrow nose is preferable for warming and moistening air before it reaches the lings, and for reducing loss of heat and moisture in expired air. In hot, humid conditions a low, broad nose serves to dissipate heat. (Wolpoff 1968; Franciscis and Long 1991)

Seems like they covered every physical difference between Australoid people and Negroid people, with the exception of hair texture.* Hiernaux continues, describing the Fulani of West Africa (one of the few populations studied in this regard):

> From the Sahelian arid zone to the rain forest, stature gradually decreases, the nose and face becomes gradually broader in proportions, and the head becomes slightly rounder. As pointed out repeatedly, the factors of these morphological clines **lay in the environment, not in gene flow from North Africa or Arabia.**[463]

Dr. Keita traces the "extreme Negroid" variant to an ancestral African population that started off in East Africa, possibly in the Sudan, then settled in the Sahara, and then migrated further west, as evidenced by genetic as well as linguistic evidence. About 5,000 years ago, these people began the Bantu expansion that spread far and

---

* Hair texture, too, has been studied as an adaptive response to environment. Tightly coiled hair is better suited to hot, humid conditions, because it allows heat to the leave the surface of the body easier.

wide across Africa, replacing many of the oldest "Paleo-African" populations.[464] The editors of the UNESCO General History of Africa agree, noting the ancestors of the Bantu must have started out in East Africa, near the Central Sudan.[465]

QUESTIONS TO CONSIDER

What other factors affected the emergence and eventual dominance of West African, or Bantu, people? Anthropologist Peter Frost says that the westward expansion of the Niger-Congo people, who brought with them the science of agriculture, "triggered a cascade of changes that would have profound behavioral and morphological consequences." What were these changes, and how did they occur? Frost notes:

> Agriculture, especially year-round agriculture, enables women to become more self-reliant in feeding themselves and their children, thus making it less costly for men to take second wives.[466] As a result, the polygyny rate is 20-50% of all marriages in sub-Saharan agricultural societies.[467]
>
> If some men have more wives, others will have to do without. In general, men will have to compete more keenly with each other for access to women. When such rivalry intensifies in non-human species, the result is an intensification of sexual selection for larger, stronger, and more muscular males. This may explain why the highly polygynous, agricultural peoples of sub-Saharan Africa are so physically robust. They and their African American descendants outclass European-descended subjects for weight, chest size, arm girth, leg girth, muscle fiber properties, and bone density.[468]
>
> This masculinization of body build may be hormonally mediated. When Winkler and Christiansen[469] studied two Namibian peoples, the weakly polygynous hunter-gatherer !Kung and the highly polygynous agricultural Kavango, the latter were found to have markedly higher levels of both total testosterone and DHT. The authors suggest that lower levels of these hormones may account for the !Kung's neotenous appearance, i.e., sparse body hair, small stature, pedomorphic morphology, and light yellowish skin.

In other words, the males with the "go get it" disposition were more likely to have multiple wives, and thus multiple children. This results in how the next generation looked, as well as their hormone levels. Several generations down the line, African agriculturalists and their descendents are noticeably different from their hunter-gatherer neighbors who aren't big on polygamy. This much seems clear.

As a result, throughout the Diaspora, young Black men have more circulating testosterone than young East Asian men, and young white men have less than pretty much everyone.[470] In Africa, Bantu men have higher levels than the Khoisan people they displaced in West and East Africa. However, the "go get it" disposition associated with high testosterone has its downside. High testosterone/DHT is associated with prostate cancer and the highest incidences in the world are among Black men.[471] Black men in America are worst off, probably due to poorer environmental and dietary factors.[472]

But was it just the advent of agriculture (and increases in polygamy) that made Bantu people more "robust"? There's significant evidence that the ancestors of the Bantu married into African populations that were older than humanity itself. That is, just as the Out-Of-Africa migration saw humans in Europe and Asia "mixing" with Neanderthals in Europe and with Denisovans in Oceania, Africans also mixed with archaic pre-human populations.[473] The rate is as high as 13% in some West African populations.

It shouldn't sound too strange. After all, these "archaic" people weren't very different from modern humans; they just descended from much older populations that predated modern humans. But what was the outcome of this admixture? Just as Neanderthal DNA made Paleolithic Eurasians more "robust," and Denisovan DNA made Australians and Melanesians more robust, did the archaic hominids in southwest Africa make the ancestors of the Bantu more robust? Did this process, in fact, give all of these human populations a serious survival advantage over their "purebred" peers? Every dog breeder knows that mutts are tougher, with stronger immune systems. We have better documentation on the results of Neanderthal and Denisovan DNA, but it's the same effect. By breeding with populations who have been around for a million years or more, your descendants adopt genetic resistance to a lot of dangerous pathogens.[474]

QUESTIONS TO CONSIDER

Does this have anything to do with the rise of the Bantu, who rapidly "re-colonized" Africa, dominating or displacing native Khoisan-speaking people and other older populations across Africa?

Is this what it took for these "mixed" populations to become the second wave of colonizers to dominate the prehistoric world, quickly displacing their unmixed predecessors? We know the DBP/Negritos of Asia (like the Andaman Islanders) lack the archaic genes found among their neighbors. Same thing with many DBP people in Central Africa. Is that why DBP people typically avoid serious conflict, or is it because the key to survival for such populations is living unobtrusively?

ABOUT THE AUTHOR

You may want to know a little more about who I am and why I wrote this book. If you've read *How to Hustle and Win*, then you already know a lot of my story. My parents are immigrants from Bangladesh, who moved to the U.S. in the 70s. I was born and raised in a predominantly Black and Latino neighborhood in Jersey City, New Jersey during the height of the crack epidemic. English isn't my first language, but I learn new things pretty quickly.

As much as my mother wanted to keep me out of trouble, my innate desire to "know" pulled me into the streets. I was always a rebellious kid, and never gelled too well with other Indians, who saw me as the "ghetto Indian." But the streets seemed like a better fit. By the time I was 14, I had been kicked out of high school and was fully immersed in the kind of lifestyle that doesn't typically have a happy ending. I didn't plan on going to college, nor did I plan on living to see 25.

I don't want to say hip-hop saved my life, but it did play a role in my redemption. I'd always been attracted to knowledge, so when Nas and Wu-Tang came out spitting Five Percent language, I immediately wanted to know more. I'd seen little bits and pieces of this information when I'd catch the train to New York, just to get away from the city (or because I'd run away from home!). I remember having deep conversations with the Black book vendors who once lined the streets, yet I never had the money to buy any books (though I always seemed to have enough for weed and alcohol).

My mother had once told me that Indian people used to be Black, but I didn't think there was anything 'deep' to the sense of solidarity I felt with other Black and brown people. I always assumed that experiencing racism from white people (which I enjoyed plenty of) was all that did it.

Things finally clicked when an older brother named Pure Sun introduced me to the culture of the Five Percent. He was immersed in the hood as well, and I can't say he was living righteously, but it's clear that he was there for a reason. Had he not been entrenched in the same streets as me, I would have never come into the knowledge of self. That's how I learned about books like *African Presence in Early Asia*, where I saw exactly "how" Indians were Black.

To be clear, Sun didn't introduce me to Five Percent literature or any Black books. He simply introduced me to the culture. As in real people, like Jersey City elders Cee Born and Earth Asia, who were more upright examples of the teachings than he was. Through them,

I met dozens of Five Percenters. They, like Sun, told me I was Black, and that I was Original. It would take some study, however, before I would really understand what that meant. At first, I assumed it was kind of like when my friends in the streets would say, "You a n*gga too." Yet it was much deeper than that.

Until this point, I had believed that the streets were my home. When I found this culture, I found my real home. I ended up graduating from high school, and – with the help of my "crisis intervention counselor" Mr. James Johnson – I went to college in Atlanta. I couldn't decide what to study, so I majored in Sociology and then Philosophy before I found my passion: History. I did most of my research papers on ancient Black history. Even got inducted into the International Honors Society.

When I graduated from college, I took a teaching job with the public school system. For eleven years since that day, I've only worked in Black and brown communities like the one I grew up in. During this time, I cofounded a nonprofit that would address youth in a way I couldn't do in the classroom.

After I earned my masters, specialist, and doctorate degrees in education, specifically focusing on curriculum designed to meet the needs of at-risk Black and brown youth, I developed a curriculum that could do what school teachers and nonprofits couldn't. This is how my first book, *How to Hustle and Win*, was born. For those who have read it, you can revisit it and see how it's designed like a true curriculum.

And that book led to an entire line of educational books, dealing with all the issues not being addressed by people in positions of power. We've covered self-empowerment, social change, physical health, mental health, the prison system, and even knowledge of self. With every book we've published, I've asked myself, what's not being said? What problems are not being addressed?

"The future emerges from the past." – Senegalese Proverb

Thus, I realized just how important it is that we cover history. In this volume of the *Science of Self* series, we're exploring not simply what it means to be Black, but how everything came to be the way that it is now. We're offering our readers a lens into the past that allows them to peer into the future. And – above all – we're destroying the myth that Black people have contributed little to world history.

In fact, there would be **no such thing as history without Black people**. Black people are the authors of world civilization, and the

Original People of the planet. Sometimes, it seems unimaginable how we grow up thinking the exact opposite. As my elder brother Runoko Rashidi often says:

> Strong people constantly talk about their history, while weak people do not. Weak people seek to downplay the past and act as if it is unimportant. Strong people do no such thing.

Rashidi asks, "What if we all grew up knowing our true history? Before slavery? What if we knew about the royalty in our blood, and how we came to be where we are today?"

In asking myself these questions while looking at the state of the world today, it is clear that the majority of Original People, not just here in America but everywhere, are out of touch with who they are and how they came to be. They don't know why they're in the conditions they're in, so they're unable to fix them. After all, you can't treat a disease if you don't know its cause. This is why this book exists.

I want to show Original People – all Original People – our common history and our shared heritage. I want to give people a reference to consult when there's confusion about who we were and what we really did. I want to give us a lens into the past so we can calculate the future. And that's what this is all about. I'm just striving to do my part in fixing this screwed-up world.

CONTACT AND BOOKING DETAILS

To have Supreme Understanding appear on your show, panel, broadcast, conference, or at any event, simply email us at booking@supremedesignonline.com with the specifics of your event or program and what you'd like to accomplish.

If you're interested in reviewing this book or using parts of it in another work, please simply give us credit for brief quotes and contact us at rights@supremedesignonline.com for longer passages.

If you're interested in ordering copies of this book or others at volume discounts for a school or university, those rates are available directly on our website. Simply find the book's page and use the drop-down menu to choose the wholesale quantity you're interested in. If you have trouble, email orders@supremedesignonline.com

INSPIRATION FOR THIS WORK

There are a few sources I'd like to identify as providing some of the needed inspiration for this work. I've already mentioned Ivan Van

Sertima and Runoko Rashidi's *African Presence* series, and quoted those works throughout this volume. I later picked up *The Destruction of Black Civilization* by Chancellor Williams. In this monumental work, Williams makes a statement that further inspired me:

> I only made passing reference in the work to Blacks scattered outside of Africa over the world, not from the slave trade, but from dispersions that began in prehistory. This fact alone indicates the great tasks of future scholarship on the real history of the race. We are actually just on the threshold, gathering up some important missing fragments. **The biggest jobs are still ahead.**
>
> Ancient China and the Far East, for example, must be a special area of African research. How do we explain such a large population of Blacks in southern China, powerful enough to form a kingdom of their own? Or the Black people of Formosa, Australia, the Malay Peninsula, Indo-China, the Andaman, and numerous other islands?
>
> The heavy concentration of Africans in India, and the evidence that the earliest Aryan chiefs were Black (which will make Hitler rise from his grave) opens still another interesting field for investigation.
>
> Even the "Negroid" finds in early Europe appear not to be as challenging as the Black population centers in Asia. For, again, reference is not made to small groups which may have wandered anywhere over the Earth; rather, our concern is with great and dominant populations. These are the Blacks who have so puzzled Western scholars that some theorize that Asia or Europe may be the homeland of Africans after all.
>
> The African populations in Palestine, Arabia, and Mesopotamia are better known, although the many centuries of Black rule over Palestine, South Arabia, and in Mesopotamia should be studied and elaborated in more detail.
>
> All of this will call for a new kind of scholarship, a scholarship without any mission other than the discovery of truth, and one that will not tremble with fear when that truth is contrary to what one prefers to believe.[475]

The reason why I've worked night after day on this book, entirely rewriting this book six times, losing sleep, wearing myself ragged, even hospitalizing myself once in the process, has been because I'd like to think that this book represents at least part of the fulfillment of that vision. And it was worth it. This is a story that deserved to be told. And it deserved to be told truthfully.

As Williams said prophetically, once Black people are afforded "a history of the Blacks that is a history of Blacks," change is on its way:

> They will be coming back, centerstage, into their own history at last. But to what end? Will it be just for the intellectual satisfaction of knowing our true history? Knowing it, but so what? The answer is

nothing, unless from history we learn what our strengths were and, especially, in what aspect we are weak and vulnerable. Our history can then become at once the foundation and guiding light for united efforts and serious planning of what we should be about now.[476]

In recent years, I've dug up a two-volume text known as *The African Abroad*, written by Black scholar William Henry Ferris in 1911. This massive series covers so much ancient (and often unknown) Black history that it's almost unimaginable. W.E.B. Du Bois' 1915 *The Negro* is comparable, but Ferris' scope and depth are unmatched.

Before I came across any of these books, however, I was a young Five Percenter, learning mostly by oral tradition. At some point in my studies, I came across a Five Percent publication titled "African or Asiatic?" by Shabazz Adew Allah.

This was the first time I'd come across the idea that Black history extended beyond the region known as Africa, and that "Africa" was in fact a relatively recent name, applied to separate Black populations from each other, both politically and subconsciously. Adew wrote:

> The primary effect of this erroneous labeling by the Europeans and Arabs has been to successfully isolate and detach the Blackman from a much larger world context and view, wherein he has suffered in his ability to relate and identify with his extended family who are located on other parts of the planet Earth besides so-called Africa.
>
> He has been made blind to the fact that the Blackman who have lived and existed in so-called Africa along with the advanced societies and civilizations that they produced only represent a small fraction of the numerous other Black people who inhabit this planet and who also in other geographical areas have made out-standing achievements of their own.
>
> In short the Blackman's mental vision and perspective has been kept confined and limited to areas solely between the boundaries of so-called Africa, and as a result he has lived blindly with the belief and misconception that his history exceeds no further than this location.
>
> It is our intention through the manifestations of teachings to emphasize the universality of the Blackman, by impressing upon all the full extent to which **the Blackman has dispersed himself to all corners of the Earth, dating back from time immemorial, from Mexico to China, from Alaska to England, from India to Australia, the Blackman was existing and building civilizations in these places thousand of years ago and many of these areas had already been lived in and abandoned by him at the time that the Europeans first made their appearance on the planet Earth.**
>
> The Blackman had even settled in regions as far North as Alaska and Greenland, which are areas usefully associated with a much colder climate, a fact that tends to dispel the popular myth that the

Blackman lost his pigmentation and became white skinned only because he had lived in this cold climate for a prolonged number of years...A noted author, Cheikh Anta Diop, in his book *The African Origin of Civilization: Myth or Reality* says in the 19th century Bory DeSaint Vincent described the Eskimos, same of whom were almost as Black as the Blackest Africans, despite the latitude....

It was partly because of the above stated circumstances why the Europeans found it necessary to fabricate the myth of a land called Africa and people called Africans. He was eager to prevent the Blacks from recognizing his true origin and roots in this world which he secretly knew extended over the entire globe and dated back into far distant past.

By creating divisions within the family of the original people that were based upon such trivial factors as geographical boundaries and locations he was triumphant in producing a mass state of separation and alienation amongst them. Also by signaling out certain customs and life styles that were common to Blacks who lived together in one area, and which were generally unknown to or not practiced by Blacks who lived in other areas, he was able to further increase the gaps and divisions that he artificially created. Because the Black people called Sumerians used a form of writing and other Black people like the Dravidians of India, or the Sabeans of South Arabia didn't, he used this as a criteria for proclaiming that they were a different people.

Before I'd read any books on the subject, this paper made me want to know more. It's been over 15 years since I began that journey, and those years have been filled with countless hours of research and analysis. This book is one of the fruits of that labor. In future Volumes, we'll address all of the questions we've left unanswered, including the problem of how and when everything changed from the time when the world was Black.

WHAT'S IN VOLUME 3, 4, AND 5?
WHAT YOU'LL LEARN IN VOLUME THREE

The third volume of the *Science of Self* series focuses on the common culture of our ancestors, the Original People, the cultural ties that still bind many indigenous people today, and their connection to Black and brown people in the West today. Because the hood retains much of this culture, whether they know it or not.

Tentative release date? We're thinking Summer of 2013, accompanied by the release of *Black God* and *Black People Invented Everything*.

WHAT YOU'LL LEARN IN VOLUME FOUR

The fourth volume of the series focuses on the origins of white people (for real), their early history (including their conquests of the world's Black civilizations), their cultural pathologies, the way they developed these pathologies, and the persistent nature of white supremacy then and now.

Tentative release date? Most likely Early Winter 2014.

WHAT YOU'LL LEARN IN VOLUME FIVE

The fifth volume of the series focuses on the "secret" history of the world within the past 2,000 years. We'll explore the origins and history of the world's secret societies, the Crusades, the Moorish Conquest of Spain, the Black Plague, the Maafa (slave trade), and everything else that was left out of our history books.

Tentative release date? Between Summer and Fall of 2014.

WHAT ARE THESE BOOKS TITLED?

We don't know yet! But you can help us choose a title by placing your vote at www.thescienceofself.com

There you'll find excerpts, videos, and other content related to these books. You'll also be able to find out exactly when they'll release and order them before anyone else.

ENDNOTES

1 Cheikh Anta Diop. (1974). African Origin of Civilization. Lawrence Hill Books.
2 Elijah Muhammad. (1965). Message to the Blackman. Elijah Muhammad Books.
3 Elijah Muhammad. (1965).
4 John W. Burgess, (1902). Reconstruction and the Constitution: 1866-1876, p. 133, cited in Novick, That Noble Dream, p. 75.
5 Hugh Trevor-Roper. (1965). The Rise of Christian Europe.
6 Bertram Lenox Putnam Weale. (1910). The conflict of colour: the threatened upheaval throughout the world. p. 232-233.
7 Laurie Pawlik-Kienlen. "Modern Mud Huts: Green Housing From the Ground". Alive. www.alive.com/articles/view/21745/modern_mud_huts
8 Visit www.blackhistorystudies.com for an article on this.
9 Charles Q. Choi. (2009). "Ancient Mayans likely had fountains and toilets." NBC News. www.msnbc.msn.com/id/34575056
10 Joseph Ki-Zerbo. (Aug-Sep 1979). "A Continent Viewed From Within." The UNESCO Courier. UNESCO.
11 Debra A. Brock, Tracy E. Douglas, David C. Queller & Joan E. Strassmann, (Jan 20 2011). "Primitive agriculture in a social amoeba," Nature 469, p. 393–396.
12 Solheim, W.G. (1972) An earlier agricultural revolution. Scientific American 226: 34-41
13 Alasdiar Wilkins. (May 25 2011) "The story behind the world's oldest museum, built by a Babylonian princess 2,500 years ago," i09, http://io9.com/5805358/the-story-behind-the-worlds-oldest-museum-built-by-a-babylonian-princess-2500-years-ago
14 Marshall Mathers. (2012). Unknown History: Unknown for a Reason. iUnicorn Press.
15 Memnon77. (1999). "Stuff I Rant About on YouTube." www.youtube.com/xgbu
16 Joe Remus (2012). Uncle Joe's Compendium of Mystic Web Wisdom. www.unclejoesgibberish.com
17 Piankhy Netertari. (2001). "Stuff I Say on my personal Website without Proof." www.ancientafricanastronautsandmixtapes.com
18 Doan Bilivmy. (1870). The Mountaineth Refluvieth: Doth it Harken Yonder? And other Anomalous Contingencies. Williams and Harkinson and Boyd.
19 Dan Rather. (2007). "Radar detects granite deposit, not pyramid." USA Today.
20 Dan Rather. (2008). "Not if you actually read the original source." BBC News.
21 All books and documentaries aren't ripoffs, of course. But any time you're being scammed, there's always some money or power involved. Sometimes, misinformation is purposely fed to our communities to keep us distracted and impotent. Other times, someone's just trying to make an easy buck.
22 J. Douglas Kenyon. (2005). Forbidden History: Prehistoric Technologies, Extraterrestrial Intervention, And The Suppressed Origins Of Civilization. Inner Traditions. p. 1
23 Jeanna Bryner. (Jul 2010). "Ancient Hunting Weapon Discovered in Melting Ice." Live Science. http://www.livescience.com/history/ancient-weapon-found-in-ice-100705.html
24 McPherron, S. et al. (2010). Evidence for stone-tool-assisted consumption of animal tissues before 3.39 million years ago at Dikika, Ethiopia Nature, 466 (7308), 857-860.
25 Cameron M. Smith, Evan T. Davies. (2009). Anthropology for Dummies. Wiley & Sons.
26 "Anthropology." (1968). International Encyclopedia of the Social Sciences. Available at www.encyclopedia.com
27 Charles Seignobos. (1906). History of Ancient Civilization. C. Scriber and Sons.
28 Charles Seignobos. (1906).
29 John G. Jackson. (1985). Ethiopia and the Origin of Civilization. Black Classic Press.
30 John G. Jackson. (1985).
31 John G. Jackson. (1985).
32 Franz Boas. (May 31 1906). "Commencement Address at Atlanta University." Atlanta University Leaflet, No. 19. www.webdubois.org/BoasAtlantaCommencement.html
33 Originally posted at www.egyptsearch.com (no longer available)

34 According to James W. Loewen in *Lies my Teacher Told Me*: "When Columbus reached Haiti, he found the Arawaks in possession of some spear points made of guanine. The Indians told members of Columbus' party that they got the guanine from Black traders who had come from the South and East. Guanine proved to be an alloy of gold, silver, and copper, identical to the gold alloy preferred by West Africans, who called it "guanine." Islamic historians have recorded stories of Black sailors going into the West. Genetic studies found that traces of diseases common in Africa were also found in pre-Columbians corpses in Brazil. Columbus' son, Ferdinand, who accompanied the admiral on his third voyage, reported that people he met or heard about in eastern Honduras, were "...almost black in color..." and probably African. The first Europeans to reach Panama, Balboa and company, reported seeing Black slaves in an Indian town. The Indians reported they had captured them from a nearby Black community." James W. Loewen. (1995). Lies my Teacher Told Me. Touchstone Books. p. 138.

35 Wesley Muhammad. (Jul 2011). "The Aryanization of Islam." http://blackarabia.blogspot.com/2011/07/aryanization-of-islam.html

36 Sujan Dass. (Ed.) (2009). Black Rebellion: Eyewitness Accounts of Major Slave Revolts. Two Horizons Press.

37 And 30 million is a conservative number. 20th century scholarly estimates range from a low of 8.4 million to a high of 112 million. William M. Denevan. (1992.) The Native Population of the Americas in 1492. University of Wisconsin Press.

38 Cheikh Anta Diop. (1974).

39 Gonder, M, et al. (2007). Whole mtDNA Genome Sequence Analysis of Ancient African Lineages. Mol Biol Evol. 24(3):757-68.

40 Tishkoff et al. (2000). Short Tandem-Repeat Polymorphism/Alu Haplotype Variation at the PLAT Locus. American Journal of Human Genetics; 67:901-925

41 Chancellor Williams, (1987). The Destruction of Black Civilization: Great Issues of a Race from 4500 B.C to 2000 A.D. Third World Press. p. 31-32

42 Richard Klein. (1999). The Human Career. Cambridge University Press. p. 502.

43 Tishkoff SA, Williams SM., (Aug 2002). Genetic analysis of African populations: human evolution and complex disease. Nature Reviews Genetics, (8):611-21.

44 Rightmire GP. New studies of post-Pleistocene human skeletal remains from the Rift Valley, Kenya. Am J Phys Anthropol. 1975 May; 42(3): 351-69.

45 Jean Hiernaux, The People of Africa (Encore Editions: 1975), pp. 17-204

46 S.O.Y. Keita. (1990). Studies of Ancient Crania from Northern Africa. Am J Phys Anthropol. 83(1):35-48. http://www.ncbi.nlm.nih.gov/pubmed/2221029

47 S.O.Y. Keita. (1993). "Studies and Comments on Ancient Egyptian Biological Relationships," History in Africa 20, 129-54; J Hum Evol. (Jul 1997), 33(1):33-82.

48 Relethford, J.H. (2000). Human skin color diversity is highest in sub-Saharan African populations. Hum Biol. 72(5):773-80.

49 Tishkoff SA, Williams SM., (Aug 2002). Genetic analysis of African populations: human evolution and complex disease. Nature Reviews, Genetics, (8):611-21.

50 Jean Hiernaux, (1975). The People of Africa. Encore Editions. p. 53, 54

51 S. Keita, (1996). "The Diversity of Indigenous Africans," in Egypt in Africa, Theodore Clenko, Editor, p. 104-105.

52 Betty Shabazz and Merit Publishers. (1970). Malcolm X: All Afro-American History, Pathfinder Press, Inc., p . 26.

53 See Chancellor Williams. (1987); Cheikh Anta Diop. (1988). Pre-Colonial Black Africa. Chicago Review Press.

54 Joseph Ki-Zerbo. (1979).

55 McPherron, S., et al. (2010). Evidence for stone-tool-assisted consumption of animal tissues before 3.39 million years ago at Dikika, Ethiopia Nature, 466 (7308), 857-860.

56 Darren Schuettler, "Ancient Tools Suggest Termite Foraging" http://abcnews.go.com/sections/scitech/DailyNews/hominid_termites.html

57 JoAnn Gutin, (Nov 17 1995). "Do Kenya Tools Root Birth of Modern Thought in Africa?" Science 270, p. 1118.

THIS BOOK WILL CHANGE THE WAY YOU SEE SCIENCE

The Science of Self is a dynamic tour of reality, covering the formation of our universe, the development of life, and the laws that govern these processes and personify themselves as Man. The book introduces readers to hundreds of scientific fields, peering into what quantum mechanics, genetics, anthropology, mathematics, and archaeology have to say about the past, present, and future of Black and brown people. As the first of a five-volume series, this text ventures beyond superficial ideas about history, science, and meta-physics, plunging into questions about the mathematical language that connects man, God, and the laws of nature.

THIS BOOK WILL CHANGE THE WAY YOU SEE HISTORY

Based on over 28 years of combined research, with over 360 references, and a dozen reviewers, this book is history in the making. No other nonfiction text has attempted to cover nearly 14 billion years of Black history. How could all that possibly be Black history? You'll have to read the book to understand.

THIS BOOK WILL CHANGE THE WAY YOU SEE REALITY

What is the origin of Blackness? Why is melanin found in space? How did life evolve from one ancestor into the diversity we see today? What does quantum physics tell us about consciousness and reality? How did the Black man shape the Earth long before he built the pyramids? What is the mathematical blueprint that is hard-wired into our consciousness? Is there a difference between the mind and the brain? What does it mean to be the Original Man and Woman? All of these questions, and hundreds more, are answered within these pages.

THIS BOOK WILL CHANGE THE WAY YOU SEE YOURSELF

WWW.THESCIENCEOFSELF.COM

supreme design
Publishing
__ OF __
500

www.SupremeDesignOnline.com

ISBN 978-1-935721-68-0

9 781935 721680

534995>

THE SCIENCE OF SELF

LIMITED EDITION

MAN, GOD, and the MATHEMATICAL LANGUAGE of NATURE

VOLUME ONE

VOL ONE

SUPREME UNDERSTANDING and C'BS ALIFE ALLAH

58 Robert G. Bednarik, (1993). "Stone Age Stone Walls," The Artefact, 16, p. 60

59 Robert G. Bednarik, (1994). "Art Origins", Anthropos, 89: 169-180, p. 170.

60 D. Mania and U. Mania and E. Vlcek, (1994). "Latest Finds of Skull Remains of from Bilzingsleben (Thruingia)", Naturwissenschaften, 81, p. 123-127; Alexander Marshack, (1972). The Roots of Civilization, McGraw-Hill Book Co., p. 139; Robert G. Bednarik, (1990). "On Lower Paleolithic Cognitive Development," 23rd Chacmool Conference Calgary, p. 427-435, p. 432; Rick Gore, (Jul 1997). "The First Europeans," National Geographic, p. 110

61 Robin Dennell, (Feb 27 1997). "The World's Oldest Spears," and Hartmut Thieme, "Lower Palaeolithic Hunting Spears form Germany," Nature, 385, p. 767; 810.

62 "Lower Paleolithic people were not scavengers, say anthropologists." (Aug 2009). Science Codex. www.sciencecodex.com/lower_paleolithic_people_were_not_scavengers_say_anthropologists

63 W.C. Pei, (1930). "Notice of the Discovery of Quartz and Other Stone artifacts in the Lower Pleistocene Hominid-Bearing Sediments of the Choukoutien Cave Deposit," Bulletin of the Geological Society of China, 11:2, 109-146.

64 Victor Barnouw, (1982). An Introduction to Anthropology: Physical Anthropology and Archaeology, Vol. 1, The Dorsey Press, p. 141

65 Juliet Clutton-Brock, (1995). "Origins of the Dog: Domestication and Early History," in James Serpell, ed. The Domestic Dog, Cambridge University Press, p. 8-10

66 P.Y. Sondaar, et al., "Middle Pleistocene faunal turnover and Colonization of Flores (Indonesia)," Comptes Rendus de l'Academie des Sciences. Paris 319: 1255-1262.

67 Bruce Bower, (Feb 23 2002). "Almond Joy, Stone Age Style," Science News, p. 117.

68 Robert G. Bednarik, (1993). "Wonders of Wonderwork Cave," The Artefact, 16, p. 61

69 Thomas Wynn, (1995). "Handaxe Enigmas," World Archaeology, 27:1, p. 10-24.

70 J. A. J. Gowlett, J. W. K. Harris, D. Walton and B. A. Wood, (Nov 12 1981). "Early archaeological sites, Hominid Remains and Traces of Fire from Chesowanja, Kenya," Nature, 294, p. 128; C. K. Brain and A. Sillen, (Dec 1 1988). "Evidence from the Swartkrans cave for the earliest use of fire," Nature, 336, p. 464-465

71 Brian Ludwig, "New Evidence for the Possible Use of Controlled Fire from ESA Sites in the Olduvai and Turkana Basins," Abstracts for the Paleoanthropology Society Meeting, The University of Pennsylvania Museum.

72 K.D. Schick, N. Toth. (1993). Making Silent Stones Speak, Simon and Schuster, p.160

73 M.D. Leakey, (1971). Olduvai Gorge 3 Excavations in Beds I and II, 1960-1693, Cambridge University Press, p. 269

74 D.C. Johanson, L. Johanson, B. Edgar, (1994). Ancestors, Villard Books, p. 163-165

75 Victor Barnouw, (1982). An Introduction to Anthropology: Physical Anthropology and Archaeology, Vol. 1, The Dorsey Press, p. 126

76 Juan Luis A. Ferreras, (May/Jun 1997). "Faces from the Past," Archaeology, p. 31-33.

77 See Cheikh Anta Diop. (1959).Cultural Unity of Black Africa. Third World Press.

78 Olivia Vlahos. (1967). African Beginnings. Fawcett Premier. p. 19-20.

79 Maya Metni Pilkington (2008). An apportionment of African genetic diversity based on mitochondrial, Y chromosomal, and X chromosomal data. PH.d Dissertation (published). University of Arizona, p. 1-9.

80 University of the Witwatersrand, Johannesburg. (Dec 2011). "Plant bedding, medicinal plant use, and settlement patterns at Sibudu." www.wits.ac.za/sibudu

81 "Stone Age Engraving Traditions Appear on Ostrich Shells," (Mar 2010). Science News. http://www.sciencenews.org/view/generic/id/56807/title/Stone_Age_engraving_traditions_appear_on_ostrich_eggshells

82 Wadley, L; Hodgskiss, T; Grant, M (Jun 2009). "From the Cover: Implications for complex cognition from the hafting of tools with compound adhesives in the Middle Stone Age, South Africa.". Proceedings of the National Academy of Sciences of the United States of America 106 (24): 9590–4. doi:10.1073/pnas.0900957106.

83 Wadley L, Hodgkiss T, Grant M. (2009). Supporting Information for Implications for complex cognition from the hafting of tools with compound adhesives in the Middle

WHY TRAVEL?

The only thing better than learning about these cultures from a distance is actually *being there*. Everywhere I've went, I've immersed myself in the culture of the people and studied their history hands-on. Many of us can't imagine traveling too far outside of our comfort zones, but everything in us tells us we should. To help people embrace the idea of seeing the world (affordably and realistically), I'm putting together a book on how to travel. Check for it at www.supremedesignonline.com this Summer.

THAILAND

JAPAN

GHANA

HAWAII

PUERTO RICO

MEXICO

COSTA RICA

Stone Age, South Africa Proc Natl Acad Sci USA. 106:9590–9594.

84 Wurz, S. (1999). "The Howiesons Poort Backed Artefacts from Klasies River: An Argument for Symbolic Behaviour Author(s)". South African Archaeological Bulletin 54 (169): 38–50. doi:10.2307/3889138.

85 Lucinda Backwell, Francesco d'Ericco and Lyn Wadley, (2008). "Middle Stone Age Bone Tools from the Howiesons Poort layers, Sibidu Cave, South Africa, Journal of Archaeological Science 35, no. 6: 1566-1580.

86 Article originally available at www.wits.ac.za, site of the University of the Witwatersrand, Johannesburg.

87 Zenobia Roberts, Richard G. Roberts. (Mar-Apr 2009). "Catalysts for Stone Age Innovations." Commun Integr Biol. 2(2): 191–193.

88 Zenobia Roberts, Richard G. Roberts. (2009).

89 Jacobs, Z; et al. (2008). "Ages for the Middle Stone Age of southern Africa: implications for human behavior and dispersal". Science 322 (5902): 733–5.

90 "African Bone Tools Dispute Key Ideas About Human Evolution." (Nov 2001). National Geographic News. news.nationalgeographic.com/news/2001/11/1108_bonetool.html

91 "African Bone Tools Dispute Key Ideas About Human Evolution." (Nov 2001).

92 Brown KS, et al. (2009). Fire As an Engineering Tool of Early Modern Humans. Science, 325: 859-862. doi:10.1126/science.1175028

93 "Deep African Roots for Toolmaking Method," (Nov 2010). Science News. www.sciencenews.org/view/generic/id/64807/

94 Richard A. Lovett. (Jul 2006). "Bigger Cities Causing Stronger Summer Storms, Experts Say, National Geographic." http://news.nationalgeographic.com/news/2006/07/060726-rain-cities.html

95 Bücher, Karl. (1901). Industrial Evolution. H. Holt and Company. p. 47.

96 The World Atlas of Archaeology. (1988). Portland House. Original published in French as Le Grand Atlas de l'archeologie by Encyclopedia Universalis.

97 Günter Berghaus. (2004). New Perspectives on Prehistoric Art. Praeger.

98 Julio Mercader, (2002). "Forest People: The Role of African Rainforests in Human Evolution and Dispersal," Evolutionary Anthropology 11, no.3: 117-124, http://ucalgary.academia.edu/juliomercader/Papers/365119/Forest_People_the_Role_of_African_Rainforests_In_Human_Evolution_and_Dispersal

99 Els Cornelissen, (Sep 2002). Human Responses to Changing Environments in Central Africa Between 40,000 and 12,000 BC, Journal of World Prehistory, Vol. 16, Iss. 3.

100 Els Cornelissen. (2002).

101 Shaw, T. (1980). Hunters, gatherers and first farmers in West Africa. In J.V.S. Megaw (Ed.) Hunters, Gatherers and First Farmers beyond Europe (p. 69-125). Leicester University Press.

102 Shaw, T. (1980). p. 111-114; Davies, O. (1968). The origins of agriculture in West Africa. Current Anthropology, 9, 479-487.

103 Posnansky, M. (1984). Early agricultural societies in Ghana. In J.D. Clark & S.A. Brandt (Eds.) From Hunters to Farmers: The Causes and Consequences of Food Production in Africa (p. 147-151). University of California Press; Stahl, A.B. (1995). Intensification in the west African Late Stone Age: a view from central Ghana. In T. Shaw, P. Sinclair, B. Andah, & A. Okpoko (Eds.) The Archaeology of Africa (p. 261-273). Routledge.

104 Cornelissen, Els (Mar 2003), "On Microlithic Quartz Industries at the End of the Pleistocene in Central Africa: The Evidence from Shum Laka (NW Cameroon)." African Archaeological Review, Vol. 20, No. 1.

105 Lavachery, P. (2001). The Holocene Archaeological Sequence of Shum Laka Rock Shelter (Grassfields, Western Cameroon). African Archaeological Review. Vol. 18, No. 4

106 Yellen, JE, et al. (28 April 1995). "A middle stone age worked bone industry from Katanda, Upper Semliki Valley, Zaire". Science 268 (5210): 553-556.

107 Shadreck Chirikure; Innocent Pikirayi (2008). "Inside and outside the dry stone walls: revisiting the material culture of Great Zimbabwe". Antiquity 82: 976–993.

108 Rincon, Paul (May 23 2003). "Oldest sculpture found in Morocco". BBC. http://news.bbc.co.uk/2/hi/science/nature/3047383.stm

109 Drusillla Dunjee Houston. (1926).

110 Larry O'Hanlon. (Feb 2010). "Steak Dinners Go Back 2.5 Million Years". Discovery News. http://news.discovery.com/animals/earliest-bull-beef-fossil.html

111 Julius Caesar. (14 AD). The Gallic Wars. (Trans. W. A. McDevitte and W. S. Bohn). Available at http://classics.mit.edu/Caesar/gallic.html

112 Nicholas Wade. (2006). Before the Dawn. Penguin. p. 94

113 Nicholas Wade, (2006). p 69.

114 Davies, G.I (1998). "Introduction to the Pentateuch". In John Barton. Oxford Bible Commentary. Oxford University Press.

115 Yosef Ben-Jochannan. (1996). We, the Black Jews. Black Classic Press.

116 Rudolph Windsor. (1998). From Babylon to Timbuktu: A History of the Ancient Black Races Including the Black Hebrews. Windsor Golden Series.

117 Cruciani F., et al., (2011). "A revised root for the human y chromosomal phylogenetic tree: The origin of patrilineal diversity in Africa," American Journal of Human Genetics 88, no. 6: 814-818. www.sciencedirect.com/science/article/pii/S0002929711001649

118 Supreme Understanding. C'BS Alife Allah. (2012). The Science of Self, Volume One: Man, God, and the Mathematical Language of Nature. Supreme Design Publishing.

119 African historian Joseph Ki-Zerbo suggests that the topography of Africa itself may have facilitated such reunions and migrations. Ki-Zerbo writes: "One example is the great meridian groove of the Rift Valley, stretching from the very centre of Africa and across the Ethiopian ridge as far as Iraq. The curve of the valleys of the Sangha, Ubangi and Zaire must have acted as a corridor in an eastwest direction. It is not by chance that the first kingdoms of black Africa developed in these more accessible regions, these Sahels at once permeable from within, to a certain extent open towards the exterior, and in contact with neighbouring regions of Africa with different and complementary resources." Joseph Ki-Zerbo. (Aug-Sep 1979). "A Continent Viewed From Within." The UNESCO Courier. UNESCO.

120 Verónica Fernandes et al, (2012). "The Arabia Cradle: Mitochondrial Relicts of the First Steps along the Southern Route out of Africa," The American Journal of Human Genetics 90: 1-9.

121 Andrew Lawler. (Jan 2011). Did Modern Humans Travel Out of Africa Via Arabia? Science 28, Vol. 331 no. 6016 p. 387 DOI: 10.1126/science.331.6016.387

122 Armitage, S., et al. (2011). The Southern Route "Out of Africa": Evidence for an Early Expansion of Modern Humans into Arabia Science, 331 (6016), 453-456.

123 Rose J.I., et al. (2011). The Nubian Complex of Dhofar, Oman: An African Middle Stone Age Industry in Southern Arabia. PLoS ONE 6:e28239.

124 Harry Hamilton Johnston. (1910). The Negro in the New World. p. 27

125 Rose J.I., et al. (2011).

126 Christopher Ehret has said: "We talk about "Islamic Civilization" or "Ancient Near Eastern Civilization" or "Western Civilization." But what are we talking about? We're talking about a bunch of different peoples who somehow have a something in common culturally, something which allows us to think of them as part of a wider grouping. If we take this model of civilization and apply it to Africa, we quickly discover that there are big groupings of people across Africa which share in underlying historical commonalities. If we go really deep, we have four traditions which diffused throughout large regions of Africa. What we can see that each of them has its roots in some particular transition that gave that group some material or economic advantage."

127 Verónica Fernandes et al, "The Arabia Cradle: Mitochondrial Relicts of the First Steps along the Southern Route out of Africa," The American Journal of Human Genetics 90 (2012): 1-9.

128 Katie Alcock, (2010). "Stone Tools 'Change Migration Story'," BBC News. http://www.bbc.co.uk/news/science-environment-11327442

129 Michael D. Petraglia, Jeffrey I. Rose. (2009). The Evolution of Human Populations in

Arabia: Paleoenvironments, Prehistory and Genetics. Springer.

130 Nicholas Wade. (2006).

131 "Supervolcano Eruption -- In Sumatra -- Deforested India 73,000 Years Ago." (Nov 2009). Science Daily. www.sciencedaily.com/releases/2009/11/091123142739.htm

132 Steve Oppenheimer. (2004). The Real Eve, p. 82

133 Hanihara T. (Mar 1996). Comparison of craniofacial features of major human groups. American Journal of Physical Anthropology, 99(3):389-412.

134 Steve Oppenheimer. (2004). p. 188.

135 Sacha Jones. (2007). "The Toba Supervolcanic Eruption," In Petraglia and Allchin (Eds.). The evolution and history of human populations in South Asia, p. 177.

136 Victor Grauer. (2011).

137 Elizabeth Culotta, (2005). "Snapshots from the Meeting," Science 308, no. 5721: 491, www.sciencemag.org/content/308/5721/491.2.full

138 W.E.B. Du Bois. (1915). The Negro.

139 Rose J.I., et al. (2011). They write: "Although southern Arabia experienced successive periods of extreme aridity after MIS 5, terrestrial archives document another increase in precipitation across the interior of Arabia during early MIS 3, enabling north-south demographic exchange between ~60–50 ka. South Arabian populations may have spread to the north at this time, taking with them a Nubian-derived Levallois technology… which is notably the hallmark of the Middle-Upper Palaeolithic transition in the Levant."

140 Michael D. Petraglia, Jeffrey I. Rose. (2009). The Evolution of Human Populations in Arabia: Paleoenvironments, Prehistory and Genetics. Springer.

141 Nicholas Wade. (2006).

142 Anna Revedin et al. (2010). Thirty thousand-year-old evidence of plant food processing PNAS:10.1073/pnas.1006993107

143 Supreme Understanding. C'BS Alife Allah. (2012). The Science of Self, Volume One: Man, God, and the Mathematical Language of Nature. Supreme Design Publishing.

144 Richards MP, et al. (June 2000). "Neanderthal diet at Vindija and Neanderthal predation: the evidence from stable isotopes." PNAS 97 (13): 7663–6.

145 Andrea Thompson. (2006) "Neanderthals were Cannibals, Study Confirms." Live Science. www.livescience.com/health/061204_neanderthal_lifestyle.html

146 Anna Revedin, et al. (2010). Thirty thousand-year-old evidence of plant food processing. PNAS:10.1073/pnas.1006993107

147 Gray, Richard (Dec 18 2011). "Neanderthals built homes with mammoth bones". Telegraph. www.telegraph.co.uk/science/science-news/8963177/Neanderthals-built-homes-with-mammoth-bones.html

148 Nicholas Wade. (2006). p. 13

149 Alasdair Wilkins, (2011). "There were just too many humans for Neanderthals to survive." http://io9.com/5826353

150 Vega Toscano, L.G, Raposo, L., & M. Santonja. (1994). Environments and settlements in the Middle Palaeolithic of the Iberian peninsula, in W. Roebroeks & C. Gamble (ed.), The Middle Palaeolithic occupation of Europe: 23-48. Universtiy of Leiden.

151 Karkanas, P.; et al. (Sep 2004). "The earliest evidence for clay hearths: Aurignacian features in Klisoura Cave 1, southern Greece." Antiquity.

152 Christine Mellot. (2008). "Stalking the ancient dog." Science News.

153 Mietje Germonpré et al. (2008). Fossil dogs and wolves from Palaeolithic sites in Belgium, the Ukraine and Russia: osteometry, ancient DNA and stable isotopes. Journal of Archaeological Science doi:10.1016/j.jas.2008.09.033.

154 Derr, Mark (2011). How the Dog Became the Dog: From Wolves to Our Best Friends. Penguin Group USA.

155 Pritchard, Hamish (Aug 3 2011). "Ancient dog skull unearthed in Siberia". BBC News; Ovodov, Nikolai D.; et al. (Jul 28 2011). "A 33,000-Year-Old Incipient Dog from the Altai Mountains of Siberia: Evidence of the Earliest Domestication Disrupted by the Last Glacial Maximum." PLoS ONE.

156 Viegas, Jennifer (Oct 7 2011). "Prehistoric dog found with mammoth bone in mouth".

Discovery News.
157 E.M. O'Brian. (Jul 1984). "What was the Acheulean Hand Ax?" Natural History, p. 18.
158 Valet, Jean-Pierre, and Hélène Valladas. (2010). "The Laschamp-Mono lake geomagnetic events and the extinction of Neanderthal: A causal link or a coincidence?" Quaternary Science Reviews.
159 The data is based on remains of Neanderthals occupying Mezmaiskaya Cave in the Russian Caucasus.
160 Golovanova, Liubov V., et al. (2010). "Significance of Ecological Factors in the Middle to Upper Paleolithic Transition." Current Anthropology. 51: 655-691.
161 Andrew Froehle and Steven E. Churchill, (2009). "Energetic Competition Between Neandertals and Anatomically Modern Humans" PaleoAnthropology: 96–116.
162 Banks WE, et al. (2008) Neanderthal Extinction by Competitive Exclusion. PLoS ONE 3(12): e3972. doi:10.1371/journal.pone.0003972
163 Robin Mckie. (2009). "How Neanderthals Met a Grisly Fate: Devoured By Humans," The Observer. http://www.guardian.co.uk/science/2009/may/17/neanderthals-cannibalism-anthropological-sciences-journal
164 Hillary Mayell. "When Did "Modern" Behavior Emerge in Humans?" National Geographic News.
165 Ker Thal, (2009). "Humans Likely Killed Neanderthal, Weapons Test Shows," National Geographic News. http://news.nationalgeographic.com/news/2009/07/090722-human-neanderthal-murder.html
166 Marlowe, F.W. (2005). "Hunter-gatherers and human evolution." Evolutionary Anthropology 14 (2): 15294. doi:10.1002/evan.20046.
167 J. Chavaillon, D. Lavallée, (1988). "Bola" in Dictionnaire de la Préhistoire, PUF.
168 McClellan (2006). Science and Technology in World History. JHU Press. p. 6–12
169 John Roach, (2006). Neanderthals' Last Stand was Gibraltar, Study Suggests," National Geographic News. http://news.nationalgeographic.com/news/2006/09/060913-neanderthals.html
170 Green RE et al. (May 2010). "A draft sequence of the Neandertal genome." Science 7;328 (5979):710-22.
171 Charles Q. Choi, "Innovative Blades May Have Led to a Stone Age Population Boom," Scientific American. http://www.scientificamerican.com/article.cfm?id=innovative-blades-may-hav
172 Robert Halliburton. (1897). How a Race of Pygmies was Found in North Africa and Spain. Arbuthnot Bros. Co. Ltd. Halliburton continues: "A young Jew now living in Manchester, but a native of Mogador, said that the Moors worshipped these Barakers, and would not talk freely about them to the Jews. He had tried to find out about them, but without success. He had constantly, when a boy, seen an old Baraker who died at Mogador about eight or ten, years ago, who was looked on as a great saint, and as such was kissed on the shoulders by the Moors as they passed him in the street. These dwarfs are supposed to bring good luck to the towns where they reside, and are guardians and protectors, resembling in this respect the Palladium of the Trojans. If strangers were to succeed in carrying them out of the country, good luck would depart with them. It is probable that some such superstitious belief was at the bottom of the difficulty which puzzled and baffled Schweinfurth in his attempt to get a sight of the dwarf Akkas of the Monbutto country, the king of which sent away by night his regiment of dwarfs, so as to keep them out of the way of his visitor."
173 Albert Churchward. (1921). The Original and Evolution of the Human Race.
174 J. T. Stock, A. B. Migliano. (Oct 2009). Stature, Mortality, and Life History among Indigenous Populations of the Andaman Islands, 1871–1986. Current Anthropology Vol. 50, No. 5.
175 John Illife. (1995). Africans: The History of a Continent. Cambridge University Press. p. 10.
176 Cavalli-Sforza, L.L. (1986). African pygmies. Academic Press.
177 Nicholas Wade. (2006). p. 90.

178 Lynn Thorndike. (1936). Short History of Civilization, p. 227.

179 Vidya Prakash Tyagi. (2009). Martial Races of Undivided India. Gyan Publishing, p. 2

180 John Block Friedman. (1981). The Monstrous Races in Medieval Art and Thought. Harvard University Press. p. 18

181 Ctesias, Ind. ii. pp. 250, 294; Philostr. Vit. Apollon. iii. 47; Plin. H. N. vi. 22

182 Ctesias, Indica (summary from Photius, Myriobiblon 72) (trans. Freese)

183 Harry Hamilton Johnston. (1910). p. 27

184 Godfrey Higgins. (1833). Anacalypsis: An Attempt to Draw Aside the Veil of the Saitic Isis; Or, An Inquiry into the Origins of Languages, Nations and Religions. To be republished by Two Horizons Press in 2013.

185 R. Thapar. (1966). A History of India.

186 Majid Husan. (2008). Geography of India. Tata McGraw-Hill.

187 Majid Husan. (2008).

188 Supreme Understanding. C'BS Alife Allah. (2012). The Science of Self, Volume One: Man, God, and the Mathematical Language of Nature. Supreme Design Publishing.

189 Pedro Soares et al. (Jun 2009). "Correcting for Purifying Selection: An Improved Human Mitochondrial Molecular Clock." http://www.ncbi.nlm.nih.gov/pubmed/19500773

190 Taylor, Thomas Griffith. (1937). Environment, race, and migration; fundamentals of human distribution. Chicago: The University of Chicago Press, p. 135

191 G. Elliot Smith (1929). The Migrations of Early Culture, Manchester University Press.

192 Victor Grauer. (2011).

193 Michael Petraglia et.al. (Jul 2007). "Middle Paleolithic Assemblages from the Indian Subcontinent Before and After the Toba Super-Eruption". Science 317, no 5834:114-116.

194 Taylor, Thomas Griffith. (1937). p. 248

195 Vidya Prakash Tyagi. (2009). p. 2

196 Cited in Majid Husan. (2008). See Guha, B. S. 1931. The racial affinities of the peoples of India. Census of India, vol. 1, Simla.

197 Taylor, Thomas Griffith. (1937).

198 Quatrefages, Armand de. (Originally published 1887, to be republished 2013). The Pygmies, Two Horizons Press. p. 184-7.

199 Quoted in John G. Jackson (1939) Ethiopia and the Origin of Civilization.

200 M. R. Verneau. (Aug 18 1924). Les recentes decouvertes prehistoriques en Indochine. Comptes Rendus Hebdomadaires des Seances de l'Acadamie des Sciences, t. 179, no. 7, p. 416-418.

201 Weber, George. (2009). "The Negrito Race." Lonely Islands: The Andamanese. http://andaman.org/book/chapter6/text6.htm

202 Coedes, G. (1969). The Making of South East Asia. trans. H. M. Wright. University of California Press. p. 21. Earlier in the text Coedes mentions a skull found in Paleolithic Laos combining characteristics of the Papuan Negroids, the Veddo-Austroloids, and the so-called Europoids (of the same type as the Indonesians and Polynesians). J. Fromaget said of this finding: "His ancestors must have had their habitat somewhere in the south of China on the borders of Yunnan and Tibet, whence they must have spread towards the east and the south throughout the whole of South East Asia, in all parts of which remains of their culture have been found."

203 Weber, George. (2009).

204 Allen, Francis A. (1879). "The Original Range of the Papuan and Negritto Races." Journal of the Anthropological Institute of Great Britain and Ireland. Vol. 8. p. 41. Of these people, Quatrefages observed in his 1885 work, The Pygmies: "As the Malay, so has the Annamite peninsula its representatives of the Negrito type, known under the name of Mois or Moys. Logan long since considered this fact as demonstrated. The doubts so often expressed in regard to this seem scarcely tenable in view of the old proofs recalled by M. Giglioli himself, of those which Earl obtained from the Annamites and Cochin-Chinese, and of the communications of two French physicians of the navy to Hamy. These last two stated to my learned colleagues that some Negro tribes live near

the northern frontiers of the Cochin-Chinese province of Bien-Hoa. The latest information furnished by Allen seems to me to remove the last doubts." p. 35.
205 Colquhoun, A.R. (1970). Amongst the Shans. Paragon Book Reprint, p. xliii.
206 Allen, Francis A. (1879). p. 41-42. Allen also notes the interesting "coincidence" that the "Negroid" Buddha himself is said to have been born to a woman named "Maia."
207 George Weber. (2009). "The Negrito of Malaysia."
www.andaman.org/BOOK/chapter35/text35.htm
208 Peter Bellwood. (2005). Economic Patterns of Early Life. The Encyclopedia of Malaysia, Volume Four: Early History. Didier Millet.
209 Peter Bellwood. (2005).
210 Comas, J. (1960). Manual of Physical Anthropology. Charles C Thomas.
211 Hooton, E. A. (1950). Up from the Ape. The Macmillan Company.
212 Von Eickstedt, E. F. Rassenkunde und Rassengeschichte der Menschheit. Ferdinand Enke Verlag, Stuttgart.
213 Schoonheyt, L.J.A. (1937). Bijdrage tot de Anthropologie der Bevolking van Batavia en Naaste Omstreken. Doctoral dissertation, Batavia-C.
214 Teuku Jacob. (Sep 1964). A Human Mandible from Anjar Urn Field, Indonesia. Journal of the National Medical Association, Vol. 56, No. 5, p. 421-426.
215 De Quatrefages, Armand. (1887). The Pygmies, Two Horizons Press. p. 25-26.
216 De Quatrefages, Armand. (1887). p. 25-26.
217 David J. de Laubenfels. (Mar 1968). Australoids, Negroids, and Negroes: A Suggested Explanation for Their Disjunct Distributions. Annals of the Association of American Geographers, Vol. 58, No. 1, p. 42-50.
218 Scott, William Henry (1984), Prehispanic Source Materials for the study of Philippine History, New Day Publishers.
219 Michael Petraglia et.al. (Jul 2007). "Middle Paleolithic Assemblages from the Indian Subcontinent Before and After the Toba Super-Eruption". Science 317, no 5834:114-116.
220 Nguyen Viet and Nguyen Thi Oan. Aug 2008. "Archaeology of Death in Vietnam". Center for SEA Prehistory. http://www.drnguyenviet.com/?id=5&cat=1&cid=22
221 Matsumura, H. and Zuraina, M. (1999). Metric analyses of an early Holocene human skeleton from Gua Gunung Runtuh, Malaysia. Am. J. Phys. Anthropol. 109: 327-340
222 Bellwood, Peter. (1985). Pre-History of the Indo-malaysian Archipelago. Australian National University.
223 Mondal PR, et al. (2011). "The genomic similarities with linguistic difference: a study among the Oraon and Munda tribes of the Ranchi district, Jharkhand, India." Genet Test Mol Biomarkers 15, no 6: 443-9.
224 Deniker, Joseph. (1900). The Races of Man: An Outline of Anthropology and Ethnography. C. Scribner's Sons.
225 Takeru Akazawa and Emőke J.E. Sathmáry. (1996). Prehistoric Mongoloid dispersals. Oxford University Press.
226 Dixon, Roland B. (1923). The Racial History of Man. Charles Scribners & Sons, p. 222. Quoted in Brunson, James E. (1985). p.15
227 Sleeboom, Margaret. (2004). Academic Nations in China and Japan. Routledge, p.56
228 Nicholas Wade. (2006).
229 James Brunson. (1985).
230 J. Lawrence Angel. (1966). Early skeletons from Tranquillity, California. Smithsonian Contributions to Anthropology, Vol. 2, No. 1. Angel writes: "This eastern Asiatic proto-Mongoloid norm does indeed show long-range resemblances to eastern Upper Paleolithics [from the Near East] and to Australoids (or Amurians and Negritoids), as well as to Palaeamericans."
231 B. A. Malyarchuk, M. A. Perkova and M. V. Derenko. On the origin of Mongoloid component in the mitochondrial gene pool of Slavs. Russian Journal of Genetics, 10.1007/s11177-008-3016-9
232 Majid Husan. (2008). Husan adds: "Their representatives are found in the sub-Himalayan region, particularly Arunachal Pradesh, Assam, and Indo-Myanmar (Burma)

border districts. Their representatives are Daflas, Garos, Kacharis, Khasis, Kuki-Nagas, Ladling, Machi, Miris, and Tipperas." If you look these people up, you will see that these are dark-skinned Mongoloid people.

233 Majid Husan. (2008).

234 Li Chi. (1928). p. 7.

235 Bo Wen et al. (Sept 2004). Genetic evidence supports demic diffusion of Han culture. Nature 431: 302. Han Chinese constitute about 92% of the population of the People's Republic of China (mainland China), 98% of the population of the Republic of China (Taiwan), 74% of the population of Singapore, 24.5% of population of Malaysia, and about 20% of the entire global human population, making it the largest ethnic group in the world. Yet there is still considerable genetic, linguistic, cultural, and social diversity among the subgroups of the Han, due to thousands of years of immigration and assimilation of various regional ethnic groups within China.

236 Latourette, Kenneth Scott. (1962). The Chinese: Their History and Culture. 4th ed. Vol. 2. The Macmillan Company. p. 438.

237 It is important to understand that the term "barbarian" was used by the ancient Chinese simply to designate alien populations, native or foreign, not necessarily in the "savage" context the term implies today. Marcel Granet called these designations "generic names without precise value." Granet, Marcel. (1930). p. 77. During the feudal period, the barbarian countries were designated as follows: *Man* in the south, *Yi* in the east, *Jung* in the west and *Ti* in the north.

238 Hsu, Cho-Yun. "The Spring and Autumn Period." *Cambridge History of Ancient China.* (1999) p. 549. Similarly, the Yi peoples were not solely isolated to the eastern shores, but there was a Western Yi recorded in the *Bamboo Annals* as well. Creel, Herrlee G. (1970) p. 199.

239 Quoted in Ivan Van Sertima and Runoko Rashidi. (Eds). African Presence in Early Asia. Transaction Publishers.

240 Schafer, Edward. (2008). *The Vermillion Bird.* University of California Press. p. 13.

241 Chai Chen Kang. (1967). p. 29.

242 Latourette, Kenneth Scott. (1962). p. 439. Again, remarks of "dark-coloured clothes," like those of the "black-haired commoners" attempt to obfuscate the racial identity of the people to whom these cleverly crafted euphemisms refer. Dark-colored clothes have never, and will never, cause any people to be regarded as "Black," just as "black hair," being a common feature of all east Asian peoples, has never been a point of reference, or reason for singling out, among observers, Chinese or otherwise. Being "black-haired" is almost certainly a euphemism for being "black-headed."

243 Lin Yueh-hwa. (Jan 1941). "The Miao-Man Peoples of Kweichow." Harvard Journal of Asiatic Studies, Vol. 5, No. 3/4, p. 279.

244 Gernet, Jacques. (1982). A History of Chinese Civilization. trans. J.R. Foster. Cambridge University Press, p. 18.

245 "Ethnologue: China." North America-China Virtual Research Centre. http://www.cic.sfu.ca/NACC/articles/minority.html The official name "Yi" has come to replace Lo-lo, Man Chia and many other such derogatory names and groupings. Most of these names originally referred to the eastern Yi people. Even the Lisu, at times, were included under the Yi designation. Thus, groups such as the Hei Lo-lo are now know as the Hei Yi (or Hei-I).

246 Peter Goullart. (1955). The Forgotten Kingdom. John Murray. p. 116.

247 Frank M. LeBar. (1964). Ethnic groups of mainland Southeast Asia.

248 Carter, George F. (2000) Earlier than you think. Texas A&M University Press. p. 300.

249 Bishop, Carl Whiting. (1934). pp. 299-300.

250 Coedes, G. (1969) The Making of South East Asia. p. 21.

251 Stoddard, Lothrop. The Rising Tide of Color Against White World-Supremacy. http://www.melvig.org/rtc/rtc_1-04.html

252 Chang Hsing-lang. "The Importation of Negro slaves to China under the T'ang Dynasty A.D. 618-907." Bulletin of the Catholic University of Peking, No. 7 (Dec.

1930). Quoted in Rogers, J.A. Sex and Race, Vol. 1. 9th ed. (1967) p. 67.

253 Imbert, H. *Les Negritos de la Chine*. (Hanoi, 1928). Quoted in Rogers, J.A. *Sex and Race*, Vol. 1. 9th ed. (1967) p. 67.

254 Li Chi. (1928) p. 245. These "black dwarfs," C.W. Bishop noted were said to have inhabited what is now Anhui province during the third century A.D. Bishop, Carl Whiting. (1934) p. 300

255 Liu, James J.Y. (1967). The Chinese Knight Errant. Routledge and Kegan Paul. According to Taoist adept Ge Hong, some hunters in the Zhongnan Mountains saw a naked man whose body appeared to be covered in black hair. Whenever they tried to capture him he "leapt over gullies and valleys as if in flight, and so could not be overtaken."

256 Li Chi. (1928). p. 259.

257 "Ethnologue: China." North America-China Virtual Research Centre. http://www.cic.sfu.ca/NACC/articles/minority.html

258 Brunson, James E. (1985). Black Jade: African Presence in the Ancient East and Other Essays. DeKalb. p. 32.

259 Li Chi. (1973). p. 8-9.

260 Weber, George. (2009). "The Negrito Race." Lonely Islands: The Andamanese. http://andaman.org/book/chapter6/text6.htm. Weber notes that the *Moi* (the *Anu-chu, Jarai*, or *Montognards*) are one of the few living DBP populations still settled within continental southeast Asia. Of other living, or until recently living, peoples with "possible Negritoid/Veddoid affiliations" in China, he listed the *Porr (Jong)*, the *Yumbri*, and the *Takkui*. A site located in the territory of the *Yumbri* and *Takkui* peoples held considerable archaeological evidence for extinct Black populations there.

261 George Weber. (2009).

262 Hotz, Robert Lee. (Sep 29 1998). "Chinese Roots Lie in Africa, Research Says." Los Angeles Times.

263 Kainer, Simon (Sep 2003). "The Oldest Pottery in the World." Current World Archaeology (Robert Selkirk): p. 44–49.

264 Chris Scarre (Ed.) (2003). Past Worlds Atlas of Archaeology. Borders Press. p. 68.

265 Chang, Kwang-Chih. (1986). The Archaeology of Ancient China. 4th ed. Yale University Press, p. 63-64.

266 Weidenreich, Franz. (1939). On the earliest representatives of modern mankind recovered on the soil of east Asia. Peking Nat. Hist. Bull., vol. 13, pt. 3, p. 163-174.

267 Peter Brown. (2012). "Liujiang." Paleohome. www-personal.une.edu.au/~pbrown3/Liujiang.html For those who want to examine the evidence for themselves, Brown's "Paleohome" website provides users access to some of the raw data on many prehistoric skulls from Australia, East Asia, and Southeast Asia.

268 J. Lawrence Angel. (1966). Early skeletons from Tranquillity, California. Smithsonian Contributions to Anthropology, Vol. 2, No. 1.

269 Stewart, D.T. 1960. A physical anthropologist's view of the peopling of the New World. Southwestern Journ. Anthropol., vol. 16, pp. 259-273. Albuquerque

270 Chai Chen Kang. (1967). Taiwan Aborigines: A Genetic Study of Tribal Variations. Harvard University Press, p. 76.

271 Chai Chen Kang. (1967) p. 210.

272 Jules Quartly. (Nov 27 2004). "In honor of the Little Black People." Taipei Times. http://www.taipeitimes.com/News/feat/archives/2004/11/27/2003212815/1

273 Jules Quartly. (2004).

274 For more on the Black gods of Japan, see Black God, a forthcoming work from Supreme Design Publishing, due to release in Summer of 2013.

275 Karl Kiyoshi Kawakami. (1903). "The Political Ideas of Modern Japan." Studies in Sociology, Economics, Politics and History, Vol. 2, No. 2. The University Press. Kawakami's name stands out to me because of its initials. It seems this name could have been a penname for a white pro-Aryan author, especially considering the time in which it was written. In fact, the author does promote an Aryan presence in Japan becoming its

"master race." However, the author does not mute the history of the DBP or Australoid People in Japan, meriting this essay worthy of our attention.

276 De Quatrefages, Armand. (1887). p. 27-28. The American translator of the book, Frederick Starr, writes: " No man has done more than he to further anthropological study in France; no man was more respected than he over the whole of Continental Europe; no European anthropologist's works have been more widely read in America.")

277 Taylor, Thomas Griffith. (1937). Environment, Race, and Migration; Fundamentals of Human Distribution. The University of Chicago Press, p. 210-211.

278 Miura T et al. (Feb 1994). Phylogenetic subtypes of human T-lymphotropic virus type I and their relations to the anthropological background. Proc Natl Acad Sci, 91(3):1124-7.

279 C.R.Smith. (2000). "Ancestors of the New World Had Many Origins". Discovery Channel Canada. http://www.cabrillo.edu/~crsmith/ancestorsmanyorigins.html

280 James Brunson. (1985).

281 Brace CL, Brace ML, Leonard WR. (Jan 1989). "Reflections on the face of Japan: a multivariate craniofacial and odontometric perspective". Am J Phys Anthropol 78, no. 1: 93-113. http://www.ncbi.nlm.nih.gov/pubmed/2648860

282 "Early Humans in Japan Produced Stone Tools," (2007). Stone Pages. http://www.stonepages.com/news/archives/002341.html

283 Kitagawa Y, Manabe Y, Oyamada J, Rokutanda A. (Jun1995). "Deciduous dental morphology of the prehistoric Jomon people of Japan: comparison of nonmetric characters". Am J Phys Anthropol 97, no. 2:101-11. For example, some of the dental traits of ancient Jōmon people resemble those of modern Mongoloid people, but when scientists looked for the most important Mongoloid trait (sinodonty), they didn't see what they expected. Instead, Jōmon teeth looked more like the teeth of Australian aborigines than modern Asian people.

284 Jared Diamond. "Japanese Roots." www2.gol.com/users/hsmr/Content/East%20Asia/Japan/History/roots.html

285 Temple DH, Auerbach BM, Nakatsukasa M, Sciulli PW, Larsen CS. (Oct 2008). "Variation in limb proportions between Jomon foragers and Yayoi agriculturalists from prehistoric Japan". Am J Phys Anthropol 137, no. 2: 164-74. doi: 10.1002/ajpa.20853

286 Sean Lee, Toshikazu Hasegawa. (May 2011). "Bayesian phylogenetic analysis supports an agricultural origin of Japonic languages." Proceedings of the Royal Society B. doi:10.1098/rspb.2011.0518

287 Hudson, Mark J. (1999). Ruins of identity: ethnogenesis in the Japanese Islands

288 Sleeboom, Margaret. (2004). Academic Nations in China and Japan. Routledge, p.56

289 Ernest Allen, Jr. (1994). "When Japan Was 'Champion of the Darker Races': Satokata Takahashi and the Flowering of Black Messianic Nationalism," Black Scholar, Vol. 24, No. 1. http://www.umass.edu/afroam/downloads/allen.tak.pdf

290 Jens Korff. (Last accessed Nov 10 2012)."Marlo Morgan-Mutant Message Down Under: Timeline. Creative Spirits". www.creativespirits.info/resources/books/marlo-morgan-mutant-message-down-under-timeline

291 Bridie Smith, (2010). "35,000 Year Old Axe Head Places Aboriginal Ancestors At the Cutting Edge of Technology," The Age. www.theage.com.au

292 Phil Mercer. (Feb 2007). "Alcohol time-bomb of Aborigines". BBC News. http://news.bbc.co.uk/2/hi/asia-pacific/6353693.stm

293 K. Langloh Parker. (1905). The Euahlayi Tribe: A Study of Aboriginal Life in Australia.

294 M. Rasmussen et al. (Oct 2011). "An Aboriginal Australian Genome Reveals Separate Human Dispersals into Asia." Science 334, 94-98.

295 Lawlor, Robert (1991). Voices of the First Day: Awakening in the Aboriginal Dreamtime. Inner Traditions International, Ltd. p. 223

296 Keith Windschuttle and Tim Gillin, (June 2002). The extinction of the Australian pygmies, Quadrant, http://www.sydneyline.com/Pygmies%20Extinction.htm

297 Taylor, Thomas Griffith. (1937). Environment, race, and migration; fundamentals of human distribution." Chicago: The University of Chicago Press, p. 100.

298 Robert J. Wenke, 1999. Patterns in Prehistory: Humankind's First Three Million Years.

Oxford University Press, p. 212-220.
299 William Whewell. (1866). History of the inductive sciences. Appleton. p. 281
300 Jennifer Bergman, "Archeoastronomy," Windows to the Universe, last accessed April 8, 2012, http://www.windows2universe.org/the_universe/uts/archeoastronomy.html
301 "Aboriginal astronomers: World's oldest?"Australian Geographic. www.australiangeographic.com.au/journal/indigenous-belief-enlightens-astronomers.htm
302 Duane W. Hamacher, David J. Frew. (Nov. 2010). An Aboriginal Australian Record of the Great Eruption of Eta Carinae. Journal for Astronomical History & Heritage, 13:3.
303 M. Griaule, G. Dieterlen, (1950). 'Un Système Soudanais de Sirius', Journal de la Société des Africainistes,' Tome XX, Fascicule 1, p. 273-94.
304 James Oberg. (1982). "The Sirius Mystery" Available at www.debunker.com/texts/dogon.html
305 Benest, D., & Duvent, J. L. (1995) "Is Sirius a triple star?" Astronomy and Astrophysics 299: 621-628.
306 Felipe F. Armesto (2003). Ideas that changed the world. Dorling Kindersley. p. 400.
307 Brian Hayden, Suzanne Villeneuve. (2011). "Astronomy in the Upper Paleolithic." Cambridge Archaeological Journal 21, no 3: 331-355.
308 Hayden, B., & Villeneuve, S. (2011). Astronomy in the Upper Palaeolithic? Cambridge Archaeological Journal, 21 (03), 331-355 DOI: 10.1017/S0959774311000400
309 Xavier Herbert. (1 November 1983). The Bulletin Literary Supplement.
310 Harry Hamilton Johnston. (1910). The Negro in the New World. p. 27
311 Quoted in Runoko Rashidi. "The African Roots of Humanity and Civilization." http://www.blackherbals.com/african_roots_of_humanity_and_ci.htm
312 Summerhayes, Glenn R., et al. "Human Adaptation and Plant Use in Highland New Guinea 49,000 to 44,000 Years Ago." Science. 330 (2010): 78-81.
313 John Hawks, (2010). "43,000 Year Old Assemblages from Highland New Guinea," http://johnhawks.net/weblog/reviews/archaeology/upper/australia/new-guinea-summerhayes-2010.html
314 Encyclopedia Britannica (1911), Volume 22, Page 679
315 Alan J. Redd and Mark Stoneking. (1999). "Peopling of the Sahul: mtDNA Variation in Aboriginal Australian and Papua New Guinean Populations," American Journal of Human Genetics, 65, p. 808.
316 Victor Grauer. (2011).
317 Runoko Rashidi. "The African Roots of Humanity and Civilization."
318 A. A. J. Jansen, Susan Parkinson, A. F. S. Robertson. (1990). Food and Nutrition in Fiji: Food production, composition, and intake, Volume One. Institute of Pacific Studies. P. 4.
319 Ian Osborn. (2008). The Rough Guide to Fiji. Penguin.
320 Runoko Rashidi. (Apr 2000). Introduction to the African Presence in Fuji. Race and History. http://www.raceandhistory.com/historicalviews/africanfiji.htm
321 Quoted in John G. Jackson (1939) Ethiopia and the Origin of Civilization: A Critical Review of the Evidence of Archaeology, Anthropology, History and Comparative Religion: According to the Most Reliable Sources and Authorities. Also see Willis N. Huggins. and John G. Jackson, (1937). An Introduction to African Civilizations, p. 188–190.
322 Robert Dixon. (1980). The Languages of Australia. University Press.
323 Thomas Huxley (1870). "On the Geographical Distribution of the Chief Modifications of Mankind" Journal of the Ethnological Society of London. The Huxley Files: Scientific Memoirs III. Available at http://aleph0.clarku.edu/huxley/SM3/GeoDis.html
324 Thomas Huxley. (1870).
325 Louis Robert Sullivan, Edward Winslow Gifford, Will Carleton McKern. (1921). A contribution to Samoan somatology. Bishop Museum Press.
326 Vandenberg N, van Oorschot RA, Tyler-Smith C, Mitchell RJ. (Dec 1999). "Y-chromosome-specific microsatellite variation in Australian aboriginals". Hum Biol 71, no. 6: 915-31. http://www.ncbi.nlm.nih.gov/pubmed/10592683
327 Elsdon Best. (1923). The Origin of the Maori: The Hidden Homeland of the Maori,

And its Probable Location. Journal of the Polynesian Society. Vol 32, No 125. p. 10-20.

328 Elsdon Best. (1923). Polynesian Voyagers. The Maori as a Deep-sea Navigator, Explorer, and Colonizer. p. 50. Available at http://nzetc.victoria.ac.nz/tm/scholarly/tei-BesPoly-t1-body-d1-d3.html

329 H. L. Shapiro. (1940). Physical Anthropology of the Maori-Moriori. Journal of the Polynesian Society, Volume 49, No. 193. p 1-16.

330 Mollison, T.H. "Beitrag zur kraniologie und osteologie der Maori." Zeitsch. f. Morph. u. Anthrop., vol. 11, 1908, pp. 529-595.

331 H. L. Shapiro. (1940). Physical Anthropology of the Maori-Moriori. Journal of the Polynesian Society, Volume 49, No. 193. p 1-16.

332 Steve Connor. (May 4 2009). "Revealed: The Face of the First European." The Independent. www.independent.co.uk/news/science/revealed-the-face--of-the-first-european-1678537.html

333 Piette, Edouard. "L'art pendant l'age du renne." Paris: Masson, 1907.

334 White, Randall. (Dec 2006) "The Women of Brassempouy: A Century of Research and Interpretation." Journal of Archaeological Method and Theory. 13(4), 276.

335 White, Randall. (Dec 2006) "The Women of Brassempouy: A Century of Research and Interpretation." Journal of Archaeological Method and Theory. 13(4), 277

336 Piette, Edouard. (1895). "La station de Brassempouy et les statuettes humaines de la periode glyptique." L'Anthropologie. 6, p. 129-130

337 Arthus Evans. (1901). Vignaud pamphlets: Crete. p. 436

338 J. Pendlebury. (1939). Archaeology of Crete. p. 39.

339 White, Randall. (Dec 2006) "The Women of Brassempouy: A Century of Research and Interpretation." Journal of Archaeological Method and Theory. 13(4), 275.

340 Arthur Evans. Palace of Minos. 45

341 Angelo Mosso. (1911). *The Dawn of Mediterranean Civilization.* p. 154

342 Angelo Mosso. (1911). p. 155

343 Angelo Mosso. (1911). p. 156

344 Thomas Griffith Taylor notes "small statues and rock paintings (found in Spain and France chiefly) which certainly point to a race akin to the Bushmen" alongside skeletons bearing matching traits. He continues, "At Willendorf (near Vienna) a statuette of a nude woman is steatopygic and has hair apparently of the peppercorn type. Similar negritoid figures come from Brassempouy and Lespugues in the south of France, and perhaps indicate a former widespread negrito stratum."

345 Don Hitchcock. (2011). "The Gravettian toolmaking and venus carving culture." http://donsmaps.com/lagravette.html According to Hitchcock, the 50-year moratorium was expected to end in 2011, but nothing was announced.

346 Nicholas Wade. (2006) p. 95. Wade begins, "For much of the period during which the exodus from Africa unfolded, from 50,000 to 30,000 years ago, people everywhere may have looked pretty much the same. Everyone outside Africa was descended from the 150 emigrants, who in turn were drawn from the host population in Africa. The first modern humans were an African species that had suddenly expanded its range. For many millennia people would presumably all have had dark skin, just as do the relict populations of Australia, New Guinea and the Andaman Islands."

347 Felix Riede, (2011). "Adaptation and Niche Construction in Human Prehistory: A Case Study From the Southern Scandanavian Late Glacial," Phil Trans R Soc B 366, no. 1566. 793-808. http://rstb.royalsocietypublishing.org/content/366/1566/793.full

348 Marcellin Boule and Henri Vallois. (trans. 1957), Fossil Men: A Textbook of Human Paleontology, Dryden Press, p. 291.

349 Harry Hamilton Johnston. (1910). The Negro in the New World. Methuen & Co. p. 27

350 Harry Hamilton Johnston. (1910). p. 27

351 Taylor, Thomas Griffith. (1937). Environment, race, and migration; fundamentals of human distribution. The University of Chicago Press, p. 257

352 Roland Burrage Dixon. (1923). The Racial History of Man.

353 Pawel Valde-Nowak, Adam Nadachowski, Mieczyslaw Wolsan. (Oct 1987). "Upper

Palaeolithic boomerang made of a mammoth tusk in south Poland," Nature 329: 436-438, www.nature.com/nature/journal/v329/n6138/abs/329436a0.html
354 Taylor, Thomas Griffith. (1937), p. 13
355 Grafton Elliot Smith, (1929).
356 Albert Churchward, (1912). The Origin and Evolution of Primitive Man, p. 73
357 John F. Hoffecker, (2009). "Out of Africa: Modern Human Origins Special Feature: The spread of Modern Humans in Europe," Proc. Natl. Acad. Sci. USA 106, no. 38:16040-16045, http://www.pnas.org/content/106/38/16040.full
358 John F. Hoffecker. (2009). "Out of Africa: Modern Human Origins Special Feature: The spread of Modern Humans in Europe". Proc. Natl. Acad. Sci. USA 106. No. 38.
359 Taylor, Thomas Griffith. (1937), p. 126.
360 Quoted in Wesley John Gaines. (1897). The Negro and the White Man. A.M.E. Publishing House.
361 Marcellin Boule and Henri Vallois, (1957), p. 291-292.
362 Cheikh Anta Diop. (1991). Civilization or Barbarism: An Authentic Anthropolog. Lawrence Hill Books. p. 15-16.
363 Encyclopedia Britannica (1911), Volume 22, p. 679
364 Brace, C. Loring (1996); Haeussler, Alice M.; Bailey, Shara E.. eds. "Cro-Magnon and Qafzeh – vive la Difference." Dental anthropology newsletter: A publication of the Dental Anthropology Association, Laboratory of Dental Anthropology, Department of Anthropology, Arizona State University, 10 (3): 2–9.
365 Trinkaus, Erik (Apr 2004); Schekman, Randy. ed. "European early modern humans and the fate of the Neandertals" Proceedings of the National Academy of Sciences USA, 104 (18): 7367–7372. Bibcode 2007PNAS..104.7367T. doi:10.1073/pnas.0702214104.
366 Trenton W. Holliday. (Mar 2000). Evolution at the Crossroads: Modern Human Emergence in Western Asia. American Anthropologist New Series, 102(1), p. 54-68.
367 Rene Verneau, (1906). Les Grottes de Grimaldi, Vol. II., Monaco.
368 Christopher Stringer, Robin McKie. (1998). African Exodus: The Origins of Modern Humanity. Macmillan. p. 162.
369 Erik Trinkaus. (1989). The Emergence of Modern Humans. School of American Research.
370 Roger Lewin. (2004). Human evolution: An illustrated introduction. Wiley-Blackwell.
371 Brace, C. Loring; et al. (2006). "The Questionable Contribution of the Neolithic and the Bronze Age to European Craniofacial Form," Proc. Natl. Acad. Sci. USA 103, no. 1: 242-247, doi: 10.1073/pnas.0509801102.
372 Lounes Chikhi, et al. (2000). Clines of nuclear DNA markers suggest a largely Neolithic ancestry of the European gene pool. Proc. Natl. Acad. Sci. USA. Vol. 95, p. 9053-9058.
373 Boyd, W. C. (1956). Genetics and the Races of Man. Little, Brown, p. 178-180.
374 Bory De Saint Vincent. (1839). Histoire et description des Iles de l'Ocean. Didot. Quoted in Cheikh Anta Diop. (1974).
375 Laylander, Don. (2000). Early Ethnography of the Californias: 1533-1825. Salinas, California.
376 Rincon, Paul. (Sep 7 2004). "Tribe challenges American origins." BBC News.
377 González-José, Rolando; et al. (2003). "Craniometric evidence for Palaeoamerican survival in Baja California". Nature 425:62-65.
378 Jeordan Legon. (Dec 3 2002). "Scientist: Oldest American skull found." CNN.
379 "Wandering the World." (Sep 2004). The Sydney Morning Herald. www.smh.com.au/articles/2004/09/10/1094789687569.html
380 Lehmann, Walter H. (1930). Die Frage völkerkundlicher Beziehungen zwischen der Südsee und Amerika. Orientalische Literaturzeitung 33(5):322-39.
381 "The Sierra de San Francisco." (Nov 2012). Bradshaw Foundation. www.bradshawfoundation.com/baja/sierra_de_san_francisco4.php
382 Gladwin, Harold S. (1947). Men Out of Asia, Whittlesey House, p. 66-67, 88-89
383 Rashidi, Runoko. (Dec. 1986). "Men Out of Asia: A Review and Update of the

Gladwin Thesis." Journal of African Civilizations, Vol. 8, No. 2. p. 254

384 Keith, Arthur. (1931) New Discoveries Relating to the Antiquity of Man. Williams & Norgate. p. 312

385 Hooton, Earnest A. (1931). Up from the Ape. Macmillan & Co. p. 650

386 Dixon, Roland B. (1923). The Racial History of Man. Scribner's Sons. p. 401-402

387 Taylor, Thomas Griffith. (1937). Environment, Race and Migration. The University of Chicago Press, p. 246

388 Dixon, Roland B. (1923). p. 459-462

389 Rashidi, Runoko. (1986). p. 256

390 Gladwin, Harold S. (1947) p. 184-185

391 J. Lawrence Angel. (1966). Early Skeletons From Tranquillity, California Smithsonian Contributions to Anthropology, Vol. 2, No. 1; Hooton, E.A. (1933). Notes on five Texas crania. Texas Archeol. Paleont. Soc. Bull., vol. 5, p. 25-39. Abilene; Hrdlicka, Ales (1906). Contribution to the physical anthropology of California. Univ. California Publ. Amer. Archeol. Ethnol., vol. 4, no. 2, p. 49-64.

392 Toyne, Sarah. (Aug 22 1999). "Aborigines were the First Americans." The Sunday Times. www.sunday-times.co.uk/news/pages/sti/99/08/22/stifgnusa02003.html?99

393 Toyne, Sarah. (1999).

394 Toyne, Sarah. (1999).

395 Neves, Walter A. et al. (1999). Lapa vermelha IV Hominid 1: Morphological affinities of the earliest known American. Genet. Mol. Biol. vol.22, n.4, p. 461-469.

396 Center for the Study of the First Americans. (2005). "A New Wind From the South Shakes Clovis." Mammoth Trumpet 20, no 3, www.centerfirstamericans.com/mammoth/issues/Volume-20/vol20_num3.pdf

397 Veronique Greenwood. (Apr 2012). "Early Skeleton Stolen From Underwater Cave in Mexico". Discover Magazine. http://blogs.discovermagazine.com/80beats/tag/young-man-of-chan-hol-ii/

398 Walter A. Neves, Mark Hubbe, (Dec 2005). "Cranial morphology of early Americans from Lagoa Santa, Brazil: Implications for the settlement of the New World" PNAS, vol. 102 no. 51 18309-18314.

399 Neves, Walter A. et al. (1999).

400 Neves WA, et al. (2003). "Early Holocene human skeletal remains from Santana do Riacho, Brazil: implications for the settlement of the New World". J Hum Evol 45, no 1:19-42, www.ncbi.nlm.nih.gov/pubmed/12890443

401 Eliza Barclay. (2008). "Oldest Skeleton in Americas Found in Underwater Cave?" National Geographic News. http://news.nationalgeographic.com/news/2008/09/080903-oldest-skeletons_2.html

402 For example, stone tools and charcoal from Serra Da Capivara, a site in remote northeast Brazil, show evidence of human habitation as long ago as 50,000 years. http://news.bbc.co.uk/1/low/sci/tech/430944.stm

403 Bower, Bruce. (1987). "Flakes, Breaks, and the First Americans," Science News, 131:172.

404 Muello, Peter. (June 16 1987). "Find Puts Man in America at Least 300,000 Years Ago," Dallas Times Herald.

405 "Underwater expedition delivers key findings in search for evidence of early Americans." (Aug 2009). Science Codex. www.sciencecodex.com/underwater_expedition_delivers_key_findings_in_search_for_evidence_of_early_americans

406 Walter Yeeling Evans-Wentz. (1911). The Fairy-Faith in Celtic Countries.

407 Donald A. Mackenzie, (1915). Myths of Babylonia and Assyria. p. 198.

408 Anonymous. (Aug 14 1937). Nature, 140, p. 291.

409 Pilapil, Virgilio R. (1991). "Was There a Prehistoric Migration of the Philippine Aetas to America?" Epigraphic Society, Occasional Papers, 20:150.

410 Taylor, Thomas Griffith. (1937). p. 11.

411 Runoko Rashidi. "The African Roots of Humanity and Civilization."

412 E. Farias, (2010). "Drought Record of the Negro River, Amazonas, Raises

Archaeological Rarities,"Acritica, http://acritica.uol.com.br/amazonia/Seca-traz-raridades_0_368963103.html

413 Fagan, Brian M. (1992). People of the Earth: An Introduction to World Prehistory, Harper Collins.

414 Merritt Ruhlen. (1998). "The origin of the Na-Dene". Proc Natl Acad Sci U S A. 95, no 23: 13994–13996. www.ncbi.nlm.nih.gov/pmc/articles/PMC25007/

415 Ruhlin, Merritt; "Voices from the Past," Natural History, 96:6, March 1987.

416 C.R. Smith. (2000).

417 Toyne, Sarah. (1999)

418 BBC News. (Aug 26 1999). 'First Americans were Australian.' http://news.bbc.co.uk/1/low/sci/tech/430944.stm

419 Smithsonian Institution, Bureau of American Ethnology. (1912). Handbook of American Indians North of Mexico: N-Z. U.S. Government Printing Office.

420 John Swanton. (1905). Haida Texts and Myths. Smithsonian Institution, Bureau of American Ethnology, Government Printing Office.

421 C.R. Smith. (2000).

422 Alice B. Kohoe. (2003). "The Fringe of American Archaeology: Transoceanic and Transcontinental Contacts in Prehistoric America". Journal of Scientific Exploration 17, no. 1: 19-36. http://www.scientificexploration.org/journal/jse_17_1_kehoe.pdf The paper includes an extensive list of transoceanic crossings made on small boats, including one made entirely from empty beer kegs and plastic bottles.

423 Alice B. Kohoe. (2003).

424 Grieder, Terence. (1982). Origins of Pre-Columbian Art. University of Texas Press.

425 C.R. Smith. (2000).

426 Alice B. Kohoe. (2003).

427 C.R. Smith. (2000).

428 James L. Guthrie. (Dec 2000-Jun 2001) 'Human lymphocyte antigens: apparent Afro-Asiatic, Southern Asian, & European HLAs in indigenous American populations', Pre-Columbiana, Vol. 2, No. 2, 3.

429 Hünmeier, Tábita et al. (Jun 2007). "Niger–Congo speaking populations and the formation of the Brazilian gene pool: mtDNA and Y-chromosome data". American Journal of Physical Anthropology 133 (2): 854–867.

430 Reich et al. (2012). "Reconstructing Native American Population History," Nature 488, no. 7411: 370-374 www.nature.com/nature/journal/v488/n7411/full/nature11258.html

431 Sa'a Naghái Bik'e Hózhó, Bik'e H0zh. (Last accessed Nov 2012). "Origins". Dykeman Roebuck Archaeology. http://drarchaeology.com/culthist/origins.htm

432 Eliza Barclay. (2008).

433 Fladmark, K. R. (1979). Routes: Alternate Migration Corridors for Early Man in North America. American Antiquity 44(1):55-69.; Fladmark, K. R. (1983). Times and Places: Environmental Correlates of Mid-to-Late Wisconsin Human Population Expansion in North America. In Early Man in the New World, ed. Richard Shutler, pp. 13-41. Beverly Hills: Sage Publications.; Fladmark, K. R. (1986). Getting One's Berings. Natural History 95(11):8-19.

434 Paul Rivet. (1925). Les Australiens an Amerique, Bull. Soc. Linguistique de Paris, 26:23-63; Morris Swadesh, (1964). "Afinidades de las lenguas amerindias," Akten des 34. Internationalen Amerikanisten Kongress, pp. 729–738; Loukotka, Cestmír (1935): Clasificación de las lenguas sudamericanas. Praga. It should be noted that Loukotka saw Australian traits in the languages of the Alakaluf, Puelche, and other Fuegians, but not the Yahgans, who are the most Mongoloid of the Fuegian people.

435 Erich M. Von Hornbostel. (Jul-Sep 1936). "Fuegian Songs." American Anthropologist. Vol. 38, Iss. 3, p. 357-367.

436 Gusinde, Martin, and Lebzelter, Viktor. (1927). Kraniologische Beobachtungen an feuerlandischen und australischen. Schadeln. In Anthropos, Bd. xxii, pp. 259-285

437 Neves W.A., Powell J.F., Ozolins E.G. (1999). "Extra-Continental Morphological Affinities of Palli Aike, Southern Chile", Intersciencia, 24/4: 258- 263. Regarding the

findings, Neves and colleagues write: "First, it shows that people similar to those that inhabited the Lagoa Santa area, in central Brazil, and the area of Sabana de Bogota, in Colombia, once had a wide distribution across South America, reaching even the southernmost region of the sub-continent. Second, but intrinsically related to the first fact, that the non-Mongoloid morphology already demonstrated to occur in tropical and subtropical areas of South America can also be found in regions characterized by very cold weather. This supports the idea that the relationship of the first known Americans with Africans and Australians cannot be explained in terms of convergent evolution due to similar climatic factors alone."

438 McCabe, Joseph. (1930). "The Story of Religious Controversy." www.infidels.org/ library/historical/joseph_mccabe/religious_controversy/chapter_02.html
439 Charles Darwin. (Apr 1890). "Darwin on the Fuegians and Patagonians." Popular Science Monthly, Volume 36.
440 McCabe, Joseph. (1926). The Human Origin of Morals. Haldeman-Julius Company.
441 "Suicide Facts: Religion and Societies History of Suicide." www.a1b2c3.com/suilodge/fachis1.htm
442 Bridges, L. (1948). Uttermost Part of the Earth. Hodder & Stoughton. p. 33-36, 166.
443 Charles Darwin. (Apr 1890). "Darwin on the Fuegians and Patagonians." Popular Science Monthly, Volume 36.
444 Snow, W.P. (1861). A few remarks on the Wild Tribes of Tierra del Fuego from Personal Observation, Transactions of the Ethnological Society of London, Vol. 1, p. 261–67.
445 David Wallechinsky & Irving Wallace. (1981). People Gone But Not Forgotten: Seven Extinct Societies. The People's Almanac.
446 Nicholas Wade. (2006).
447 George Weber. (2009). www.andaman.org/BOOK/chapter8/text8.htm Meanwhile Bantu, which simply means "people" comes from from ba-, the plural prefix, and ntu, which means "a man or a person."
448 Nicholas Wade. (2006). They also use !ohm to describe some Bantu people, to whom they'd lost a great deal of their ancestral territory before Europeans came.
449 Supreme Understanding and Alife Allah (2012). p. 121.
450 Supreme Understanding and Alife Allah (2012). p. 171.
451 Paola Spinozzi, Alessandro Zironi. (2010). Origins as a Paradigm in the Sciences and in the Humanities. Vandenhoeck & Ruprecht. pp. 48-50
452 Grafton Elliot Smith, (1929).
453 Doron M. Behar et al. The Dawn of Human Matrilineal Diversity. The American Journal of Human Genetics, Volume 82, Issue 5, 1130-1140, 24 April 2008. doi:10.1016/j.ajhg.2008.04.002
454 Paul Rincon. (last updated Apr 2008). "Human line 'nearly split in two'". BBC News. http://news.bbc.co.uk/2/hi/science/nature/7358868.stm
455 Fulvio Cruciani, Piero Santolamazza, Peidong Shen, et. al. (May 2002). "A Back Migration from Asia to Sub-Saharan Africa Is Supported by High- Resolution Analysis of Human Y-Chromosome Haplotypes," Am J Hum Genet. 70(5): 1197-1214.
456 S.O.Y. Keita, (1993). History in Africa, Vol. 20, 129-154
457 D.D. Styndera, R.R. Ackermanna and J.C. Sealy. "Early to mid-Holocene South African Later Stone Age human crania exhibit a distinctly Khoesan morphological pattern."
458 Colin P. Groves and Alan Thorne. "Terminal Pleistocene and early Holocene populations of Northern Africa."
459 F. E. Grine, et al. (Jan 12 2007). "Late Pleistocene Human Skull from Hofmeyr, South Africa, and Modern Human Origins". Science 315 (5809): 226–229.
460 Fulvio Cruciani, et. al. (2004). "Phylogeographic Analysis of Haplogroup E3b (E-M215) Y Chromosomes Reveals Multiple Migratory Events Within and Out Of Africa," Am. J. Hum. Genet. 74:1014-1022
461 Jean Hiernaux, (1975). The People of Africa. Encore Editions, p. 42-43, 62-63.

462 Jean Hiernaux, (1975), p. 82-83.

463 Jean Hiernaux, (1975), p. 156-157.

464 S.O.Y. Keita, (2004). "Exploring Northeast African Metric Craniofacial Variation at the Individual Level: A Comparative Study Using Principal Components Analysis," American Journal of Human Biology 16:679–689.

465 G. Mokhtar. (1990). UNESCO General History of Africa, Vol. II (Ancient Africa). Cambridge University Press.

466 van den Berghe, P.L. (1979). Human Family Systems: An Evolutionary View. Elsevier.

467 Pebley, A. R., and Mbugua, W. (1989). Polygyny and Fertility in Sub-Saharan Africa. In R. J. Lesthaeghe (Ed.), Reproduction and Social Organization in Sub-Saharan Africa, University of California Press, p. 338-364.

468 Ama, P. F. M., et al. (1986). Skeletal muscle characteristics in sedentary Black and Caucasian males. Journal of Applied Physiology, 61, 1758-1761; Ettinger, B., et al. (1997). Racial differences in bone density between young adult black and white subjects persist after adjustment for anthropometric, lifestyle, and biochemical differences. Journal of Clinical Endocrinology & Metabolism, 82, 429-434; Himes, J. H. (1988). Racial variation in physique and body composition. Canadian Journal of Sport Sciences, 13, 117-126; Hui, S.L., et al. (2003). Difference in bone mass between Black and White American children: Attributable to body build, sex hormone levels, or bone turnover? Journal of Clinical Endocrinology & Metabolism, 88, 642–649; Junker, H. (1921). The first appearance of the Negroes in history. Journal of Egyptian Archaeology, 7, 121-132; Meredith, H.V., and Spurgeon, J.H. (1980). Somatic comparisons at age 9 years for South Carolina White Girls and girls of other ethnic groups. Human Biology, 52, 401 411; Pollitzer, W. S. and Anderson, J. JB. (1989). Ethnic and genetic differences in bone mass: a review with a hereditary vs environmental perspective. American Journal of Clinical Nutrition, 50, 1244-1259; Todd, T.W. & Lindala, A. (1928). Dimensions of the body: Whites and American Negroes of both sexes. American Journal of Physical Anthropology, 12, 35-101; Wagner, D.R., and Heyward, V.H. (2000). Measures of body composition in blacks and whites: a comparative review. American Journal of Clinical Nutrition, 71, 1392-1402; Wright, N.M., et al. (1995). Greater secretion of growth hormone in black than in white men: possible factor in greater bone mineral density. Journal of Clinical Endocrinology & Metabolism, 80, 2291-2297.

469 Winkler, E-M., and Christiansen, K. (1993). Sex hormone levels and body hair growth in !Kung San and Kavango men from Namibia. American Journal of Physical Anthropology, 92, 155-164.
Wolff, G. & Steggerda, M. (1943). Female-male index of body build in Negroes and Whites: An interpretation of anatomical sex differences. Human Biology, 15, 127-152.

470 Pettaway, C.A. (1999). Racial differences in the androgen/androgen receptor pathway in prostate cancer. Journal of the National Medical Association, 91, 653-660; Ross, R.K., et al. (1992). 5-apha-reductase activity and risk of prostate cancer among Japanese and US white and black males. Lancet, 339, 887-889.

471 Glover, F., Coffey, D., et al. (1998). The epidemiology of prostate cancer in Jamaica. Journal of Urology, 159, 1984-1987; Ogunbiyi, J. and Shittu, O. (1999). Increased incidence of prostate cancer in Nigerians. Journal of the National Medical Association, 3, 159-164; Osegbe, D. (1997). Prostate cancer in Nigerians: facts and non-facts. Journal of Urology, 157, 1340.

472 Brawley, O.W. and Kramer B.S. (1996). Epidemiology of prostate cancer. In Volgelsang, N.J., Scardino, P.T., Shipley, W.U., and Coffey, D.S. (eds). Comprehensive textbook of genitourinary oncology. Baltimore: Williams and Wilkins.

473 Michael F. Hammer et al. (Sep 13 2011). Genetic evidence for archaic admixture in Africa. PNAS. *vol. 108 no. 37 15123-15128.*

474 See Supreme Understanding and Alife Allah (2012). The Science of Self, Vol. 1 for details on Neanderthal-human admixture.

475 Chancellor Williams. (1987). p. 41-42

476 Chancellor Williams. (1987). p. 42

ALSO FROM OUR COMPANY

How to Hustle and Win, Part 1: A Survival Guide for the Ghetto

By Supreme Understanding
Foreword by the Real Rick Ross
This is the book that started it all. Now an international bestseller, this book has revolutionized the way people think of "urban literature." It offers a street-based analysis of social problems, plus practical solutions that anyone can put to use.

CLASS	PAGES	RETAIL	RELEASE
I-1	336	$14.95	Jun. 2008

ISBN: 978-0-9816170-0-8

How to Hustle and Win, Part 2: Rap, Race, and Revolution

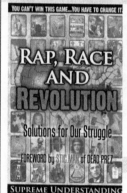

By Supreme Understanding
Foreword by Stic.man of Dead Prez
Seen here in its original green cover, the controversial follow-up to *How to Hustle and Win* digs even deeper into the problems we face, and how we can solve them. Part One focused on personal change, and Part Two explores the bigger picture of changing the entire hood.

CLASS	PAGES	RETAIL	RELEASE
I-1	384	$14.95	Apr. 2009

ISBN: 978-0-9816170-9-1

Knowledge of Self: A Collection of Wisdom on the Science of Everything in Life

Edited by Supreme Understanding, C'BS Alife Allah, and Sunez Allah, Foreword by Lord Jamar of Brand Nubian
Who are the Five Percent? Why are they here? In this book, over 50 Five Percenters from around the world speak for themselves, providing a comprehensive introduction to the esoteric teachings of the Nation of Gods and Earths.

CLASS	PAGES	RETAIL	RELEASE
I-2	256	$14.95	Jul. 2009

ISBN: 978-0-9816170-2-2

The Hood Health Handbook, Volume One (Physical Health)

Edited by Supreme Understanding and C'BS Alife Allah, Foreword by Dick Gregory

Want to know why Black and brown people are so sick? This book covers the many "unnatural causes" behind our poor health, and offers hundreds of affordable and easy-to-implement solutions.

CLASS	PAGES	RETAIL	RELEASE
PH-1	480	$19.95	Nov. 2010

ISBN: 978-1-935721-32-1

The Hood Health Handbook, Volume Two (Mental Health)

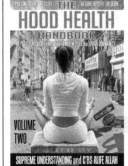

Edited by Supreme Understanding and C'BS Alife Allah

This volume covers mental health, how to keep a healthy home, raising healthy children, environmental issues, and dozens of other issues, all from the same down-to-earth perspective as Volume One.

CLASS	PAGES	RETAIL	RELEASE
MH-1	480_	$19.95	Nov. 2010

ISBN: 978-1-935721-33-8

A Taste of Life: 1,000 Vegetarian Recipes from Around the World

Edited by Supreme Understanding and Patra Afrika

This cookbook makes it easy to become vegetarian. In addition to over 1,000 recipes from everywhere you can think of, plus over 100 drink and smoothie recipes, this book also teaches how to transition your diet, what to shop for, how to cook, as well as a guide to nutrients and vitamins.

CLASS	PAGES	RETAIL	RELEASE
W-1	400	$19.95	Jun. 2011

ISBN: 978-1-935721-10-9

La Brega: Como Sobrevivir En El Barrio

By Supreme Understanding

Thanks to strong demand coming from Spanish-speaking countries, we translated our groundbreaking How to Hustle and Win into Spanish, and added new content specific to Latin America. Because this book's language is easy to follow, it can also be used to brush up on your Spanish.

CLASS	PAGES	RETAIL	RELEASE
0-1	336	$14.95	Jul. 2009

ISBN: 978-0981617-08-4

Locked Up but Not Locked Down: A Guide to Surviving the American Prison System

By Ahmariah Jackson and IAtomic Allah
Foreword by Mumia Abu Jamal

This book covers what it's like on the inside, how to make the most of your time, what to do once you're out, and how to stay out. Features contributions from over 50 insiders, covering city jails, state and federal prisons, women's prisons, juvenile detention, and international prisons.

CLASS	PAGES	RETAIL	RELEASE
J-1	288	$14.95	Jul. 2012

ISBN: 978-1935721-00-0

The Science of Self: Man, God, and the Mathematical Language of Nature

By Supreme Understanding and C'BS Alife Allah

How did the universe begin? Is there a pattern to everything that happens? What's the meaning of life? What does science tell us about the depths of our SELF? Who and what is God? This may be one of the deepest books you can read.

CLASS	PAGES	RETAIL	RELEASE
I-4	360	$19.95	Jun. 2012

ISBN: 978-1935721-67-3

The Science of Self: Man, God, and the Mathematical Language of Nature (Hardcover Edition)

By Supreme Understanding

A beautiful hardcover edition of the bestselling work, *The Science of Self*. Under the full-color dust jacket is an embossed clothbound hard cover. Autographed and numbered as part of a special limited edition series, this book also includes the 16 full-color inserts found in the paperback edition.

CLASS	PAGES	RETAIL	RELEASE
I-4	360	$34.95	Jun. 2012

Only available direct from publisher.

365 Days of Real Black History Calendar (2012 Edition)

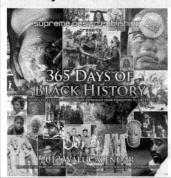

By Supreme Understanding and Robert Bailey

A calendar that'll never be out-dated! Over 365 important facts and quotes covering little-known, but important, moments in Black history. Written in brief chunks and easy language for all audiences.

CLASS	PGS	PRICE	RELEASE
I-2	26	$2.95	2011

Only available direct from publisher.

365 Days of Real Black History Calendar (2013 Edition)

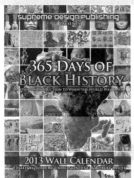

By Supreme Understanding

Our 2013 calendar and planner was also designed to be timeless, as it's a beautifully-designed companion to *When the World was Black*. You'll find dozens of striking full-color images that help tell the stories of global Black history.

CLASS	PAGES	PRICE	RELEASE
I-2	26	$4.95	2012

Only available direct from publisher.

When the World was Black, Part One: Prehistoric Cultures

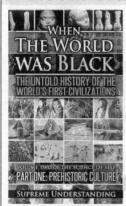

By Supreme Understanding
Foreword by Runoko Rashid

When does Black history begin? Certainly not with slavery. In two volumes, historian Supreme Understanding explores over 200,000 years of Black history from every corner of the globe. Part One covers the first Black communities to settle the world, establishing its first cultures and traditions. Their stories are remarkable.

CLASS	PAGES	RETAIL	RELEASE
I-3	400	$19.95	Feb. 2013

ISBN: 978-1-935721-04-8

When the World Was Black, Part Two: Ancient Civilizations

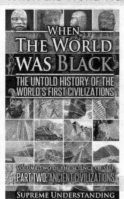

By Supreme Understanding

Part Two covers the ancient Black civilizations that gave birth to the modern world. Black people built the first urban civilizations in Africa, Asia, Europe, and the Americas. And every claim in these books is thoroughly documented with reputable sources. Do you want to know the story of your ancestors? You should. We study the past to see what the future will bring.

CLASS	PAGES	RETAIL	RELEASE
I-3	400	$19.95	Feb. 2013

ISBN: 978-1-935721-05-5

When the World was Black, Parts One and Two (Hardcover)

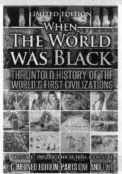

By Supreme Understanding

An incredible limited edition that combines Part One and Part Two into a single book, cased in an embossed clothbound hardcover and dust jacket. Autographed and numbered, this collector's item also includes both sets of full-color inserts.

CLASS	PAGES	RETAIL	RELEASE
I-3	800	$19.95	Dec. 2013

Only available direct from publisher.

Black Rebellion: Eyewitness Accounts of Major Slave Revolts

Edited by Dr. Sujan Dass

Who will tell the stories of those who refused to be slaves? What about those who fought so effectively that they forced their slavers to give up? Black Rebellion is a collection of historical "eyewitness" accounts of dozens of major revolts and uprisings, from the U.S. to the Caribbean, as well as a history of slavery and revolt.

CLASS	PAGES	RETAIL	RELEASE
P-3	272	$14.95	May 2010

ISBN: 978-0-981617-04-6

The Heroic Slave

By Frederick Douglass

Most people don't know that Douglass wrote a novel...or that, in this short novel, he promoted the idea of violent revolt. By this time in his life, the renowned abolitionist was seeing things differently. This important piece of history comes with *David Walker's Appeal*, all in one book.

CLASS	PAGES	RETAIL	RELEASE
P-3	160	$14.95	Apr. 2011

ISBN: 978-1-935721-27-7

David Walker's Appeal

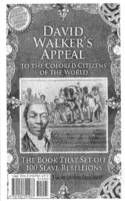

By David Walker

This is one of the most important, and radical, works ever published against slavery. Rather than call for an end by peaceful means, Walker called for outright revolution. His calls may have led to over 100 revolts, including those described in *Black Rebellion*. This important piece of history comes with Douglass' *The Heroic Slave*, which it may have helped inspire.

CLASS	PAGES	RETAIL	RELEASE
P-3	160	$14.95	Apr. 2011

ISBN: 978-1-935721-27-7

Darkwater: Voices from Within the Veil, Annotated Edition

By W.E.B. Du Bois

This book makes Du Bois' previous work, like *Souls of Black Folk*, seem tame by comparison. *Darkwater* is revolutionary, uncompromising, and unconventional in both its content and style, addressing the plight of Black women, the rise of a Black Messiah, a critical analysis of white folks, and the need for outright revolution.

CLASS	PAGES	RETAIL	RELEASE
I-4	240	$14.95	Jun. 2011

ISBN: 978-0-981617-07-7

The African Abroad: The Black Man's Evolution in Western Civilization, Volume One

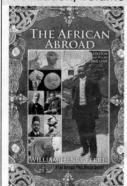

By William Henry Ferris

Who would think a book written in 1911 could cover so much? Ferris, chairman of the UNIA, speaks up for the Black man's role in Western civilization. He discusses a wealth of history, as well as some revolutionary Black theology, exploring the idea of man as God and God as man.

CLASS	PAGES	RETAIL	RELEASE
I-5	570	$29.95	Oct. 2012

ISBN: 978-1935721-66-6

The African Abroad: Volume Two

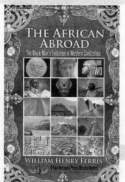

By William Henry Ferris

The second volume of Ferris' epic covers important Black biographies of great leaders, ancient and modern. He tells the stories of forty "Black Immortals." He also identifies the African origins of many of the world's civilizations, including ancient Egypt, Akkad, Sumer, India, and Europe.

CLASS	PAGES	RETAIL	RELEASE
I-5	330	$19.95	Oct. 2012

ISBN: 978-1-935721-69-7

From Poverty to Power: The Realization of Prosperity and Peace

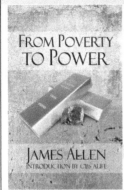

By James Allen

Want to transform your life? James Allen, the author of the classic *As a Man Thinketh,* explores how we can turn struggle and adversity into power and prosperity. This inspirational text teaches readers about their innate strength and the immense power of the conscious mind.

CLASS	PAGES	RETAIL	RELEASE
I-3	144	$14.95	May 2010

ISBN: 978-0-981617-05-3

Daily Meditations: A Year of Guidance on the Meaning of Life

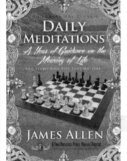

By James Allen

Need a guidebook to a productive and healthy year? This is it. James Allen delivers another great work in this book, this time offering 365 days of inspiration and guidance on life's greatest challenges. This book includes sections for daily notes.

CLASS	PAGES	RETAIL	RELEASE
C-3	208	$14.95	Apr. 2013

ISBN: 978-1-935721-08-6

The Kybalion: The Seven Ancient Egyptian Laws _

By the Three Initiates

Thousands of years ago, the ancients figured out a set of principles that govern the universe. In *The Kybalion*, these laws are explored and explained. This edition includes research into the authorship of the book, and where the laws came from.

CLASS	PAGES	RETAIL	RELEASE
C-4	130	$14.95	Oct. 2012

ISBN: 978-1-935721-25-3

Real Life is No Fairy Tale (w/ Companion CD)

By Sujan Dass and Lord Williams

Looking for a children's book that teaches about struggle? Written for school age children, this full-color hardcover book is composed entirely in rhyme, and the images are as real as they get. Includes a CD with an audio book, animated video, review questions, and printable worksheets and activities.

CLASS	PGS	RETAIL	RELEASE
CD-4	36+	$16.95	Jun. 2010

ISBN: 978-0-9816170-2-2

Aesop's Fables: 101 Classic Tales and Timeless Lessons

Edited by Dr. Sujan Dass

What's better to teach our children than life lessons? This easy-to-read collection of classic tales told by an African storyteller uses animals to teach valuable moral lessons. This edition includes dozens of black-and-white images to accompany the timeless fables. Color them in!

CLASS	PAGES	RETAIL	RELEASE
CD-3	112	$14.95	Feb. 2013

ISBN: 978-1-935721-07-9

Heritage Playing Cards (w/ Companion Booklet)

Designed by Sujan Dass

No more European royalty! This beautiful deck of playing cards features 54 full-color characters from around the world and a 16-page educational booklet on international card games and the ethnic backgrounds of the people on the cards.

CLASS	PGS	RETAIL	RELEASE
CD-2	16+	$6.95	May 2010

UPC: 05105-38587

Black God: An Introduction to the World's Religions and their Black Gods

By Supreme Understanding

Have you ever heard that Christ was Black? What about the Buddha? They weren't alone. This book explores the many Black gods of the ancient world, from Africa to Europe, Asia, and Australia, all the way to the Americas. Who were they? Why were they worshipped? And what does this mean for us today?

CLASS	PAGES	RETAIL	RELEASE
C-3	200	$19.95	Jan. 2014

ISBN: 978-1-935721-12-3

Black People Invented Everything

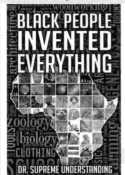

By Supreme Understanding

In *The Science of Self* we began exploring the origins of everything that modern civilization depends on today. In this book, we get into specifics, showing how Black people invented everything from agriculture to zoology, with dozens of pictures and references to prove it!

CLASS	PAGES	RETAIL	RELEASE
I-3	180	$14.95	Feb. 2014

NOT YET PUBLISHED

The Yogi Science of Breath: A Complete Manual of the Ancient Philosophy of the East

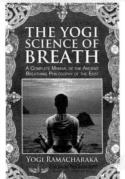

By Yogi Ramacharaka

A classic text on the science of breathing, one of the most ignored, yet important, aspects of our physical and emotional health. This book has been used by both martial arts experts and legendary jazz musicians. This edition explores the "secret science" of breath, and where its mysterious author learned such teachings.

CLASS	PAGES	RETAIL	RELEASE
PH-4	112	$14.95	Apr. 2012

ISBN: 978-1-935721-34-5

How to Get Our Books

To better serve our readers, we've streamlined the way we handle book orders. Here are some of the ways you can find our books.

In Stores

You can find our books in just about any Black bookstore or independent bookseller. If you don't find our titles on the shelves, just request them by name and publisher. Most bookstores can order our titles directly from us (via our site) or from the distributors listed below. We also provide a listing of retailers who carry our books at www.bestblackbooks.com

Online (Wholesale)

Now, you can visit our sites (like www.supremeunderstanding.com or www.bestblackbooks.com) to order wholesale quantities direct from us, the publisher. From our site, we ship heavily discounted case quantities to distributors, wholesalers, retailers, and local independent resellers (like yourself – just try it!). The discounts are so deep, you can afford to GIVE books away if you're not into making money.

Online (Retail)

If you're interested in single "retail" copies, you can now find them online at Amazon.com, or you can order them via mail order by contacting one of the mail order distributors listed below. You can also find many of our titles as eBooks in the Amazon Kindle, Nook, or Apple iBooks systems. You may also find full-length videobook or audiobook files available, but nothing beats the pass-around potential of a real book!

By Mail Order

Please contact any of the following Black-owned distributors to order our books! For others, visit our site.

Lushena Books
607 Country Club Dr
Bensenville, IL 60106
(800) 785-1545

Afrikan World Books
2217 Pennsylvania Ave.
Baltimore, MD 21217
(410) 383-2006

Special Needs X-Press
3128 Villa Ave
Bronx, NY 10468
(718) 220-3786

About the Publishers

Two Horizons Press is an imprint of Supreme Design, LLC. **Two Horizons Press** is a publisher of educational content that may go back more than 100 years. By republishing classic works that have gone ignored for political reasons, THP brings timeless information back to the public eye.

Supreme Design is the parent company for Supreme Design Publishing, Two Horizons Press, and Proven Publishing. Supreme Design was founded as a media firm in 2006 to improve society and eliminate oppression through transformative content and targeted delivery.

As an independent publisher of cutting-edge educational materials for urban families, **Supreme Design Publishing** engages difficult issues like racial justice and capitalism in the language of modern hiphop culture. Visit www.supremedesignonline.com to learn more!

Proven Publishing, another subsidiary of Supreme Design, offers our low-cost and high-quality publishing services to authors looking for greater control of their content. Proven Publishing provides the "proven" body of best practices that bring books from both Supreme Design Publishing and Two Horizons Press to life.

Visit www.provenpublishing.com to learn more!

These independent, family-run, community-based businesses are built and run according to the principles of honor and ethics of the **#360Movement**. For explanations of this cultural change campaign and its many manifestations, visit www.the360movement.com